The Inventor Mentor

*Programming Object-Oriented 3D Graphics
with Open Inventor, Release 2*

Josie Wernecke
Open Inventor Architecture Group

Addison-Wesley Publishing Company
Reading, Massachusetts Menlo Park, California
New York Don Mills, Ontario Wokingham, England
Amsterdam Bonn Sydney Singapore Tokyo Madrid
San Juan Paris Seoul Milan Mexico City Taipei

Library of Congress Cataloging-in-Publication Data

Wernecke, Josie.
    The Inventor mentor : programming Object-oriented 3D graphics
  with Open Inventor, release 2 / Josie Wernecke.
      p. cm.
    Includes index.
    ISBN 0-201-62495-8
    1. Object-oriented programming (Computer science) 2. Open
  Inventor. 3. Computer graphics. I. Title.
QA76.64.W48 1994
006.6'6--dc20
                                         93-41976
                                          CIP

Author: Josie Wernecke
Sponsoring Editor: Keith Wollman
Project Editor: Joanne Clapp Fullagar
Cover Image: Rikk Carey
Cover Design: Jean Seal
Text Design: Electric Ink, Ltd., and Kay Maitz

Set in 10-point Stone Serif

Addison-Wesley books are available for bulk purchases by corporations, institutions, and other organizations. For more information, please contact the Corporate, Government and Special Sales Department at (617) 944-3700 x2915.

3 4 5 6 7 8-CRS-9998979695
Third printing, August 1995

To my family—Steve, Jeff, and Evan

—JW

About This Book

The Inventor Mentor introduces graphics programmers and application developers to Open Inventor, an object-oriented 3D toolkit. Open Inventor is a library of objects and methods used for interactive 3D graphics. Although it is written in C++, Open Inventor also includes C bindings.

For the sake of brevity, the examples included in this book are in C++. All C++ examples, as well as equivalent examples written in C, are available on-line. If you are new to the C++ language, see Appendix A to help you understand the references to classes, subclasses, and other object-oriented concepts used throughout this book. If you are using the C application programming interface, also see Appendix B.

What This Book Contains

This book describes how to write applications using the Open Inventor toolkit. *The Inventor Toolmaker*, a companion book for the advanced programmer, describes how to create new Inventor classes and how to customize existing classes.

The Inventor Mentor contains the following parts and chapters:

Part I, "**Getting Started**," has two chapters:

- Chapter 1, "**Overview**," provides a general description of Open Inventor concepts and classes and how Inventor relates to OpenGL and the X Window System.

- Chapter 2, "**An Inventor Sampler**," presents a short program that creates a simple object. This program is then modified to show the use of important Inventor objects: engines, manipulators, and components.

Part II, "**Building a Scene Graph**," has three chapters:

- Chapter 3, "**Nodes and Groups**," introduces the concept of a scene graph and shows how to create nodes and combine them into different kinds of groups.

- Chapter 4, "**Cameras and Lights**," describes the camera nodes used to view a scene and the light nodes that provide illumination.

- Chapter 5, "**Shapes, Properties, and Binding**," describes how to create both simple and complex shapes and how to use property nodes, including material, draw style, and lighting model nodes. Binding materials and surface normals to shape nodes is also explained.

Part III, "**More About Nodes**," has three chapters:

- Chapter 6, "**Text**," shows the use of 2D and 3D text nodes.

- Chapter 7, "**Textures**," describes how to apply textures to the surfaces of objects in a scene.

- Chapter 8, "**Curves and Surfaces**," explains how to use NURBS curves and surfaces.

Part IV, "**Using a Scene Graph**," has three chapters:

- Chapter 9, "**Applying Actions**," describes how operations are applied to an Inventor scene graph. Actions include OpenGL rendering, picking, calculating a bounding box, calculating a transformation matrix, writing to a file, and searching the scene graph for certain types of nodes.

- Chapter 10, "**Handling Events and Selection**," explains how Inventor receives events from the window system. It also describes how the selection node manages a selection list and performs highlighting.

- Chapter 11, "**File Format**," describes Inventor's interchange file format, used for reading files into Inventor, writing files out from Inventor, and data exchanges such as copy and paste.

Part V, "**Application Tools**," has four chapters:

- Chapter 12, "**Sensors**," describes how Inventor sensors watch for certain types of events and invoke user-supplied callback functions when these events occur.

- Chapter 13, "**Engines**," describes how you can use Inventor engines to animate parts of a scene graph, or to create interdependencies among the nodes in the graph.

- Chapter 14, **"Node Kits,"** introduces node kits, a convenient mechanism for creating groups of related Inventor nodes. Each node kit contains a catalog of nodes from which you select the desired nodes.

- Chapter 15, **"Draggers and Manipulators,"** describes how to use draggers and manipulators, which are special objects in the scene graph that respond to user events. Manipulators are nodes with field values that can be edited directly by the user.

Part VI, **"Using the Toolkit with Other Libraries,"** has two chapters:

- Chapter 16, **"Inventor Component Library,"** shows how to use Inventor's Xt components, which are program modules with a built-in user interface for changing the scene graph interactively. It also describes the Xt utility functions and render area.

- Chapter 17, **"Using Inventor with OpenGL,"** discusses how to use Inventor with the OpenGL Library.

There are three appendices:

- Appendix A, **" Introduction to Object-Oriented Programming for C Programmers,"** describes basic concepts of object-oriented programming, including data abstraction and inheritance.

- Appendix B, **"Introduction to the C API,"** explains the differences between the Open Inventor C and C++ interfaces.

- Appendix C, **"Error Handling,"** describes Inventor's error handling mechanism.

How to Use This Book

It's unrealistic to expect anyone to read a lengthy programmer's guide from start to finish. After you read a few basic chapters, you can skim others and skip around, depending on your particular needs and goals. Here are a few suggested paths for making your way through this book.

For a basic understanding of how to create nodes and connect them into scene graphs, read Chapters 1 through 5. Then read Chapter 9, "Applying Actions," and Chapter 10, "Handling Events and Selection."

If you are mainly interested in reading files into the Inventor database, read Chapters 1 and 2 for an overview of Inventor, and then jump to Chapter 11, "File Format."

If you are an experienced OpenGL programmer, Chapters 1, 2, 10, and 17, "Using Inventor with OpenGL," are important chapters to begin with. Again, for a basic understanding of building a scene graph, you also need to read Chapters 3 through 5 and Chapter 9.

Chapter 15, "Draggers and Manipulators," and Chapter 16, "Inventor Component Library," describe the programming aspects of Inventor that have an associated user interface. The user interface for individual components is described in the on-line HELP cards provided for each class.

Once you understand the basic material presented in Chapters 1 through 5, you can skip to Chapter 13, "Engines," and Chapter 14, "Node Kits." Engines, like nodes, are basic building blocks in the scene graph. They allow you to animate parts of the scene graph and to incorporate additional behavior into scene graph objects. If you are creating scene graphs, node kits offer many shortcuts.

What You Should Know
Before Reading This Book

This book assumes you are familiar with basic concepts of 3D graphics programming. For example, it assumes you have a reasonable understanding of the following terms: *lighting, rendering, vertex, polygon, light source, picking, matrix, OpenGL, pixel, surface normal.* If these terms are new to you, consult one or two of the sources listed in "Suggestions for Further Reading," later in this introduction.

In addition, this book assumes you have some familiarity with concepts related to object-oriented programming. See "Suggestions for Further Reading" as well as Appendices A and B for good background information.

Conventions Used in This Book

This book uses **boldface text** font for all Inventor classes, methods, and field names: **SoNode, SoMaterial, getValue(), setValue(), ambientColor,** and **center**. Parentheses indicate methods. Code examples are in Courier font.

Tips

Several icons are used in the margins to highlight different kinds of text. Programming tips are marked with their own heading and the icon shown at the right.

Advanced Information

Information that is considered advanced, and could be skipped during your first reading, is marked with the icon shown at the right. This icon can apply to a single paragraph or to an entire section or chapter.

Key to Scene Graph Diagrams

Figure I-1 shows the symbols used in the scene graph diagrams that appear throughout this guide.

Suggestions for Further Reading

For a general introduction to computer graphics, see the following:

- Foley, J.D., A. van Dam, S. Feiner, and J.F. Hughes, *Computer Graphics Principles and Practice*, 2e. Reading, Mass.: Addison-Wesley, 1990.

- Neider, Jackie, Tom Davis, Mason Woo, *OpenGL Programming Guide*. Reading, Mass.: Addison-Wesley, 1993.

- Newman, W., and R. Sproull, *Principles of Interactive Computer Graphics*, 2e. New York: McGraw-Hill, 1979.

For an introduction to the C++ language, see the following:

- Lippman, Stanley B., *A C++ Primer*, 2e. Reading, Mass.:Addison-Wesley, 1991.

- Shapiro, Jonathan, *A C++ Toolkit*. Englewood Cliffs, N.J.: Prentice-Hall, Inc., 1991.

For an introduction to object-oriented programming, see

- Meyer, Bertrand, *Object-Oriented Software Construction*. London: Prentice Hall International, 1988.

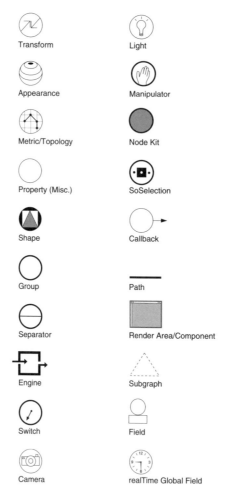

Figure I-1   Scene Graph Symbols

Acknowledgments

As a student of the Open Inventor toolkit, I am deeply indebted to the original Inventor mentors, who contributed so much to the development and content of this book: Rikk Carey, Gavin Bell, Alain Dumesny, Dave Immel, Paul Isaacs, Howard Look, David Mott, Paul Strauss, and Helga Thorvaldsdóttir. Even under the pressures of tight deadlines and numerous competing responsibilities, the members of the Inventor team consistently met my demands: they answered all questions, reviewed numerous drafts, and created the code examples that are the core of this book. Rikk Carey provided dynamic leadership for the Open Inventor project, rigorously questioning and challenging each decision. Paul Strauss, one of the chief architects of Inventor, probably read the most drafts and definitely added the most red (and green) ink to those drafts. His insightful and literate reviews were invaluable to me. Additional eagle-eyed reviewers included Ronen Barzel, Sam Chen, Beth Fryer, and Kevin Goldsmith.

Putting all the pieces of the puzzle together—screen shots, line art, color plates, text, code examples—also required a large cast of people. Rikk Carey created the cover image. Catherine Madonia used Rikk's scene to create the black-and-white images for the part- and chapter-title pages. Paul Isaacs showed his creative genius—not to mention his ability to work under brutal deadlines—in creating the many models and scenes for the images shown in Plates 1 through 21. I'm also grateful to Maria Mortati, who designed the color plate section and persuaded me to make massive edits to the figure captions. Catherine Madonia helped by creating conceptual images and by taking snapshots of the example programs. The many details of dealing with vendors, coordinating printer tests and schedules, and producing the book were ably handled by Laura Cooper and Lorrie Williams. Line art was drawn by Kay Maitz, Cheri Brown, Dan Young, Howard Look, and Lorrie Williams. Helga Thorvaldsdóttir paid special attention to the code examples: writing many of them, and revising and polishing to the bitter end.

Many thanks to Kirk Alexander, of the Interactive Computer Graphics Laboratory at Princeton University, who supplied numerous images and revisions to satisfy our requests precisely. The Out-of-Box Experience, an application originally designed for the Silicon Graphics Indy workstation, shown in Plates 37 through 40, was created by Leo Blume, Mark Daly, Kevin Goldsmith, Howard Look, and Chee Yu of Silicon Graphics, and Brad de Graf, Shari Glusker, Jill Huchital, Karen Hughes, Peter Oppenheimer, Mark Swain, Drew Takahashi, and Phil Zucco of (Colossal) Pictures. The art gallery tour shown in Plate 30 is the work of Gavin Bell, Mark Daly, Kevin Goldsmith, and Linda Roy, all of Silicon Graphics. Many of the models used in the cover scene were created by Acuris, Inc.

I'd also like to thank Jackie Neider, manager of Developer Publications in the Visual Magic Division of Silicon Graphics, and the other members of my department—Patricia Creek, Arthur Evans, Liz Deeth, Beth Fryer, Jed Hartman, Ken Jones, John Stearns, Eleanor Bassler, and Carol Geary—for their consistent support and encouragement during the course of this project (and for sharing the high-speed printer).

And, most important, thanks to my husband, Steve, and my sons, Jeff and Evan, for a warm dinner and cheerful conversation at the end of some very long days.

Contents

Part IV: Using a Scene Graph

Figures

Tables

Examples

Part I

Getting Started

## Chapter 1

Overview

Chapter Objectives

After reading this chapter, you'll be able to do the following:

- Identify the key elements that constitute the Open Inventor toolkit
- Explain the relationship of Open Inventor to OpenGL
- Describe several ways to extend Open Inventor

This chapter describes the key elements in Open Inventor and briefly outlines how you can tailor your use of this toolkit to a particular set of needs. It explains how Inventor relates to programming tools you may already be familiar with, such as OpenGL and the X Window System. Most of the topics mentioned in this chapter are covered in detail in later chapters of this book.

What Is Open Inventor?

The Inventor Mentor introduces graphics programmers and application developers to Open Inventor, an object-oriented 3D toolkit. Open Inventor is a library of objects and methods used to create interactive 3D graphics applications. Although it is written in C++, Inventor also includes C bindings.

Open Inventor is a set of building blocks that enables you to write programs that take advantage of powerful graphics hardware features with minimal programming effort. Based on OpenGL, the toolkit provides a library of objects that you can use, modify, and extend to meet new needs. Inventor objects include *database primitives,* including shape, property, group, and engine objects; interactive *manipulators*, such as the handle box and trackball; and *components*, such as the material editor, directional light editor, and examiner viewer.

Inventor offers the economy and efficiency of a complete object-oriented system. In addition to simplifying application development, Inventor facilitates moving data between applications with its 3D interchange file format. End users of 3D programs can cut and paste 3D scene objects and share them among a variety of programs on the desktop.

As shown in Figure 1-1, Inventor's foundation is supplied by OpenGL and UNIX. Inventor represents an object-oriented *application policy* built on top of OpenGL, providing a programming model and user interface for OpenGL programs.

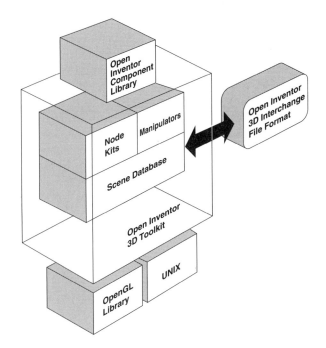

Figure 1-1   Inventor Architecture

The Inventor toolkit is window system–independent. A component library is helpful for using Inventor with specific window systems. This book describes one component library provided with the toolkit, which facilitates programming in Inventor using Xt windows and events. A companion to this book, *The Inventor Toolmaker*, provides details on how to extend Inventor to work with other window systems.

Objects, not Drawings

Inventor focuses on creating *3D objects*. All information about these objects—their shape, size, coloring, surface texture, location in 3D space—is stored in a scene database. This information can be used in a variety of ways. The most common use is to display, or *render*, an image of the 3D objects on the screen.

For many 3D graphics packages, this image is the ultimate goal—a photorealistic representation on the screen of a 3D scene. But what if a user wants to move one of the objects to a different location, and perhaps view another object from a slightly different viewpoint? What if the user wants to experiment with a different range of colors for the objects and the background of the scene? What if a chemist wants to rearrange how two molecules align with each other? What if an airplane designer wants to redesign the curve of the airplane's wing? If the image exists only as a drawing on the screen, the programmer must write complicated code to implement these functions. Additional code is required to animate parts of the scene. With Open Inventor, the ability to make these changes is built into the programming model. Changing the objects in the scene, adding to the scene, and interacting with the objects becomes a simple process because such changes are part of Inventor's well-defined interface, and because they are anticipated by Inventor's basic design.

Using Database Objects in a Variety of Ways

Because the Inventor database holds information about the objects as they exist in their own 3D "world," not just as a 2D array of pixels drawn on the screen, other operations in addition to rendering can be performed on the objects. The objects in the scene can be picked, highlighted, and manipulated as discrete entities. Bounding-box calculations can be performed on them. They can be printed, searched for, read from a file, and written to a file. Each of these built-in operations opens up a flexible and powerful arena for the application programmer. In addition, this programming model is intuitive because it is based on the physical and mechanical world we live in.

Animation

Inventor objects can also encapsulate behavior into the description stored in the scene database. Example 1-1, an excerpt from an Inventor file, describes a windmill whose blades spin at a specified rate. When this file is read into an Inventor program and displayed on the screen, the windmill is drawn and the blades are animated. No additional application code is used to make the blades spin; this description is part of the windmill object itself. Figure 1-2 shows an image of this windmill.

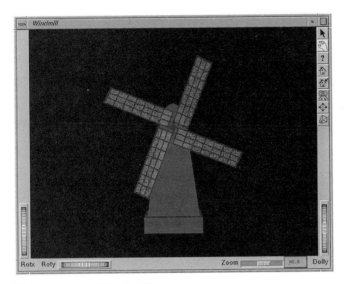

Figure 1-2   Windmill

Example 1-1   File Describing a Spinning Windmill

```
#Inventor V2.0 ascii

Separator {
   Separator {
      RotationXYZ {
         axis Z
         angle 0 =
            ElapsedTime {      # Engine to rotate blades
               speed 0.4
            }
            . timeOut          # Engine output connected to
                               # angle of rotation
      }
      Transform {
         translation 0 0 0.5
      }
      Separator {# Shaft for blades
         Material {
            diffuseColor 0.05 0.05 0.05
         }
```

```
            Transform {
                rotation 1 0 0 1.5708
                scaleFactor 0.2 0.5 0.2
            }
            Cylinder {
            }
        }
        DEF Blade Separator { # Blade geometry and properties
            Transform {        # Blade interior
                translation 0.45 2.9 0.2
                rotation 0 1 0 0.3
            }
            Separator {
                Transform {
                    scaleFactor 0.6 2.5 0.02
                }
                Material {
                    diffuseColor 0.5 0.3 0.1
                    transparency 0.3
                }
                Cube {
                }
            }
            Separator {        # Blade frame
                # .... (Details omitted)
            }
        }
        Separator {            # Second blade
            RotationXYZ {
                axis Z
                angle 1.5708
            }
            USE Blade
        }
        Separator {            # Third blade
            RotationXYZ {
                axis Z
                angle 3.14159
            }
            USE Blade
        }
```

```
    Separator {                   # Fourth blade
        RotationXYZ {
            axis Z
            angle -1.5708
        }
        USE Blade
    }
}
Separator {                       # Windmill tower
    # ... (Details omitted)
}
}
```

How Does Open Inventor Relate to OpenGL?

If you are familiar with OpenGL, you are probably curious about how OpenGL relates to Open Inventor. This section supplies an overview of how the two libraries interrelate. Chapter 17 provides additional information on how to use Open Inventor and OpenGL in a single program—taking advantage of the fast, flexible 3D rendering of OpenGL and the high-level objects and versatile scene database offered by Inventor.

Open Inventor uses OpenGL for rendering. In OpenGL, however, rendering is explicit, whereas in Inventor, rendering, along with other operations such as picking, reading, writing, and calculating a bounding box, is encapsulated in the objects.

OpenGL provides immediate-mode access to the frame buffer. It can also use a display list to record drawing commands for objects. This display list can then be played back on demand.

Open Inventor does not provide immediate access to the frame buffer. As described previously in the section "Objects, not Drawings," it is based on an object-oriented programming model that creates high-level, editable objects stored in a database. Each of these objects encapsulates a set of operations that can be applied to it: rendering, picking, database querying and searching, and bounding-box calculation. In Inventor, rendering to the frame buffer occurs when the render action is invoked. If an Inventor program never issues this command (either directly or indirectly), no drawing will appear.

A simple analogy may help to convey a feel for how Open Inventor contrasts to OpenGL. Suppose it is the year 2020 and you have the time, money, and skills required to build your dream house. You can choose one of two basic approaches, or you can combine elements of both approaches.

The first approach is to go to the Handyperson Builder's Emporium and purchase all the required materials separately—nails, wood, pipes, wires, switches, concrete, and so on. This approach gives you complete flexibility, but it also requires detailed knowledge and skill on your part to determine which parts you need and how to construct all elements of the house.

The second approach is to order a collection of prebuilt units from the *Dream Home Catalog*, published by a ten-year-old firm that bases its product on concepts of Japanese home building, modular office construction, and the highly successful prefabricated window companies of the 90s. The catalog provides a wide variety of wall-frame units, concrete forms, siding packages, windows, and doors.

The first approach—starting with raw materials—is analogous to using OpenGL for interactive graphics applications. Building a house with this method, you have complete flexibility over how the raw materials are used. You need to be familiar with the details of home construction, and you need different skills to build each part of the home from scratch— plumbing, electrical, carpentry.

The second approach—selecting prebuilt units from a catalog—is loosely analogous to creating an application with Inventor. The wall panels are prewired with the electrical, security, and plumbing connections. This prewiring can be compared to the built-in event model provided by Inventor. In addition, the complete inventory of parts, sizes, and costs is automatically computed by the catalog firm when you place the order. In a similar way, all operations (rendering, picking, bounding-box calculation, and so on) are built into Inventor objects. You do not need to add extra code (or, in the case of the house, perform extra calculations) to obtain this information. Because the catalog company has been buying parts from the Handyperson Builder's Emporium for years, it knows the exact material and sizes to use for maximum economy and minimum waste. Similarly, Open Inventor achieves high performance from its use of OpenGL.

Although the catalog offers a collection of ready-made modules, you have choices about which modules you use and how to put them together. Whenever you purchase modules from the *Dream Home Catalog*, standard sizes are used to facilitate replacing, repairing, and updating different parts of the house. With Open Inventor, applications achieve a common look and feel because Inventor provides a set of components with a unified user interface.

If you require parts not available in the catalog, the company also allows you to design your own custom parts and buy the pieces directly from the Handyperson Builder's Emporium. Perhaps you want curved corners on your wall units rather than right-angled corners. Inventor, too, allows you to design your own objects (through *subclassing*, described in *The Inventor Toolmaker*). With this added flexibility, you are not constrained to the catalog parts, but you can use them to save time and money when they're suitable.

If you want to save even more time, you can choose a complete house kit from the *Dream Home Catalog*. It offers many different models: A-frame, Ranch, Victorian, Colonial. These house kits are analogous to Inventor's *node kits*, which provide packaged sets of objects commonly used together.

When each house has been completed, it takes a highly trained eye to determine which house was constructed from raw materials and which was constructed with catalog parts. Both houses have fine quality finishing, are made of the best materials, and exhibit sturdy construction. Both exhibit touches of creativity and distinctive design.

The same could be said of applications built with OpenGL and those built with Open Inventor. The approach taken must suit the needs of the builder, and the two approaches can be combined as desired, using a combination of prebuilt Inventor objects and components and OpenGL commands.

The Inventor Toolkit

Inventor provides programming support at a variety of levels. At the end-user interface level, Inventor offers a unified look and feel for 3D graphics interfaces. At the programming level, the Inventor toolkit (shown previously in Figure 1-1) offers the following tools, which are explained in greater detail later in this chapter:

- A *3D scene database* that includes shape, property, group, engine, and sensor objects, used to create a hierarchical 3D scene

- A set of *node kits* that provide a convenient mechanism for creating prebuilt groupings of Inventor nodes

- A set of *manipulators,* including the handle box and trackball, which are objects in a scene database that the user can interact with directly

- An *Inventor Component Library* for Xt, including a render area (a window used for rendering), material editor, viewers, and utility functions, used to provide some high-level interactive tasks

This book explains Open Inventor from the bottom up, starting with the 3D scene database.

The Scene Database

The *node* is the basic building block used to create three-dimensional scene databases in Inventor. Each node holds a piece of information, such as a surface material, shape description, geometric transformation, light, or camera. All 3D shapes, attributes, cameras, and light sources present in a scene are represented as nodes.

An ordered collection of nodes is referred to as a *scene graph*. (Figure 1-3 shows a simple scene graph. Figure I-1, in "About This Book," has the key to the icons used in scene graph diagrams throughout this book.) This scene graph is stored in the Inventor *database*. Inventor takes care of storing and managing the scene graph in the database. The database can contain more than one scene graph.

After you have constructed a scene graph, you can apply a number of operations or *actions* to it, including rendering, picking, searching, computing a bounding box, and writing to a file.

Classes of database primitives include *shape nodes* (for example, sphere, cube, cylinder, quad mesh), *property nodes* (for example, material, lighting model, textures, environment), and *group nodes* (for example, separator, level-of-detail, and switch). Other special database primitives are *engines* and *sensors*. Engines are objects that can be connected to other objects in the scene graph and used to animate parts of the scene or constrain certain parts of the scene in relation to other parts (see Chapter 13). A sensor is an object that detects when something in the database changes and calls a function supplied by the application. Sensors can respond to specified timing requirements (for example, "Do this every *n* seconds") or to changes in the scene graph data (see Chapter 12).

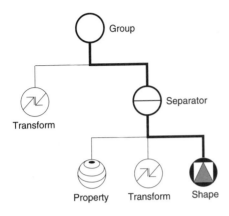

Transform

Separator

Property   Transform   Shape

Group

——— Path

Figure 1-3   Example of a Scene Graph

Node Kits

Node kits facilitate the creation of structured, consistent databases. Each node kit is a collection of nodes with a specified arrangement. A template associated with the node kit determines which nodes can be added when necessary and where they should be placed. For example, the **SoShapeKit** node kit is used for any Inventor shape object. If you use this node kit, you don't have to create and arrange each node individually. By default, the template for the **SoShapeKit** contains an **SoCube** node, and it allows a material, geometric transformation, and other properties to be inserted in the correct place when required.

Another use of node kits is to define application-specific objects and semantics. For example, a flight-simulation package might include a variety of objects representing airplanes. Each of these airplanes consists of the same general scene graph structure—for example, fuselage, wings, and landing gear—as well as some airplane-specific methods—for example, **bankLeft()**, **raiseLandingGear()**. To an application writer using this package, each type of airplane can be dealt with in a similar way. There is no need to know the details of the structure of the subgraph representing the landing gear to raise it, since the general method, **raiseLandingGear()**, exists. Creating these new objects and methods requires extending Open Inventor by subclassing, which is described in *The Inventor Toolmaker*. It is highly recommended that you use some form of node kits in your application to maintain order and policy.

Manipulators

A manipulator is a special kind of node that reacts to user interface events and can be edited directly by the user. Manipulators typically have parts that render in the scene and provide a means for translating events into changes to the database. An example of a manipulator is the *handle box*, which is a bounding box of another object with handles at the corners and sides. In Figure 1-4, handle boxes surround the knights. By picking on a handle and dragging it, the user can change the scale or position of the box and thus the object inside it. Manipulators provide an easy way for applications to incorporate direct 3D interaction.

Figure 1-4   Handle-Box Manipulator

Inventor Component Library

The Inventor Component Library provides window-system support and integration with the X Window System. This library includes the following features:

- A render area (window) object

- Main loop and initialization convenience routines

- An event translator utility

- Editors

- Viewers

The render area accepts an X event, translates it into an Inventor event, and then passes it to "smart" objects, such as manipulators, that may handle the event.

The Inventor Component Library also contains a set of viewers and editors that fall into the general category of *components*. Components are reusable modules that contain both a render area and a user interface. They are used for editing scene graph nodes (materials, lights, transformations) as well as for viewing scenes in different ways. Rather than solving the same problems over and over again, you can simply select an Inventor component and plug it into your application. If you need added functionality, you can write your own component and add it to Inventor (see *The Inventor Toolmaker*). Examples of components are the material editor, directional light editor (see Figure 1-5), fly viewer ("flies" through the scene), and examiner viewer (looks at a single object from any perspective).

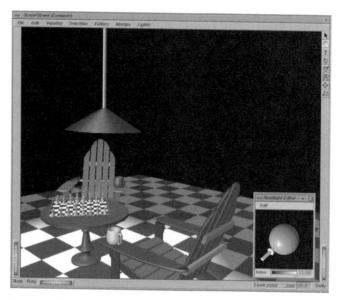

Figure 1-5   Example of a Component: Directional Light Editor (lower right)

Inventor Class Tree

Figure 1-6 summarizes the Inventor class tree. Base classes are at the left, and derived classes are at the right. **SoBase** is the base class for **SoFieldContainer**, from which both nodes and engines are derived. Action classes are derived from **SoAction**. **SoXtComponent** is another base class. The Xt render area, as well as the viewers and editors, are all derived from **SoXtComponent**. Classes to the right in the tree *inherit* the fields and methods of the classes they are derived from.

Extending the Toolkit

One of the most important aspects of Inventor is the ability to program new objects and operations as extensions to the toolkit. One way to extend the set of objects provided by Inventor is to derive new classes from existing ones. See *The Inventor Toolmaker* for specific examples of creating new classes.

Another way to include new features in Inventor is by using *callback functions*, which provide an easy mechanism for introducing specialized behavior into a scene graph or prototyping new nodes without subclassing. A callback function is a user-written function that is called under certain conditions. Callback functions provided by Inventor include the following:

- **SoCallback**—a generic node in the database that provides a callback function for all database actions (see Chapter 17)

- **SoCallbackAction**—generic traversal of the database with a callback function at each node (see Chapter 9)

- **SoEventCallback**—a node in the database that calls a user-defined function when it receives an event (see Chapter 10)

- **SoSelection**—selection callback node (see Chapter 10)

- Manipulators—provide callback functions for event processing (see Chapter 15)

- **SoXt** components—support their own callback functions when a change occurs (see Chapter 16)

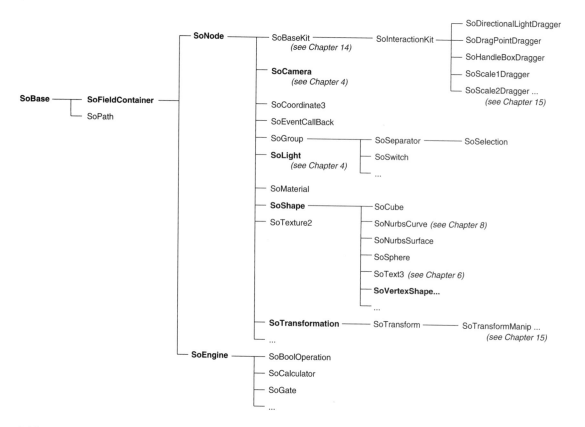

boldface = abstract class

Figure 1-6   Inventor Class Tree Summary (Part 1 of 3)

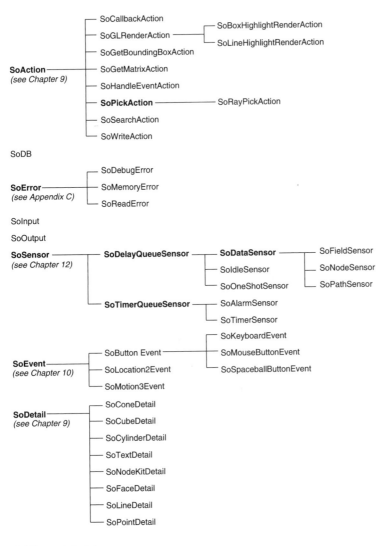

SoDB

SoInput

SoOutput

boldface = abstract class

Figure 1-7   Inventor Class Tree Summary (Part 2 of 3)

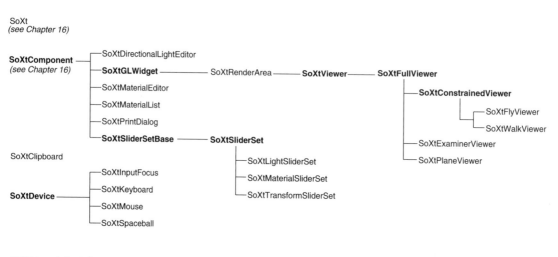

SoXt
(see Chapter 16)

SoXtComponent
(see Chapter 16)
- SoXtDirectionalLightEditor
- **SoXtGLWidget** — SoXtRenderArea — **SoXtViewer** — **SoXtFullViewer**
    - **SoXtConstrainedViewer**
        - SoXtFlyViewer
        - SoXtWalkViewer
    - SoXtExaminerViewer
    - SoXtPlaneViewer
- SoXtMaterialEditor
- SoXtMaterialList
- SoXtPrintDialog
- **SoXtSliderSetBase** — **SoXtSliderSet**
    - SoXtLightSliderSet
    - SoXtMaterialSliderSet
    - SoXtTransformSliderSet

SoXtClipboard

SoXtDevice
- SoXtInputFocus
- SoXtKeyboard
- SoXtMouse
- SoXtSpaceball

boldface = abstract class

Figure 1-8   Inventor Class Tree Summary (Part 3 of 3)

## Chapter 2

An Inventor Sampler

Chapter Objectives

After reading this chapter, you'll be able to do the following:

- Explain the basic structure of an Inventor program
- Describe the conventions used by Inventor

This chapter provides an overview of the 5 percent of Inventor that is part of any program. It includes a short program that draws a red cone in a window. This program is gradually augmented to show the use of some important Inventor objects: engines, manipulators, and components. Inventor naming conventions and basic data types are also described.

"Hello, Cone"

This chapter begins with a set of sample programs that illustrate the key aspects of Inventor. Example 2-1 creates a red cone and then renders it in a window (Figure 2-1). This example uses an Inventor Xt window, which is part of the Inventor Component Library. This library provides utilities for window management and event processing and also contains a set of Inventor components (viewers and editors).

The code shown in Example 2-1 constructs a simple scene graph composed of a camera node, a light node, a material node, and a cone node. Later chapters go into specifics on creating nodes, setting values in fields, structuring the database, and applying actions. The purpose of this chapter is simply to convey a feel for the tools Inventor offers and to help you get started writing an Inventor program.

A Red Cone

The first example program illustrates the basic steps in writing an Inventor program.

1. Create a window where the scene will be rendered. This example uses **SoXtRenderArea**, the Inventor Xt window.

2. Build the scene graph by creating property and shape nodes and combining them into groups.

Example 2-1 gives the code to create the cone shown in Figure 2-1.

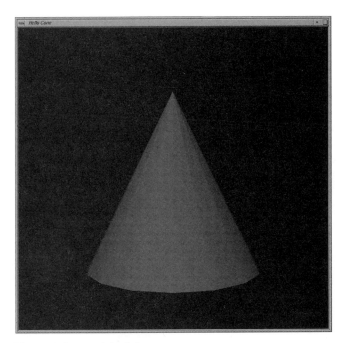

Figure 2-1   A Red Cone

Example 2-1   Basic "Hello, Cone" Program

```
#include <Inventor/Xt/SoXt.h>
#include <Inventor/Xt/SoXtRenderArea.h>
#include <Inventor/nodes/SoCone.h>
#include <Inventor/nodes/SoDirectionalLight.h>
#include <Inventor/nodes/SoMaterial.h>
#include <Inventor/nodes/SoPerspectiveCamera.h>
#include <Inventor/nodes/SoSeparator.h>

main(int , char **argv)
{
   // Initialize Inventor. This returns a main window to use.
   // If unsuccessful, exit.
   Widget myWindow = SoXt::init(argv[0]); // pass the app name
   if (myWindow == NULL) exit(1);

   // Make a scene containing a red cone
   SoSeparator *root = new SoSeparator;
   SoPerspectiveCamera *myCamera = new SoPerspectiveCamera;
```

```
    SoMaterial *myMaterial = new SoMaterial;
    root->ref();
    root->addChild(myCamera);
    root->addChild(new SoDirectionalLight);
    myMaterial->diffuseColor.setValue(1.0, 0.0, 0.0);    // Red
    root->addChild(myMaterial);
    root->addChild(new SoCone);

    // Create a renderArea in which to see our scene graph.
    // The render area will appear within the main window.
    SoXtRenderArea *myRenderArea = new SoXtRenderArea(myWindow);

    // Make myCamera see everything.
    myCamera->viewAll(root, myRenderArea->getViewportRegion());

    // Put our scene in myRenderArea, change the title
    myRenderArea->setSceneGraph(root);
    myRenderArea->setTitle("Hello Cone");
    myRenderArea->show();

    SoXt::show(myWindow);   // Display main window
    SoXt::mainLoop();       // Main Inventor event loop
}
```

Using Engines to Make the Cone Spin

Example 2-2 illustrates how to use engines to make the cone spin. An engine is attached to the angle field of an **SoRotationXYZ** node in the scene graph. The engine changes the angle value in the rotationXYZ node in response to changes in the real-time clock, which in turn causes the cone to rotate. After each change, the scene is automatically rendered again by the render area. Successive rotations give the desired effect of a spinning cone.

Example 2-2   "Hello, Cone" Using Engines

```
#include <Inventor/Xt/SoXt.h>
#include <Inventor/Xt/SoXtRenderArea.h>
#include <Inventor/engines/SoElapsedTime.h>
#include <Inventor/nodes/SoCone.h>
#include <Inventor/nodes/SoDirectionalLight.h>
#include <Inventor/nodes/SoMaterial.h>
#include <Inventor/nodes/SoPerspectiveCamera.h>
#include <Inventor/nodes/SoRotationXYZ.h>
#include <Inventor/nodes/SoSeparator.h>
```

```
main(int , char **argv)
{
   // Initialize Inventor and Xt
   Widget myWindow = SoXt::init(argv[0]);
   if (myWindow == NULL) exit(1);

   SoSeparator *root = new SoSeparator;
   root->ref();
   SoPerspectiveCamera *myCamera = new SoPerspectiveCamera;
   root->addChild(myCamera);
   root->addChild(new SoDirectionalLight);

   // This transformation is modified to rotate the cone
   SoRotationXYZ *myRotXYZ = new SoRotationXYZ;
   root->addChild(myRotXYZ);

   SoMaterial *myMaterial = new SoMaterial;
   myMaterial->diffuseColor.setValue(1.0, 0.0, 0.0);   // Red
   root->addChild(myMaterial);
   root->addChild(new SoCone);

   // An engine rotates the object. The output of myCounter
   // is the time in seconds since the program started.
   // Connect this output to the angle field of myRotXYZ
   myRotXYZ->axis = SoRotationXYZ::X;       // rotate about X axis
   SoElapsedTime *myCounter = new SoElapsedTime;
   myRotXYZ->angle.connectFrom(&myCounter->timeOut);

   SoXtRenderArea *myRenderArea = new SoXtRenderArea(myWindow);
   myCamera->viewAll(root, myRenderArea->getViewportRegion());
   myRenderArea->setSceneGraph(root);
   myRenderArea->setTitle("Engine Spin");
   myRenderArea->show();

   SoXt::show(myWindow);
   SoXt::mainLoop();
}
```

Adding a Trackball Manipulator

The next two examples show additional methods for editing a node in the scene graph. Example 2-3 adds a manipulator (a trackball) to the first example (see Figure 2-2). The trackball itself appears as three rings around the cone. When the left mouse button is pressed on the trackball, it highlights itself in a different color to show it is active. While it is active, the mouse can be used to rotate the trackball and the object (here, the cone) inside it. In this example, a trackball is constructed instead of the **SoRotationXYZ** node in Example 2-2. Each time the user rotates the trackball, its values change and the cone rotates as well. Because the render area has a sensor attached to the scene graph, the scene is automatically rendered again after each edit, and the cone appears to move.

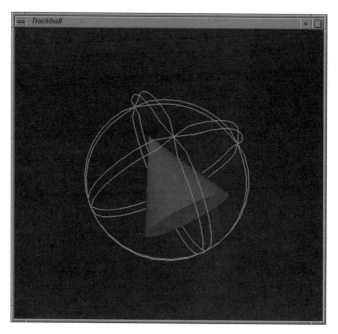

Figure 2-2   Cone with Trackball Manipulator

Example 2-3 "Hello, Cone" with a Trackball Manipulator

```
#include <Inventor/Xt/SoXt.h>
#include <Inventor/Xt/SoXtRenderArea.h>
#include <Inventor/manips/SoTrackballManip.h>
#include <Inventor/nodes/SoCone.h>
#include <Inventor/nodes/SoDirectionalLight.h>
#include <Inventor/nodes/SoMaterial.h>
#include <Inventor/nodes/SoPerspectiveCamera.h>
#include <Inventor/nodes/SoSeparator.h>

main(int , char **argv)
{
   // Initialize Inventor and Xt
   Widget myWindow = SoXt::init(argv[0]);
   if (myWindow == NULL) exit(1);

   SoSeparator *root = new SoSeparator;
   root->ref();

   SoPerspectiveCamera *myCamera = new SoPerspectiveCamera;
   root->addChild(myCamera);                  // child 0
   root->addChild(new SoDirectionalLight); // child 1
   root->addChild(new SoTrackballManip);      // child 2

   SoMaterial *myMaterial = new SoMaterial;
   myMaterial->diffuseColor.setValue(1.0, 0.0, 0.0);
   root->addChild(myMaterial);
   root->addChild(new SoCone);

   SoXtRenderArea *myRenderArea = new SoXtRenderArea(myWindow);
   myCamera->viewAll(root, myRenderArea->getViewportRegion());
   myRenderArea->setSceneGraph(root);
   myRenderArea->setTitle("Trackball");
   myRenderArea->show();

   SoXt::show(myWindow);
   SoXt::mainLoop();
}
```

Adding the Examiner Viewer

Example 2-4 replaces the render area in the first example with the examiner viewer, a component. This viewer, shown in Figure 2-3, modifies the camera node, which lets you view the cone from different positions. It provides a user interface that allows use of the mouse to modify camera placement in the scene. (Note that this example looks similar to the trackball in Example 2-3. Here, however, the camera is moving, not the cone itself.) This program does not need to set up a camera and call **viewAll()** because the viewer does this automatically.

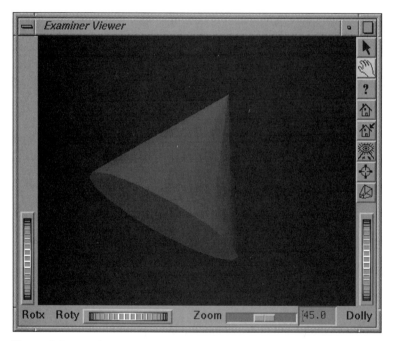

Figure 2-3   Cone with Examiner Viewer

Example 2-4   "Hello, Cone" Using the Examiner Viewer

```
#include <Inventor/Xt/SoXt.h>
#include <Inventor/Xt/viewers/SoXtExaminerViewer.h>
#include <Inventor/nodes/SoCone.h>
#include <Inventor/nodes/SoDirectionalLight.h>
#include <Inventor/nodes/SoMaterial.h>
#include <Inventor/nodes/SoPerspectiveCamera.h>
```

```
#include <Inventor/nodes/SoSeparator.h>

main(int , char **argv)
{
    Widget myWindow = SoXt::init(argv[0]);
    if (myWindow == NULL) exit(1);

    SoSeparator *root = new SoSeparator;
    root->ref();
    SoMaterial *myMaterial = new SoMaterial;
    myMaterial->diffuseColor.setValue(1.0, 0.0, 0.0);
    root->addChild(myMaterial);
    root->addChild(new SoCone);

    // Set up viewer:
    SoXtExaminerViewer *myViewer =
            new SoXtExaminerViewer(myWindow);
    myViewer->setSceneGraph(root);
    myViewer->setTitle("Examiner Viewer");
    myViewer->show();

    SoXt::show(myWindow);
    SoXt::mainLoop();
}
```

Naming Conventions

Basic types in Inventor begin with the letters **Sb** (for scene basic; see the next section, "Scene Basic Types"). For example:

- SbColor

- SbViewVolume

All other classes in Inventor are prefixed with the letters **So** (for scene object). For example:

- SoCone

- SoPerspectiveCamera

- SoMaterial

- SoTransform

Methods and variables begin with a lowercase letter. Each word within a class, method, or variable name begins with an uppercase letter. For example:

- getNormal()
- setSceneGraph()
- myCube

Enumerated type values are in UPPERCASE. For example:

- FILLED
- PER_PART

Scene Basic Types

This section discusses Inventor's **Sb** classes, a set of basic types that are used in many Inventor objects. Inventor includes useful methods for converting between different types and performing specific 3D operations on them.

Inventor defines the following types:

SbBool	Boolean value (TRUE or FALSE)
SbBoxnx	2D or 3D box that has planes parallel to the major axes and is specified by two points on a diagonal (includes **SbBox3f**, **SbBox2f**, **SbBox2s**); n is the number of values in the type (2 or 3), and x is the value type (f for float, s for short)
SbColor	RGB (red/green/blue) color value with conversion routines to other color spaces
SbCylinder	cylinder
SbLine	directed 3D line
SbMatrix	4×4 matrix
SbName	character string stored in a special table for fast and easy comparison, typically for identifiers
SbPList	list of generic (**void ***) pointers
SbPlane	oriented 3D plane
SbRotation	representation of a 3D rotation about an arbitrary axis

SbSphere	sphere
SbString	"smart" character strings that have many convenience methods for easy string manipulation
SbTime	representation of time—in seconds; seconds and microseconds; or using the **timeval** structure
SbVec_nx_	2D or 3D vector, used to represent points or directions (includes **SbVec2f**, **SbVec3f**, **SbVec2s**); _n_ is the number of values in the type (2, 3, or 4), and _x_ is the value type (f for float; s for short)
SbViewportRegion	
	active viewport region within a display window
SbViewVolume	view volume (for example, see **SoCamera**'s **getViewVolume**() method in the _Open Inventor C++ Reference Manual_)

Methods

Each **Sb** class has useful operators associated with it. For example, you can negate a variable of type **SbVec3f**, multiply it by a matrix, or normalize it to unit length. The following code creates a unit-length vector, based on the specified direction:

```
SbVec3f v(1.0, 2.0, 3.0); // declares and initializes the vector

v.normalize(); // normalizes the vector to unit length
```

Similarly, **SbMatrix** has useful methods including **multVecMatrix**(), which multiplies a row vector by the matrix and returns the result, and **rotate**(), which sets the matrix to rotate by a given amount. See the _Open Inventor C++ Reference Manual_ for a complete description of the available methods for each **Sb** class.

Types versus Fields

Chapter 3 contains a complete discussion of *fields*, which are the structures that store parameters for nodes. A field contains a value of a certain type. Fields are always contained within Inventor nodes. Many fields contain a corresponding **Sb** type. For example:

- A field of type **SoSFVec3f** contains an **SbVec3f**

- A field of type **SoSFRotation** contains an **SbRotation**

- A field of type **SoSFName** contains an **SbName**

Coordinate Systems in Inventor

Inventor uses a right-handed coordinate system for 3D data, with +*z* coming out of the screen. All angles are specified in radians. Objects are described in their own local coordinate space, known as *object coordinate space*. After all transformations have been applied to the objects in the scene graph, they are said to be in *world coordinate space*. This world coordinate space includes the camera and lights.

Include Files

Inventor contains include files for every class. You need to include the appropriate file for each class used in your program. For example, **SoSphere** and **SoTransform** nodes require you to include the files *SoSphere.h* and *SoTransform.h*. Most include files are found in a subdirectory—for example, *nodes/SoSphere.h* and *sensors/SoNodeSensor.h*.

In addition, you need to include the *SoXt.h* file if you are writing an interactive program that uses the Inventor Component Library.

If you are programming using the C application programming interface, use the *Inventor_c* directory instead of the *Inventor* directory.

Part II

Building a Scene Graph

Nodes and Groups

Chapter Objectives

After reading this chapter, you'll be able to do the following:

- Build scene graphs using shape, property, and group nodes
- Explain how nodes inherit values in the scene graph
- Describe why separator nodes are useful
- Explain the advantages of shared instancing of nodes in the scene graph
- Define the term *path* and explain why paths are needed
- Set and query field values
- Ignore specified fields in a node
- Explain how nodes are deleted in Open Inventor
- Use Inventor's runtime type-checking mechanism

This chapter illustrates how to construct scene graphs from shape, property, and group nodes. It explains general rules for traversing a scene graph, focusing on GL rendering traversal. The concepts of database actions and traversal state are introduced.

The Scene Database

The Inventor *scene database* consists of information representing one or more 3D scenes. This database, **SoDB**, can contain several *scene graphs*, as shown in Figure 3-1. Each scene graph consists of a related set of 3D objects and attributes. In Figure 3-1, for example, the scene graphs might represent a car, a small house, another car, a large house, and a person.

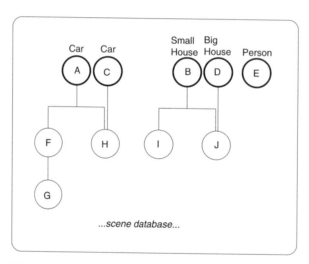

Figure 3-1   An Inventor Database

You can perform two basic operations, or *methods*, directly on the scene database. First, you *initialize* it:

```
SoDB::init()
```

This must be the first Inventor call you make. If you use the Inventor Component Library, the database is initialized automatically when you call **SoXt::init()** (see Chapter 16). If you are not using components, but you are using interaction or node kits, or both, call **SoInteraction::init()**, which initializes the database, interaction, and node kits.

Second, you can *read* from a file into the scene database, which adds new scene graphs to it:

SoSeparator **readAll**(SoInput *in*)

or

SbBool **read**(SoInput *in*, SoNode *&*rootNode*) const

or

SbBool **read**(SoInput *in*, SoPath *&*path*) const

Using the first syntax, Inventor reads all graphs from a file specified by *in* and returns a pointer to a separator that contains the root nodes of all the scene graphs in the file. Using the second syntax, Inventor reads from a file specified by *in* and returns a pointer to the resulting root node (*rootNode*). Using the third syntax, Inventor reads a file specified by *in* and returns a pointer to the resulting path (*path*). (See "Paths" on page 58.) If an error occurs, the methods return FALSE. (Also see Chapter 11 for more information on **SoInput**.)

Scene Graphs

A scene graph consists of one or more *nodes*, each of which represents a geometry, property, or grouping object. Hierarchical scenes are created by adding nodes as children of grouping nodes, resulting in a *directed acyclic graph*.

Note: Although Inventor nodes are organized into graphs, Inventor has no enforced policy on how the scene database is organized. You could, for example, create your own nodes that are organized into structures that are not graphs. (See *The Inventor Toolmaker* for more information on extending the Open Inventor toolkit.)

Figure 3-1 shows a simple database containing five scene graphs. The top node of a scene graph is called a *root node* (nodes A through E). Notice how node H is connected to two different parent nodes. This is called *shared instancing*. Also note that node E is not connected to any other node in the database. Usually this is a temporary state, and the node is attached to other nodes as you build the scene graph.

Types of Nodes

A *node* is the fundamental element of a scene graph. It contains data and methods that define some specific 3D shape, property, or grouping. When a node is created, it is automatically inserted into the database as a root node. Usually, you connect the node to other nodes in the database to construct a hierarchy.

Nodes are divided into three basic categories:

- *Shape nodes*, which represent 3D geometric objects
- *Property nodes*, which represent appearance and other qualitative characteristics of the scene
- *Group nodes*, which are containers that collect nodes into graphs

These categories are not strict and are used only to help you learn about Inventor classes.

Creating Nodes

Use the **new** operator to create nodes. For example:

```
SoSphere *headSphere = new SoSphere;
```

Do not allocate nodes in arrays. (See "How Nodes Are Deleted" on page 70.)

Note: Although you create nodes using the **new** operator, you cannot delete them using **delete**. See "How Nodes Are Deleted" on page 70 for a description of how and when nodes are deleted in Inventor. An understanding of reference counting is vital to your use of Inventor, since you must be aware of the conditions under which a node is automatically deleted.

What's in a Node?

Each node is composed of a set of data elements, known as *fields*, that describe the parameters of the node. For example, a point light-source node (of class **SoPointLight**) contains four fields: *intensity, color, location,* and *on*. The **intensity** field contains a value from 0.0 (no illumination) to 1.0 (maximum illumination). The **color** field specifies a Red/Green/Blue illumination color for the light source. The **location** field specifies the position of the light. The **on** field specifies whether the light is on.

Inventor defines a number of field types. Each field type has unique methods to get and set its values. Within each node, the fields are named according to their usage. For example, here are a few nodes and their fields:

Node	Fields
SoCoordinate3	point
SoNormal	vector
SoMaterial	ambientColor
	diffuseColor
	specularColor
	emissiveColor
	shininess
	transparency
SoPerspectiveCamera	
	viewportMapping
	position
	orientation
	aspectRatio
	nearDistance
	farDistance
	focalDistance
	heightAngle

Note that fields that contain multiple values, such as the **point** field in **SoCoordinate3**, have singular names.

What Happens When You Apply an Action to a Node?

Each node implements its own action behavior. When you want to perform a particular action on a scene, you create an instance of the action class (for example, **SoGLRenderAction** or **SoGetBoundingBoxAction**) and then apply it to the root node of the scene graph. For each action, the database manages a *traversal state*, which is a collection of elements or parameters in the action at a given time. Typically, executing an action involves traversing the graph from top to bottom and left to right. During this traversal, nodes can modify the traversal state, depending on their particular behavior for that action.

This chapter focuses on the *OpenGL rendering action*, since one of the primary reasons for constructing a 3D database is to view and manipulate objects. The rendering traversal state consists of a set of elements, each of which can be altered by a given class of nodes. When a rendering action is applied, each element is used and interpreted in a specified manner. A few of the elements in the traversal state include the following:

- Current geometric transformation
- Current material components
- Current lighting model
- Current drawing style
- Current text font
- Current coordinates
- Current normals
- Current lights
- Current viewing specification

An **SoMaterial** node, for example, sets the current values in the various material elements of the traversal state. An **SoDrawStyle** node sets the current value in the drawing-style element of the traversal state. Shape nodes, such as **SoSphere**, are especially important in rendering traversal, since they cause their shape to be drawn, using the current values in the traversal state.

Shape Nodes

Shape nodes represent 3D geometric objects. They are unique because they describe physical matter that is affected by property and group nodes, and during a rendering action, they actually cause their shape to be drawn on the screen. Classes of shape nodes include **SoSphere**, **SoIndexedFaceSet**, and **SoText3**. Figure 3-2 shows the portion of the class tree that contains the shape-node classes.

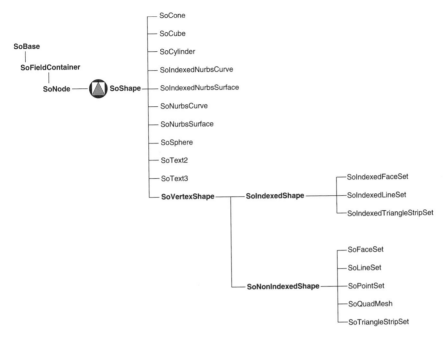

Figure 3-2   Shape-Node Classes

Property Nodes

Property nodes represent appearance and qualitative characteristics of the scene, such as surface material, drawing style, or geometric transformation. Figure 3-3 shows the portion of the class tree that contains the property-node classes. Since property nodes fall naturally into several subgroupings, the scene graph diagrams use three different icons for property nodes:

- The *transform* icon is used for nodes that perform transformations, such as **SoTransform**, **SoRotation**, **SoScale**, **SoTranslation**, **SoRotationXYZ**, and **SoResetTransform**. These nodes are all derived from **SoTransformation**.

- The *appearance* icon is used for nodes that modify an object's appearance, such as **SoMaterial**, **SoMaterialBinding**, **SoBaseColor**, **SoComplexity**, **SoDrawStyle**, **SoLightModel**, and **SoFont**.

- The *metrics* icon is used for nodes that contain coordinate, normal, and other geometric information, such as **SoCoordinate3**, **SoCoordinate4**, **SoProfileCoordinate2**, **SoProfileCoordinate3**, **SoNormal**, and **SoNormalBinding**.

In general, a property node *replaces* the values in a corresponding element of the traversal state with its own new values. Geometric transformations are one exception to this rule. They *concatenate* with the current transformation.

Let's take the material node as an example. This node represents the surface and spectral (color) properties of an object. To create a bronze material, first create the material node and then set the field values appropriately:

```
SoMaterial *bronze = new SoMaterial;

// set field values
bronze->ambientColor.setValue(.33, .22, .27);
bronze->diffuseColor.setValue(.78, .57, .11);
bronze->specularColor.setValue(.99, .94, .81);
bronze->shininess = .28;
```

If you do not explicitly set the field values for a particular node, Inventor uses the default values for those fields (see the *Open Inventor C++ Reference Manual* for individual nodes). For example, in the preceding example, transparency remains 0.0.

SoTransform nodes, which produce geometric transformations, include fields for scaling, rotating, and translating. The following code defines a transform node that translates −1 in the *y* direction:

```
SoTransform *myXform = new SoTransform;

// set field value
myXform->translation.setValue(0.0, -1.0, 0.0);
```

In order for this translation to take effect, it must be inserted appropriately into a scene graph (that is, *before* the shape node to translate).

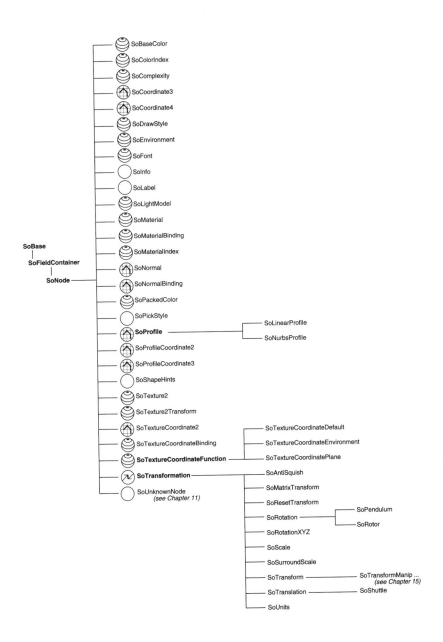

SoBase
|
SoFieldContainer
|
SoNode —

- SoBaseColor
- SoColorIndex
- SoComplexity
- SoCoordinate3
- SoCoordinate4
- SoDrawStyle
- SoEnvironment
- SoFont
- SoInfo
- SoLabel
- SoLightModel
- SoMaterial
- SoMaterialBinding
- SoMaterialIndex
- SoNormal
- SoNormalBinding
- SoPackedColor
- SoPickStyle
- **SoProfile**
  - SoLinearProfile
  - SoNurbsProfile
- SoProfileCoordinate2
- SoProfileCoordinate3
- SoShapeHints
- SoTexture2
- SoTexture2Transform
- SoTextureCoordinate2
- SoTextureCoordinateBinding
- **SoTextureCoordinateFunction**
  - SoTextureCoordinateDefault
  - SoTextureCoordinateEnvironment
  - SoTextureCoordinatePlane
- **SoTransformation**
  - SoAntiSquish
  - SoMatrixTransform
  - SoResetTransform
  - SoRotation
    - SoPendulum
    - SoRotor
  - SoRotationXYZ
  - SoScale
  - SoSurroundScale
  - SoTransform ——— SoTransformManip ...
    (see Chapter 15)
  - SoTranslation ——— SoShuttle
  - SoUnits
- SoUnknownNode
  (see Chapter 11)

Figure 3-3   Property-Node Classes

Types of Nodes   **43**

Groups

A *group node* is a container for collecting child objects. Groups collect property, shape, and other group nodes into graphs. Figure 3-4 shows the portion of the class tree that contains the group-node classes. There are a variety of different group-node classes, each with a specialized grouping characteristic.

When a group node is created, it has no children. The base class for all group nodes is **SoGroup**, and all nodes derived from it have an **addChild()** method.

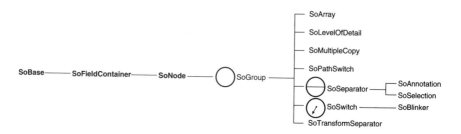

Figure 3-4   Group-Node Classes

Creating Groups

Suppose you want to combine the transform node, the material node, and the sphere node created earlier into a single group, the "head" group for a robot object. First, create the **SoGroup**. Then use the **addChild()** method for each child node, as follows:

```
SoGroup *head = new SoGroup;

head->addChild(myXform);
head->addChild(bronze);
head->addChild(headSphere);
```

Figure 3-5 shows a diagram of this group. All scene graph diagrams use the icons shown in Figure I-1. By convention, all figures show the first child in the group on the left, and ordering of children is from left to right.

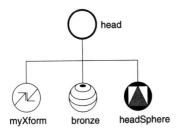

head

myXform   bronze   headSphere

Figure 3-5   Simple Group

Ordering of Children

The **addChild()** method adds the specified node to the *end* of the list of children in the group, as shown in the preceding code. Each child added to the group has an associated index. The first child in a group has an index of 0, the second child in a group has an index of 1, and so on.

The **insertChild()** method

void **insertChild**(SoNode *child*, int *newChildIndex*);

inserts a child node into a group at the location specified by *newChildIndex*. For example,

```
SoDrawStyle *wireStyle;

wireStyle = new SoDrawStyle;
wireStyle->style = SoDrawStyle::LINES;
// Insert as child 1 (the node right after the first child,
// which is child 0.
body->insertChild(wireStyle, 1);
```

inserts a wireframe drawing-style node as the second child of the body group.

Other group methods allow you to find out how many children are in a group, to find the index of a particular child, to access the child with a given index, and to remove children.

Why Is Order Important?

Each node class has its own way of responding to a given database action. For this discussion, assume you are dealing only with the *GL rendering* action (here called simply *rendering*).

- If the node to be rendered is a *group node*, it invokes the rendering action on each of its children in order, typically from left to right in the scene graph.

- Each child node in turn executes its own rendering method, which then affects the traversal state in some way (see Chapter 9). If the child node is a *property node*, it modifies one or more elements in the traversal state, such as the value used for diffuse color, the value used for scaling an object, or the value used for line width. Most property nodes simply *replace* the values for an element in the traversal state. (A bronze material node replaces values in the material element with its own new values.) Geometric transformations are exceptions because they *combine* with each other to make composite transformations.

- If the child node is a *shape node*, it draws itself using the current traversal state.

During rendering, the scene graph is traversed, starting from the root node, from left to right and from top to bottom. Nodes to the right (and down) in the graph inherit the traversal state set by nodes to the left (and above).

Figure 3-6 shows how nodes inherit state. When the *waterMolecule* node is rendered, it visits its first child, *oxygen*. The *oxygen* group then visits each of its children, as follows:

1. The material node (*redPlastic*) changes the material element to a shiny red surface.

2. The sphere node (*sphere1*) causes a sphere to be rendered using the current traversal state. A shiny red sphere is drawn at the origin.

The graph traversal continues to the next group on the right, *hydrogen1*, which in turn visits each of its children in order from left to right:

3. The transform node (*hydrogenXform1*) modifies the transformation matrix (let's say it scales by a factor of 0.75 in *x*, *y*, and *z*). It also modifies the transformation matrix by adding a translation of 0.0, -1.2, 0.0 (in *x*, *y*, and *z*).

4. The material node (*whitePlastic*) changes the material element to a shiny white surface.

5. The sphere node (*sphere2*) causes another sphere to be rendered using the modified traversal state. This sphere is white. Additionally, *sphere2* appears in a new location and is scaled down in size, the result of the **SoTransform** node in its group.

Next, the *hydrogen2* group visits its children, from left to right:

6. The transform node (*hydrogenXform2*) modifies the transformation matrix, translating in the +*x* and +*y* directions.

7. The sphere node (*sphere3*) causes the third sphere to be rendered using the modified traversal state. This sphere is still white and scaled by 0.75 because it inherits these attributes from the *hydrogen1* group.

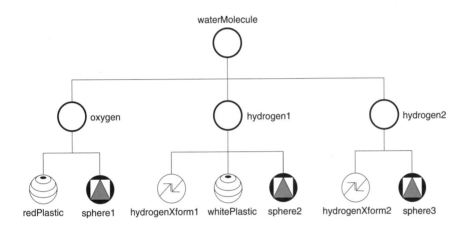

Figure 3-6   Combining Groups

Example 3-1 shows the code to create this molecule.

Example 3-1   Molecule.c++

```cpp
// Construct all parts
SoGroup *waterMolecule = new SoGroup;        // water molecule

SoGroup *oxygen = new SoGroup;               // oxygen atom
SoMaterial *redPlastic = new SoMaterial;
SoSphere *sphere1 = new SoSphere;

SoGroup *hydrogen1 = new SoGroup;            // hydrogen atoms
SoGroup *hydrogen2 = new SoGroup;
SoTransform *hydrogenXform1 = new SoTransform;
SoTransform *hydrogenXform2 = new SoTransform;
SoMaterial *whitePlastic = new SoMaterial;
SoSphere *sphere2 = new SoSphere;
SoSphere *sphere3 = new SoSphere;

// Set all field values for the oxygen atom
redPlastic->ambientColor.setValue(1.0, 0.0, 0.0);
redPlastic->diffuseColor.setValue(1.0, 0.0, 0.0);
redPlastic->specularColor.setValue(0.5, 0.5, 0.5);
redPlastic->shininess = 0.5;

// Set all field values for the hydrogen atoms
hydrogenXform1->scaleFactor.setValue(0.75, 0.75, 0.75);
hydrogenXform1->translation.setValue(0.0, -1.2, 0.0);
hydrogenXform2->translation.setValue(1.1852, 1.3877, 0.0);
whitePlastic->ambientColor.setValue(1.0, 1.0, 1.0);
whitePlastic->diffuseColor.setValue(1.0, 1.0, 1.0);
whitePlastic->specularColor.setValue(0.5, 0.5, 0.5);
whitePlastic->shininess = 0.5;

// Create a hierarchy
waterMolecule->addChild(oxygen);
waterMolecule->addChild(hydrogen1);
waterMolecule->addChild(hydrogen2);

oxygen->addChild(redPlastic);
oxygen->addChild(sphere1);
hydrogen1->addChild(hydrogenXform1);
hydrogen1->addChild(whitePlastic);
hydrogen1->addChild(sphere2);
hydrogen2->addChild(hydrogenXform2);
hydrogen2->addChild(sphere3);
```

Separators

To isolate the effects of nodes in a group, use an **SoSeparator** node, which is a subclass of **SoGroup**. Before traversing its children, an **SoSeparator** saves the current traversal state. When it has finished traversing its children, the **SoSeparator** restores the previous traversal state. Nodes within an **SoSeparator** thus do not affect anything above or to the right in the graph.

Figure 3-7, for example, shows the body and head for a robot. The *body* group, a separator, contains **SoTransform** and **SoMaterial** nodes that affect the traversal state used by the cylinder in that group. These values are restored when all children in the *body* group have been visited, so the *head* group is unaffected by the *body*-group nodes. Because the *head* group is also a separator group, the traversal state is again saved when group traversal begins and restored when group traversal finishes.

Separators are inexpensive to use and help to structure scene graphs. You will probably use them frequently.

Tip: The root node of a scene graph should be a separator if you want the state to be reset between successive renderings.

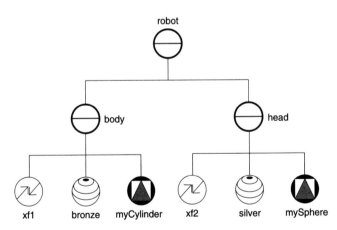

Figure 3-7   Separator Groups

Code for the robot body and head groups is shown below:

```
// create body parts
SoTransform *xf1 = new SoTransform;
xf1->translation.setValue(0.0, 3.0, 0.0);

SoMaterial *bronze = new SoMaterial;
bronze->ambientColor.setValue(.33, .22, .27);
bronze->diffuseColor.setValue(.78, .57, .11);
bronze->specularColor.setValue(.99, .94, .81);
bronze->shininess = .28;

SoCylinder *myCylinder = new SoCylinder;
myCylinder->radius = 2.5;
myCylinder->height = 6;

// construct body out of parts
SoSeparator *body = new SoSeparator;
body->addChild(xf1);
body->addChild(bronze);
body->addChild(myCylinder);

// create head parts
SoTransform *xf2 = new SoTransform;
xf2->translation.setValue(0, 7.5, 0);
xf2->scaleFactor.setValue(1.5, 1.5, 1.5);

SoMaterial *silver = new SoMaterial;
silver->ambientColor.setValue(.2, .2, .2);
silver->diffuseColor.setValue(.6, .6, .6);
silver->specularColor.setValue(.5, .5, .5);
silver->shininess = .5;

SoSphere *mySphere = new SoSphere;

// construct head out of parts
SoSeparator *head = new SoSeparator;
head->addChild(xf2);
head->addChild(silver);
head->addChild(mySphere);

// add head and body
SoSeparator *robot = new SoSeparator;
robot->addChild(body);
robot->addChild(head);
```

Other Subclasses of SoGroup

In addition to **SoSeparator**, other subclasses of **SoGroup** include the following:

- SoSwitch
- SoLevelOfDetail
- SoSelection (see Chapter 10)

In the robot example, **SoSeparator** nodes are used to contain the effects of nodes within a particular group in the scene graph; you do not want the head to inherit the transformation or material attributes from the body group. Conversely, the molecule example uses **SoGroup** nodes to accumulate a set of properties to apply to other nodes later in the graph.

SoSwitch

An **SoSwitch** node is exactly like an **SoGroup** except that it visits only one of its children. It contains one field, **whichChild**, which specifies the index of the child to traverse. For example, the following code specifies to visit node *c* of switch *s*:

```
SoSwitch *s = new SoSwitch;

s->addChild(a);            // this child has an index of 0
s->addChild(b);            // this child has an index of 1
s->addChild(c);            // this child has an index of 2
s->addChild(d);            // this child has an index of 3
s->whichChild = 2;         // specifies to visit child(c)
```

The default setting of **whichChild** is SO_SWITCH_NONE, which specifies to traverse none of the group's children.

You can use an **SoSwitch** node to switch between several different camera nodes for viewing a scene. You can also use an **SoSwitch** node for rudimentary animation. By cycling through a series of groups, you can, for example, make the wings on a duck flap up and down or make a robot walk across the screen. **SoBlinker**, derived from **SoSwitch**, cycles among its children (see Chapter 13) and provides some additional controls useful for animation.

SoLevelOfDetail

The **SoLevelOfDetail** node allows you to specify the same object with varying levels of detail. The children of this node are arranged from highest to lowest level of detail. The size of the objects when projected into the viewport determines which child to use. This node is very useful for applications requiring the fastest rendering possible. It has one field:

screenArea (SoMFFloat)

> areas on the screen to use for comparison with the bounding box of the level-of-detail group. By default, this value is 0.0, so the first child in the group is traversed.

To determine which child to traverse, Inventor computes the 3D bounding box of all children in the level-of-detail group. It projects that bounding box onto the viewport and then computes the area of the screen-aligned rectangle that surrounds the bounding box. This area is then compared to the areas stored in the **screenArea** field. For example, Figure 3-8 shows a level-of-detail node with three children. Suppose the **screenArea** field contains the values [400.0, 100.0]. If the bounding-box projection of the group is 390.0 square pixels (that is, less than 400.0 but greater than 100.0), then *childB* is traversed. If the bounding-box projection of the group is 450.0 pixels (that is, greater than 400.0, then *childA* is traversed. If the bounding-box projection is less than 100.0, *childC* is traversed.

The **SoComplexity** node, discussed in Chapter 5, also affects the child selection for the level-of-detail node. If complexity is 0.0 or is of type BOUNDING_BOX, the last child in **SoLevelOfDetail** is always traversed. If complexity is 1.0, the first child is always used. If the complexity value is greater than 0.0 and less than 0.5, the computed size of the bounding rectangle is scaled down appropriately to use a less detailed representation. If the complexity value is greater than 0.5, the size of the bounding rectangle is scaled up appropriately. If the complexity is 0.5, Inventor uses the computed size of the bounding rectangle as is.

Figure 3-9 shows an object modeled with different levels of detail. Each group of candlesticks is arranged with the most detailed model at the left, a medium level of detail in the middle, and the least detailed model at the right. When the candlestick is close to the camera (as in the first group at the left of Figure 3-9), the most detailed model would be used. This model uses a texture on the base of the candlestick and has a detailed candle with a wick. When the object is farthest away, the least detailed model can be used since the details are not visible anyway. When the object is mid-range (the center group of Figure 3-9), the middle model would be used.

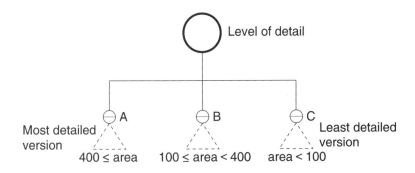

Figure 3-8   Scene Graph with Level-of-Detail Node

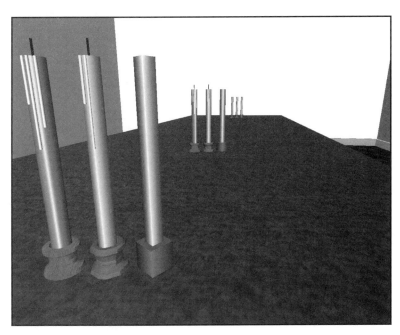

Figure 3-9   Different Levels of Detail for an Object

Shared Instancing of Nodes

You can add any node to more than one group. A bicycle, for example, might use the same basic wheel group for both the front and rear wheels, with slight modifications for size and location of the two wheels. The term *shared instancing* refers to such cases, where a single node has more than one parent.

The robot example can instance the *leg* group twice to form a left and right leg, as shown in Figure 3-10. The basic *leg* group contains nodes for a cylinder (the thigh), a transformed cylinder (the calf), and a transformed cube (the foot). The left and right leg groups (the parents: *rightLeg* and *leftLeg*) each contain an additional **SoTransform** node to position the complete legs correctly onto the robot's body.

Any change made within the *leg* group is reflected in all instances of it. Here, for example, if the height of the cube in the *foot* node is doubled, both the left and right feet double in height.

Shared instancing offers database and program economy, since objects can be reused without duplicating them. You save both time and space by reusing nodes (and groups) when possible.

Do not, however, create cycles within a given scene graph. A node can connect to multiple parents but should not be a child of itself or any of its descendants.

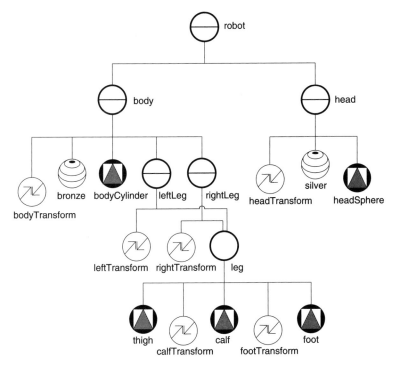

Figure 3-10   Scene Graph Showing Shared Instancing of the Leg Group

Example 3-2 shows the code for the robot as described up to this point. The rendered image is shown in Figure 3-11.

Example 3-2   Robot.c++

```
// Robot with legs

// Construct parts for legs (thigh, calf and foot)
SoCube *thigh = new SoCube;
thigh->width = 1.2;
thigh->height = 2.2;
thigh->depth = 1.1;

SoTransform *calfTransform = new SoTransform;
calfTransform->translation.setValue(0, -2.25, 0.0);
```

```
SoCube *calf = new SoCube;
calf->width = 1;
calf->height = 2.2;
calf->depth = 1;

SoTransform *footTransform = new SoTransform;
footTransform->translation.setValue(0, -2, .5);

SoCube *foot = new SoCube;
foot->width = 0.8;
foot->height = 0.8;
foot->depth = 2;

// Put leg parts together
SoGroup *leg = new SoGroup;
leg->addChild(thigh);
leg->addChild(calfTransform);
leg->addChild(calf);
leg->addChild(footTransform);
leg->addChild(foot);

SoTransform *leftTransform = new SoTransform;
leftTransform->translation = SbVec3f(1, -4.25, 0);

// Left leg
SoSeparator *leftLeg = new SoSeparator;
leftLeg->addChild(leftTransform);
leftLeg->addChild(leg);

SoTransform *rightTransform = new SoTransform;
rightTransform->translation.setValue(-1, -4.25, 0);

// Right leg
SoSeparator *rightLeg = new SoSeparator;
rightLeg->addChild(rightTransform);
rightLeg->addChild(leg);

// Parts for body
SoTransform *bodyTransform = new SoTransform;
bodyTransform->translation.setValue(0.0, 3.0, 0.0);
```

```
SoMaterial *bronze = new SoMaterial;
bronze->ambientColor.setValue(.33, .22, .27);
bronze->diffuseColor.setValue(.78, .57, .11);
bronze->specularColor.setValue(.99, .94, .81);
bronze->shininess = .28;

SoCylinder *bodyCylinder = new SoCylinder;
bodyCylinder->radius = 2.5;
bodyCylinder->height = 6;

// Construct body out of parts
SoSeparator *body = new SoSeparator;
body->addChild(bodyTransform);
body->addChild(bronze);
body->addChild(bodyCylinder);
body->addChild(leftLeg);
body->addChild(rightLeg);

// Head parts
SoTransform *headTransform = new SoTransform;
headTransform->translation.setValue(0, 7.5, 0);
headTransform->scaleFactor.setValue(1.5, 1.5, 1.5);

SoMaterial *silver = new SoMaterial;
silver->ambientColor.setValue(.2, .2, .2);
silver->diffuseColor.setValue(.6, .6, .6);
silver->specularColor.setValue(.5, .5, .5);
silver->shininess = .5;

SoSphere *headSphere = new SoSphere;

// Construct head
SoSeparator *head = new SoSeparator;
head->addChild(headTransform);
head->addChild(silver);
head->addChild(headSphere);

// Robot is just head and body
SoSeparator *robot = new SoSeparator;
robot->addChild(body);
robot->addChild(head);
```

❖ **Tip:** When constructing a complicated scene graph, you may want to define the graph using the Inventor file format (see Chapter 11) and read the graph from a file or from a string in memory. This approach can be easier and less error-prone than constructing the scene graph programmatically.

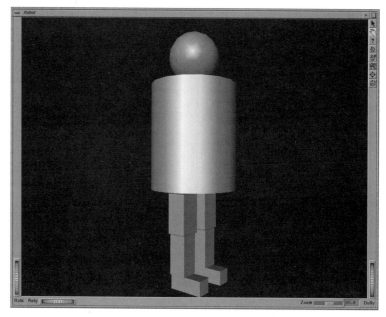

Figure 3-11   Rendered Image of the Robot

Paths

Paths are used to isolate particular objects in the scene graph. Suppose you want to refer to the left foot of the robot. Which node in Figure 3-10 represents the left foot? You can't refer simply to the *foot* node, since that node is used for both the left and right feet. The answer is that the left foot is represented by the path, or chain, starting at the *robot* node (the root), and leading all the way down the graph to the *foot* node. Figure 3-12 indicates the path for the left *foot* node.

A path contains references to a chain of nodes, each of which is a child of the previous node. A path represents a scene graph or *subgraph* (part of a scene graph). In scene graph diagrams in this book, a path is represented by a heavy line that connects the chain of nodes.

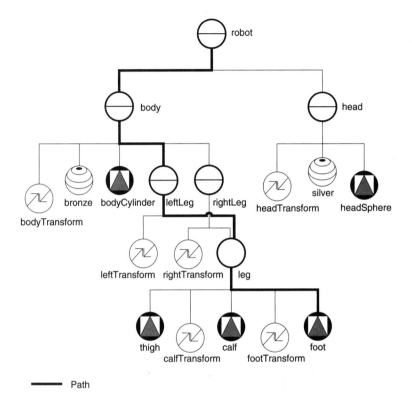

Figure 3-12 Path Representing the Left Foot

Where Do Paths Come From?

Paths are returned by a *picking* or *search* action, and you can construct your own path. (See Chapter 9 for a detailed description of interactive picking.) The user of an interactive application might click the mouse over an object on the screen, causing the object to be picked, and then perform an operation on that object—for example, moving it, changing its color, or deleting it. The selection node manages a list of paths as the currently selected objects.

What Are Paths Used For?

All actions that can be performed on a node can also be performed on a path. These actions include calculating a bounding box and origin for the path, accumulating a transformation matrix for it, and writing the path to a file.

How you use the information included in a path depends on your application. You may use the whole path, or only part of the path. If your user clicks the mouse on the robot's left foot, is the user selecting the whole robot, the left leg, or just the left foot? (Perhaps one click selects the whole robot, and subsequent clicks select parts of the robot that are lower in the graph, such as the left leg and foot.)

Fields within a Node

When you create a node, its fields are already set to predefined values. Afterward, you can change the values in its fields directly. The syntax for setting the value of a field depends on the type of the field and whether it is a single-value or multiple-value field. The following example creates a drawing-style node and sets its fields:

```
SoDrawStyle *d = new SoDrawStyle;

d->style.setValue(SoDrawStyle::LINES) ;
d->lineWidth.setValue(3) ;
d->linePattern.setValue(0xf0f0);
```

The current drawing style is now nonfilled, dashed outlines, with a line width of 3 pixels. If you do not set the field values explicitly, Inventor uses the default values for that node. Default values for **SoDrawStyle** nodes are as follows:

Field	Default Values
style	SoDrawStyle::FILLED
lineWidth	1
linePattern	0xffff (solid)
pointSize	1

The following sections discuss setting and getting values for different types of fields. See also Chapter 13, which discusses field-to-field connections as well as several special types of fields—*global* fields and *trigger* fields.

Why Fields?

You may be wondering why Inventor nodes have fields instead of simple member variables. This section outlines a few of the mechanisms provided by fields. *The Inventor Toolmaker* provides additional background on these topics.

First, fields provide consistent methods for setting and inquiring values, as described in the following sections and in the *Open Inventor C++ Reference Manual*. Second, fields provide a mechanism for Inventor to detect changes to the database. Third, you can connect fields in one node to fields in another node, as described in Chapter 13. Finally, fields provide a consistent and automatic way to read and write node values.

Single- versus Multiple-Value Fields

A single-value field has one value of a given type. Single-value fields include the letters **SF** in their class name. For example:

SoSFBool   contains an **SbBool**

SoSFFloat   contains a single **float**

SoSFRotation   contains an **SbRotation**

SoSFName   contains an **SbName**

SoSFColor   contains a single **SbColor**

Single-value fields are used for nodes that have no use for arrays of values, such as a line pattern, a translation value, a rotation value, or a camera aspect ratio.

A multiple-value field contains an array of values. Multiple-value fields include the letters **MF** in their class name—for example, **SoMFBool**, **SoMFFloat**, **SoMFVec3f**, and **SoMFColor**. Multiple-value fields are used for coordinate points and normal vectors. They are also used for materials, so that you can assign different colors to different vertices. Most fields have both **SF** and **MF** forms. See the *Open* Inventor *C++ Reference Manual* for descriptions of fields within each node class.

Single-Value Fields: Setting and Getting Values

The examples earlier in this chapter show how to declare and create nodes. This section provides additional examples of the syntax for setting and getting values for single-value fields within the nodes. (Most fields have a **setValue()** and **getValue()** method and can also use the = operator to set values.)

Floats, Longs, and Shorts

This first example sets the value in the **height** field of an **SoOrthographicCamera** node through use of the **setValue()** method. This field is of type **SoSFFloat**:

```
SoOrthographicCamera *cam = new SoOrthographicCamera;

cam->height.setValue(1.);
```

or

```
cam->height = 1.; // = operator has been defined for this field
```

To get the value for this field, use the **getValue()** method:

```
float result = cam->height.getValue();
```

Vectors

You can specify an **SoSFVec3f** field in several different formats. Each defines a 3D vector:

- You can set it from a vector (an **SbVec3f**).

- You can set it from three floats (either a vector or three separate values).

- You can set it from an array of three floats.

The following examples show how to set values for **SoSFVec3f** fields. An **SoTransform** node has a field, **translation**, which is an **SoSFVec3f** field that contains one value of type **SbVec3f**. The variable *xform* is a transform-node instance.

```
SoTransform *xform = new SoTransform;

//(1) Setting the field from a vector

SbVec3f vector;
vector.setValue(2.5, 3.5, 0.0);
```

```
xform->translation.setValue(vector);
// or: xform->translation = vector;


//(2a) Setting the field from a vector of three floats

xform->translation.setValue(SbVec3f(2.5, 3.5, 0.0));
// or: xform->translation = SbVec3f(2.5, 3.5, 0.0);


//(2b) Setting the field from three floats

float x = 2.5, y = 3.5, z = 0.0;
xform->translation.setValue(x, y, z);


//(3) Setting the field from an array of three floats

float floatArray[3];
floatArray[0] = 2.5;
floatArray[1] = 3.5;
floatArray[2] = 0.0;
xform->translation.setValue(floatArray);
```

Use the **getValue()** method to get values for a field. This example copies the vector, changes it, and copies it back:

```
SbVec3f t = xform->translation.getValue();

t[0] += 1.0;
xform->translation.setValue(t);
// or: xform->translation = t;
```

Rotations

A rotation field specifies a rotation in 3D space. Since an **SbRotation** represents rotation around an axis by an angle, you can set its value by specifying the axis and angle:

```
SbRotation r;
SbVec3f axis(0., 1., 0.);
float angle = M_PI; //from math.h
r.setvalue(axis, angle);

// or SbRotation r(SbVec3f(0., 1., 1.), M_PI);
```

You can also define a rotation to rotate one direction vector into another, as follows:

```
SbRotation r(SbVec3f(0.0, 0.0, 1.0), SbVec3f(0.0, 1.0, 0.0));
```

To set the value of the **rotation** field of an **SoTransform** node:

```
SoTransform *xform = new SoTransform;

xform ->rotation = r;
```

You can also use **setValue()** to set the value of a **rotation** field and supply an axis and angle, a quaternion, or two vectors.

The = (assignment) operator can be used to set a field's value from another field of the same type. As with vectors, **getValue()** returns the value of the field.

 Tip: If you want to specify a rotation as an axis/angle, you must pass an **SbVec3f** and a float. Passing four floats specifies a quaternion.

Multiple-Value Fields: Setting and Getting Values

The **SoMaterial** node contains the following fields:

Field Name	Class
ambientColor	SoMFColor
diffuseColor	SoMFColor
specularColor	SoMFColor
emissiveColor	SoMFColor
shininess	SoMFFloat
transparency	SoMFFloat

These examples show different styles for setting the fields of an **SoMaterial** node. The **transparency** field is of type **SoMFFloat**, so it contains one or more values of type **float**. The **diffuseColor** field is of type **SoMFColor**, so it contains one or more values of type **SbColor**. The syntax for setting multiple values in an **SoMFFloat** field is as follows:

nodeName->fieldName.**setValues**(*starting index, number of values, pointer to array of values*);

For example:

```
SoMaterial *mtl;
float vals[3];

vals[0] = 0.2;
vals[1] = 0.5;
vals[2] = 0.9;

mtl->transparency.setValues(0, 3, vals);
```

Space for the array is reallocated when necessary. The values are copied in from the array. An example of setting a multiple-value field that uses an **Sb** type is as follows:

```
SoMaterial *mtl;
SbVec3f vals[3];

vals[0].setValue(1.0, 0.0, 0.0);
vals[1].setValue(0.0, 1.0, 0.0);
vals[2].setValue(0.0, 0.0, 1.0);
mtl->diffuseColor.setValues(0, 3, vals);
```

If you want to set only one value in an **SoMFFloat** field, you can use the following shorthand method:

nodeName->fieldName.**setValue**(*value1*);

For example:

```
mtl->transparency.setValue(.25);
//or mtl->transparency = .25;
```

This short method sets the number of values equal to 1 and sets the field to the specified value. However, it also throws away any subsequent values that were previously set in the array, so you should use it only to set the field to have one value. Use the longer method (**setValues**) or the **set1Value()** method if you want to change one value in the array and preserve the rest of the values.

You can use the [ ] operator to get a particular value within a multiple-value field as follows:

```
f = myMtl->transparency[13]; // get 14th value of array
```

You can also create loops to access all values in the field:

```
for (i = 0; i < myMtl->transparency.getNum(); i++) {
    printf("transparency value %d is %g\n", i,
            myMtl->transparency[i]);
}
```

To insert values in the middle of a field:

```
float newValues[2];
newValues[0] = 0.1;
newValues[1] = 0.2;

// First, make space; after this, myMtl->transparency[10]
// and myMtl->transparency[11] will have arbitrary values:

myMtl->transparency.insertSpace(10, 2);

// Set the space created to the right values:

myMtl->transparency.setValues(10, 2, newValues);
```

To delete values from a field:

```
// Delete myMtl->transparency[8] and myMtl->transparency[9];
// the values in myMtl->transparency[10] on up will be moved
// down to fill in the missing space, and the transparency
// array will have two fewer values.

myMtl->transparency.deleteValues(8, 2);
```

See the *Open Inventor C++ Reference Manual* for additional methods used to edit **MF** fields.

Ignore Flag

Every field has an Ignore flag associated with it. Use the **setIgnored()** method to set or reset the Ignore flag. When this flag is set, the field is disregarded. This flag enables you to ignore certain fields in a node and to use others. For example, to ignore the specular color field in a material node so the value is inherited from the previous material:

```
SoMaterial *bronze = new SoMaterial;

bronze->ambientColor.setValue(.33, .22, .27);
bronze->diffuseColor.setValue(.78, .57, .11);
bronze->specularColor.setIgnored(TRUE);
bronze->shininess = .28;
```

To turn the Ignore flag off:

```
bronze->specularColor.setIgnored(FALSE);
```

The **isIgnored()** method returns TRUE if the Ignore flag for this field is set:

```
if (bronze->specularColor.isIgnored()) {
    printf("Yes, specular is ignored\n");
}
```

Some fields are not inherited and are thus not affected by the Ignore flag. Examples of fields that are *not* inherited are the fields of shape nodes, light-source nodes, some groups, and cameras, as well as the fields in the **SoEnvironment** node. If you set the Ignore flag for a field whose values are not inherited, Inventor simply uses the field's default values.

Override Flag

Every node has an Override flag associated with it. The Override flag is a powerful mechanism typically used (sparingly) near the top of a scene graph. When this flag is set, any nodes of the same type encountered later in the graph are ignored even if they also have their Override flag set. For example, you might insert a line-style **SoDrawStyle** node at the top of a graph to ensure that the whole scene is drawn as wireframe objects, regardless of drawing styles specified lower in the scene graph. Use the **setOverride()** method to set and reset the Override flag. The **isOverride()** method returns the state of the Override flag.

For example:

```
// This function toggles the given draw-style node between
// overriding any other draw-style nodes below it in the scene
// graph, and not having any effect at all on the scene graph.
//
void
toggleWireframe(SoDrawStyle *myDrawStyle)
{
   if (myDrawStyle->isOverride()) {
      myDrawStyle->style.setIgnored(TRUE);
      myDrawStyle->setOverride(FALSE);
   } else {
      myDrawStyle->style = SoDrawStyle::LINES;
      myDrawStyle->style.setIgnored(FALSE);
      myDrawStyle->setOverride(TRUE);
   }
}
```

Normally, the Override flag is not used within a scene graph for modeling. Use it in applications where you need to specify a temporary change to the whole graph.

Note: The Override flag is not written to a file (see Chapter 11).

Setting the Override flag on a node whose field values are not inherited (for example, on a sphere with a radius of 7) has no effect on other nodes in the graph of that type.

References and Deletion

Although nodes are created in the usual C++ fashion, the procedure for deleting nodes differs from the C++ style. The following discussion explains how a node counts references to itself and when these references are incremented and decremented. It outlines the proper procedure for unreferencing a node, which results in the node's deletion.

Reference Counting

Each node stores the number of references made to that node within the database. There are several different types of references for nodes:

- Parent-child link

- Path-node link

Engines also store a reference count (see Chapter 13). This count is incremented when the output of an engine is connected to a field. You can also increment or decrement the reference count manually, by calling **ref()** or **unref()**.

Figure 3-13 shows the reference counts for nodes in a small subgraph. Whenever you create a reference to a node, you increment its count. The action

```
A->addChild(B)
```

adds node B to node A and also increments the reference count for node B by 1. In Figure 3-13 node C has a reference count of 2 because it has been added to two different parent groups. At this point, nodes A and D contain 0 references.

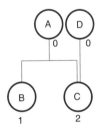

Figure 3-13   Reference Counts

Referencing a node in a path also increments the node's reference count, as shown in Figure 3-14. The reference count for node A now becomes 1, and the reference count for node B becomes 2.

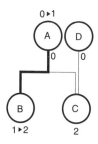

— Path

Figure 3-14   Incrementing the Reference Count

❖ **Tip:** Be sure to reference the root of the scene graph: `root->ref()`. This node is not referenced by being a child of anything else.

How Nodes Are Deleted

Inventor uses a reference-counting mechanism to delete nodes and subgraphs of nodes. To understand how nodes are deleted, you need to know how a node's reference count is incremented and decremented, as detailed in this section.

When you remove a reference to a node, its reference count is decremented. Removing a child decrements the reference count. When a node's count returns to 0, it is deleted from the database. Consider the following cases, however, where deleting a node causes problems (refer to Figure 3-13 for this discussion):

Problem 1:	If you remove node B from node A, the reference count for node B goes to 0 and the node is deleted. But what if you still want to use node B?
Problem 2:	How do you delete node A? Its reference count has always been 0.
Problem 3:	What if someone applies an action to a node that has a reference count of 0? The action creates a path, which references the node. When the action finishes, the path is removed, and the node is deleted.

The solution to these problems is that when you want to prevent a node from being deleted, you reference it:

```
B->ref();
```

Referencing a node increments its count by 1 and ensures that the node is not accidentally deleted. After you have explicitly referenced node B, you can safely remove it as a child of A without fear of deleting node B (Problem 1).

Similarly, to prevent node A from being deleted (Problem 3), you reference it:

```
A->ref();
```

If you want to delete A (Problem 2), you can unreference it, which decrements the reference count. Node A is now deleted, since you were the only one with a reference to it:

```
A->unref();
```

When a group is deleted, all of its children are removed and their reference counts are decremented by 1. In Figure 3-15, for example, if you specify

```
P->unref(); // reference count for P goes to 0
```

the reference counts for the child nodes are decremented as follows:

1. Q goes to 0

      2. S goes to 1

3. R goes to 0

      4. S goes to 0

Since all reference counts now equal 0, all nodes are deleted.

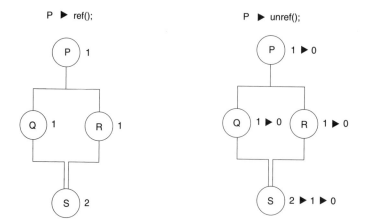

Figure 3-15   Decrementing the Reference Count

❖ **Tip:** Do not allocate nodes, paths, or engines in arrays. This creates problems when one reference count goes to 0 and Inventor tries to free the space allocated for one object in the array.

When you apply an action to a node, the action automatically creates a path that references the node. When the action finishes, it automatically removes the path, and thus decrements the node's reference count. Here again, if the node originally has a reference count of 0, it is deleted when the action finishes.

❖ **Tip:** Random memory errors are often caused by unreferenced nodes that have been deleted. If such errors occur, check your program to be sure that it is not trying to use nodes that have been deleted. The debugging version of the Inventor library catches many common reference-counting mistakes.

Nodes with Zero References

A node, path, or engine should be created only with **new** and never declared on the stack. These objects should be freed only when their reference count goes to 0, not when they go out of scope.

A newly created node has a reference count of 0. This does not mean that it immediately disappears, since a node is deleted only when the reference count is *decremented* to 0. Sometimes it is important to be able to restore a node to its original state (that is, reference count equals 0, but it still exists). For example:

```
// Create a sphere of a certain radius and returns its bounding
// box. NOTE: BUGGY VERSION; provided for discussion only!

SoSphere *makeSphere(float radius, SbBox3f &box)
{
   sphere = new SoSphere;// reference count of 0
   sphere->radius.setValue(radius);

   ba = new SoGetBoundingBoxAction;
   ba->apply(sphere);// does a ref/unref
   box = ba->getBoundingBox();

   return  sphere; // ERROR! returning node that
       // was deleted when ref count
       // went back to zero!
}
```

In this example, the sphere node is referenced and unreferenced by **SoGetBoundingBoxAction**. When unreferenced, the sphere's reference count goes to 0, and it is deleted. The sphere needs to be referenced before the action is applied.

You can use the **unrefNoDelete()** method in cases such as this one, where you want to return the sphere to its original "fresh" state, with a reference count of 0 (but not deleted). Here is an example of using **unrefNoDelete()**:

```
// Create a sphere of a certain radius and returns its bounding
// box. NOTE: CORRECT VERSION

SoSphere *makeSphere(float radius, SbBox3f &box)
{
   sphere = new SoSphere;// reference count of 0
   sphere->ref();// we want it to stay around
   sphere->radius.setValue(radius);

   ba = new SoGetBoundingBoxAction;
   ba->apply(sphere);// does a ref/unref
   box = ba->getBoundingBox();

   sphere->unrefNoDelete();// ref count goes to zero,
// but sphere stays around
   return  sphere;// returns sphere with ref
// count of zero
}
```

Summary of References and Deletion

Table 3-1 summarizes the occurrences that increment and decrement reference counts of nodes and engines. Note that connecting an engine to a field in a node does not increment the node's reference count. (Engines are discussed in Chapter 13.)

Increments Reference Count by 1	Decrements Reference Count by 1
Adding a node as a child of another node increments child's reference count	Removing a node as a child of another node
Adding a node to a path	Removing a node from a path
Applying an action to a node or path increments reference count of all nodes that are traversed	When traversal for the action finishes, all nodes that were traversed are unreferenced
Adding a node to an SoNodeList node	Removing a node from an SoNodeList
Setting an SoSFNode or SoMFNode value to point to a node	Changing an SoSFNode or SoMFNode value to point to a different node or to NULL, or deleting the value
Connecting an output of an engine to a field in a node or engine increments the engine's reference count	Disconnecting an engine's output from the field decrements the engine's reference count

Table 3-1   References and Deletion

Node Types

Inventor provides runtime type-checking through the **SoType** class. Use the **getTypeId()** method on an instance to obtain the **SoType** for that instance. Runtime type-checking is available for most Inventor classes, including nodes, engines, actions, details, and events.

The **SoType** class has methods that enable you to find the parent class of a type (**getParent()**), to create an instance of a particular type (**createInstance()**), and to obtain an **SbName** for the class type (**getName()**). For example, the following code returns a name, such as

Material or Group, which you could then use to print some information about the node:

```
node->getTypeId().getName();
```

The following two statements both return the **SoType** for an **SoMaterial** node (the first is more efficient):

```
// (1)
SoMaterial::getClassTypeId();

// (2)
SoType::fromName("Material");
```

To determine whether an instance is of a particular type, use the == operator, as follows:

```
if (myNode->getTypeId() == SoGroup::getClassTypeId())
      // Is this an SoGroup?
```

To determine whether an instance is of the same type or derived from a particular class, use the **isOfType()** method or the **SoType::derivedFrom()** method (the two methods have the same effects):

```
// (1)
if (myNode->isOfType(SoGroup::getClassTypeId()))
    // Is this an SoGroup, SoSeparator, SoSwitch, and so on

// (2)
if (myNode->getTypeId().isDerivedFrom(
      SoGroup::getClassTypeId()))
```

Also see the description in Chapter 9 of the **SoSearchAction**, which allows you to search the scene graph for nodes of a particular type, or derived from a type.

Naming Nodes

You can assign a name to a node, path, or engine and then search for the object by name. Because the names are preserved when the objects are written to or read from files, they are also a useful way of identifying objects. The base class **SoBase** provides the **setName()** method, which allows you to specify a name for a node, path, or engine. It also provides the **getName()** method, which returns the name for the given object.

Any node, path, or engine has one name, which does not have to be unique. Names can be any **SbName**. An **SbName** can start with any uppercase or lowercase letter (A-Z) or an underscore (_). All characters in an **SbName** must be digits 0-9, upper/lowercase A-Z, or underscores. The default name for an object is the empty string ("").

Use the **SoNode** method **getByName()** to find a node or nodes with a given name. (**SoPath** and **SoEngine** provide similar **getByName()** methods.) The search action also allows you to search for an object or objects with a given name (see Chapter 9).

An example of how names might be used is a slot-car racer program that allows users to create their own slot cars, following simple conventions for how big the cars are, which direction is up, and how the standard nodes or engines in the slot cars are named. For example, the guidelines might specify that the **SoTransform** node that is the steering wheel's rotation is always named *SteeringWheelRotation*. The slot-car program could then read in the scene graph for a given car, search for the *SteeringWheelRotation* node, and then animate the steering wheel using that node.

Example 3-3 shows naming several nodes with **setName()**, then using **getByName()** to return specific nodes. The child node named *MyCube* is removed from the parent named *Root*.

Example 3-3   Naming Nodes

```
#include <Inventor/SoDB.h>
#include <Inventor/nodes/SoCube.h>
#include <Inventor/nodes/SoSeparator.h>
#include <Inventor/nodes/SoSphere.h>
#include <Inventor/sensors/SoNodeSensor.h>

void RemoveCube();   // Defined later...

main( int , char ** )
{
    SoDB::init();

    // Create some objects and give them names:
    SoSeparator *root = new SoSeparator;
    root->ref();
    root->setName("Root");

    SoCube *myCube = new SoCube;
    root->addChild(myCube);
    myCube->setName("MyCube");
```

```
    SoSphere *mySphere = new SoSphere;
    root->addChild(mySphere);
    mySphere->setName("MySphere");

    RemoveCube();
}

void
RemoveCube()
{
    // Remove the cube named 'MyCube' from the separator named
    // 'Root'.  In a real application, isOfType() would probably
    // be used to make sure the nodes are of the correct type
    // before doing the cast.

    SoSeparator *myRoot;
    myRoot = (SoSeparator *)SoNode::getByName("Root");

    SoCube *myCube;
    myCube = (SoCube *)SoNode::getByName("MyCube");

    myRoot->removeChild(myCube);
}
```

## Chapter 4

Cameras and Lights

Chapter Objectives

After reading this chapter, you'll be able to do the following:

- Add different types of cameras to a scene, experimenting with a variety of camera positions, orientations, and viewport mappings

- Add different types of lights to a scene, experimenting with a variety of light types, intensities, and colors

Chapters 4 through 8 focus on several different classes of nodes. Cameras and lights are discussed first because the objects you create are not visible without them. Then, in the following chapters, you learn more about other kinds of nodes in the scene database, including shapes, properties, bindings, text, textures, and NURBS curves and surfaces. Feel free to read selectively in this group of chapters, according to your interests and requirements.

Using Lights and Cameras

The previous chapters introduced you to group, property, and shape nodes and showed you how to create a scene graph using these nodes. Now you'll move on to two classes of nodes that affect how the 3D scene appears: *lights* and *cameras*. In Inventor, as in the real world, lights provide illumination so that you can view objects. If a scene graph does not contain any lights and you're using the default lighting model (Phong lighting), the objects are in darkness and cannot be seen. Just as the real world provides a variety of illumination types—light bulbs, the sun, theatrical spotlights—Inventor provides different classes of lights for you to use in your scene.

Cameras are our "eyes" for viewing the scene. Inventor provides a class of camera with a lens that functions just as the lens of a human eye does, and it also provides additional cameras that create a 2D "snapshot" of the scene with other kinds of lenses. This chapter discusses cameras first and assumes that the scene has at least one light at the top of the scene graph.

❖ **Tip:** Viewer components create their own camera and light automatically. See Chapter 16 for more information on viewers.

Cameras

A camera node generates a picture of everything after it in the scene graph. Typically, you put the camera near the top left of the scene graph, since it must *precede* the objects you want to view. A scene graph should contain only one active camera, and its *position* in space is affected by the current geometric transformation.

❖ **Tip:** A switch node can be used to make one of several cameras active.

SoCamera

Camera nodes are derived from the abstract base class **SoCamera** (see Figure 4-1).

Figure 4-1   Camera-Node Classes

SoCamera has the following fields:

viewportMapping (SoSFEnum)
>   treatment when the camera's aspect ratio is different from the viewport's aspect ratio. (See "Mapping the Camera Aspect Ratio to the Viewport" on page 85.)

position (SoSFVec3f)
>   location of the camera viewpoint. This location is modified by the current geometric transformation.

orientation (SoSFRotation)
>   orientation of the camera's viewing direction. This field describes how the camera is rotated with respect to the default. The default camera looks from (0.0, 0.0, 1.0) toward the origin, and the up direction is (0.0, 1.0, 0.0). This field, along with the current geometric transformation, specifies the orientation of the camera in world space.

aspectRatio (SoSFFloat)
>   ratio of the camera viewing width to height. The value must be greater than 0.0. A few of the predefined camera aspect ratios included in *SoCamera.h* are
>
>   SO_ASPECT_SQUARE (1/1)
>   SO_ASPECT_VIDEO (4/3)
>   SO_ASPECT_HDTV (16/9)

nearDistance (SoSFFloat)
>   distance from the camera viewpoint to the near clipping plane.

farDistance (SoSFFloat)
> distance from the camera viewpoint to the far clipping plane.

focalDistance (SoSFFloat)
> distance from the camera viewpoint to the point of focus (used by the examiner viewer).

Figures 4-2 and 4-3, later in this chapter, show the relationship between the camera position, orientation, near and far clipping planes, and aspect ratio.

When a camera node is encountered during rendering traversal, Inventor performs the following steps:

1. During a rendering action, the camera is positioned in the scene (based on its specified position and orientation, which are modified by the current transformation).

2. The camera creates a *view volume*, based on the near and far clipping planes, the aspect ratio, and the height or height angle (depending on the camera type). A view volume, also referred to as a *viewing frustum*, is a six-sided volume that contains the geometry to be seen (refer to sections on each camera type, later in this chapter, for diagrams showing how the view volume is created). Objects outside of the view volume are *clipped*, or thrown away.

3. The next step is to compress this 3D view volume into a 2D image, similar to the photographic snapshot a camera makes from a real-world scene. This 2D "projection" is now easily mapped to a 2D window on the screen. (See "Mapping the Camera Aspect Ratio to the Viewport" on page 85.)

4. Next, the rest of the scene graph is rendered using the projection created by the camera.

You can also use the **pointAt()** method to replace the value in a camera's **orientation** field. This method sets the camera's orientation to point toward the specified target point. If possible, it keeps the up direction of the camera parallel to the positive *y*-axis. Otherwise, it makes the up direction of the camera parallel to the positive *z*-axis.

The syntax for the **pointAt()** method is as follows:

void   **pointAt**(const SbVec3f &*targetPoint*)

Two additional methods for **SoCamera** are **viewAll()** and **getViewVolume()**. The **viewAll()** method is an easy way to set the camera to view an entire scene graph using the current orientation of the camera. You provide the root node of the scene to be viewed (which usually contains the camera) and a reference to the viewport region used by the render action. The *slack* parameter is used to position the near and far clipping planes. A *slack* value of 1.0 (the default) positions the planes for the "tightest fit" around the scene. The syntax for **viewAll()** is as follows:

void **viewAll**(SoNode *sceneRoot*, const SbViewportRegion &*vpRegion*,
          float *slack* = 1.0)

The **viewAll()** method modifies the camera **position**, **nearDistance**, and **farDistance** fields. It does not affect the camera orientation. An example showing the use of **viewAll()** appears in "Viewing a Scene with Different Cameras" on page 86.

The **getViewVolume()** method returns the camera's view volume and is usually used in relation to picking.

Subclasses of SoCamera

The **SoCamera** class contains two subclasses, as shown in Figure 4-1:

- SoPerspectiveCamera
- SoOrthographicCamera

SoPerspectiveCamera

A camera of class **SoPerspectiveCamera** emulates the human eye: objects farther away appear smaller in size. Perspective camera projections are natural in situations where you want to imitate how objects appear to a human observer.

An **SoPerspectiveCamera** node has one field in addition to those defined in **SoCamera**:

heightAngle (SoSFFloat)
          specifies the vertical angle in radians of the camera view volume.

The view volume formed by an **SoPerspectiveCamera** node is a truncated pyramid, as shown in Figure 4-2. The height angle and the aspect ratio determine the width angle as follows:

widthAngle = heightAngle * aspectRatio

SoOrthographicCamera

In contrast to perspective cameras, cameras of class **SoOrthographic-Camera** produce *parallel* projections, with no distortions for distance. Orthographic cameras are useful for precise design work, where visual distortions would interfere with exact measurement.

An **SoOrthographicCamera** node has one field in addition to those defined in **SoCamera**:

height (SoSFFloat) specifies the height of the camera view volume.

The view volume formed by an **SoOrthographicCamera** node is a rectangular box, as shown in Figure 4-3. The height and aspect ratio determine the width of the rectangle:

width = height * aspectRatio

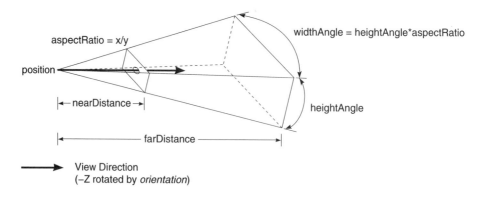

Figure 4-2   View Volume and Viewing Projection for an
SoPerspectiveCamera Node

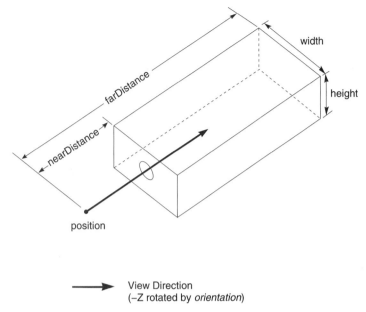

width

farDistance

height

nearDistance

position

→ View Direction
(–Z rotated by *orientation*)

Figure 4-3   View Volume and Viewing Projection for an
SoOrthographicCamera Node

Mapping the Camera Aspect Ratio to the Viewport

A *viewport* is the rectangular area where a scene is rendered. By default, the viewport has the same dimensions as the window (**SoXtRenderArea**). The viewport is specified when the **SoGLRenderAction** is constructed (see Chapter 9).

The **viewportMapping** field of **SoCamera** allows you to specify how to map the camera projection into the viewport when the aspect ratios of the camera and viewport differ. The first three choices crop the viewport to fit the camera projection. The advantage to these settings is that the camera aspect ratio remains unchanged. (The disadvantage is that there is dead space in the viewport.)

- CROP_VIEWPORT_FILL_FRAME adjusts the viewport to fit the camera (see Figure 4-4). It draws the viewport with the appropriate aspect ratio and fills in the unused space with gray.

- CROP_VIEWPORT_LINE_FRAME adjusts the viewport to fit the camera. It draws the border of the viewport as a line.

- CROP_VIEWPORT_NO_FRAME adjusts the viewport to fit the camera. It does not indicate the viewport boundaries.

These two choices adjust the camera projection to fit the viewport:

- ADJUST_CAMERA adjusts the camera to fit the viewport (see Figure 4-4). The projected image is not distorted. (The actual values stored in the **aspectRatio** and **height/heightAngle** fields are not changed. These values are temporarily overridden if required by the viewport mapping.) This is the default setting.

- LEAVE_ALONE does not modify anything. The camera image is resized to fit the viewport. A distorted image is produced (see Figure 4-4).

Figure 4-4 shows the different types of viewport mapping. In this example, the camera aspect ratio is 3 to 1 and the viewport aspect ratio is 1.5 to 1. The top camera uses CROP_VIEWPORT_FILL_FRAME viewport mapping. The center camera uses ADJUST_CAMERA. The bottom camera uses LEAVE_ALONE. Figure 4-4 also shows three stages of mapping. At the left is the initial viewport mapping. The center column of drawings shows how the mapping changes if the viewport is compressed horizontally. The right-hand column shows how the mapping changes if the viewport is compressed vertically.

Viewing a Scene with Different Cameras

Example 4-1 shows a scene viewed by an orthographic camera and two perspective cameras in different positions. It uses a blinker node (described in Chapter 13) to switch among the three cameras. The scene (a park bench) is read from a file. Figure 4-5 shows the scene graph created by this example. Figure 4-6 shows the image created by this example.

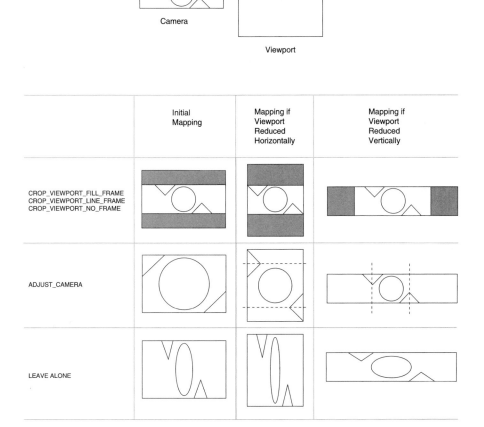

Figure 4-4   Mapping the Camera Aspect Ratio to the Viewport

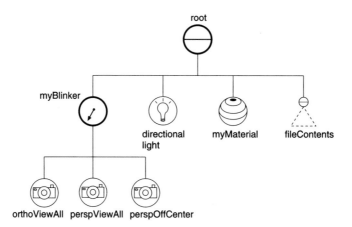

myBlinker

directional light

myMaterial

fileContents

orthoViewAll   perspViewAll   perspOffCenter

Figure 4-5   Scene Graph for Camera Example

Example 4-1   Switching among Multiple Cameras

```
#include <Inventor/SbLinear.h>
#include <Inventor/SoDB.h>
#include <Inventor/SoInput.h>
#include <Inventor/Xt/SoXt.h>
#include <Inventor/Xt/SoXtRenderArea.h>
#include <Inventor/nodes/SoBlinker.h>
#include <Inventor/nodes/SoDirectionalLight.h>
#include <Inventor/nodes/SoMaterial.h>
#include <Inventor/nodes/SoOrthographicCamera.h>
#include <Inventor/nodes/SoPerspectiveCamera.h>
#include <Inventor/nodes/SoSeparator.h>
#include <Inventor/nodes/SoTransform.h>

main(int, char **argv)
{
   // Initialize Inventor and Xt
   Widget myWindow = SoXt::init(argv[0]);
   if (myWindow == NULL)
      exit(1);

   SoSeparator *root = new SoSeparator;
   root->ref();
```

Figure 4-6   Camera Example

```
// Create a blinker node and put it in the scene. A blinker
// switches between its children at timed intervals.
SoBlinker *myBlinker = new SoBlinker;
root->addChild(myBlinker);

// Create three cameras. Their positions will be set later.
// This is because the viewAll method depends on the size
// of the render area, which has not been created yet.
SoOrthographicCamera *orthoViewAll = new SoOrthographicCamera;
SoPerspectiveCamera *perspViewAll = new SoPerspectiveCamera;
SoPerspectiveCamera *perspOffCenter = new SoPerspectiveCamera;
myBlinker->addChild(orthoViewAll);
myBlinker->addChild(perspViewAll);
myBlinker->addChild(perspOffCenter);

// Create a light
root->addChild(new SoDirectionalLight);

// Read the object from a file and add to the scene
SoInput myInput;
if (! myInput.openFile("parkbench.iv"))
   return 1;
SoSeparator *fileContents = SoDB::readAll(&myInput);
if (fileContents == NULL)
   return 1;

SoMaterial *myMaterial = new SoMaterial;
myMaterial->diffuseColor.setValue(0.8, 0.23, 0.03);
root->addChild(myMaterial);
root->addChild(fileContents);

SoXtRenderArea *myRenderArea = new SoXtRenderArea(myWindow);
```

```
// Establish camera positions.
// First do a viewAll() on all three cameras.
// Then modify the position of the off-center camera.
SbViewportRegion myRegion(myRenderArea->getSize());
orthoViewAll->viewAll(root, myRegion);
perspViewAll->viewAll(root, myRegion);
perspOffCenter->viewAll(root, myRegion);
SbVec3f initialPos;
initialPos = perspOffCenter->position.getValue();
float x, y, z;
initialPos.getValue(x,y,z);
perspOffCenter->position.setValue(x+x/2., y+y/2., z+z/4.);

myRenderArea->setSceneGraph(root);
myRenderArea->setTitle("Cameras");
myRenderArea->show();

SoXt::show(myWindow);
SoXt::mainLoop();
}
```

After you view this example, experiment by modifying the fields in each camera node to see how changes in camera position, orientation, aspect ratio, location of clipping planes, and camera height (or height angle) affect the images on your screen. Then try using the **pointAt()** method to modify the orientation of the camera node. Remember that a scene graph includes only *one* active camera at a time, and it must be placed *before* the objects to be viewed.

Lights

With the default lighting model (Phong), a scene graph also needs at least one light before you can view its objects. During a rendering action, traversing a light node in the scene graph turns that light on. The position of the light node in the scene graph determines two things:

- *What the light illuminates*—a light illuminates everything that follows it in the scene graph. (The light is part of the traversal state, described in Chapter 3. Use an **SoSeparator** node to isolate the effects of a particular light from the rest of the scene graph.)

- *Where the light is located in 3D space*—certain light-source nodes (for example, **SoPointLight**) have a **location** field. This light location is affected by the current geometric transformation. Other light-source nodes have a specified **direction** (for example, **SoDirectionalLight**), which is also affected by the current geometric transformation.

Another important fact about all light-source nodes is that lights accumulate. Each time you add a light to the scene graph, the scene appears brighter. The maximum number of active lights is dependent on the OpenGL implementation.

In some cases, you may want to separate the position of the light in the scene graph from what it illuminates. Example 4-2 uses the **SoTransformSeparator** node to move only the position of the light. Sensors and engines are also a useful way to affect a light's behavior. For example, you can attach a sensor to a sphere object; when the sphere position changes, the sensor can change the light position as well. Or, you can use an engine that finds the path to a given object to affect the location of the light that illuminates that object (see **SoComputeBoundingBox** in the *Open Inventor C++ Reference Manual*).

SoLight

All lights are derived from the abstract base class **SoLight**. This class adds no new methods to **SoNode**. Its fields are as follows:

on (SoSFBool)   whether the light is on.

intensity (SoSFFloat)

> brightness of the light. Values range from 0.0 (no illumination) to 1.0 (maximum illumination).

color (SoSFColor)   color of the light.

Subclasses of SoLight

The **SoLight** class contains three subclasses, as shown in Figure 4-7:

- SoPointLight
- SoDirectionalLight
- SoSpotLight

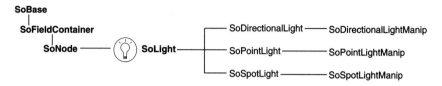

Figure 4-7   Light-Node Classes

Figure 4-8 shows the effects of each of these light types. The left side of the figure shows the direction of the light rays, and the right side shows the same scene rendered with each light type. Plates 1 through 3 show additional use of these light types.

❖ **Tip:** Directional lights are typically faster than point lights for rendering. Both are typically faster than spotlights. To increase rendering speed, use fewer and simpler lights.

SoPointLight

A light of class **SoPointLight**, like a star, radiates light equally in all directions from a given location in 3D space. An **SoPointLight** node has one additional field:

location (SoSFVec3f)
> 3D location of a point light source. (This location is affected by the current geometric transformation.)

SoDirectionalLight

A light of class **SoDirectionalLight** illuminates uniformly along a particular direction. Since it is infinitely far away, it has no location in 3D space. An **SoDirectionalLight** node has one additional field:

direction (SoSFVec3f)
> specifies the direction of the rays from a directional light source. (This direction is affected by the current geometric transformation.)

Ambient Light

(See Chapter 5)

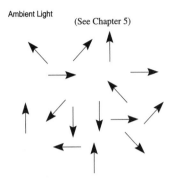

Point Light

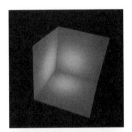

Directional Light

Spot Light

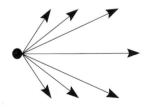

Figure 4-8   Light Types

Tip: A surface composed of a single polygon (such as a large rectangle) with one normal at each corner will not show the effects of a point light source, since lighting is computed (by OpenGL) only at vertices. Use a more complex surface to show this effect.

With an **SoDirectionalLight** source node, all rays of incident light are parallel. They are reflected equally from all points on a flat polygon, resulting in flat lighting of equal intensity, as shown in Figure 4-8. In contrast, the intensity of light from an **SoPointLight** source on a flat surface would vary, because the angle between the surface normal and the incident ray of light is different at different points of the surface.

SoSpotLight

A light of class **SoSpotLight** illuminates from a point in space along a primary direction. Like a theatrical spotlight, its illumination is a cone of light diverging from the light's position. An **SoSpotLight** node has four additional fields (see Figure 4-9):

location (SoSFVec3f)

> 3D location of a spotlight source. (This location is affected by the current geometric transformation.)

direction (SoSFVec3f)

> primary direction of the illumination.

dropOffRate (SoSFFloat)

> rate at which the light intensity drops off from the primary direction (0.0 = constant intensity, 1.0 = sharpest drop-off).

cutOffAngle (SoSFFloat)

> angle, in radians, outside of which the light intensity is 0.0. This angle is measured from one edge of the cone to the other.

Using Multiple Lights

You can now experiment by adding different lights to a scene. Example 4-2 contains two light sources: a stationary red directional light and a green point light that is moved back and forth by an **SoShuttle** node (see Chapter 13). Figure 4-10 shows the scene graph created by this example.

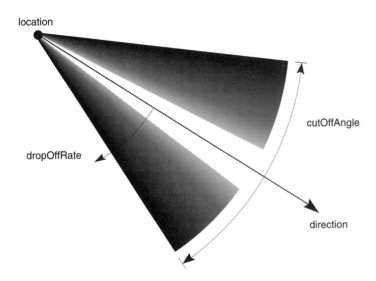

location

cutOffAngle

dropOffRate

direction

Figure 4-9   Fields for SoSpotLight Node

Example 4-2   Using Different Types of Lights

```
#include <Inventor/SoDB.h>
#include <Inventor/Xt/SoXt.h>
#include <Inventor/Xt/viewers/SoXtExaminerViewer.h>
#include <Inventor/nodes/SoCone.h>
#include <Inventor/nodes/SoDirectionalLight.h>
#include <Inventor/nodes/SoMaterial.h>
#include <Inventor/nodes/SoPointLight.h>
#include <Inventor/nodes/SoSeparator.h>
#include <Inventor/nodes/SoShuttle.h>
#include <Inventor/nodes/SoTransformSeparator.h>

main(int , char **argv)
{
   // Initialize Inventor and Xt
   Widget myWindow = SoXt::init(argv[0]);
   if (myWindow == NULL)
      exit(1);

   SoSeparator *root = new SoSeparator;
   root->ref();
```

```
// Add a directional light
SoDirectionalLight *myDirLight = new SoDirectionalLight;
myDirLight->direction.setValue(0, -1, -1);
myDirLight->color.setValue(1, 0, 0);
root->addChild(myDirLight);

// Put the shuttle and the light below a transform separator.
// A transform separator pushes and pops the transformation
// just like a separator node, but other aspects of the state
// are not pushed and popped. So the shuttle's translation
// will affect only the light. But the light will shine on
// the rest of the scene.
SoTransformSeparator *myTransformSeparator =
    new SoTransformSeparator;
root->addChild(myTransformSeparator);

// A shuttle node translates back and forth between the two
// fields translation0 and translation1.
// This moves the light.
SoShuttle *myShuttle = new SoShuttle;
myTransformSeparator->addChild(myShuttle);
myShuttle->translation0.setValue(-2, -1, 3);
myShuttle->translation1.setValue( 1,  2, -3);

// Add the point light below the transformSeparator
SoPointLight *myPointLight = new SoPointLight;
myTransformSeparator->addChild(myPointLight);
myPointLight->color.setValue(0, 1, 0);
```

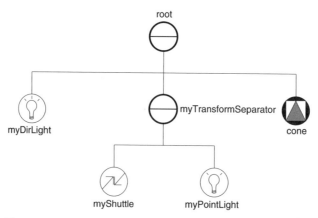

Figure 4-10   Scene Graph for Light Example

```
      root->addChild(new SoCone);

      SoXtExaminerViewer *myViewer =
               new SoXtExaminerViewer(myWindow);
      myViewer->setSceneGraph(root);
      myViewer->setTitle("Lights");
      myViewer->setHeadlight(FALSE);
      myViewer->show();

      SoXt::show(myWindow);
      SoXt::mainLoop();
}
```

Chapter 5

Shapes, Properties, and Binding

Chapter Objectives

After reading this chapter, you'll be able to do the following:

● Use a variety of shapes in the scene, including complex shapes that use information from coordinate and normal nodes

● Explain how indexed shapes specify their own order for using coordinate, material, normal, and texture values

● Experiment with different effects for color values, shininess, and transparency

● Render a scene using different drawing styles for different parts of the scene

● Render a scene using different light models

● Create a scene with fog in it

● Use the shape hints, complexity, and level-of-detail nodes to speed up performance

● Experiment with different types of material and normal binding

For convenience, shapes are divided into two categories: *simple shapes* and *complex shapes*. Simple shapes are self-contained nodes that hold their own geometrical parameters. Complex shapes, in contrast, may refer to other nodes for their coordinates and normals. This chapter also discusses important property nodes, including material, draw-style, and lighting-style nodes. Other chapter examples illustrate key concepts pertaining to *geometric transformations* and to *binding nodes* for materials and normals.

Simple Shapes

All shape nodes are derived from the abstract base class **SoShape**. Inventor provides the following simple shapes:

- Cube (you specify the width, height, and depth)
- Cone (you specify the height and bottom radius)
- Sphere (you specify the radius)
- Cylinder (you specify the height and the radius)

Figure 5-1 shows the portion of the class tree that contains shape classes.

Complex Shapes

Complex shapes, such as triangle strip sets and face sets, require at least a set of coordinates. If the lighting is set to PHONG, complex shapes also require a set of surface normals, as shown in Figure 5-2. Coordinates and normals are defined by separate nodes in the scene graph so that this information can be shared by other nodes.

Examples of complex shapes include the following:

- Face set, indexed face set
- Line set, indexed line set
- Triangle strip set, indexed triangle strip set
- Point set
- Quad mesh
- NURBS curve and surface

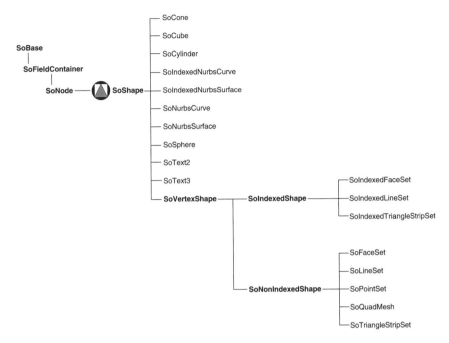

Figure 5-1   Shape-Node Classes

An **SoCoordinate3** node sets the current coordinates in the rendering state to the specified points. This node contains one field (**point**), which is of type **SoMFVec3f**. For example:

```
SbVec3f verts[6];
SoCoordinate3 *coord = new SoCoordinate3;

// ...Initialize vertices array ...

coord->point.setValues(0, 6, verts);
```

An **SoNormal** node sets the current surface normals in the rendering state to the specified vectors. This node contains one field, **vector**, of type **SoMFVec3f**.

Tip: Normals can also be generated automatically by Inventor, in which case ❖
you do not need an **SoNormal** node. See "Generating Normals
Automatically" on page 132 for further information.

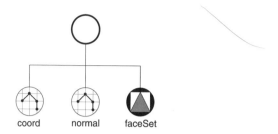

Figure 5-2   Nodes Used to Create a Simple Indexed Face Set

Face Set

An **SoFaceSet** is a shape node that represents a polygonal object formed by constructing faces out of the current coordinates, current normals, current materials, and current textures. It uses the values within each node in the order they are given. (To use coordinates, normals, and materials in a different order, use the **SoIndexedFaceSet** node, described in the next section.)

Example 5-1 creates an obelisk using a face set composed of eight faces. The scene graph for this example is shown in Figure 5-3. Ignore the normal binding node for now. This node is explained in "Binding Nodes" on page 126. Figure 5-4 shows the image created by this example.

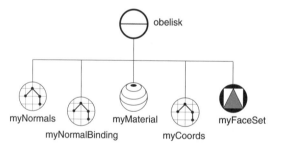

Figure 5-3   Scene Graph for Face Set Example

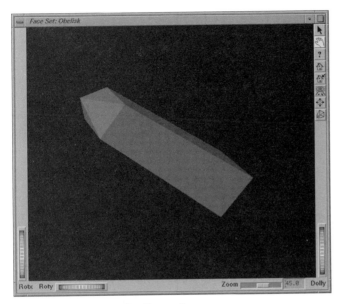

Figure 5-4   Face-Set Example

Example 5-1   Creating a Face Set

```
//  Eight polygons. The first four are triangles
//  The second four are quadrilaterals for the sides.
static float vertices[28][3] =
{
    { 0, 30, 0}, {-2,27, 2}, { 2,27, 2},          //front tri
    { 0, 30, 0}, {-2,27,-2}, {-2,27, 2},          //left  tri
    { 0, 30, 0}, { 2,27,-2}, {-2,27,-2},          //rear  tri
    { 0, 30, 0}, { 2,27, 2}, { 2,27,-2},          //right tri
    {-2, 27, 2}, {-4,0, 4}, { 4,0, 4}, { 2,27, 2},  //front quad
    {-2, 27,-2}, {-4,0,-4}, {-4,0, 4}, {-2,27, 2},  //left  quad
    { 2, 27,-2}, { 4,0,-4}, {-4,0,-4}, {-2,27,-2},  //rear  quad
    { 2, 27, 2}, { 4,0, 4}, { 4,0,-4}, { 2,27,-2}   //right quad
};

// Number of vertices in each polygon:
static long numvertices[8] = {3, 3, 3, 3, 4, 4, 4, 4};

// Normals for each polygon:
static float norms[8][3] =
{
    {0, .555,  .832}, {-.832, .555, 0}, //front, left tris
    {0, .555, -.832}, { .832, .555, 0}, //rear, right tris
```

```
        {0, .0739,  .9973}, {-.9972, .0739, 0},//front, left quads
        {0, .0739, -.9973}, { .9972, .0739, 0},//rear, right quads
};

SoSeparator *
makeObeliskFaceSet()
{
    SoSeparator *obelisk = new SoSeparator();
    obelisk->ref();

    // Define the normals used:
    SoNormal *myNormals = new SoNormal;
    myNormals->vector.setValues(0, 8, norms);
    obelisk->addChild(myNormals);
    SoNormalBinding *myNormalBinding = new SoNormalBinding;
    myNormalBinding->value = SoNormalBinding::PER_FACE;
    obelisk->addChild(myNormalBinding);

    // Define material for obelisk
    SoMaterial *myMaterial = new SoMaterial;
    myMaterial->diffuseColor.setValue(.4, .4, .4);
    obelisk->addChild(myMaterial);

    // Define coordinates for vertices
    SoCoordinate3 *myCoords = new SoCoordinate3;
    myCoords->point.setValues(0, 28, vertices);
    obelisk->addChild(myCoords);

    // Define the FaceSet
    SoFaceSet *myFaceSet = new SoFaceSet;
    myFaceSet->numVertices.setValues(0, 8, numvertices);
    obelisk->addChild(myFaceSet);

    obelisk->unrefNoDelete();
    return obelisk;
}
```

❖ **Tip:** When you construct a scene graph, be sure that you have used as few
nodes as possible to accomplish your goals. For example, to create a
multifaceted polygonal shape, it's best to put all the coordinates for the
shape into one **SoCoordinate** node and put the description of all the
face sets into a single **SoFaceSet** (or **SoIndexedFaceSet**) node rather
than using multiple nodes for each face.

Indexed Face Set

An **SoIndexedFaceSet** node is a shape node that represents a polygonal object formed by constructing faces out of the current coordinates, using the current surface normals, current materials, and current texture. In contrast to the **SoFaceSet** node, this node can use those values in any order. This node class contains four fields with indices that specify the ordering:

coordIndex (SoMFLong)

contains indices into the coordinates list. These indices connect coordinates to form a set of faces. A value of SO_END_FACE_INDEX (–1) indicates the end of one face and the start of the next face. This field is always used.

materialIndex (SoMFLong)

contains indices into the current material(s) for the materials of the face set. This field is used only when some type of indexed material binding is specified in the **SoMaterialBinding** node. See "Binding Nodes" on page 126.

normalIndex (SoMFLong)

contains indices into the current normals for the vertices of the face set. This field is used only when indexed normal binding (either per vertex or per face) is specified in the **SoNormalBinding** node. See "Binding Nodes" on page 126.

textureCoordIndex (SoMFLong)

contains indices of the texture coordinates that are applied to the shape (see Chapter 7).

Be sure that the indices contained in the indexed face set can actually be found in the coordinates and normals lists, or errors will occur.

Note: If you use the **SoShapeHints** node to specify that the vertices are counterclockwise, you must specify the vertex indices according to the *right-hand rule*. The right-hand rule states that if you place the fingers of your right hand around the face following the direction in which the vertices are specified, your thumb points in the general direction of the geometric normal. Alternatively, you can specify the vertices in clockwise order. In this case, the direction of the geometric normal is determined by the left-hand rule.

Example 5-2 creates the first stellation of the dodecahedron from an indexed face set. Each of the twelve intersecting faces is a pentagon. The scene graph diagram for this example is shown in Figure 5-5. Figure 5-6 shows the image created by this example.

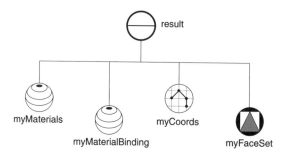

Figure 5-5   Scene Graph for Indexed Face-Set Example

Example 5-2   Creating an Indexed Face Set

```
// Positions of all of the vertices:
//
static float vertexPositions[12][3] =
{
    { 0.0000,   1.2142,   0.7453},   // top

    { 0.0000,   1.2142,  -0.7453},   // points surrounding top
    {-1.2142,   0.7453,   0.0000},
    {-0.7453,   0.0000,   1.2142},
    { 0.7453,   0.0000,   1.2142},
    { 1.2142,   0.7453,   0.0000},

    { 0.0000,  -1.2142,   0.7453},   // points surrounding bottom
    {-1.2142,  -0.7453,   0.0000},
    {-0.7453,   0.0000,  -1.2142},
    { 0.7453,   0.0000,  -1.2142},
    { 1.2142,  -0.7453,   0.0000},

    { 0.0000,  -1.2142,  -0.7453},   // bottom
};
```

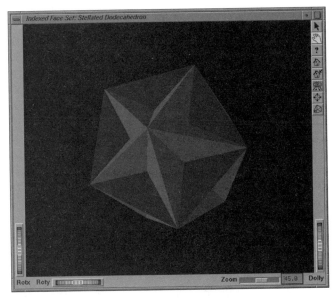

Figure 5-6   Indexed Face-Set Example

```
// Connectivity, information; 12 faces with 5 vertices each },
// (plus the end-of-face indicator for each face):

static long indices[72] =
{
   1,   2,   3,   4, 5, SO_END_FACE_INDEX, // top face

   0,   1,   8,   7, 3, SO_END_FACE_INDEX, // 5 faces about top
   0,   2,   7,   6, 4, SO_END_FACE_INDEX,
   0,   3,   6, 10, 5, SO_END_FACE_INDEX,
   0,   4, 10,   9, 1, SO_END_FACE_INDEX,
   0,   5,   9,   8, 2, SO_END_FACE_INDEX,

   9,   5,   4,   6, 11, SO_END_FACE_INDEX, // 5 faces about bottom
  10,   4,   3,   7, 11, SO_END_FACE_INDEX,
   6,   3,   2,   8, 11, SO_END_FACE_INDEX,
   7,   2,   1,   9, 11, SO_END_FACE_INDEX,
   8,   1,   5, 10, 11, SO_END_FACE_INDEX,

   6,   7,   8,   9, 10, SO_END_FACE_INDEX, // bottom face
};
```

```
// Colors for the 12 faces
static float colors[12][3] =
{
    {1.0, .0, 0}, { .0,  .0, 1.0}, {0, .7,  .7}, { .0, 1.0,  0},
    { .7, .7, 0}, { .7,  .0,  .7}, {0, .0, 1.0}, { .7,  .0, .7},
    { .7, .7, 0}, { .0, 1.0,  .0}, {0, .7,  .7}, {1.0,  .0,  0}
};

// Routine to create a scene graph representing a dodecahedron
SoSeparator *
makeStellatedDodecahedron()
{
    SoSeparator *result = new SoSeparator;
    result->ref();

    // Define colors for the faces
    SoMaterial *myMaterials = new SoMaterial;
    myMaterials->diffuseColor.setValues(0, 12, colors);
    result->addChild(myMaterials);
    SoMaterialBinding *myMaterialBinding = new SoMaterialBinding;
    myMaterialBinding->value = SoMaterialBinding::PER_FACE;
    result->addChild(myMaterialBinding);

    // Define coordinates for vertices

    // Define coordinates for vertices
    SoCoordinate3 *myCoords = new SoCoordinate3;
    myCoords->point.setValues(0, 12, vertexPositions);
    result->addChild(myCoords);

    // Define the IndexedFaceSet, with indices into
    // the vertices:
    SoIndexedFaceSet *myFaceSet = new SoIndexedFaceSet;
    myFaceSet->coordIndex.setValues(0, 72, indices);
    result->addChild(myFaceSet);

    result->unrefNoDelete();
    return result;
}
```

Triangle Strip Set

The **SoTriangleStripSet** node constructs triangle strips out of the vertices located at the current coordinates. It is one of the fastest ways to draw polygonal objects in Inventor. The triangle strip set uses the current coordinates, in order, starting at the index specified by the **startIndex** field. (If no index is specified, it starts at the first index.)

The **numVertices** field indicates the number of vertices to use for each triangle strip in the set. The triangle strip set is described as follows:

```
static long numVertices[2] =

{
    32, // flag
     8  // pole
};

SoTriangleStripSet *myStrips = new SoTriangleStripSet;
myStrips->numVertices.setValues(0, 2, numVertices);
```

Because the **numVertices** field contains an array with two values, two triangle strips are created. The first strip (the flag) is made from the first 32 coordinate values. The second strip (the flagpole) is made from the next 8 coordinates. Face 0 determines the vertex ordering—in this case, counterclockwise.

Tip: Triangle strip sets and quad meshes are generally faster to render than face sets.

Example 5-3 shows the code for creating a pennant-shaped flag. Figure 5-7 shows the scene graph for this example. Figure 5-8 shows the resulting image.

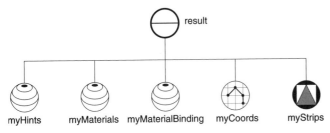

Figure 5-7   Scene Graph for Triangle Strip Set Example

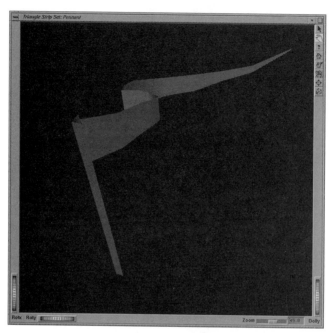

Figure 5-8   Triangle Strip Set Example

Example 5-3   Creating a Triangle Strip Set

```
// Positions of all of the vertices:

static float vertexPositions[40][3] =
{
    {  0,   12,    0 }, {  0,   15,    0},
    {2.1, 12.1,  -.2 }, { 2.1, 14.6,  -.2},
    {  4, 12.5,  -.7 }, {   4, 14.5,  -.7},
    {4.5, 12.6,  -.8 }, { 4.5, 14.4,  -.8},
    {  5, 12.7,   -1 }, {   5, 14.4,   -1},
    {4.5, 12.8, -1.4 }, { 4.5, 14.6, -1.4},
    {  4, 12.9, -1.6 }, {   4, 14.8, -1.6},
    {3.3, 12.9, -1.8 }, { 3.3, 14.9, -1.8},
    {  3,   13, -2.0 }, {   3, 14.9, -2.0},
    {3.3, 13.1, -2.2 }, { 3.3, 15.0, -2.2},
    {  4, 13.2, -2.5 }, {   4, 15.0, -2.5},
    {  6, 13.5, -2.2 }, {   6, 14.8, -2.2},
    {  8, 13.4,   -2 }, {   8, 14.6,   -2},
```

```
    { 10, 13.7, -1.8 }, {  10, 14.4, -1.8},
    { 12,   14, -1.3 }, {  12, 14.5, -1.3},
    { 15, 14.9, -1.2 }, {  15,   15, -1.2},

    {-.5, 15,   0 }, { -.5, 0,   0},    // the flagpole
    {  0, 15,  .5 }, {   0, 0,  .5},
    {  0, 15, -.5 }, {   0, 0, -.5},
    {-.5, 15,   0 }, { -.5, 0,   0}
};


// Number of vertices in each strip.
static long numVertices[2] =
{
    32, // flag
    8   // pole
};

// Colors for the 12 faces
static float colors[2][3] =
{
    { .5, .5,  1 }, // purple flag
    { .4, .4, .4 }, // grey flagpole
};

// Routine to create a scene graph representing a pennant.
SoSeparator *
makePennant()
{
    SoSeparator *result = new SoSeparator;
    result->ref();

    // A shape hints tells the ordering of polygons.
    // This ensures double-sided lighting.
    SoShapeHints *myHints = new SoShapeHints;
    myHints->vertexOrdering = SoShapeHints::COUNTERCLOCKWISE;
    result->addChild(myHints);

    // Define colors for the strips
    SoMaterial *myMaterials = new SoMaterial;
    myMaterials->diffuseColor.setValues(0, 2, colors);
    result->addChild(myMaterials);
    SoMaterialBinding *myMaterialBinding = new SoMaterialBinding;
    myMaterialBinding->value = SoMaterialBinding::PER_PART;
    result->addChild(myMaterialBinding);
```

```
    // Define coordinates for vertices
    SoCoordinate3 *myCoords = new SoCoordinate3;
    myCoords->point.setValues(0, 40, vertexPositions);
    result->addChild(myCoords);

    // Define the TriangleStripSet, made of two strips.
    SoTriangleStripSet *myStrips = new SoTriangleStripSet;
    myStrips->numVertices.setValues(0, 2, numVertices);
    result->addChild(myStrips);

    result->unrefNoDelete();
    return result;
}
```

Quad Mesh

The **SoQuadMesh** node constructs quadrilaterals from the vertices located at the current coordinates. It uses the coordinates in order, starting at the index specified by the **startIndex** field. (If no index is specified, it starts at the first index.)

The **verticesPerColumn** and **verticesPerRow** fields indicate the number of vertices in the columns and rows of the mesh. Example 5-4 creates a quad mesh as follows:

```
SoQuadMesh *myQuadMesh = new SoQuadMesh;
myQuadMesh->verticesPerRow = 12;
myQuadMesh->verticesPerColumn = 5;
```

Each row in this quad mesh contains 12 vertices. Each column contains 5 vertices. Figure 5-9 shows the scene graph for this example. Figure 5-10 shows the resulting image.

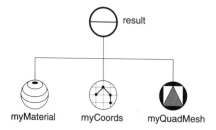

Figure 5-9   Scene Graph for Quad Mesh Example

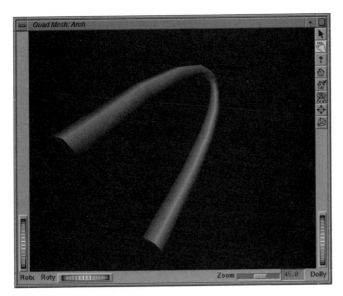

Figure 5-10   Quad Mesh Example

Example 5-4   Creating a Quad Mesh

```
// Positions of all of the vertices:

static float vertexPositions[160][3] =
{   // 1st row
    {-13.0,   0.0, 1.5}, {-10.3, 13.7, 1.2}, { -7.6, 21.7, 1.0},
    { -5.0, 26.1, 0.8}, { -2.3, 28.2, 0.6}, { -0.3, 28.8, 0.5},
    {  0.3, 28.8, 0.5}, {  2.3, 28.2, 0.6}, {  5.0, 26.1, 0.8},
    {  7.6, 21.7, 1.0}, { 10.3, 13.7, 1.2}, { 13.0,   0.0, 1.5},
    // 2nd row
    {-10.0,   0.0, 1.5}, { -7.9, 13.2, 1.2}, { -5.8, 20.8, 1.0},
    { -3.8, 25.0, 0.8}, { -1.7, 27.1, 0.6}, { -0.2, 27.6, 0.5},
    {  0.2, 27.6, 0.5}, {  1.7, 27.1, 0.6}, {  3.8, 25.0, 0.8},
    {  5.8, 20.8, 1.0}, {  7.9, 13.2, 1.2}, { 10.0,   0.0, 1.5},
    // 3rd row
    {-10.0,   0.0,-1.5}, { -7.9, 13.2,-1.2}, { -5.8, 20.8,-1.0},
    { -3.8, 25.0,-0.8}, { -1.7, 27.1,-0.6}, { -0.2, 27.6,-0.5},
    {  0.2, 27.6,-0.5}, {  1.7, 27.1,-0.6}, {  3.8, 25.0,-0.8},
    {  5.8, 20.8,-1.0}, {  7.9, 13.2,-1.2}, { 10.0,   0.0,-1.5},
```

```
   // 4th row
   {-13.0,  0.0,-1.5}, {-10.3, 13.7,-1.2}, { -7.6, 21.7,-1.0},
   { -5.0, 26.1,-0.8}, { -2.3, 28.2,-0.6}, { -0.3, 28.8,-0.5},
   {  0.3, 28.8,-0.5}, {  2.3, 28.2,-0.6}, {  5.0, 26.1,-0.8},
   {  7.6, 21.7,-1.0}, { 10.3, 13.7,-1.2}, { 13.0,  0.0,-1.5},
   // 5th row
   {-13.0,  0.0, 1.5}, {-10.3, 13.7, 1.2}, { -7.6, 21.7, 1.0},
   { -5.0, 26.1, 0.8}, { -2.3, 28.2, 0.6}, { -0.3, 28.8, 0.5},
   {  0.3, 28.8, 0.5}, {  2.3, 28.2, 0.6}, {  5.0, 26.1, 0.8},
   {  7.6, 21.7, 1.0}, { 10.3, 13.7, 1.2}, { 13.0,  0.0, 1.5}
};

// Routine to create a scene graph representing an arch.
SoSeparator *
makeArch()
{
   SoSeparator *result = new SoSeparator;
   result->ref();

   // Define the material
   SoMaterial *myMaterial = new SoMaterial;
   myMaterial->diffuseColor.setValue(.78, .57, .11);
   result->addChild(myMaterial);

   // Define coordinates for vertices
   SoCoordinate3 *myCoords = new SoCoordinate3;
   myCoords->point.setValues(0, 60, vertexPositions);
   result->addChild(myCoords);

   // Define the QuadMesh.
   SoQuadMesh *myQuadMesh = new SoQuadMesh;
   myQuadMesh->verticesPerRow = 12;

   myQuadMesh->verticesPerColumn = 5;
   result->addChild(myQuadMesh);

   result->unrefNoDelete();
   return result;
}
```

Property Nodes

This section describes a number of important property classes, all of which are derived from **SoNode**:

- **SoMaterial**, which sets the ambient color, diffuse color, specular color, emissive color, shininess, and transparency of the current material

- **SoDrawStyle**, which tells shape nodes which drawing technique to use during rendering

- **SoLightModel**, which tells shape nodes how to compute lighting calculations during rendering

- **SoEnvironment**, which allows you to simulate various atmospheric effects, such as fog, haze, pollution, and smoke, and to describe other global environmental attributes such as ambient lighting and light attenuation

- **SoShapeHints**, which provides additional information regarding vertex shapes to allow Inventor to optimize certain rendering features

- **SoComplexity**, which allows you to specify the extent to which shape objects are subdivided into polygons, as well as the general degree of texture complexity and level of detail

- **SoUnits**, which allows you to define a standard unit of measurement for all subsequent shapes in the scene graph

Each of these classes affects different elements of the rendering state, as described later in this section. Figure 5-11 shows the portion of the class tree for property nodes.

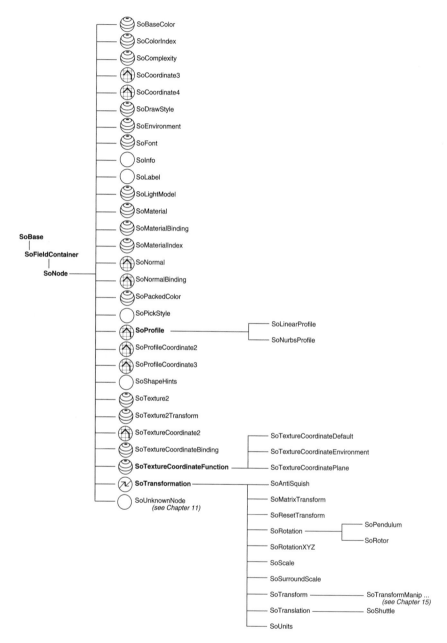

Figure 5-11   Property-Node Classes

Material Node

An **SoMaterial** node includes the following fields:

ambientColor (SoMFColor)

>reflected color of an object in response to the ambient lighting in the scene. The default value for this field is [0.2, 0.2, 0.2].

diffuseColor (SoMFColor)

>an object's base color. The default value for this field is [0.8, 0.8, 0.8].

specularColor (SoMFColor)

>reflective quality of an object's highlights. The default value for this field is [0.0, 0.0, 0.0].

emissiveColor (SoMFColor)

>light produced by an object. The default value for this field is [0.0, 0.0, 0.0].

shininess (SoMFFloat)

>degree of shininess of an object's surface, ranging from 0.0 for a diffuse surface with no shininess to a maximum of 1.0 for a highly polished surface. The default value for this field is 0.2.

transparency (SoMFFloat)

>degree of transparency of an object's surface, ranging from 0.0 for an opaque surface to 1.0 for a completely transparent surface. The default value for this field is 0.0.

Tip: The transparency type is specified in the render action (see Chapter 9).

An example of setting values in an **SoMaterial** node is the following:

```
SoMaterial *gold  = new SoMaterial;

//Set material values

gold->ambientColor.setValue(.3, .1, .1);
gold->diffuseColor.setValue(.8, .7, .2);
gold->specularColor.setValue(.4, .3, .1);
gold->shininess = .4;
```

Since gold is opaque, you can use the default value of 0.0 for the transparency field.

SoBaseColor, another class derived from **SoNode**, replaces only the diffuse color field of the current material and has no effect on other material fields.

❖ **Tip:** If you are changing only the diffuse color of an object, use an **SoBaseColor** node in place of an **SoMaterial** node. For example, to represent a complex terrain that uses many different diffuse colors, use one **SoMaterial** node for the ambient, specular, and emissive color values, and then use one **SoBaseColor** node with multiple values for the changing diffuse colors. The **SoBaseColor** class is also useful when the light model is BASE_COLOR (see "Light-Model Node" on page 120).

Draw-Style Node

An **SoDrawStyle** node includes the following fields:

style (SoSFEnum)   current drawing style. Values for this field are

SoDrawStyle::FILLED
filled regions (default)

SoDrawStyle::LINES
nonfilled outlines

SoDrawStyle::POINTS
points

SoDrawStyle::INVISIBLE
not drawn at all

pointSize (SoSFFloat)
(for POINTS style) radius of points, in printer's points. The default value is 0.0. A value of 0.0 indicates to use the fastest value for rendering, which is typically 1.0. If this value is not 0.0, the point size is scaled by the amount required to keep it a constant size, which depends on the pixels per inch of the viewport region.

❖ **Tip:** Draw-style LINES and POINTS look best with a BASE_COLOR lighting model.

lineWidth (SoSFFloat)

(for LINES style) line width, in printer's points (1 inch = 72.27 printer's points). Values can range from 0.0 to 256.0. The default value is 0.0, which indicates to use the fastest value for rendering.

linePattern (SoSFUShort)

(for LINES style) current line-stipple pattern. Values can range from 0 (invisible) to 0xffff (solid). The default value is 0xffff.

Figure 5-12 shows the same object rendered in different drawing styles.

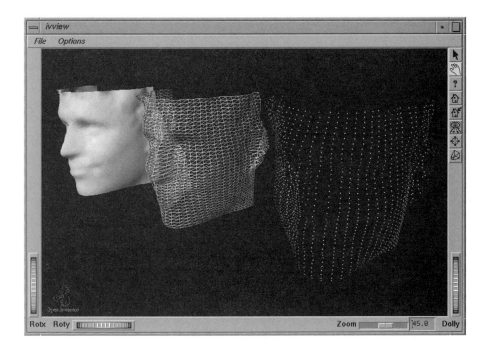

Figure 5-12   Drawing Styles (FILLED, LINES, POINTS)

Light-Model Node

An **SoLightModel** node includes the following field:

model (SoSFEnum)

current lighting model applied to all subsequent shape nodes in the scene graph. The lighting model tells the shape node how to compute lighting calculations during rendering. Values for this field are as follows:

SoLightModel::BASE_COLOR
ignores light sources and uses only the diffuse color and transparency of the current material.

SoLightModel::PHONG
uses the OpenGL Phong lighting model, which takes into account all light sources in the scene and the object's surface orientation with respect to the lights. This lighting model (the default) usually requires at least one light in the scene. (There may be emissive color and ambient lighting also.)

Note: In Inventor, shading (such as Gouraud or flat) is dictated by the combination of the material specification of the object, the lighting model, and the normal bindings. A shading model is not explicitly specified.

Plates 4 and 5 show the same scene with the different lighting models. (Plate 4 uses BASE_COLOR, and Plate 5 uses PHONG.)

SoMaterial and **SoBaseColor** can be used along with any drawing style and any lighting model. In some cases, however, some of the material attributes might be ignored. For example, if you specify BASE_COLOR for the **SoLightModel model** field, only the diffuse color and transparency of the current material are used. But what happens if you specify only a base color (with **SoBaseColor**) and subsequently select the Phong lighting model for **SoLightModel**? In this case, Inventor uses the base color for the diffuse color and the default or current material element values for the other **SoMaterial** fields.

Note: By default, the light model is PHONG. For images to render correctly, you need to specify normals and light sources. If you want to see only colored objects, change the light model to BASE_COLOR and use **SoBaseColor** to specify only the base (diffuse) color.

Environment Node

You can use the **SoEnvironment** node to simulate various atmospheric effects such as fog, haze, pollution, and smoke. For general purposes, these atmospheric effects are grouped under the term *fog*. The difference between fog and haze, for example, is simply the color and density.

Specifically, the **SoEnvironment** node allows you to specify the color and intensity of the ambient lighting, the light attenuation for point lights and spotlights, and the type, color, and visibility factor for fog. Plate 6 shows the effects of an **SoEnvironment** node. This image uses a value of FOG for the fog type. The **fogColor** is (0.2, 0.2, 0.46).

An **SoEnvironment** node includes the following fields:

ambientIntensity (SoSFFloat)
> intensity of ambient light in the scene. This field is used with Phong lighting.

ambientColor (SoSFColor)
> color of ambient light in the scene. This field is used with Phong lighting.

attenuation (SoSFVec3f)
> defines how light drops off with distance from a light source. You can specify squared, linear, and constant attenuation coefficients with respect to the distance of the light from the object's surface. (The three components of the vector are the squared, linear, and constant coefficients, in that order.) This field is used with Phong lighting.

fogType (SoSFEnum)
> type of fog. Values for this field are
>
> SoEnvironment::NONE
> no fog (default)
>
> SoEnvironment::HAZE
> opacity of the fog increases linearly with the distance from the camera
>
> SoEnvironment::FOG
> opacity of the fog increases exponentially with the distance from the camera

SoEnvironment::SMOKE
increase in fog opacity is an exponential-squared increase with the distance from the camera

fogColor (SoSFColor)
color of the fog.

fogVisibility (SoSFFloat)
the distance at which fog totally obscures the objects in the scene. For the default value (0.0), this distance is adjusted to equal the far plane of the camera. Otherwise, it is used as is.

❖ **Tip:** For realistic scenes, clear the window to the fog color before drawing the fogged objects (see the **SoXtRenderArea::setBackgroundColor()** method.)

Shape-Hints Node

By default, Inventor does not assume anything about how the vertices in a vertex shape are ordered, whether its surface is closed or open, or whether the faces of the shape are convex or concave. If you know that the vertices are in a consistent order, that the shape is closed, or that the shape faces are convex, you can use the **SoShapeHints** node to notify Inventor so that it can optimize certain rendering features.

The **SoShapeHints** node has four fields:

vertexOrdering (SoSFEnum)
provides hints about the ordering of the faces of a vertex-based shape derived from **SoVertexShape**. This field describes the ordering of all the vertices of all the faces of the shape when it is viewed from the outside.

Values for this field are

SoShapeHints::UNKNOWN_ORDERING
the ordering of the vertices is not known (the default)

SoShapeHints::CLOCKWISE
the vertices for each face are specified in clockwise order

SoShapeHints::COUNTERCLOCKWISE
the vertices for each face are specified in counterclockwise order

shapeType (SoSFEnum)

> SoShapeHints::UNKNOWN_SHAPE_TYPE
> the shape type is not known (the default)

> SoShapeHints::SOLID
> the shape is a solid object (not an open surface)

faceType (SoSFEnum)

> SoShapeHints::UNKNOWN_FACE_TYPE
> the face type is not known

> SoShapeHints::CONVEX
> all faces of the shape are convex
> (the default)

creaseAngle (SoSFFloat)

> used for automatic normal generation. See "Generating
> Normals Automatically" on page 132.

If the **shapeType** is SOLID and the **vertexOrdering** is either CLOCKWISE
or COUNTERCLOCKWISE, Inventor turns on backface culling and turns off
two-sided lighting. If the **shapeType** is not SOLID and the **vertexOrdering**
is either CLOCKWISE or COUNTERCLOCKWISE, Inventor turns off
backface culling and turns on two-sided lighting. In all other cases, backface
culling and two-sided lighting are both off. If you use the **SoShapeHints**
node, be sure to describe the object accurately; otherwise, objects may be
rendered incorrectly.

Tip: In general, the more information you specify with the shape-hints
node, the faster the rendering speed. The exception to this rule is when
shapeType is not SOLID and the **vertexOrdering** is either
CLOCKWISE or COUNTERCLOCKWISE. In this case, rendering may be
slower because two-sided lighting is automatically turned on and
backface culling is turned off.

Complexity Node

Use the **SoComplexity** node to indicate the amount of subdivision into polygons for subsequent shape nodes in the scene graph. This node has three fields:

type (SoSFEnum)   general type of complexity. Values for this field are

>SoComplexity::OBJECT_SPACE
>(the default) bases the subdivision on the object itself, regardless of where it is on the screen or which parts are closer to the viewer.

>SoComplexity::SCREEN_SPACE
>bases the complexity on the amount of screen space occupied by the object. Objects requiring the full screen require more detail; small objects require less detail. The result is that objects that are closer to the viewer usually receive more detail than objects that are farther away. This type of complexity is more expensive to compute than the others. In addition, it invalidates the render cache when the camera moves (see the discussion of render caching in Chapter 9).

>SoComplexity::BOUNDING_BOX
>renders a bounding box in place of the shape. This type is used for speed, when exact shapes are not required. It uses the current drawing style to render the box.

value (SoSFFloat)   a value that provides a hint about the amount of subdivision desired, where 0.0 is minimum complexity and 1.0 is maximum complexity. The default is 0.5.

textureQuality (SoSFFloat)
>a value that provides a hint about the quality of texture mapping used on the object. The trade-off is between speed of rendering and quality of texturing. A value of 0.0 indicates maximum speed (possibly turning off texturing completely), and 1.0 indicates finest texture quality. The default is 0.5.

Figure 5-13 shows the same object with different levels of complexity. The spheres at the left use object-space complexity and a complexity value of .5. The spheres at the right use screen-space complexity and a complexity value of .06. The NURBS examples in Chapter 8 use the **SoComplexity** node.

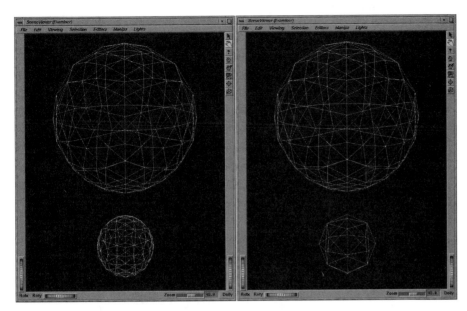

Figure 5-13   Specifying Different Levels of Complexity (left: OBJECT_SPACE; right: SCREEN_SPACE)

Tip: Simpler scenes render more quickly than complex scenes. For example,
  . to increase rendering speed, use fewer lights, turn off textures or
  specify a lower texture-quality value, and choose a simpler drawing
  style, such as wireframe, and a lower complexity value. The viewer
  pop-up menu allows you to disable certain of these features for faster
  rendering.

Units Node

Inventor lets you define your data in a variety of different units. It uses
meters as its default units, but you can use the **SoUnits** node to specify a
different unit of measurement. The units node acts like a scale node by
scaling subsequent shapes into the specified units. **SoUnits** can adjust the
amount it scales an object by checking to see if any other units have been
defined. The units node adjusts the scale so that the previously defined
units are no longer in effect.

The **SoUnits** node has one field:

units (SoSFEnum) defines the current unit of measurement to be applied to all subsequent shapes in the scene graph. Possible values are as follows:

SoUnits::METERS
SoUnits::CENTIMETERS
SoUnits::MILLIMETERS
SoUnits::MICROMETERS
SoUnits::MICRONS
SoUnits::NANOMETERS
SoUnits::ANGSTROMS
SoUnits::KILOMETERS
SoUnits::FEET
SoUnits::INCHES
SoUnits::POINTS
SoUnits::YARDS
SoUnits::MILES
SoUnits::NAUTICAL_MILES

To render your data in units other than these, use an **SoUnits** node to set the current units back to meters, followed by a scale node that scales from meters into the desired units.

Binding Nodes

Materials and normals are bound to shape nodes in different ways. The first part of this discussion focuses on *material binding*, which is how the current materials specified in an **SoMaterial** node are mapped onto the geometry of the shape nodes that use that particular material. Since normal binding is analogous to material binding, this initial discussion focuses on material binding. (See Example 5-1 earlier in this chapter for an example of using a normal binding node.)

An **SoMaterialBinding** node contains a value that describes how to bind materials to shapes. These values include the following:

SoMaterialBinding::DEFAULT
> uses the "best" binding for each shape. Most shapes interpret this binding as OVERALL.

SoMaterialBinding::NONE
> uses no material.

SoMaterialBinding::OVERALL
> uses the first current material for the entire shape.

SoMaterialBinding::PER_PART
> binds one material to each part in the shape. The definition of *part* depends on the shape. For face sets and cubes, a part is a face. For line sets, a part is a line segment. For cylinders, a part is the sides, top, or bottom.

SoMaterialBinding::PER_PART_INDEXED
> binds one material to each part by index.

SoMaterialBinding::PER_FACE
> binds one material to each face in the shape.

SoMaterialBinding::PER_FACE_INDEXED
> binds one material to each face by index (for indexed vertex shapes).

SoMaterialBinding::PER_VERTEX
> binds one material to each vertex in the shape.

SoMaterialBinding::PER_VERTEX_INDEXED
> binds one material to each vertex by index (for indexed vertex shapes).

Each shape node interprets the binding type somewhat differently. For example, an **SoSphere** node does not have parts, faces, or indices, so those binding types (PER_PART, PER_FACE, PER_VERTEX) are meaningless for spheres. You can regard the value specified in the material-binding node as a *hint* to the shape about binding. If you specify a value that makes no sense for a particular shape, such as PER_FACE for a cylinder, the shape interprets the information the best it can (in this case, it uses OVERALL, since a cylinder has no faces). See the *Open Inventor C++ Reference Manual* for information on how each shape interprets the different binding types.

Suppose you specify PER_PART for a cylinder. The cylinder has three parts (sides, top, bottom). If the current material contains three values—for example, orange, purple, yellow—those values are used for the three parts of the cylinder, producing orange sides, a purple top, and a yellow bottom. But what happens if the number of current materials is greater than the number of parts? As you might guess, Inventor simply ignores the extra materials if they're not required. (If the current material list contains five values, your cylinder ignores the last two values.)

If the current material contains *fewer* values than the binding requires, Inventor cycles through the current values as often as needed. For example, if you specify PER_FACE for a cube and the current materials list contains three values (violet, periwinkle, teal), the results are as follows:

Face 1	violet
Face 2	periwinkle
Face 3	teal
Face 4	violet
Face 5	periwinkle
Face 6	teal

Indexed Binding

So far, you've been using the values in the current material *in order*. You can, however, also use the current material values in a new order if you specify either PER_FACE_INDEXED or PER_VERTEX_INDEXED for an indexed vertex shape or PER_PART_INDEXED for a shape that has parts. When you use these types of binding, Inventor refers to the materials-index field of the shape node (for example, **SoIndexedFaceSet**, **SoIndexedLineSet**). Instead of starting with the first material and working through the list, Inventor indexes into the materials list in whatever order you specify.

As an example, consider a tetrahedron, represented as an **SoIndexedFaceSet**. The current materials list (in an **SoMaterial** node) contains the following values:

Material List	0	peach
	1	khaki
	2	white

and the **materialIndex** field (in an **SoIndexedFaceSet** node) contains these values:

Material Index	1
	1
	0
	2

If you specify PER_FACE (not indexed), Inventor ignores the **materialIndex** field and cycles through the materials list in order:

Face 1	peach
Face 2	khaki
Face 3	white
Face 4	peach

On the other hand, if you specify PER_FACE_INDEXED, Inventor uses the **materialIndex** field to pull values out of the materials list as follows:

Face 1	khaki
Face 2	khaki
Face 3	peach
Face 4	white

This indexing is economical, since you can use a single, small set of materials for a wide variety of objects and purposes.

Binding per Vertex

Inventor offers two types of per-vertex binding: PER_VERTEX and PER_VERTEX_INDEXED. With nonindexed material binding per vertex, Inventor simply selects materials in order from the materials list and assigns a material to each vertex of the shape node. It then interpolates the materials between the vertices and across the faces of the shape.

 ## Nuances

An **SoMaterial** node contains six fields, each of which holds multiple values. However, the number of values in these six fields may not be equal. You might have five different values in the ambient, diffuse, specular, and emissive fields, but only two values in the shininess field and one in the transparency field. In such cases, Inventor chooses a cycle equal to the field with the greatest number of values (in this case, five). In a field with fewer values, its last value is repeated until the end of the cycle.

When PER_VERTEX binding is specified, a value of −1 (the default) for the **materialIndex** field or the **normalIndex** field in an **SoIndexedFaceSet** (or any other indexed shape node) indicates to use the coordinate indices for materials or normals. The defined constants SO_END_LINE_INDEX, SO_END_FACE_INDEX, and SO_END_STRIP_INDEX can be used for this specification. This saves time and space and ensures that the indices match up. When you use a "special" coordinate index (such as SO_END_FACE_INDEX), the corresponding material index is skipped over so that the arrays of indices match.

 Tip: For better performance, use PER_FACE or PER_FACE_INDEXED binding with one material node and one face-set node that defines multiple polygons, instead of OVERALL binding with multiple material nodes and multiple face set nodes.

Using a Material-Binding Node

Example 5-5 illustrates different types of material binding using the dodecahedron created in Example 5-2 (the common code has been omitted here). The scene graph for the example is shown in Figure 5-14. When you run the program, you can type a number to select the type of material binding, as follows:

- **0** for PER_FACE (see Plate 7)

- **1** for PER_VERTEX_INDEXED (see Plate 8)

- **2** for PER_FACE_INDEXED (see Plate 9)

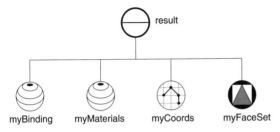

Figure 5-14   Scene Graph for Material Binding Example

Example 5-5   Using Different Material Bindings

```
// Which material to use to color the faces
// half red & half blue
static long materialIndices[12] = {
   0, 0, 0, 0, 0, 0,
   1, 1, 1, 1, 1, 1,
};

switch(whichBinding) {
  case 0:
    // Set up binding to use a different color for each face
    myBinding->value = SoMaterialBinding::PER_FACE;
    break;
  case 1:
    // Set up binding to use a different color at each
    // vertex, BUT, vertices shared between faces will
    // have the same color.
    myBinding->value = SoMaterialBinding::PER_VERTEX_INDEXED;
    break;
  case 2:
    myBinding->value = SoMaterialBinding::PER_FACE_INDEXED;
    myIndexedFaceSet->materialIndex.setValues(
            0, 12, materialIndices);
    break;
}
```

Normal Binding

Normals are bound to shapes in almost the same manner as materials. The type of normal binding specified in an **SoNormalBinding** node is a *hint* to the shape node about how to apply the current normals to that shape. Indexed shape nodes such as **SoIndexedFaceSet** and **SoIndexedTriangle-StripSet** contain a **normalIndex** field used to store indices into the normals list (in an **SoNormal** node). If the type of binding specified does not require indices (for example, PER_VERTEX), the **normalIndex** field is not used.

The main difference between indexed normals and indexed materials is that indexed normals do not cycle. If used, normals must match up exactly with the faces, vertices, or parts of the object. If the normals do not match exactly, then default normals are generated (see the following section). You *must* specify enough normals to bind to faces, parts, or vertices.

Generating Normals Automatically

Normals can be generated automatically for any shape derived from **SoVertexShape**. Because this process involves a great deal of computation, we recommend that you use automatic caching or explicitly turn on render caching so that the results are saved and can be reused (see Chapter 9 for more information on caching). Inventor generates normals automatically if needed for rendering and

- DEFAULT normal binding is used and

- You do not specify any normals *or* the number of normals is different from the number of vertices

When Inventor generates normals automatically, it looks at the **creaseAngle** field of the **SoShapeHints** node. The *crease angle* is defined as the angle between the normals for two adjoining faces. This angle indicates the maximum angle size at which separate normals are drawn for adjoining faces. For example, if the crease angle is one radian and the normals for two adjoining faces form an angle less than or equal to one radian, the faces share the same normal, which causes the edge to be shaded smoothly. If the normals for the faces form an angle greater than one radian, Inventor calculates separate normals for each face, which creates a crease. If you want an object to appear sharply faceted, specify 0 as the **creaseAngle**. If you want an object to appear completely smooth, specify PI as the **creaseAngle**.

Transformations

Unlike other property nodes, transformation nodes do not *replace* the current geometric transformation element in the action state. Instead, they have a *cumulative* effect on the current geometric transformation. In Figure 5-15, for example, the transformations in node *xfm1* are applied first, followed by the transformations in node *xfm2*.

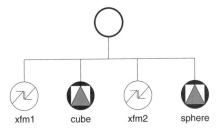

Figure 5-15   Cumulative Effect of Transformation Nodes

The cube is affected by only the transformation in *xfm1*. The sphere, however, is affected by both *xfm1* and *xfm2*.

SoTransform Node

An **SoTransform** node includes the following fields:

translation (SoSFVec3f)
> the translation in *x*, *y*, and *z*. The default value is [0.0 0.0 0.0].

rotation (SoSFRotation)
> the rotation in terms of an axis and an angle. The default value is [0.0 0.0 1.0], 0.0.

scaleFactor (SoSFVec3f)
> the scaling factor in *x*, *y*, and *z*. The default value for this field is [1.0 1.0 1.0].

scaleOrientation (SoSFRotation)
> the rotation to apply *before* the scale is applied. The default value is [0.0 0.0 1.0], 0.0.

center (SoSFVec3f)
> the center point for rotation and scaling. The default value for this field is [0.0 0.0 0.0].

❖ **Tip:** If you are using only one of the fields in an **SoTransform** node, you can substitute the corresponding "lightweight" version. For rotations, use **SoRotation** or **SoRotationXYZ**; for translations, use **SoTranslation**; and for scaling, use **SoScale**.

Order of Transformations

Within each **SoTransform** node, the fields are applied so that the last field in the node (the **center**) affects the shape object *first*. The order is first the center, followed by the scale orientation, the scaling factor, the rotation, and the translation.

Figure 5-16 and Figure 5-17 show how different ordering of transformations produces different results. At the left of Figure 5-17, the temple is scaled, rotated, and then translated. The transform node *closest* to the shape object affects the object *first*. You thus need to read backward through the code to see how the effects of the transformations are felt. At the right of Figure 5-17, the temple is rotated, then scaled and translated. Example 5-6 shows the code for the two sets of transformations.

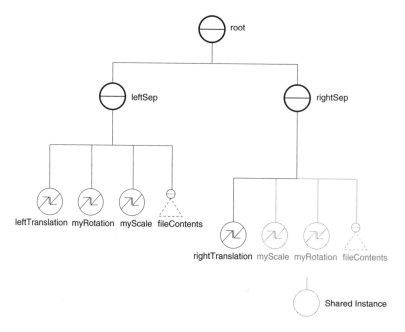

Figure 5-16   Two Groups with Transformations in Different Order

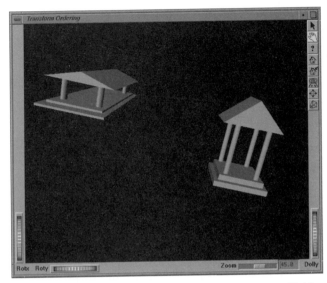

Figure 5-17   Effects of Ordering Transformation Fields

Example 5-6   Changing the Order of Transformations

```
#include <Inventor/Xt/SoXt.h>
#include <Inventor/Xt/viewers/SoXtExaminerViewer.h>
#include <Inventor/SoDB.h>
#include <Inventor/nodes/SoMaterial.h>
#include <Inventor/nodes/SoRotationXYZ.h>
#include <Inventor/nodes/SoScale.h>
#include <Inventor/nodes/SoSeparator.h>
#include <Inventor/nodes/SoTranslation.h>

main(int, char **argv)
{
   // Initialize Inventor and Xt
   Widget myWindow = SoXt::init(argv[0]);
   if (myWindow == NULL) exit(1);

   SoSeparator *root = new SoSeparator;
   root->ref();

   // Create two separators, for left and right objects.
   SoSeparator *leftSep = new SoSeparator;
   SoSeparator *rightSep = new SoSeparator;
   root->addChild(leftSep);
   root->addChild(rightSep);
```

```
// Create the transformation nodes.
SoTranslation *leftTranslation  = new SoTranslation;
SoTranslation *rightTranslation = new SoTranslation;
SoRotationXYZ *myRotation = new SoRotationXYZ;
SoScale *myScale = new SoScale;

// Fill in the values.
leftTranslation->translation.setValue(-1.0, 0.0, 0.0);
rightTranslation->translation.setValue(1.0, 0.0, 0.0);
myRotation->angle = M_PI/2;    // 90 degrees
myRotation->axis = SoRotationXYZ::X;
myScale->scaleFactor.setValue(2., 1., 3.);

// Add transforms to the scene.
leftSep->addChild(leftTranslation);   // left graph
leftSep->addChild(myRotation);        // then rotated
leftSep->addChild(myScale);           // first scaled

rightSep->addChild(rightTranslation); // right graph
rightSep->addChild(myScale);          // then scaled
rightSep->addChild(myRotation);       // first rotated

// Read an object from file. (as in example 4.2.Lights)
SoInput myInput;
if (!myInput.openFile("temple.iv"))
   return (1);
SoSeparator *fileContents = SoDB::readAll(&myInput);
if (fileContents == NULL) return (1);

// Add an instance of the object under each separator.
leftSep->addChild(fileContents);
rightSep->addChild(fileContents);

// Construct a renderArea and display the scene.
SoXtExaminerViewer *myViewer =
        new SoXtExaminerViewer(myWindow);
myViewer->setSceneGraph(root);
myViewer->setTitle("Transform Ordering");
myViewer->viewAll();
myViewer->show();

SoXt::show(myWindow);
SoXt::mainLoop();
}
```

## Part III

More About Nodes

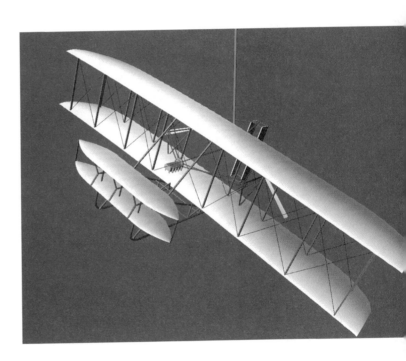

## Chapter 6

Text

Chapter Objectives

After reading this chapter, you'll be able to do the following:

- Add 2D text annotations to a scene
- Add 3D text to a scene, using a variety of customized profiles and fonts

This chapter describes the use of 2D and 3D text. Inventor's 2D text provides you with a simple, quick method for annotating your graphics. For greater embellishment and flexibility, use 3D text, which offers you a wide range of possibilities for shaping the profiles of 3D fonts. Key concepts introduced in this chapter include *justification, spacing, font type* and *size,* and *profiles.* Although the topic of NURBS curves and surfaces is mentioned, that subject is explained fully in Chapter 8.

The first part of this chapter focuses on 2D text and introduces certain concepts common to both 2D and 3D text, such as justification, spacing, and font type and size. The second part of the chapter describes the use of 3D text. The main additional concept in the use of 3D text is defining the cross-sectional *profile* for the text. You can create profiles that are straight, curved, or a combination of the two.

Two-Dimensional Text

The text node, **SoText2**, defines text strings that are rendered as 2D screen-aligned text. Just as other shape nodes cause their shape to be drawn when encountered during rendering traversal, an **SoText2** node causes text to be drawn, using the current values for font and color. Text attributes used by **SoText2** are specified in the **SoFont** node. These attributes include font type and point size. Two-dimensional text does not scale in size according to changes in distance from the camera.

SoText2 has the following fields:

string (SoMFString)

> the text string or strings to display. You can specify multiple strings.

spacing (SoSFFloat)

> the spacing between lines of text. The default interval is 1.0. For a multiple-string field, the vertical distance from the top of one line to the top of the next line is equal to **spacing** times the font size.

justification (SoSFEnum)

> alignment of the text strings relative to the text origin. Justification can be LEFT (the default), RIGHT, or CENTER.

The *text origin* is positioned at (0, 0, 0), transformed by the current geometric transformation. Text is drawn relative to the text origin, according to the specified justification. For example, if you specify RIGHT justification, the right side of the text aligns with the text origin.

Font Type and Size

Use the **SoFont** node to specify a font type and size for subsequent text nodes (both 2D and 3D) in the scene graph. This node contains the following fields:

name (SoSFName)
> font name. Check your release documentation for a list of font types that are supported on your system.

size (SoSFFloat)
> for **SoText2**, the point size in printer's points. For **SoText3**, the size in object space units (default = 10.0).

For example, to specify 140-point Courier bold italic:

```
SoFont *font = new SoFont;
font->name.setValue("Courier-BoldOblique");
font->size.setValue(140);
```

Using 2D Text

Example 6-1 renders a globe and uses 2D text to label the continents Africa and Asia. The **SoFont** node specifies 24-point Times Roman as the current font. Figure 6-1 shows the scene graph for this example. Figure 6-2 shows the image produced by this program.

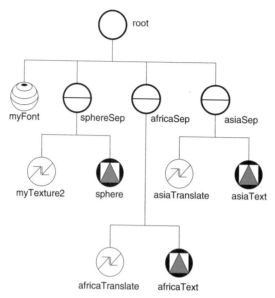

Figure 6-1   2D Text Example

Example 6-1   Using 2D Text

```
#include <Inventor/nodes/SoFont.h>
#include <Inventor/nodes/SoGroup.h>
#include <Inventor/nodes/SoSeparator.h>
#include <Inventor/nodes/SoSphere.h>
#include <Inventor/nodes/SoText2.h>
#include <Inventor/nodes/SoTexture2.h>
#include <Inventor/nodes/SoTranslation.h>

#include <Inventor/Xt/SoXt.h>
#include <Inventor/Xt/viewers/SoXtExaminerViewer.h>

main(int argc, char **argv)
{
   Widget myWindow = SoXt::init(argv[0]);
   if(myWindow == NULL) exit(1);

   SoGroup *root = new SoGroup;
   root->ref();
```

```
// Choose a font.
SoFont *myFont = new SoFont;
myFont->name.setValue("Times-Roman");
myFont->size.setValue(24.0);
root->addChild(myFont);

// Add the globe, a sphere with a texture map.
// Put it within a separator.
SoSeparator *sphereSep = new SoSeparator;
SoTexture2   *myTexture2 = new SoTexture2;
root->addChild(sphereSep);
sphereSep->addChild(myTexture2);
sphereSep->addChild(new SoSphere);
myTexture2->filename = "globe.rgb";

// Add Text2 for AFRICA, translated to proper location.
SoSeparator *africaSep = new SoSeparator;
SoTranslation *africaTranslate = new SoTranslation;
SoText2 *africaText = new SoText2;
africaTranslate->translation.setValue(.25,.0,1.25);
africaText->string = "AFRICA";
root->addChild(africaSep);
africaSep->addChild(africaTranslate);
africaSep->addChild(africaText);
```

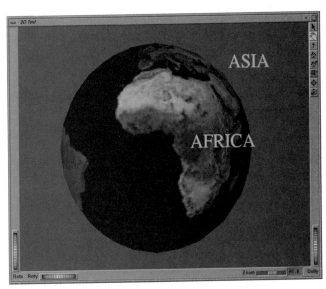

Figure 6-2   Simple Text

```
    // Add Text2 for ASIA, translated to proper location.
    SoSeparator *asiaSep = new SoSeparator;
    SoTranslation *asiaTranslate = new SoTranslation;
    SoText2 *asiaText = new SoText2;
    asiaTranslate->translation.setValue(.8,.8,0);
    asiaText->string = "ASIA";
    root->addChild(asiaSep);
    asiaSep->addChild(asiaTranslate);
    asiaSep->addChild(asiaText);

    SoXtExaminerViewer *myViewer =
            new SoXtExaminerViewer(myWindow);
    myViewer->setSceneGraph(root);
    myViewer->setTitle("2D Text");
    myViewer->setBackgroundColor(SbColor(0.35, 0.35, 0.35));
    myViewer->show();
    myViewer->viewAll();

    SoXt::show(myWindow);
    SoXt::mainLoop();
}
```

Three-Dimensional Text

In contrast to 2D text, 3D text scales in size according to changes in distance from the camera and does not always stay parallel to the screen. Three-dimensional text has depth. The face of a 3D letter can join its sides at right angles (the default). Or you can bevel the edges of the letter by specifying your own text profile, as shown at the right of Figure 6-3, which shows a beveled letter A.

The chief advantages of 2D text are that it is faster than 3D text and, because it remains parallel to the screen, is always readable. Advantages of 3D text are that it can be scaled and is generally prettier than 2D text.

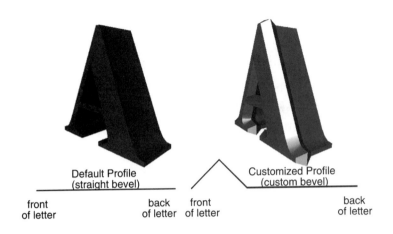

Default Profile
(straight bevel)

Customized Profile
(custom bevel)

front
of letter

back
of letter

front
of letter

back
of letter

Figure 6-3   Defining a Customized Profile for 3D Text

SoText3 has the following fields:

string (SoMFString)

the text string or strings to display. You can specify
multiple strings.

spacing (SoSFFloat)

the spacing between lines of text. The default interval is
1.0. For a multiple-string field, the vertical distance
from the top of one line to the top of the next line is
equal to **spacing** times the font size.

justification (SoSFEnum)

alignment of the text strings relative to the text origin.
Justification can be LEFT (the default), RIGHT, or
CENTER. LEFT means that the bottom-left front of the
first character in the first line is at (0.0, 0.0, 0.0).
Successive lines start under the first character. RIGHT
means that the bottom-right of the last character is at
(0.0, 0.0, 0.0). Successive lines end under the last
character of the first line. CENTER means that the center
of each line is at (0.0, 0.0, 0.0).

parts (SoSFBitMask)

visible parts of the text (FRONT, SIDES, BACK, or ALL).
The default is FRONT.

Parts of 3D Text

Three-dimensional text has three parts: front, sides, and back. Text uses the current material. If material binding is specified as PER_PART, the front uses the first material, the sides use the second material, and the back uses the third material.

❖ **Tip:** Be aware that when you turn on SIDES and BACK of 3D text, you draw three times more polygons than with FRONT only, so performance is slower.

Profile

The profile describes the cross-section of the letter, as shown in Figure 6-3. The profile is drawn in its own 2D plane. This plane is perpendicular to the face of the text, as shown in Figure 6-4. The origin of this plane is at the edge of the letter. In this coordinate system, capital letters are one unit high. The profile coordinates thus need to be in the range of 0.0 to about 0.3 or 0.4 times the size of the font.

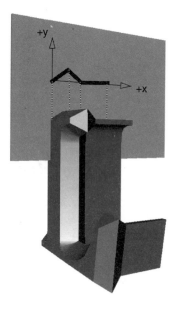

Figure 6-4   2D Plane for Drawing a Text Profile

Linear Profiles

Profiles are constructed from the current *profile coordinates*. If the profile is a collection of connected straight-line segments, use the **SoLinearProfile** node to specify how the coordinates are connected. The profile coordinates are specified in an **SoProfileCoordinate2** node, which precedes the **SoLinearProfile** node in the scene graph (see Example 6-3).

Curved Profiles

If the profile is curved, use the **SoNurbsProfile** node to specify how the coordinates are used. If you are interested in creating curved profiles, first read Chapter 8 for detailed conceptual information on NURBS curves. The coordinates themselves are specified in the **SoProfileCoordinate2** node or the **SoProfileCoordinate3** node, depending on whether the curve is nonrational or rational. (The terms *nonrational* and *rational* are also explained in Chapter 8.)

Linking Profiles

If your text profile is a combination of linear and curved lines, you can join the linear profile to the curved profile. The base profile class, **SoProfile**, includes a **linkage** field that is inherited by both **SoLinearProfile** and **SoNurbsProfile**. This field indicates whether the profile is START_FIRST (begin the first profile for the text), START_NEW (begin a new profile; for NURBS trimming only), or ADD_TO_CURRENT (append this profile to the previous one).

Simple Use of 3D Text

Example 6-2 illustrates a simple use of 3D text. It renders a globe and then uses 3D text to label the continents Africa and Asia. The **SoFont** node specifies Times Roman as the current font. Figure 6-5 shows the scene graph for this example. Figure 6-6 shows the image produced by this program.

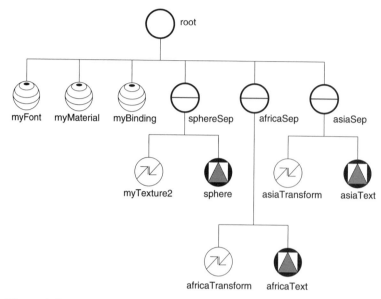

Figure 6-5   Scene Graph for Simple 3D Text Example

Example 6-2   Using 3D Text

```
#include <Inventor/Xt/SoXt.h>
#include <Inventor/Xt/viewers/SoXtExaminerViewer.h>
#include <Inventor/nodes/SoFont.h>
#include <Inventor/nodes/SoGroup.h>
#include <Inventor/nodes/SoMaterial.h>
#include <Inventor/nodes/SoMaterialBinding.h>
#include <Inventor/nodes/SoSeparator.h>
#include <Inventor/nodes/SoSphere.h>
#include <Inventor/nodes/SoText3.h>
#include <Inventor/nodes/SoTexture2.h>
#include <Inventor/nodes/SoTransform.h>


main(int, char **argv)
{
   Widget myWindow = SoXt::init(argv[0]);
   if(myWindow == NULL) exit(1);

   SoGroup *root = new SoGroup;
   root->ref();
```

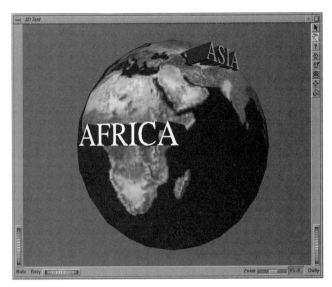

Figure 6-6   Simple 3D Text Example

```
// Choose a font.
SoFont *myFont = new SoFont;
myFont->name.setValue("Times-Roman");
myFont->size.setValue(.2);
root->addChild(myFont);

// We'll color the front of the text white, and the sides
// dark grey. So use a materialBinding of PER_PART and
// two diffuseColor values in the material node.
SoMaterial        *myMaterial = new SoMaterial;
SoMaterialBinding *myBinding = new SoMaterialBinding;
myMaterial->diffuseColor.set1Value(0,SbColor(1,1,1));
myMaterial->diffuseColor.set1Value(1,SbColor(.1,.1,.1));
myBinding->value = SoMaterialBinding::PER_PART;
root->addChild(myMaterial);
root->addChild(myBinding);

// Create the globe.
SoSeparator *sphereSep = new SoSeparator;
SoTexture2  *myTexture2 = new SoTexture2;
root->addChild(sphereSep);
sphereSep->addChild(myTexture2);
sphereSep->addChild(new SoSphere);
myTexture2->filename = "globe.rgb";
```

```
// Add Text3 for AFRICA, transformed to proper location.
SoSeparator *africaSep = new SoSeparator;
SoTransform *africaTransform = new SoTransform;
SoText3 *africaText = new SoText3;
africaTransform->rotation.setValue(SbVec3f(0,1,0),.4);
africaTransform->translation.setValue(.25,.0,1.25);
africaText->parts = SoText3::ALL;
africaText->string = "AFRICA";
root->addChild(africaSep);
africaSep->addChild(africaTransform);
africaSep->addChild(africaText);

// Add Text3 for ASIA, transformed to proper location.
SoSeparator *asiaSep = new SoSeparator;
SoTransform *asiaTransform = new SoTransform;
SoText3 *asiaText = new SoText3;
asiaTransform->rotation.setValue(SbVec3f(0,1,0),1.5);
asiaTransform->translation.setValue(.8,.6,.5);
asiaText->parts = SoText3::ALL;
asiaText->string = "ASIA";
root->addChild(asiaSep);
asiaSep->addChild(asiaTransform);
asiaSep->addChild(asiaText);

SoXtExaminerViewer *myViewer =
        new SoXtExaminerViewer(myWindow);
myViewer->setSceneGraph(root);
myViewer->setTitle("3D Text");
myViewer->setBackgroundColor(SbColor(0.35, 0.35, 0.35));
myViewer->show();
myViewer->viewAll();

SoXt::show(myWindow);
SoXt::mainLoop();
}
```

 ## Advanced Use of 3D Text

Example 6-3 illustrates additional features available with 3D text. It
specifies a beveled cross-section for the text using the **SoProfile-
Coordinate2** and **SoLinearProfile** nodes. The text uses two different
materials— one for the front of the text, and one for the back and sides. The
font node specifies the Times Roman font. Figure 6-7 shows the scene graph
for this figure. Figure 6-8 shows the rendered image.

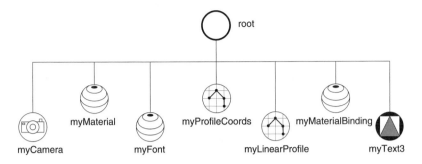

Figure 6-7   Scene Graph for Advanced 3D Text Example

Example 6-3   Creating Beveled 3D Text

```
#include <Inventor/Xt/SoXt.h>
#include <Inventor/Xt/viewers/SoXtExaminerViewer.h>
#include <Inventor/nodes/SoFont.h>
#include <Inventor/nodes/SoGroup.h>
#include <Inventor/nodes/SoLinearProfile.h>
#include <Inventor/nodes/SoMaterial.h>
#include <Inventor/nodes/SoMaterialBinding.h>
#include <Inventor/nodes/SoPerspectiveCamera.h>
#include <Inventor/nodes/SoProfileCoordinate2.h>
#include <Inventor/nodes/SoText3.h>

main(int argc, char **argv)
{

   Widget myWindow = SoXt::init(argv[0]);
   if(myWindow == NULL) exit(1);

   SoGroup *root = new SoGroup;
   root->ref();

   // Set up camera.
   SoPerspectiveCamera*myCamera = new SoPerspectiveCamera;
   myCamera->position.setValue(0, -(argc - 1) / 2, 10);
   myCamera->nearDistance.setValue(5.0);
   myCamera->farDistance.setValue(15.0);
   root->addChild(myCamera);
```

Figure 6-8   Advanced 3D Text Example

```
// Let's make the front of the text green,
// and the sides and back shiny gold.
SoMaterial *myMaterial = new SoMaterial;
SbColor colors[3];
// diffuse
colors[0].setValue(1, 1, 1);
colors[1].setValue(1, 1, 0);
colors[2].setValue(1, 1, 0);
myMaterial->diffuseColor.setValues(0, 3, colors);
// specular
colors[0].setValue(1, 1, 1);
colors[1].setValue(1, 1, 0);
colors[2].setValue(1, 1, 0);
myMaterial->specularColor.setValues(0, 3, colors);
myMaterial->shininess.setValue(.1);
root->addChild(myMaterial);

// Choose a font.
SoFont *myFont = new SoFont;
myFont->name.setValue("Times-Roman");
root->addChild(myFont);
```

```
// Specify a beveled cross-section for the text.
SoProfileCoordinate2 *myProfileCoords =
          new SoProfileCoordinate2;
SbVec2f coords[4];
coords[0].setValue(.00, .00);
coords[1].setValue(.25, .25);
coords[2].setValue(1.25, .25);
coords[3].setValue(1.50, .00);
myProfileCoords->point.setValues(0, 4, coords);
root->addChild(myProfileCoords);

SoLinearProfile *myLinearProfile = new SoLinearProfile;
long    index[4] ;
index[0] = 0;
index[1] = 1;
index[2] = 2;
index[3] = 3;
myLinearProfile->index.setValues(0, 4, index);
root->addChild(myLinearProfile);

// Set the material binding to PER_PART.
SoMaterialBinding *myMaterialBinding = new SoMaterialBinding;
myMaterialBinding->
          value.setValue(SoMaterialBinding::PER_PART);
root->addChild(myMaterialBinding);

// Add the text.
SoText3 *myText3 = new SoText3;
myText3->string.setValue("Beveled Text");
myText3->justification.setValue(SoText3::CENTER);
myText3->parts.setValue(SoText3::ALL);
root->addChild(myText3);

SoXtExaminerViewer *myViewer =
          new SoXtExaminerViewer(myWindow);
myViewer->setSceneGraph(root);
myViewer->setTitle("Complex 3D Text");
myViewer->show();
myViewer->viewAll();

SoXt::show(myWindow);
SoXt::mainLoop();
}
```

## Chapter 7

Textures

Chapter Objectives

After reading this chapter, you'll be able to do the following:

- Apply textures to objects in the scene graph using the default values for texture mapping

- Apply textures to objects in the scene graph by specifying texture coordinates explicitly

- Use texture-coordinate functions such as **SoTextureCoordinatePlane** and **SoTextureCoordinateEnvironment** to map textures onto objects

- Create a texture map that can be stored in memory and applied to an object

- Wrap a texture around an object so that the image is repeated

- Specify how a texture affects the underlying shaded color of an object

This chapter explains how to use textures, which allow you to add realism and detail to scenes. In Inventor, you create a 2D texture image and then apply this texture to the surface of a 3D shape object. The rectangular patch of texture you define is stretched and compressed to "fit" the 3D shape according to your specifications. Key concepts introduced in this chapter include *texture map, wrapping textures, texture model, texture components*, and *environment mapping*.

Creating Textured Objects

Using textures, you can create a table with a wood grain, an orange with a dimpled, shiny surface, and a field of grass. To do so, first create wood, orange peel, and grass textures and then apply the textures to the various shape objects. Figure 7-1 contrasts two sets of objects: the objects on the right use texture mapping, and the objects on the left do not use textures.

Figure 7-1   Texture Mapping

What Is a Texture Map?

A *texture map* is a 2D array of pixel information for a particular pattern, or texture. Inventor, like OpenGL, uses the letter *s* for the horizontal texture coordinate and *t* for the vertical texture coordinate. A texture map is a 1×1 square, with coordinates ranging from 0.0 to 1.0 in both the *s* and *t* dimensions, as shown in Figure 7-2. Texture coordinates are assigned to each vertex of a polygon (this assignment is done either explicitly by you, or automatically by Inventor). If the pixels in the texture do not match up exactly with the pixels in the polygon, Inventor uses a filtering process to assign texture pixels to the object. The texture is read from a file or from memory.

Nodes Used for Texture Mapping

This section describes use of the following node classes:

SoTexture2
: specifies a 2D texture map to be used and associated parameters for texture mapping.

SoTextureCoordinate2
: explicitly defines the set of 2D texture coordinates to be used by subsequent vertex shapes.

SoTextureCoordinateBinding
: specifies how the current texture coordinates are to be bound to subsequent shape nodes.

SoTextureCoordinatePlane
SoTextureCoordinateEnvironment
: allow you to use a function to map from spatial coordinates to texture coordinates.

SoTextureCoordinateDefault
: turns off any previous texture-coordinate function so that all following shapes use their default texture coordinates.

SoTexture2Transform
: defines a 2D transformation for the texture map.

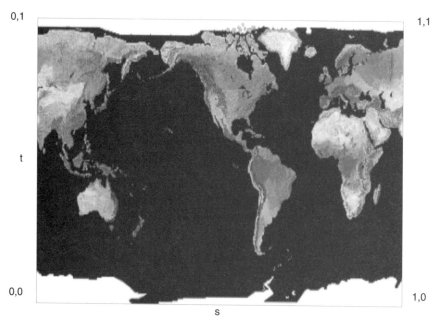

0,1

1,1

t

0,0

1,0

s

Figure 7-2   Texture Coordinates

The **SoComplexity** node has a **textureQuality** field that relates to texture mapping as well. It allows you to specify a value between 0.0 and 1.0, with 0.0 for the fastest rendering and 1.0 for the finest texturing. (In general, there is a trade-off between speed and the quality of texturing.) The default value for this field is 0.5.

Using the Defaults

Although you can affect how a texture is applied to an object in many ways, the simplest way to use textures is to use the default values. If you use textures, you need only an **SoTexture2** node (for the texture) and a shape node (the target object). Example 7-1, which displays a textured cube, illustrates this method. See "SoTexture2 Node" on page 165 for a detailed description of the **SoTexture2** node and its defaults.

Example 7-1   Using the Default Texture Values

```
#include <Inventor/Xt/SoXt.h>
#include <Inventor/Xt/viewers/SoXtExaminerViewer.h>
#include <Inventor/nodes/SoCube.h>
#include <Inventor/nodes/SoSeparator.h>
#include <Inventor/nodes/SoTexture2.h>

main(int , char **argv)
{
   Widget myWindow = SoXt::init(argv[0]);
   if(myWindow == NULL) exit(1);

   SoSeparator *root = new SoSeparator;
   root->ref();

   // Choose a texture
   SoTexture2 *rock = new SoTexture2;
   root->addChild(rock);
   rock->filename.setValue("brick.1.rgb");

   // Make a cube
   root->addChild(new SoCube);

   SoXtExaminerViewer *myViewer =
           new SoXtExaminerViewer(myWindow);
   myViewer->setSceneGraph(root);
   myViewer->setTitle("Default Texture Coords");
   myViewer->show();

   SoXt::show(myWindow);
   SoXt::mainLoop();
}
```

Tip: If several nodes use the same texture, position the texture node so that ❖ it can be used by all the nodes. When possible, group nodes to share textures first, then to share materials, because it is expensive to switch textures.

Key Concepts

This section explains some special ways you can change how a texture is applied to a shape object. These variations include the following:

- How the texture wraps around the object

- How the texture affects the object's underlying colors

In addition, this section explains how to specify the pixels for a texture image to be stored in memory.

Wrapping a Texture around an Object

Texture coordinates range from 0.0 to 1.0 in each dimension (see "What Is a Texture Map?" on page 157). What happens, then, if your polygon texture coordinates range from 0.0 to 2.0 in some dimension? In such cases, you have a choice:

- The texture can either be *repeated* as many times as necessary to cover the face (or stretched to cover the face)

- Or the last row of pixels can be repeated to cover the rest of the face (called *clamping*)

Figure 7-3 shows examples of both types of wrapping. The cylinder on the left has the texture repeated twice along its length and around its circumference. The cylinder on the right has the top scanline clamped, by setting **wrapT** to CLAMP. See "SoTexture2 Node" on page 165 for a description of the **wrapS** and **wrapT** fields.

How a Texture Affects the Underlying Colors

You can specify one of three texture *models* to use (see "SoTexture2 Node" on page 165). Each model causes the texture map to affect the underlying colors of the polygon in different ways. The model types are as follows:

MODULATE   multiplies the shaded color by the texture color (the default). If the texture has an alpha component, the alpha value modulates the object's transparency.

DECAL	replaces the shaded color with the texture color. If the texture has an alpha component, the alpha value specifies the texture's transparency, allowing the object's color to show through the texture.
BLEND	uses the texture intensity to blend between the shaded color and a specified constant blend color.

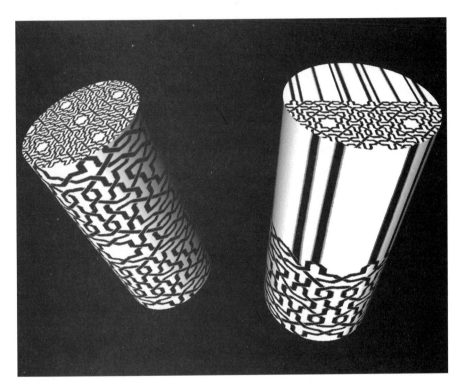

Figure 7-3   Wrapping the Texture around the Object

The MODULATE model can be used with any texture file. The BLEND model is used with one- or two-component files. The DECAL model is used with three- or four-component files. See "Components of a Texture" on page 162.

Tip: MODULATE works best on bright materials because the texture intensity, which is less than or equal to 1.0, is multiplied by the shaded color.

Plates 10 through 13 show examples of each texture model. The image in Plate 10 shows the scene without a texture. The image in Plate 11 uses a MODULATE model, so the color of the building is a combination of the texture and material colors. The image in Plate 12 uses a DECAL model, so the color of the building is determined completely by the texture map. The image in Plate 13 uses the BLEND model, so the color of the building blends between the underlying material color and the blend color value (gold).

❖ **Tip:** To create bright green polka dots on an object, create a black and white texture with white dots. Then use the BLEND texture model with a green blend color.

See the **glTexEnv()** function in the *OpenGL Reference Manual* for the actual equations used to calculate the final textured object colors.

❖ **Tip:** If you use MODULATE, you may want to surround your texture images with a one-pixel border of white pixels and set **wrapS** and **wrapT** to CLAMP so that the object's color is used where the texture runs out.

Storing an Image

Texture maps are read from a file or from memory. For information on what image file formats your platform supports, see your release documentation.

You can store a texture map as an **SoSFImage** and then specify the image in the **image** field of the **SoTexture2** node. This section provides details on how to store the texture-map pixels in memory. The texture, whether stored in a file or in memory, can contain from one to four components, as described in the following section.

Components of a Texture

A texture can be one of the following types:

- *One-component texture*—contains only an intensity value. This type of texture is often referred to as an *intensity map*. For example, an image of a mountain could use a one-component texture and vary the intensity of a constant-color polygon to make the image more realistic.

- *Two-component texture*—contains an intensity value and an alpha (transparency) value. For example, you can create a tree with leaves made of polygons of varying intensity, from dark green to bright green. Then, you can vary the transparency at the edges of the leaf area, so that you can see around the edges of the leaves to the objects behind them.

- *Three-component texture*—contains red, green, and blue values. This is a red-green-blue image, such as a photo or a commonly used texture such as brick, concrete, or cloth.

- *Four-component texture*—contains red, green, blue, and alpha (transparency) values. This texture is similar to the RGB three-component texture, but also contains transparency information. You can use a four-component texture to create a colorful New England maple tree in October using the technique described previously for two-component textures.

Tip: One- and two-component textures are generally faster than three- and four-component textures, since they require less computation. ❖

Storing an Image in Memory

Use the **setValue()** method to assign the value to the **SoSFImage**. This method requires you to supply the size of the texture (*width* ∗ *height*, in pixels), the number of components in the texture, and the values of the components for each pixel (as an array of unsigned chars, with values 0 to 255).

For a one-component texture, each byte in the array stores the intensity value for one pixel. As shown in Figure 7-4, byte 0 is the lower left corner of the pixel map, and numbering of bytes is from left to right within each row.

For example, to store a one-component texture, the code would be

```
SoTexture2 *textureNode = new SoTexture2;

// A 3-by-2 array of black and white pixels; the array is
//upside-down here (the first pixel is the lower left corner)
unsigned char image [] = {
    255, 0,
    0, 255,
    255, 0
};
//Set the image field:
textureNode->image.setValue(SbVec2s(3,2), 1, image);
```

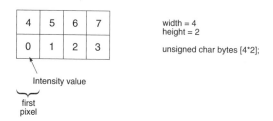

width = 4
height = 2

unsigned char bytes [4*2];

Intensity value

first
pixel

Figure 7-4   Format for Storing a One-Component Texture in Memory

For a two-component texture, byte 0 is the intensity of the first pixel, and byte 1 is the alpha (transparency) value for the first pixel. Bytes 2 and 3 contain the information for pixel 2, and so on (see Figure 7-5).

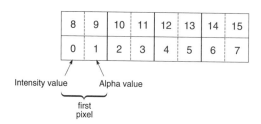

Intensity value   Alpha value

first
pixel

Figure 7-5   Format for Storing a Two-Component Texture in Memory

A three-component texture requires three bytes to store the information for each pixel. For the first pixel, byte 0 contains the red value, byte 1 contains the green value, and byte 2 contains the blue value (see Figure 7-6). A four-component texture requires four bytes for each pixel (red, green, blue, and alpha values).

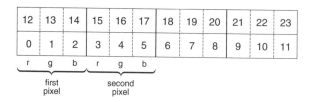

r   g   b   r   g   b

first   second
pixel   pixel

Figure 7-6   Format for Storing a Three-Component Texture in Memory

SoTexture2 Node

An **SoTexture2** node specifies the image for the texture map, how the texture wraps around the object, and the texture model to use.

Fields of an SoTexture2 Node

The **SoTexture2** node has the following fields:

filename (SoSFName)

specifies the name of the file to use as a texture map. See your release documentation for information on what file formats your system supports. You specify either a file name or an image (see next field) for the texture map.

If the **filename** field is set, the image file is read and the **image** field is set to the pixels in that file. If the **image** field is set, the **filename** field is set to " " (an empty string; the default value). This behavior assures that there is no ambiguity about which field is used for the texture.

image (SoSFImage)

specifies the color and number of pixels in the texture map.

wrapS (SoSFEnum)
wrapT (SoSFEnum)

specifies how the image wraps in the *s* (horizontal) and *t* (vertical) directions (see Figure 7-3). Possible values are as follows:

REPEAT	specifies to repeat the map to fill the shape (the default)
CLAMP	specifies to repeat the last row of pixels

model (SoSFEnum)

        specifies the texture model to use. Possible values are as follows:

MODULATE	multiplies the shaded color times the texture color (the default)
DECAL	replaces the shaded color with the texture color
BLEND	blends between the shaded color and the specified blend color (see the **blendColor** field)

blendColor (SoSFColor)

        specifies the color to blend when using the BLEND texture model.

The **textureQuality** field of the **SoComplexity** node controls the quality of filtering used to apply the texture. A value of 0.0 disables texturing completely, and a value of 1.0 specifies to use the highest quality of texturing. The default value for this field is 0.5.

Transforming a Texture Map

You can transform the texture map by inserting an **SoTexture2Transform** node into the scene graph before the shape node. This node has a cumulative effect and is applied to the texture coordinates. As shown in Figure 7-7, the relationship between the **SoTexture2Transform** node and the **SoTextureCoordinate2** node is analogous to the relationship between the **SoTransform** nodes and the **SoCoordinate** nodes.

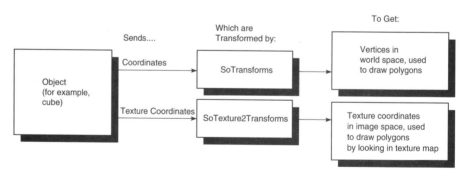

Figure 7-7   How the SoTexture2Transform Node Relates to the Texture Coordinates

The fields of the **SoTexture2Transform** node are as follows:

translation (SoSFVec2f)
> specifies a translation of the object's texture coordinates.

rotation (SoSFFloat)
> specifies a rotation of the object's texture coordinates. The rotation angle is in radians.

scaleFactor (SoSFVec2f)
> specifies how to scale the texture on the object. The object's s and t coordinates are multiplied by the scale factor. A scale factor of (2.0, 2.0) thus makes the texture appear smaller on the object (see left side of Figure 7-8). A scale factor of (0.5, 0.5) makes the texture appear larger (see right side of Figure 7-8).

center (SoSFVec2f)
> specifies the center of the rotation and scale transformations. The default is (0.0, 0.0), the lower left corner of the texture.

In Figure 7-8, the sphere on the left has a texture **scaleFactor** of (2.0, 2.0), so the texture is repeated twice in s and t. The sphere on the right has a texture **scaleFactor** of (0.5, 0.5), so only half the texture is used in both the s and t directions.

scaleFactor = (2.0, 2.0)   scaleFactor = (0.5, 0.5)

Figure 7-8   Effects of Different Scale Factors on a Texture Map

Mapping the Texture onto the Object

You can choose one of three techniques for mapping the 2D texture space onto the 3D object space:

1. Use the default texture coordinates. The texture is applied in different ways for different shapes, as described later in this section.

2. For shapes derived from **SoVertexShape**, you can specify the texture coordinates explicitly. With this method, you create an **SoTextureCoordinate2** node and specify a texture coordinate for each vertex in the shape.

3. Use one of the texture-coordinate functions to map the texture to the shape:

    SoTextureCoordinatePlane
    SoTextureCoordinateEnvironment

Techniques 1 and 3 are automatic, and hence easy to use. Technique 2 requires explicit coordinates generated by you and is thus harder to use but gives more explicit control. Each of these three techniques is described in detail in the following sections.

Using the Default Texture Mapping

Inventor uses the same technique for generating default texture coordinates for any shape that is derived from **SoVertexShape**. First, it computes the bounding box of the object. Then, it uses the longest edge of the box as the horizontal (s) axis of the texture. It uses the next longest edge as the vertical (t) axis of the texture. The value of the s coordinate ranges from 0.0 to 1.0, from one end of the bounding box to the other. The value of t ranges from 0 to n, where n equals the ratio of the second longest side of the bounding box to the longest side (the effect is that the texture is applied to the longest side of the box, without distortion).

For shapes that are not derived from **SoVertexShape**, the default texture coordinates are generated differently for each shape. These shapes include **SoCone, SoCube, SoCylinder, SoNurbsSurface, SoSphere**, and **SoText3**. Default texture mapping for each of these shapes is described in the following paragraphs.

SoSphere

For example, if your scene graph contains an **SoTexture2** node followed by an **SoSphere** node, the texture is applied to the sphere using default texture coordinates. The texture covers the entire surface of the sphere, wrapping counterclockwise from the back of the sphere (see Figure 7-9). The texture wraps around and connects to itself. A visible seam can result if the texture is nonrepeating.

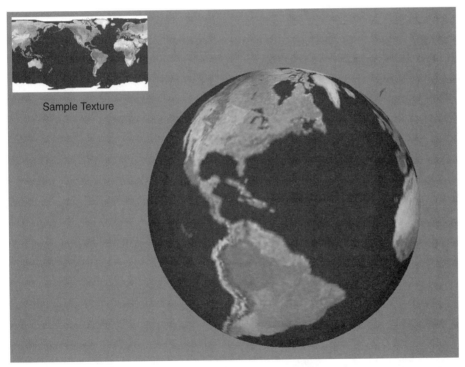

Sample Texture

Figure 7-9   Default Texture Mapping for SoSphere

Tip: Increasing the complexity of a simple shape improves the appearance ❖ of a texture on it.

SoCube

When a texture is applied to an **SoCube** using the default texture coordinates, the entire texture is applied to each face. On the front, back, right, and left sides of the cube, the texture is applied right-side up. On the top, the texture appears right-side up if you tilt the cube toward you. On the bottom, the texture appears right-side up if you tilt the cube away from you (see Figure 7-10).

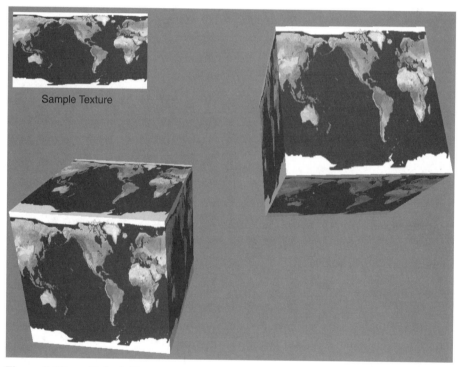

Sample Texture

Figure 7-10   Default Texture Mapping for SoCube

SoCylinder

When a texture is applied to an **SoCylinder** using the default texture coordinates, the texture wraps around the sides in a counterclockwise direction, beginning at the −z axis. A circle cut from the center of the texture square is applied to the top and bottom of the cylinder. When you look at the cylinder from the +z axis, the texture on the top appears right-side up when the cylinder tips towards you. The texture on the bottom appears right-side up when the cylinder tips away from you (see Figure 7-11).

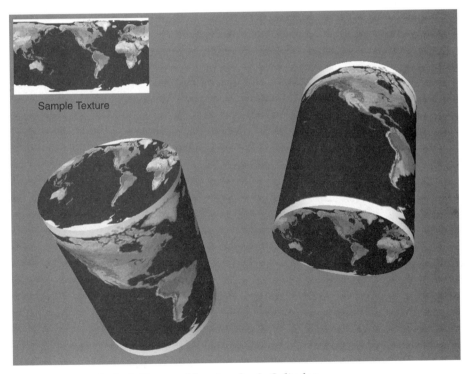

Sample Texture

Figure 7-11   Default Texture Mapping for SoCylinder

SoCone

When a texture is applied to an **SoCone** using the default texture coordinates, the texture wraps counterclockwise around the sides of the cone, starting at the back of the cone. The texture wraps around and connects to itself. A visible seam can result if the texture is nonrepeating. A circle cut from the center of the texture square is applied to the bottom of the cone just as it is applied to the bottom of a cylinder (see Figure 7-12).

❖ **Tip:** Increasing the complexity of a textured cone is especially important because of the way the texture is mapped near the tip of the cone.

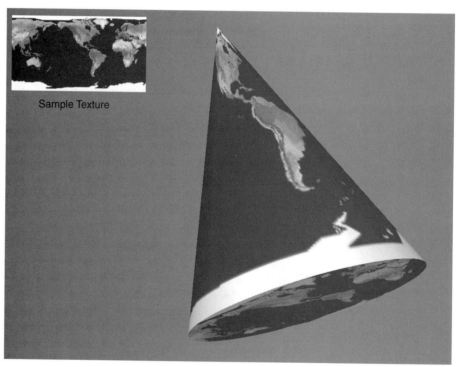

Sample Texture

Figure 7-12   Default Texture Mapping for SoCone

SoNurbsSurface

When a texture is applied to a NURBS surface using the default texture coordinates, the edges of the texture square are stretched to fit the NURBS patch (see Figure 7-13). A surface can be made up of many patches, like the teapot. If the NURBS surface is trimmed, so is the texture.

Sample Texture

Figure 7-13   Default Texture Mapping for SoNurbsSurface

SoText3

When a texture is applied to the front of an **SoText3** surface using the default texture coordinates, texture coordinate (0,0) is at the text's origin. The distance from 0.0 to 1.0 in *s* and *t* texture coordinates is equal to the font size. For the sides of an **SoText3** surface, using default texture mapping, the *s* coordinate extends forward along the text profile, starting with texture coordinate 0.0 at the back of the letter and increasing to the front. A *font-size* distance along the profile is a texture coordinate distance of 1.0. The *t* coordinates extend around the outline of the character clockwise in a similar fashion. (See Figure 7-14.)

Figure 7-14   Default Texture Mapping for SoText3

Specifying Texture Coordinates Explicitly

Sometimes, you may want to explicitly specify the texture coordinates for each vertex of an object. In this case, create an **SoTextureCoordinate2** node and specify the set of 2D texture coordinates to be applied to the vertices of the shape.

When you use this technique, you must specify a texture coordinate for each vertex in the shape. The coordinates are specified in pairs: the *s* coordinate followed by the *t* coordinate.

Example 7-2 shows specifying texture coordinates explicitly. It uses an **SoTextureCoordinateBinding** node to index into the texture-coordinates list.

Example 7-2 Specifying Texture Coordinates Explicitly

```
#include <Inventor/Xt/SoXt.h>
#include <Inventor/Xt/viewers/SoXtExaminerViewer.h>
#include <Inventor/nodes/SoCoordinate3.h>
#include <Inventor/nodes/SoFaceSet.h>
#include <Inventor/nodes/SoNormal.h>
#include <Inventor/nodes/SoNormalBinding.h>
#include <Inventor/nodes/SoSeparator.h>
#include <Inventor/nodes/SoTexture2.h>
#include <Inventor/nodes/SoTextureCoordinate2.h>
#include <Inventor/nodes/SoTextureCoordinateBinding.h>

main(int , char **argv)
{
   Widget myWindow = SoXt::init(argv[0]);
   if(myWindow == NULL) exit(1);

   SoSeparator *root = new SoSeparator;
   root->ref();

   // Choose a texture
   SoTexture2 *brick = new SoTexture2;
   root->addChild(brick);
   brick->filename.setValue("brick.1.rgb");

   // Define the square's spatial coordinates
   SoCoordinate3 *coord = new SoCoordinate3;
   root->addChild(coord);
   coord->point.set1Value(0, SbVec3f(-3, -3, 0));
   coord->point.set1Value(1, SbVec3f( 3, -3, 0));
```

```
coord->point.set1Value(2, SbVec3f( 3,   3, 0));
coord->point.set1Value(3, SbVec3f(-3,   3, 0));

// Define the square's normal
SoNormal *normal = new SoNormal;
root->addChild(normal);
normal->vector.set1Value(0, SbVec3f(0, 0, 1));

// Define the square's texture coordinates
SoTextureCoordinate2 *texCoord = new SoTextureCoordinate2;
root->addChild(texCoord);
texCoord->point.set1Value(0, SbVec2f(0, 0));
texCoord->point.set1Value(1, SbVec2f(1, 0));
texCoord->point.set1Value(2, SbVec2f(1, 1));
texCoord->point.set1Value(3, SbVec2f(0, 1));

// Define normal and texture coordinate bindings
SoNormalBinding *nBind = new SoNormalBinding;
SoTextureCoordinateBinding *tBind =
        new SoTextureCoordinateBinding;
root->addChild(nBind);
root->addChild(tBind);
nBind->value.setValue(SoNormalBinding::OVERALL);
tBind->value.setValue
        (SoTextureCoordinateBinding::PER_VERTEX);

// Define a FaceSet
SoFaceSet *myFaceSet = new SoFaceSet;
root->addChild(myFaceSet);
myFaceSet->numVertices.set1Value(0, 4);

SoXtExaminerViewer *myViewer =
        new SoXtExaminerViewer(myWindow);
myViewer->setSceneGraph(root);
myViewer->setTitle("Texture Coordinates");
myViewer->show();

SoXt::show(myWindow);
SoXt::mainLoop();
}
```

Using a Texture-Coordinate Function

A third way to map texture coordinates onto an object is through the use of a *texture-coordinate function*. A texture-coordinate function defines the texture coordinates for an object based on the position of each vertex in the object. Each texture-coordinate function uses a different algorithm for calculating the texture coordinates, as described in detail in the following subsections. These functions allow you to specify texture mapping in a general way, without requiring you to define explicit texture coordinates. The texture-coordinate function ignores the current texture coordinates specified by an **SoTextureCoordinate2** node.

Inventor includes two texture-coordinate functions:

SoTextureCoordinatePlane

          projects a texture map through a plane.

SoTextureCoordinateEnvironment

          specifies that objects should look as if they reflect their environment (also known as *reflection mapping* or *environment mapping*).

To use the default texture coordinates (in effect, to "turn off" the effect of any previous texture-coordinate node in the scene graph without using a separator), use the **SoTextureCoordinateDefault** node.

SoTextureCoordinatePlane

SoTextureCoordinatePlane, probably the most commonly used texture-coordinate function, projects a texture plane onto a shape object, as shown in Plate 14. You define an *s* and a *t* direction, which are used to define a plane for the texture. The texture coordinate (*s*) is then defined by the following equation, where *coord* is a coordinate in the object:

$$s = \left(\frac{1}{directionS} \right) * \quad coord$$

The fields for **SoTextureCoordinatePlane** are as follows:

directionS (SoSFVec3f)

> projection direction of *s* coordinate
> (default = 1.0, 0.0, 0.0)

directionT (SoSFVec3f)

> projection direction of *t* coordinate
> (default = 0.0, 1.0, 0.0)

The length of the direction vector equals the repeat interval of the texture (see Example 7-3).

Example 7-3 shows the use of **SoTextureCoordinatePlane** (see Figure 7-15). It draws three texture-mapped spheres, each with a different repeat frequency as defined by the fields of the **SoTextureCoordinatePlane** node.

Example 7-3   Using SoTextureCoordinatePlane

```
#include <Inventor/nodes/SoMaterial.h>
#include <Inventor/nodes/SoSeparator.h>
#include <Inventor/nodes/SoSphere.h>
#include <Inventor/nodes/SoTexture2.h>
#include <Inventor/nodes/SoTexture2Transform.h>
#include <Inventor/nodes/SoTextureCoordinatePlane.h>
#include <Inventor/nodes/SoTranslation.h>

#include <Inventor/Xt/SoXt.h>
#include <Inventor/Xt/viewers/SoXtExaminerViewer.h>

main(int , char **argv)
{
   Widget myWindow = SoXt::init(argv[0]);
   if(myWindow == NULL) exit(1);

   SoSeparator *root = new SoSeparator;
   root->ref();

   // Choose a texture.
   SoTexture2 *faceTexture = new SoTexture2;
   root->addChild(faceTexture);
   faceTexture->filename.setValue("sillyFace.rgb");
   // Make the diffuse color pure white
   SoMaterial *myMaterial = new SoMaterial;
   myMaterial->diffuseColor.setValue(1,1,1);
   root->addChild(myMaterial);
```

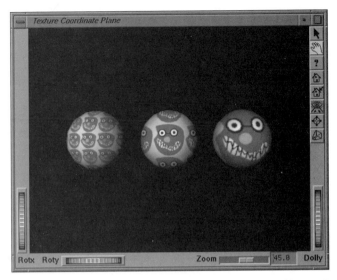

Figure 7-15   SoTextureCoordinatePlane with Different Repeat Frequencies

```
// This texture2Transform centers the texture about (0,0,0)
SoTexture2Transform *myTexXf = new SoTexture2Transform;
myTexXf->translation.setValue(.5,.5);
root->addChild(myTexXf);

// Define a texture coordinate plane node.  This one will
// repeat with a frequency of two times per unit length.
// Add a sphere for it to affect.
SoTextureCoordinatePlane *texPlane1 = new
          SoTextureCoordinatePlane;
texPlane1->directionS.setValue(SbVec3f(2,0,0));
texPlane1->directionT.setValue(SbVec3f(0,2,0));
root->addChild(texPlane1);
root->addChild(new SoSphere);

// A translation node for spacing the three spheres.
SoTranslation *myTranslation = new SoTranslation;
myTranslation->translation.setValue(2.5,0,0);
```

```
// Create a second sphere with a repeat frequency of 1.
SoTextureCoordinatePlane *texPlane2 = new
        SoTextureCoordinatePlane;
texPlane2->directionS.setValue(SbVec3f(1,0,0));
texPlane2->directionT.setValue(SbVec3f(0,1,0));
root->addChild(myTranslation);
root->addChild(texPlane2);
root->addChild(new SoSphere);

// The third sphere has a repeat frequency of .5
SoTextureCoordinatePlane *texPlane3 = new
        SoTextureCoordinatePlane;
texPlane3->directionS.setValue(SbVec3f(.5,0,0));
texPlane3->directionT.setValue(SbVec3f(0,.5,0));
root->addChild(myTranslation);
root->addChild(texPlane3);
root->addChild(new SoSphere);

SoXtExaminerViewer *myViewer = new SoXtExaminerViewer(myWindow);
myViewer->setSceneGraph(root);
myViewer->setTitle("Texture Coordinate Plane");
myViewer->show();

SoXt::show(myWindow);
SoXt::mainLoop();
}
```

SoTextureCoordinateEnvironment

The **SoTextureCoordinateEnvironment** node specifies that subsequent objects should reflect their environment, just as a shiny round Christmas ornament reflects its surroundings. For best results, the texture map specified should be a spherical reflection map. See the *OpenGL Programming Guide*, Chapter 9, for tips on how to create a spherical reflection map.

When **SoTextureCoordinateEnvironment** is used, a calculation is made at each vertex of the polygon to determine where a vector from the viewpoint to the vertex would be reflected. This reflection point defines the texture coordinate for that point on the polygon. See Plates 16 and 17.

Because of the way environment mapping is implemented in OpenGL, environment maps are accurate only if the camera does not move relative to the environment being reflected.

Chapter 8

Curves and Surfaces

Chapter Objectives

After reading this chapter, you'll be able to do the following:

- Create a variety of curves and surfaces
- Trim areas of NURBS surfaces
- Use NURBS profiles to specify the beveled edges of 3D text

Curves and curved surfaces provide a convenient mathematical means of describing a geometric model. Instead of using drawings, metal strips, or clay models, designers can use these mathematical expressions to represent the surfaces used on airplane wings, automobile bodies, machine parts, or other smooth curves and surfaces. Inventor uses a particular type of parametric polynomial, a NURBS (Non-Uniform Rational B-Spline), to represent curves and surfaces. This entire chapter can be considered advanced material.

Overview

To use NURBS curves and surfaces in an Inventor program, you need to develop an intuitive feel for a number of basic concepts. This section defines these key concepts and shows how they pertain to the various Inventor NURBS-related classes. For a more rigorous mathematical description of a NURBS, see "Suggestions for Further Reading" on page 207 at the end of this chapter.

Classes Used with NURBS Shapes

This chapter describes use of the following classes:

SoNurbsCurve   represents a NURBS curve. (This is where the knot sequence is specified.)

SoNurbsSurface   represents a NURBS surface. (This is where the knot sequence is specified.)

SoNurbsProfile   trims regions from a NURBS surface using a NURBS curve.

SoLinearProfile   trims regions from a NURBS surface using connected line segments.

SoProfileCoordinate2
                      specifies 2D coordinates for trim curves.

SoProfileCoordinate3
                      specifies rational 2D coordinates for trim curves.

SoCoordinate3   specifies the control points of a NURBS surface or curve.

SoCoordinate4   specifies rational control points of a NURBS surface or curve.

Parametric Curves

For simplicity, this discussion first explains the important NURBS concepts in terms of *curves*, which are lines in 3D space, such as a helix. Once you understand how to define a NURBS curve, defining a NURBS surface is a simple extension of your knowledge (see "NURBS Surfaces" on page 199).

A NURBS curve or surface is *parametric*—that is, the equations that describe it depend on variables (or *parameters*) that are not explicitly part of the geometry. A NURBS curve is described in terms of one parameter, u. The following three functions map this single parameter into x-y-z space:

$x = f(u)$
$y = g(u)$
$z = h(u)$

By sweeping through different values of u (that is, through parameter space), it is possible to evaluate the equations and determine the x, y, and z values for points on the curve in object space. Figure 8-1 represents this mapping of parameter space to object space.

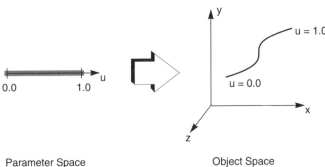

Parameter Space   Object Space

Figure 8-1   Mapping a Parametric Curve to Object Space

Key Concepts

Your job as programmer is to define the components that make up the parametric functions, referred to as *f()*, *g()*, and *h()* in the previous section. Instead of explicitly specifying the equations, you specify the following three things:

- Control points—using **SoCoordinate3** or **SoCoordinate4** nodes

- Knot sequence—using **SoNurbsCurve** or **SoIndexedNurbsCurve** nodes

- Order—implicitly defined by number of control points and number of knots

A brief description of each is provided in this section, along with discussions of how they are related and how continuity is defined. A more elaborate description is provided in "Basis Function" on page 187.

Control points are points in object space that affect the shape of the curve in some way. The curve may pass near the control points, as shown at the left in Figure 8-2, or pass through some of them, as shown at the right in the figure. The control points can be a set of data points through which you want to fit a curve, or a grid of points used to describe a curved surface such as the hood of a car. In Inventor, control points are specified in an **SoCoordinate3** or **SoCoordinate4** node.

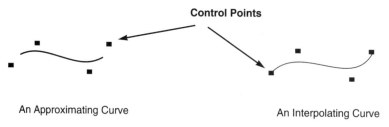

An Approximating Curve   An Interpolating Curve

Figure 8-2   Using Control Points to Shape the Curve

The *knot sequence* defines how the control points affect the curve. The knot sequence is simply a list of nondecreasing numbers. These numbers determine whether the curve passes through and interpolates between some of the control points (an interpolating curve) or passes near the control points (an approximating curve). In Inventor, the knot sequence is specified in an **SoNurbsCurve** or **SoNurbsSurface** (or **SoIndexedNurbsCurve**, **SoIndexedNurbsSurface**) node.

The *order* of a curve determines the form of the parametric equations. The order is equal to one plus the maximum exponent (*degree*) of the variables in the parametric equations. For example, the parametric equations of a cubic curve (*degree* = 3, *order* = 4) have the following form:

$$x(u) = A_x u^3 + B_x u^2 + C_x u + D_x$$
$$y(u) = A_y u^3 + B_y u^2 + C_y u + D_y$$
$$z(u) = A_z u^3 + B_z u^2 + C_z u + D_z$$

Similarly, the parametric equations of a quadratic curve (*degree* = 2, *order* = 3) have the following form:

$$x(u) = A_x u^2 + B_x u + C_x$$
$$y(u) = A_y u^2 + B_y u + C_y$$
$$z(u) = A_z u^2 + B_z u + C_z$$

Alternatively, you may wish to think of the order as the number of coefficients in the parametric equation. The order of a curve affects how smooth the curve can be (see "Continuity of a Curve" on page 186).

In Inventor, the order of a curve is not explicitly specified. Order is equal to

number_of_knots − number_of_control_points

Control Points and Order

The order of the curve determines the minimum number of control points necessary to define the curve. You must have at least *order* control points to define a curve. (So for a curve of order 4, you must have at least four control points.) To make curves with more than *order* control points, you can join two or more curve segments into a *piecewise curve* (see Figure 8-3).

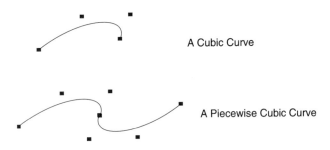

A Cubic Curve

A Piecewise Cubic Curve

Figure 8-3   Piecewise Cubic Curve

The order of the curve also affects how the curve behaves when a control point is moved. In Inventor, a NURBS curve can have an order up to 8. However, higher orders introduce oscillation into the curve and can behave unpredictably when a control point moves. *Cubic curves* (order of 4) are the most commonly used curves, since they provide enough control for most geometric modeling applications without the drawbacks of higher-order curves.

Continuity of a Curve

A *breakpoint* is where two curve segments meet within a piecewise curve. The *continuity* of a curve at a breakpoint describes how those curves meet at the breakpoint. Figure 8-4 shows four possible types of continuity:

No continuity	The curves do not meet at all.
C^0 *continuity*	The endpoints of the two curves meet (the curves have positional continuity only). There may be a sharp point where they meet.
C^1 *continuity*	The curves have identical tangents at the breakpoint. (The tangent is the *slope* at the breakpoint.) The curves join smoothly. C^1 curves also have positional continuity.
C^2 *continuity*	The curves have identical curvature at the breakpoint. (*Curvature* is defined as the rate of change of the tangents.) Curvature continuity implies both tangential and positional continuity.

The order of a curve determines the maximum continuity possible. Thus, you may need a higher order curve if you need more continuity. The maximum continuity is *order* − 2. For example, for cubic curves, the maximum continuity possible is C^2 (curvature continuity).

Chapter 8: Curves and Surfaces

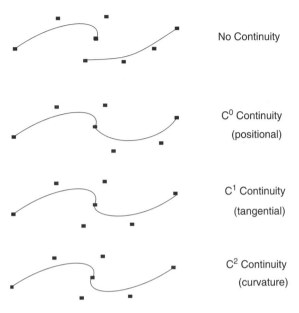

No Continuity

C^0 Continuity
(positional)

C^1 Continuity
(tangential)

C^2 Continuity
(curvature)

Figure 8-4   Continuity of a Curve

Basis Function

Each control point is like a magnet tugging on the curve (see Figure 8-5). The strength and extent of these magnets is described mathematically by a particular basis function. For a NURBS, this function is the *B-spline* basis function. (See "Suggestions for Further Reading" on page 207 for references presenting a more thorough derivation of the B-spline basis function.)

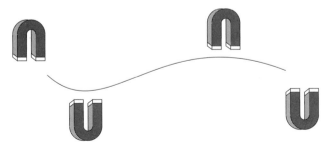

Figure 8-5   Control Points Influence the Curve

The B-spline basis function (Figure 8-6) describes the curve in parameter (*u*) space. For each value of *u*:

*contribution_of_each_control_point = location * its_basis _function*

The resulting curve is equal to the *sum* of the contributions from each control point. Note that often a control point (a "magnet") affects the entire curve, although its influence becomes weaker as you move away from it. The exact extent of the influence is determined by the knot sequence.

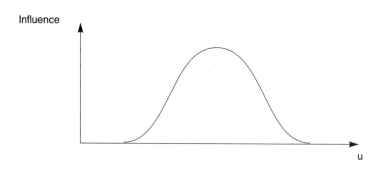

Figure 8-6   B-Spline Basis Function

Knot Sequence

The distribution of basis functions in parameter space is controlled by the *knot sequence* (also referred to as the *knot vector*, or *the knots*). The knot sequence is a list of nondecreasing values. Each knot defines the beginning and end of a basis function. There must be exactly *(order + number of control points)* values in the knot sequence. The curve is defined only where *order* basis functions overlap (as shown in Figure 8-7). If the knot values are singular (no repeating values) and regularly spaced, the curve is a *uniform B-spline* (as shown in Figure 8-7).

Figure 8-7 shows a uniform knot sequence. Four control points are defined (in object space). The top of the figure illustrates the four basis functions for each of the control points. The basis functions overlap where *u* = 3.0 to *u* = 4.0, as indicated by the shaded portion. This figure also illustrates another important NURBS relationship: at any point where the curve is defined, the sum of all basis functions is equal to 1.

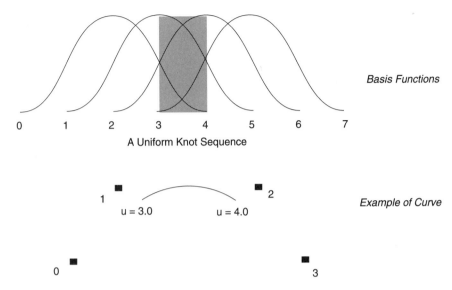

Figure 8-7   Uniform Knot Sequence

Knot Multiplicity

Distinct knot values define *segments*. A basis function always spans *order* segments. In Figure 8-7, for example, the basis function beginning at 0 and ending at 4 spans four segments (knot 0 to knot 1; knot 1 to knot 2; knot 2 to knot 3; and knot 3 to knot 4).

Duplicating values in the knot sequence increases that value's *multiplicity* and causes more than one basis function to start at that point. This also causes a corresponding decrease in the continuity of the curve. Figure 8-8 uses the same two sets of control points, with different knot sequences for the top and bottom curves. Notice how the bottom curve has C^0 continuity, and the top curve has C^2 continuity. This relationship between multiplicity and the continuity of the curve can be expressed mathematically as follows:

$$C^{ORD - (M + 1)}$$

where *ORD* equals the order of the curve and *M* is the multiplicity.

The maximum multiplicity (maximum times you can repeat a knot) is *order*. Table 8-1 shows knot multiplicity and the resulting continuity.

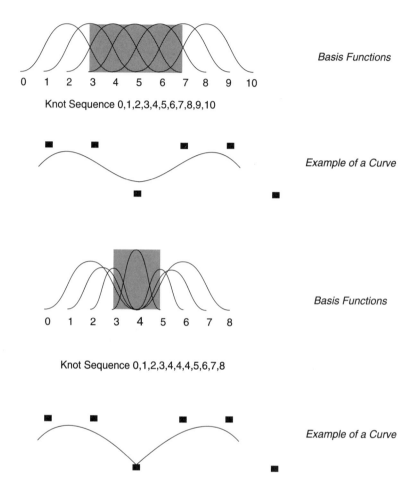

Knot Sequence 0,1,2,3,4,5,6,7,8,9,10

Basis Functions

Example of a Curve

Knot Sequence 0,1,2,3,4,4,4,5,6,7,8

Basis Functions

Example of a Curve

Figure 8-8   Knot Multiplicity

Knot Multiplicity	Continuity Conditions	Continuity
1	positional tangential curvature	C^2
2	positional tangential	C^1
3	positional	C^0
4	none	none

Table 8-1   Continuity and Knot Multiplicity for Cubic Curves

Common Knot Sequences

Several common knot sequences are extremely useful for a wide variety of applications:

Uniform cubic B-spline
> knots are uniformly spaced; single multiplicity (for example, 0, 1, 2, 3, 4, 5, 6, 7)

Cubic Bezier curve   multiplicity = 4 at beginning and end (for example, 0, 0, 0, 0, 1, 1, 1, 1)

Uniform cubic B-spline that passes through endpoints
> multiplicity= 4 at beginning and end; uniformly spaced single knots between (for example, 0, 0, 0, 0, 1, 2, 3, 4, 5, 5, 5, 5)

The behavior of the Bezier curve and the uniform cubic B-spline makes them ideal for geometric modeling and CAD applications. The curve passes through the first and last control points (see Figure 8-9). A line drawn through the first and second control points determines the tangent at the first endpoint. A line drawn through the last two control points determines the tangent at the second endpoint.

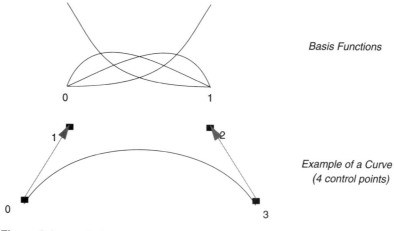

Basis Functions

Example of a Curve
(4 control points)

Figure 8-9   Cubic Bezier Curve

Summary of NURBS Relationships

The previous pages have outlined important relationships among NURBS parameters. They can be summarized as follows:

- *order* = *degree* + 1, where
  degree is the maximum exponent in the parametric equations
- To define a curve, you need at least *order* control points
- Maximum continuity = *order* − 2
- Number of knots = *order* + number of control points
- Knot values must be nondecreasing
- Maximum knot multiplicity = *order*
- Continuity = *order* − (multiplicity + 1)

Thus, for cubic curves, the order equals 4. You need at least four control points to define a cubic curve. The maximum continuity for cubics is C^2 continuity. You need a minimum of eight knots in the knot sequence. The maximum knot multiplicity of cubics is 4.

Rational Curves

Each control point has an associated *weight* that influences the shape of its basis function. As shown in Figure 8-10, this is analogous to having magnets of differing sizes tugging on the curve. For *nonrational* curves, all control points have a weight of 1.0. For *rational* curves, the control points have differing weights. If a control point has a weight greater than 1.0, its influence on the curve is greater than that of control points with weights of 1.0.

The parametric equations for rational curves have both a numerator and a denominator, which results in a *ratio*. (The numerator is the original parametric equation. The denominator is another parametric equation that takes the weight into account.) We recommend that the weight be a value greater than 0. Use an **SoCoordinate4** node to specify x, y, z, and w (weight) values.

Rational curves and surfaces are required to accurately represent conic sections, spheres, and cylinders. For more information, see "Suggestions for Further Reading" on page 207.

w = 10.0

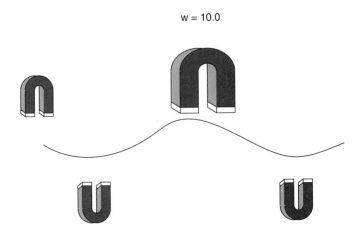

Figure 8-10   Rational Curves

N-U-R-B-S Spells NURBS

If you've made it this far into the discussion of the NURBS, you now understand all the buzzwords that form this acronym:

Non-Uniform   Knot spacing need not be *uniform*.

Rational   The parametric equations describing the curve can have a denominator (that is, they can be *ratios*).

B-Spline   The influence of the control points is based on the *B-spline* basis function.

Examples of NURBS Curves

This section provides two examples of NURBS curves: a B-spline curve and a uniform B-spline curve that passes through the end control points.

B-Spline Curve

Example 8-1 creates and displays a B-spline curve. Seven control points are defined. The knot vector contains ten knots. Since

number_of_knots = order + number_of_control_points

this curve has an order of 3. It has a multiplicity of 2 (one knot is used twice). This curve has a continuity of C^0.

Figure 8-11 shows the scene graph for the nodes in this example. Figure 8-12 shows the resulting curve.

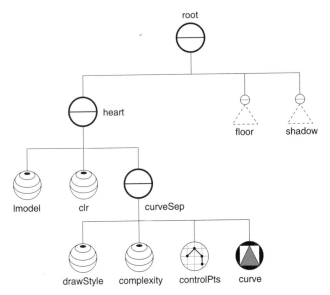

Figure 8-11   Scene Graph for B-Spline Curve Example

Example 8-1   Creating a B-Spline Curve

```
// The control points for this curve
float pts[7][3] = {
    { 4.0, -6.0,  6.0},
    {-4.0,  1.0,  0.0},
    {-1.5,  5.0, -6.0},
    { 0.0,  2.0, -2.0},
    { 1.5,  5.0, -6.0},
    { 4.0,  1.0,  0.0},
    {-4.0, -6.0,  6.0}};

// The knot vector
float knots[10] = {1, 2, 3, 4, 5, 5, 6, 7, 8, 9};

// Create the nodes needed for the B-Spline curve.
SoSeparator *
makeCurve()
{
    SoSeparator *curveSep = new SoSeparator();
    curveSep->ref();
```

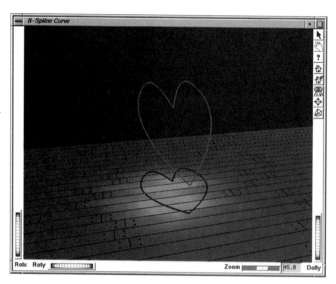

Figure 8-12   B-Spline Curve

```
// Set the draw style of the curve.
SoDrawStyle *drawStyle  = new SoDrawStyle;
drawStyle->lineWidth = 4;
curveSep->addChild(drawStyle);

// Define the NURBS curve including the control points
// and a complexity.
SoComplexity  *complexity = new SoComplexity;
SoCoordinate3 *controlPts = new SoCoordinate3;
SoNurbsCurve  *curve       = new SoNurbsCurve;
complexity->value = 0.8;
controlPts->point.setValues(0, 7, pts);
curve->numControlPoints = 7;
curve->knotVector.setValues(0, 10, knots);
curveSep->addChild(complexity);
curveSep->addChild(controlPts);
curveSep->addChild(curve);

curveSep->unrefNoDelete();
return curveSep;
}
```

Uniform B-Spline Curve Passing through Endpoints

Example 8-2 creates a uniform B-spline curve that passes through the end control points. The knot sequence has a multiplicity of 4 at the beginning and end, which causes the curve to pass through the first and last control points. In between, the curve is uniform.

The scene graph for the nodes in this example has the same structure as the scene graph shown in Figure 8-11. Figure 8-13 shows the resulting curve.

Example 8-2   Creating a Uniform B-Spline Curve

```
// The control points for this curve
float pts[13][3] = {
    { 6.0,   0.0,   6.0},
    {-5.5,   0.5,   5.5},
    {-5.0,   1.0,  -5.0},
    { 4.5,   1.5,  -4.5},
    { 4.0,   2.0,   4.0},
    {-3.5,   2.5,   3.5},
    {-3.0,   3.0,  -3.0},
    { 2.5,   3.5,  -2.5},
    { 2.0,   4.0,   2.0},
    {-1.5,   4.5,   1.5},
    {-1.0,   5.0,  -1.0},
```

Figure 8-13   A Uniform B-Spline Curve that Passes through the Endpoints

```
                { 0.5,   5.5,  -0.5},
                { 0.0,   6.0,   0.0}};

   // The knot vector
   float knots[17] = {
      0, 0, 0, 0, 1, 2, 3, 4, 5, 6, 7, 8, 9, 10, 10, 10, 10};

   // Create the nodes needed for the B-Spline curve.
   SoSeparator *
   makeCurve()
   {
       SoSeparator *curveSep = new SoSeparator();
       curveSep->ref();

       // Set the draw style of the curve.
       SoDrawStyle *drawStyle  = new SoDrawStyle;
       drawStyle->lineWidth = 4;
       curveSep->addChild(drawStyle);

       // Define the NURBS curve including the control points
       // and a complexity.
       SoComplexity  *complexity = new SoComplexity;
       SoCoordinate3 *controlPts = new SoCoordinate3;
       SoNurbsCurve  *curve      = new SoNurbsCurve;
       complexity->value = 0.8;
       controlPts->point.setValues(0, 13, pts);
       curve->numControlPoints = 13;
       curve->knotVector.setValues(0, 17, knots);
       curveSep->addChild(complexity);
       curveSep->addChild(controlPts);
       curveSep->addChild(curve);

       curveSep->unrefNoDelete();
       return curveSep;
   }
```

NURBS Surfaces

A surface differs from a curve only in that it has two parametric directions (*u* and *v*) instead of one (Figure 8-14), and that the order and knot vector must be specified for both parameters.

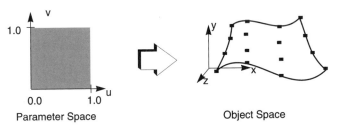

Figure 8-14   Curved Surfaces

The two parametric dimensions, *u* and *v*, are mapped to 3D object space. As with curves, control points are specified in object space. The *u* and *v* parameters can have a different order, and a different knot sequence, although they are often the same. The order for each dimension is specified as

order = number_of_knots – number_of_control_points

Tip: Put NURBS shapes under their own separator to facilitate caching.

Bezier Surface

Example 8-3 creates a plain Bezier surface. The knot vectors define a cubic Bezier surface (multiplicity 4 at beginning and end). The surface is order 4 with 16 control points arranged in a four-by-four grid. The *u* and *v* knot vectors each have a length of 8. Figure 8-15 shows the scene graph for the nodes in this example. Notice that the points used as control points (*controlPts*) must precede the NURBS node (*surface*) in the scene graph. Figure 8-16 shows the rendered image.

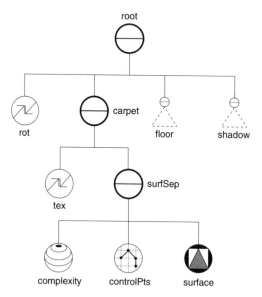

Figure 8-15   Scene Graph for a Bezier Surface

Example 8-3   Bezier Surface

```
// The control points for this surface
float pts[16][3] = {
    {-4.5,  -2.0,   8.0},
    {-2.0,   1.0,   8.0},
    { 2.0,  -3.0,   6.0},
    { 5.0,  -1.0,   8.0},
    {-3.0,   3.0,   4.0},
    { 0.0,  -1.0,   4.0},
    { 1.0,  -1.0,   4.0},
    { 3.0,   2.0,   4.0},
    {-5.0,  -2.0,  -2.0},
    {-2.0,  -4.0,  -2.0},
    { 2.0,  -1.0,  -2.0},
    { 5.0,   0.0,  -2.0},
    {-4.5,   2.0,  -6.0},
    {-2.0,  -4.0,  -5.0},
    { 2.0,   3.0,  -5.0},
    { 4.5,  -2.0,  -6.0}};

// The knot vector
float knots[8] = {
    0, 0, 0, 0, 1, 1, 1, 1};
```

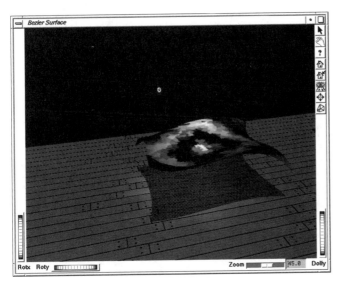

Figure 8-16   Bezier Surface

```
// Create the nodes needed for the Bezier surface.
SoSeparator *
makeSurface()
{
   SoSeparator *surfSep = new SoSeparator();
   surfSep->ref();

   // Define the Bezier surface including the control
   // points and a complexity.
   SoComplexity  *complexity = new SoComplexity;
   SoCoordinate3 *controlPts = new SoCoordinate3;
   SoNurbsSurface  *surface  = new SoNurbsSurface;
   complexity->value = 0.7;
   controlPts->point.setValues(0, 16, pts);
   surface->numUControlPoints = 4;
   surface->numVControlPoints = 4;
   surface->uKnotVector.setValues(0, 8, knots);
   surface->vKnotVector.setValues(0, 8, knots);
   surfSep->addChild(complexity);
   surfSep->addChild(controlPts);
   surfSep->addChild(surface);

   surfSep->unrefNoDelete();
   return surfSep;
}
```

❖ **Tip:** If a NURBS surface is changing, inserting an **SoComplexity** node with SCREEN_SPACE specified as the **type** may improve performance, especially if the NURBS surfaces are far away.

Trimming NURBS Surfaces

Profile curves are used to trim (cut areas away from) a NURBS surface. Profile curves themselves are not rendered; they are simply used to trim any subsequent NURBS surfaces in the scene graph. Like transformations, profile curves are pushed and popped by separator groups, yet they accumulate with each other.

Profile curves are often used to perform a stencil operation, such as cutting a shape out of a cloth surface with a pair of scissors. They are also used to remove sharp corners from a NURBS surface. See also Example 6-3, which uses a profile curve with 3D text.

Trimming NURBS surfaces is considered an advanced topic. If this is your first exposure to a NURBS, experiment first with curves and surfaces, then move on to trimmed surfaces.

A profile curve can consist of a linear profile curve (**SoLinearProfile**), a NURBS curve (**SoNurbsProfileCurve**), or a combination of the two. For coordinates, it uses either **SoProfileCoordinate2** (for nonrational profile curves) or **SoProfileCoordinate3** (for rational profile curves). The main requirement is that the composite profile curve make a complete loop, with its first point repeated as its last point. In addition, it cannot be self-intersecting.

❖ **Tip:** If you want your profile curve to be straight but follow the surface, use an **SoNurbsProfileCurve** with an order 2 curve. (See Example 8-4.) Linear profiles create straight trim edges in object space that do not follow the surface. You will seldom use an **SoLinearProfile** to trim a NURBS surface.

The direction in which the points of a profile curve are defined is significant. If the profile curve is defined in a clockwise direction, the area inside the curve is discarded and the area outside the curve is retained. If the profile curve is defined in a counterclockwise direction, the area inside is retained and the area outside is discarded. Profile curves can be nested inside each other but cannot intersect each other. The outermost profile curve must be defined in a counterclockwise direction (see Example 8-4).

Profile curves are defined in parameter space, which is mapped to object space.

Example 8-4 adds profile curves to the surface created in Example 8-3. Figure 8-17 shows the scene graph for the nodes in this example. Notice that the points used as control points (*controlPts*) must precede the NURBS node (*surface*) in the scene graph. Similarly, the points that define the profile curve (*trimPts*) must precede the profile-curve nodes (*nTrim1*, *nTrim2*, and *nTrim3*). And, naturally, the profile-curve nodes must precede the NURBS surface to be trimmed.

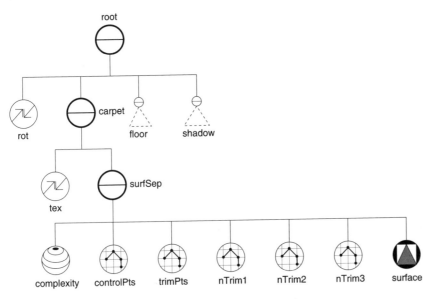

Figure 8-17   Scene Graph for Trimmed Bezier Surface

Figure 8-18 shows the trim curves used in Example 8-4, mapped in parameter (*u/v*) space. This example uses three NURBS profile curves. Each curve has its own knot vector. The first curve, *nTrim1*, has four segments and five control points (it starts and ends at the same point). It is an order 2 curve that passes through the endpoints. The second profile curve, *nTrim2*, is also linear. It passes through the endpoints and has three segments. The third profile curve, *nTrim3*, is a cubic curve (order = 4). It has a multiplicity 4 at beginning and end (which makes it a Bezier curve that passes through the endpoints).

Notice that these trim curves are nested inside each other and that the outermost curve is counterclockwise. They do not intersect each other. Figure 8-19 shows the trimmed Bezier surface produced by Example 8-4.

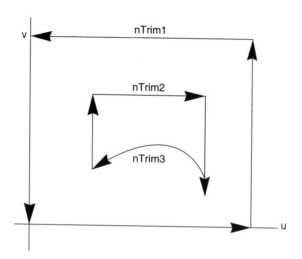

Figure 8-18   Trim Curves Used in Example 8-4

Example 8-4   Trimming a Bezier Surface

```
// The array of trim coordinates
float tpts[12][2] = {
      {0.0, 0.0},
      {1.0, 0.0},
      {1.0, 1.0},
      {0.0, 1.0},
      {0.2, 0.2},
      {0.2, 0.7},
      {0.9, 0.7},
      {0.9, 0.2},
      {0.7, 0.0},
      {0.4, 0.8}};

// The 16 coordinates defining the Bezier surface.
float pts[16][3] = {
      {-4.5, -2.0,  8.0},
      {-2.0,  1.0,  8.0},
      { 2.0, -3.0,  6.0},
```

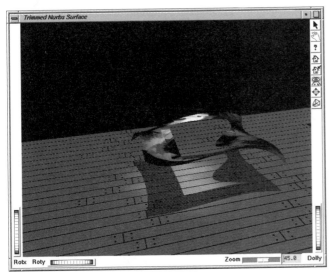

Figure 8-19   A Trimmed Bezier Surface

```
       { 5.0,  -1.0,   8.0},
       {-3.0,   3.0,   4.0},
       { 0.0,  -1.0,   4.0},
       { 1.0,  -1.0,   4.0},
       { 3.0,   2.0,   4.0},
       {-5.0,  -2.0,  -2.0},
       {-2.0,  -4.0,  -2.0},
       { 2.0,  -1.0,  -2.0},
       { 5.0,   0.0,  -2.0},
       {-4.5,   2.0,  -6.0},
       {-2.0,  -4.0,  -5.0},
       { 2.0,   3.0,  -5.0},
       { 4.5,  -2.0,  -6.0}};

// The 3 knot vectors for the 3 trim curves.
float tknots1[7] = {0, 0, 1, 2, 3, 4, 4};
float tknots2[6] = {0, 0, 1, 2, 3, 3};
float tknots3[8] = {0, 0, 0, 0, 1, 1, 1, 1};

// The Bezier knot vector for the surface.
// This knot vector is used in both the U and
// V directions.
float knots[8] = {0, 0, 0, 0, 1, 1, 1, 1};
```

```
// Create the nodes needed for the Bezier patch
// and its trim curves.
SoSeparator *
makeSurface()
{
   SoSeparator *surfSep = new SoSeparator();
   surfSep->ref();

   // Define the Bezier surface including the control
   // points, trim curve, and a complexity.
   SoComplexity   *complexity    = new SoComplexity;
   SoCoordinate3 *controlPts     = new SoCoordinate3;
   SoNurbsSurface *surface       = new SoNurbsSurface;
   complexity->value = 0.7;
   controlPts->point.setValues(0, 16, pts);
   surface->numUControlPoints.setValue(4);
   surface->numVControlPoints.setValue(4);
   surface->uKnotVector.setValues(0, 8, knots);
   surface->vKnotVector.setValues(0, 8, knots);
   surfSep->addChild(complexity);
   surfSep->addChild(controlPts);

   SoProfileCoordinate2 *trimPts = new SoProfileCoordinate2;
   SoNurbsProfile *nTrim1        = new SoNurbsProfile;
   SoNurbsProfile *nTrim2        = new SoNurbsProfile;
   SoNurbsProfile *nTrim3        = new SoNurbsProfile;
   long trimInds[5];

   trimPts->point.setValues(0, 12, tpts);
   trimInds[0] = 0;
   trimInds[1] = 1;
   trimInds[2] = 2;
   trimInds[3] = 3;
   trimInds[4] = 0;
   nTrim1->index.setValues(0, 5, trimInds);
   nTrim1->knotVector.setValues(0, 7, tknots1);
   trimInds[0] = 4;
   trimInds[1] = 5;
   trimInds[2] = 6;
   trimInds[3] = 7;
   nTrim2->linkage.setValue(SoProfile::START_NEW);
   nTrim2->index.setValues(0, 4, trimInds);
   nTrim2->knotVector.setValues(0, 6, tknots2);
   trimInds[0] = 7;
   trimInds[1] = 8;
   trimInds[2] = 9;
   trimInds[3] = 4;
```

```
nTrim3->linkage.setValue(SoProfile::ADD_TO_CURRENT);
nTrim3->index.setValues(0, 4, trimInds);
nTrim3->knotVector.setValues(0, 8, tknots3);

surfSep->addChild(trimPts);
surfSep->addChild(nTrim1);
surfSep->addChild(nTrim2);
surfSep->addChild(nTrim3);
surfSep->addChild(surface);

surfSep->unrefNoDelete();
return surfSep;
}
```

Suggestions for Further Reading

The following texts provide more detailed information on NURBS curves and surfaces:

Bartels, R., J. Beatty, and B. Barsky, *An Introduction to Splines for Use in Computer Graphics and Geometric Modeling.* Los Altos, Ca.: Morgan Kaufmann, 1987.

Farin, G., *Curves and Surfaces for Computer Aided Geometric Design*, 2e. San Diego, Ca.: Academic Press, Inc., 1990.

Part IV

Using a Scene Graph

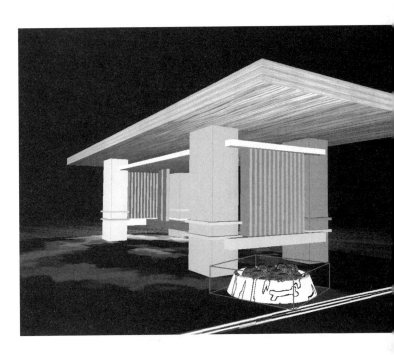

## Chapter 9

Applying Actions

Chapter Objectives

After reading this chapter, you'll be able to do the following:

- Draw, or *render*, all or part of a scene graph

- Print a scene graph

- Create a texture map from a rendering of a scene graph

- Compute a 3D bounding box for objects in a scene graph

- Compute a cumulative transformation matrix (and its inverse) for objects in a scene graph

- Write a scene graph to a file

- Search for nodes, types of nodes, or nodes with specific names in a scene graph

- Pick objects in a scene graph and obtain information about them

- Perform your own action by writing callback functions that can be invoked during scene graph traversal

- Write callback functions that use the primitives (points, lines, triangles) generated by Inventor shapes

This chapter describes how actions are applied to an Inventor scene graph. Earlier chapters introduced you to the most commonly used action, GL rendering, which traverses the scene graph and draws it using the OpenGL Library. This chapter outlines a general model for performing any action and highlights important concepts related to other Inventor actions, including picking, calculating a bounding box, calculating a transformation matrix, writing to a file, and searching the scene graph for certain nodes.

Inventor Actions

The preceding chapters focused on building a scene graph using group, property, and shape nodes. Once you have created this scene graph, you can apply *actions* to it. Table 9-1 summarizes some of the ways you can use the scene graph and the specific Inventor action to use.

You Can Perform This Task	Using This Action
Draw, or *render*, the scene graph	SoGLRenderAction
Compute a 3D bounding box for objects in the scene graph	SoGetBoundingBoxAction
Compute a cumulative transformation matrix (and its inverse)	SoGetMatrixAction
Write the scene graph to a file	SoWriteAction
Search for paths to specific nodes, types of nodes, or nodes with specific names in the scene graph	SoSearchAction
Allow objects in the scene graph to handle an event (see Chapter 10)	SoHandleEventAction
Pick objects in the scene graph along a ray	SoRayPickAction
Traverse the scene graph and accumulate traversal state, then perform your own action using callback functions	SoCallbackAction

Table 9-1   Using Inventor Actions

Figure 9-1 shows the portion of the class tree for actions.

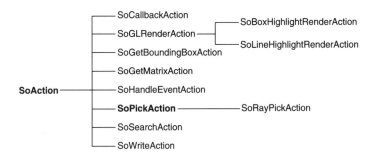

Figure 9-1   Action Classes

General Model

Performing any action on the scene graph follows the general model described in this section.

1. Initialize the action by constructing an instance of the action class. You can construct the action on the stack as follows:

    ```
    SbViewportRegion region(300, 200);

    SoGLRenderAction renderAction(region);
    ```

    You can also use the **new** operator to allocate an instance of the action:

    ```
    renderAction = new SoGLRenderAction(region);
    ```

    If you create the action with **new**, don't forget to delete the action when you finish using it.

2. Set up special parameters for the action. For example, the constructor for **SoGLRenderAction** allows you to specify the viewport region as well as whether to inherit the current OpenGL settings. If you specify

    ```
    SoGLRenderAction renderAction(region, TRUE);
    ```

    you can use the current OpenGL values for line width, material, and so on. If you specify FALSE (or omit this parameter), Inventor sets up its own defaults.

3. Apply the action to a node, a path, or a path list. For example:

```
renderAction->apply(root);
```

4. Obtain the results of the action, if applicable. Some actions have additional methods that can be used with them. For example, the **SoGetBoundingBoxAction** has one method, **getBoundingBox()**, that returns the bounding box computed by the action and another method, **getCenter()**, that returns the computed center.

Applying an Action

When an action is applied to a scene graph, each node encountered in the graph implements its own action behavior. In some cases, a particular type of node does nothing for a particular action. **SoMaterial** does nothing when an **SoGetBoundingBoxAction** is applied, for example. In other cases, the action behavior is relatively simple. For example, for most actions, all classes derived from **SoGroup** do little except traverse their children in a specified order.

When an action is applied, the Inventor database manages a *traversal state* (similar to the rendering state of OpenGL). The traversal state is an internal class used by Inventor to store transient state elements (parameters) during execution of the action. Typically, this management involves traversing the scene graph from top to bottom and from left to right. The elements in the traversal state are modified by the nodes encountered during this traversal. For certain actions, such as writing to a file (**SoWriteAction**) and accumulating a transformation matrix (**SoGetMatrixAction**), little or no traversal state is maintained. In these cases, the database does not need to keep track of all parameters inherited by nodes lower in the graph from the nodes above them.

The following sections focus on individual actions and how they are implemented by different nodes. You don't need to worry about exactly *how* the database manages the traversal state. You need only a general idea of which nodes implement a given action and how they implement it.

An action can be applied to a node, a path, or a path list. When an action is applied to a node, the graph rooted by that node is traversed. When the action is applied to a path, all nodes in the path chain itself are traversed, as well as all nodes, if any, under the last node in the path. In addition, all nodes that affect the nodes in the path chain are also traversed (typically, these nodes are to the left and above the nodes in the path). Applying an action to a path list is similar to applying the action to each path, except that subgraphs common to two or more paths are traversed only once.

Rendering

Chapters 3 through 8 illustrated how different nodes implement the **SoGLRenderAction**. This action draws the objects represented by a scene graph. Here is how various nodes implement the **SoGLRenderAction**:

- If the node is a *group* node, it visits each of its children in a specified order. If it is an **SoSeparator** node, it saves the traversal state before traversing its children and restores it after traversing its children.

- If the node is a *property* node, it often replaces a value in the corresponding element of the traversal state (other property nodes, such as **SoTransform**, may have different behaviors). For example:

  SoMaterial replaces the values for the current material.

  SoLightModel replaces the values for the current lighting model.

  SoDrawStyle replaces the values for the current drawing style.

  SoCoordinate3 replaces the values for the current coordinates.

- If the node is derived from **SoTransformation**, it modifies the current transformation matrix. Each new set of values is preconcatenated onto the existing transformation matrix.

- If the node is a *shape* node, it causes its shape to be drawn, using the current elements in the traversal state. Figure 9-2 shows an indexed face set instanced in two different groups. When rendered as part of *group1*, it uses the current elements of the traversal state, causing a red wireframe face set to be drawn. Because subsequent nodes in *group2* modify the current material, drawing style, and transformation matrix, the next instance of the indexed face set, later in the graph, appears green and filled. It is also twice as big as the red face set and translated to a new location.

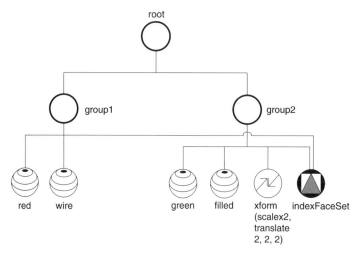

Figure 9-2   Shared Instances of a Shape Node

Setting the Transparency Quality

Use the **setTransparencyType()** method of the render action to specify the quality of rendering for transparent objects. Inventor uses three general types of transparency rendering. *Screen-door transparency* uses a fill pattern to simulate transparency. *Additive blending* adds the transparent object to the colors already in the frame buffer. *Alpha blending* uses a multiplicative algorithm for combining source and destination colors and alpha factor. Within these general categories, there are three types of additive blending and three types of alpha blending, depending on the degree of realism and amount of speed required for a particular rendering job.

See the *OpenGL Programming Guide* for a discussion of alpha blending.

Transparency Levels

In Inventor, the transparency quality level can be specified as follows:

SCREEN_DOOR   use OpenGL stipple patterns for screen-door transparency.

ADD   use additive OpenGL alpha blending.

DELAYED_ADD   use additive blending; render opaque objects first and transparent objects last.

SORTED_OBJECT_ADD
use additive blending. Draw opaque objects first, then transparent objects. Sort the transparent objects by their distance from the camera and draw them from back to front (same as DELAYED_ADD because adding is commutative).

BLEND use OpenGL alpha blending. (See Plate 18.)

DELAYED_BLEND
use OpenGL alpha blending; render opaque objects first and transparent objects last. (See Plate 19.)

SORTED_OBJECT_BLEND
use OpenGL alpha blending. Draw opaque objects first, then transparent objects. Sort the transparent objects by their distance from the camera and draw them from back to front. (See Plate 20.)

Trade-offs

Transparency rendering with the ADD (or BLEND) level of transparency, however, works only if the transparent object is being blended into something *already* in the frame buffer. This type of transparency rendering computes the transparency in the order in which the objects are rendered.

To ensure that transparent objects are rendered last, use the DELAYED_ADD (or DELAYED_BLEND) level. For example, if you draw a transparent cube first and then draw an opaque cylinder behind the cone, you won't see the transparency with the ADD level of transparency. In this case, you must use DELAYED_ADD (or DELAYED_BLEND). The delayed levels require more time than ADD or BLEND, but the realism is greater. (Compare Plates 18 and 19.)

For the highest degree of realism in rendering transparent objects, specify SORTED_OBJECT_ADD (or SORTED_OBJECT_BLEND). This level requires the most time but produces the best results. It renders the transparent objects after the opaque objects and also sorts the objects by distance from the camera, drawing them from back to front. (See Plate 20.)

Tip: Objects such as face sets do not sort within themselves, so the faces in ❖ a face set may not be drawn in the correct order for transparency. If the object is solid, using the **SoShapeHints** node with the proper hints may improve the picture.

Note to OpenGL programmers: If you are using delayed or sorted transparency levels, Inventor does not update the z buffer for transparent objects so that they can be drawn in any order.

If you are using an **SoXtRenderArea**, you can use the **setTransparency-Type()** method to set the quality level for rendering transparent objects.

Antialiasing

The **SoGLRenderAction** class also provides methods for *antialiasing*, techniques used to eliminate or reduce jagged lines and make objects drawn on the screen appear smooth. You can choose from two antialiasing methods:

- *Smoothing*, which is relatively "cheap" in terms of processing time. Smoothing applies to lines and points only.

- *Using the accumulation buffer*, which requires more processing time than smoothing but applies to the whole image and results in superior antialiasing. This technique requires an OpenGL window that supports an accumulation buffer.

Method 1: Smoothing

Use the **SoGLRenderAction::setSmoothing()** method to turn on smoothing. The **isSmoothing()** method returns the current state of the Smoothing flag. This form of antialiasing is for lines and points only. Because it requires alpha or additive blending, Inventor changes the transparency type if necessary when you turn on smoothing.

Method 2: Using the Accumulation Buffer

Normally, Inventor performs one rendering pass each time a render action is applied. You can use the **SoGLRenderAction::setNumPasses()** method to increase the number of rendering passes for accumulation buffer antialiasing. Inventor then renders the scene multiple times, moving the camera a little bit each time, and averages the results. The more times Inventor renders a scene, the better the antialiasing. The trade-off is that increasing the number of passes also increases the amount of time required to render the scene. The number of passes can be from 1 to 255, inclusive. Specifying 1 disables multipass antialiasing.

In addition, if you specify TRUE for the **SoGLRenderAction::setPass-Update()** method, the current contents of the accumulation buffer are copied into the currently active drawing buffer after each rendering pass. This technique slows things down but allows you to watch what happens between the incremental rendering passes. The default for **setPassUpdate()** is FALSE.

Tip: Use the **SoXtRenderArea::setAntialiasing()** method to turn on ❖ smoothing and to specify the number of passes for accumulation buffer antialiasing. You can specify either smoothing or accumulation buffer antialiasing, or both.

Printing and Off-screen Rendering

To print all or part of an Inventor scene graph, use the **SoOffscreen-Renderer** class, which in turn uses an **SoGLRenderAction** to render an image into an off-screen memory buffer. This rendering buffer can be used both to generate an image to send to a PostScript printer (see Example 9-1) and to generate an image to be used as a texture map (see Example 9-2).

The image rendered into the buffer can be one of four component types:

LUMINANCE   one component (grayscale)

LUMINANCE_TRANSPARENCY
                     two components (grayscale with alpha value)

RGB   three components (full color)

RGB_TRANSPARENCY
                     four components (full color with alpha value)

Use the **SoOffscreenRenderer::setComponents()** method to specify the components in the image generated before you render the image. To print black and white, use LUMINANCE. To print color, use RGB. To generate images with transparency information, use LUMINANCE_TRANSPARENCY or RGB_TRANSPARENCY.

Tip: If you want the output to go directly to a printer, use the ❖ **SoXtPrintDialog**, an Xt component. See the *Open Inventor C++ Reference Manual* for more information.

How to Generate a File for Printing

To write a scene graph to a file in Encapsulated PostScript (EPS) format, you first render the scene with the off-screen renderer. Then you use the **writeToPostScript()** method to generate the PostScript output and write it to the given file.

For example, suppose you want to print a screen area that is 300 pixels by 400 pixels. Use the **setWindowSize()** method on **SbViewportRegion** to specify the size of the viewport to be printed:

```
SbViewportRegion vp;
vp.setWindowSize(SbVec2s(300, 400));

rootNode = getMyScene();

SoOffscreenRenderer renderer(vp);
renderer->render(rootNode);
renderer->writeToPostScript(stdout);
```

This code fragment assumes the default pixels per inch (approximately 72). To change the number of pixels per inch, use the **setPixelsPerInch()** method on **SbViewportRegion**. Typically, you use the resolution of the printer. For a 300 dots-per-inch (DPI) printer, you would specify the following:

```
vp.setPixelsPerInch(300);
```

This resolution affects line width, the size of 2D text, and point size, which are all specified in pixels.

You may want the printed image to be the same size as the image rendered on the screen. To determine the size of the image on the screen, first use the **getViewportSizePixels()** method on **SbViewportRegion** to obtain the number of pixels (in x and y) of the viewport region. Then use the **getScreenPixelsPerInch()** method on **SoOffscreenRenderer** to find out the screen resolution in pixels.

```
screenVp = renderArea->getViewportRegion();
SbVec2s screenSize = screenVp.getViewportSizePixels();
float screenPixelsPerInch =
        SoOffscreenRenderer::getScreenPixelsPerInch();
```

Now you can calculate the size of the screen image in pixels by dividing x and y by *screenPixelsPerInch*. If you have a 300-by-400-pixel viewport on a screen with a resolution of 100 pixels per inch, your image is 3 by 4 inches.

To print this image at the same size, you specify the following:

vp.**setWindowSize**(SbVec2s(*x_in_inches* * *printer_DPI*,
                             y_in_inches * *printer_DPI*));

vp.**setPixelsPerInch**(*printer_DPI*);

Your OpenGL implementation may restrict the maximum viewport size. Use **getMaximumResolution**() to obtain the maximum resolution possible for a viewport in your window system.

Example 9-1 shows a simple function that renders a given scene graph and then saves it in a file that can be sent to a printer.

Example 9-1   Printing

```
SbBool
printToPostScript (SoNode *root, FILE *file,
    SoXtExaminerViewer *viewer, int printerDPI)
{
    // Calculate size of the image in inches which is equal to
    // the size of the viewport in pixels divided by the number
    // of pixels per inch of the screen device.  This size in
    // inches will be the size of the Postscript image that will
    // be generated.
    const SbViewportRegion &vp  = viewer->getViewportRegion();
    const SbVec2s &imagePixSize = vp.getViewportSizePixels();
    SbVec2f imageInches;
    float pixPerInch;

    pixPerInch = SoOffscreenRenderer::getScreenPixelsPerInch();
    imageInches.setValue((float)imagePixSize[0] / pixPerInch,
                    (float)imagePixSize[1] / pixPerInch);

    // The resolution to render the scene for the printer
    // is equal to the size of the image in inches times
    // the printer DPI;
    SbVec2s postScriptRes;
    postScriptRes.setValue((short)(imageInches[0])*printerDPI,
                    (short)(imageInches[1])*printerDPI);

    // Create a viewport to render the scene into.
    SbViewportRegion myViewport;
    myViewport.setWindowSize(postScriptRes);
    myViewport.setPixelsPerInch((float)printerDPI);
```

```
// Render the scene
SoOffscreenRenderer *myRenderer =
        new SoOffscreenRenderer(myViewport);
if (!myRenderer->render(root)) {
   delete myRenderer;
   return FALSE;
}

// Generate PostScript and write it to the given file
myRenderer->writeToPostScript(file);

delete myRenderer;
return TRUE;
}
```

Generating a Texture Map

You can also use the off-screen renderer to render an image to be used as a texture map. In this case, use the **SoOffscreenRenderer::render()** method to render the image. Then use the **getBuffer()** method to obtain the buffer.

Example 9-2 shows the typical sequence for using the rendering buffer to generate a texture map.

Example 9-2   Generating a Texture Map

```
#include <Inventor/SoDB.h>
#include <Inventor/SoInput.h>
#include <Inventor/Xt/SoXt.h>
#include <Inventor/Xt/viewers/SoXtExaminerViewer.h>
#include <Inventor/SbViewportRegion.h>
#include <Inventor/misc/SoOffscreenRenderer.h>
#include <Inventor/nodes/SoCube.h>
#include <Inventor/nodes/SoDirectionalLight.h>
#include <Inventor/nodes/SoPerspectiveCamera.h>
#include <Inventor/nodes/SoRotationXYZ.h>
#include <Inventor/nodes/SoSeparator.h>
#include <Inventor/nodes/SoTexture2.h>
```

```
SbBool
generateTextureMap (SoNode *root, SoTexture2 *texture,
    short textureWidth, short textureHeight)
{

    SbViewportRegion myViewport(textureWidth, textureHeight);

    // Render the scene
    SoOffscreenRenderer *myRenderer =
            new SoOffscreenRenderer(myViewport);
    myRenderer->setBackgroundColor(SbColor(0.3, 0.3, 0.3));
    if (!myRenderer->render(root)) {
        delete myRenderer;
        return FALSE;
    }
    // Generate the texture
    texture->image.setValue(SbVec2s(textureWidth, textureHeight),
            SoOffscreenRenderer::RGB, myRenderer->getBuffer());

    delete myRenderer;
    return TRUE;
}

main(int, char **argv)
{
    // Initialize Inventor and Xt
    Widget appWindow = SoXt::init(argv[0]);
    if (appWindow == NULL)
        exit(1);

    // Make a scene from reading in a file
    SoSeparator *texRoot = new SoSeparator;
    SoInput in;
    SoNode *result;

    texRoot->ref();
        in.openFile("jumpyMan.iv");
    SoDB::read(&in, result);

    SoPerspectiveCamera *myCamera = new SoPerspectiveCamera;
    SoRotationXYZ *rot = new SoRotationXYZ;
    rot->axis  = SoRotationXYZ::X;
    rot->angle = M_PI_2;
    myCamera->position.setValue(SbVec3f(-0.2, -0.2, 2.0));
    myCamera->scaleHeight(0.4);
```

```
texRoot->addChild(myCamera);
texRoot->addChild(new SoDirectionalLight);
texRoot->addChild(rot);
texRoot->addChild(result);

// Generate the texture map
SoTexture2 *texture = new SoTexture2;
texture->ref();
if (generateTextureMap(texRoot, texture, 64, 64))
   printf ("Successfully generated texture map\n");
else
   printf ("Could not generate texture map\n");
texRoot->unref();

// Make a scene with a cube and apply the texture to it
SoSeparator *root = new SoSeparator;
root->ref();
root->addChild(texture);
root->addChild(new SoCube);

// Initialize an Examiner Viewer
SoXtExaminerViewer *viewer =
        new SoXtExaminerViewer(appWindow);
viewer->setSceneGraph(root);
viewer->setTitle("Offscreen Rendered Texture");
viewer->show();

SoXt::show(appWindow);
SoXt::mainLoop();
}
```

Caching

Caching saves the result of an operation so that it doesn't need to be repeated. Inventor provides two kinds of caching: *render caching* and *bounding-box caching*. (See "Calculating a Bounding Box" on page 229 for a description of the **SoGetBoundingBoxAction**.) For both the render action and the bounding-box action, you can specify that the results of the traversal be saved in a *cache*. The render cache, for example, contains an OpenGL display list that results from traversing the scene graph to be rendered. If the scene graph does not change, Inventor can use the contents of this cache for subsequent renderings, without traversing the scene graph at all.

An **SoSeparator** node has two fields that are used for caching. Possible values for these fields are AUTO, ON, or OFF. AUTO is the default value.

renderCaching (SoSFEnum)
> specifies whether render caching is used. AUTO turns on caching when the scene graph below the separator is not changing. ON specifies to always try to build a cache, regardless of whether it is efficient. OFF specifies not to build or use a cache.

boundingBoxCaching (SoSFEnum)
> specifies whether bounding-box caching is used.

The **SoSeparator** class has a **setNumRenderCaches()** method that allows you to specify how many render caches each separator node will have. The greater the number of render caches that are built, the more memory used. You might use two caches, for example, if a viewer switches between wireframe and filled draw-styles, and the draw-style is set outside the cache. This method affects only the separator nodes that are created after it is called. Setting the number of render caches to 0 before any separators are created turns off render caching. The default number of render caches is 2.

Tip: If render caching is AUTO, it will take several renderings for caching to take effect. The caching mechanism requires several renderings for comparison to determine that nothing is changing and the scene can be cached.

How Caching Works

The caching process begins with the separator group, as follows:

1. The separator group checks whether a valid cache exists.

2. If a valid cache exists, the separator group ignores the scene graph below it and uses the contents of the cache.

3. If a valid cache does not exist, the separator group checks the appropriate field to see if it should create a cache.

4. If caching is ON, it opens a cache, traverses the nodes under the separator group, records the results in the cache, and then calls the cache. If caching is AUTO, Inventor uses a special set of conditions to determine whether it is efficient to create a cache.

The nodes under the separator group may inherit values from nodes that appear before the separator group in the graph. For example, materials, coordinates, texture coordinates, complexity nodes, normals, and bindings tend to be used by each shape. If these values change, the cache needs to change. (Note that if a texture outside the cache changes, the cache is still valid because the shape does not send the texture calls to OpenGL. The texture is sent directly to OpenGL when the **SoTexture2** node is traversed.)

Be aware that these changes also invalidate the cache:

- For **SoText2**, changing the font or camera (because the text is screen-aligned)

- For **SoText3**, changing the profile coordinates or type of profile

Inventor is conservative in determining whether the current cache is valid (that is, caches may be invalidated and rebuilt even if inherited values have not changed).

Figure 9-3 shows a scene graph with a transform node whose values are changing frequently and a cube. In this case, turn on caching at the separator above the cube so that the changing transform values do not invalidate the cache.

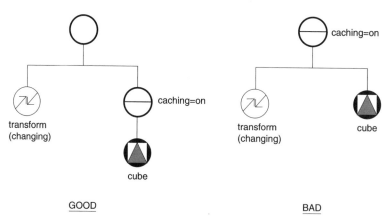

GOOD   BAD

Figure 9-3   Caching a Shape

Figure 9-4 shows a scene graph with a complexity node whose values are changing frequently and a cube. Here, you would include both the property node and the shape in the same cache, since the shape always uses the property node when it is rendered.

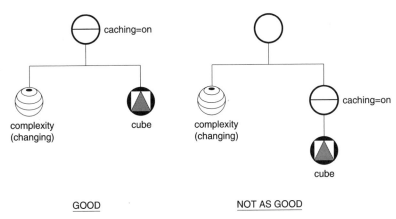

GOOD   NOT AS GOOD

Figure 9-4   Caching a Shape along with a Changing Property Node

Trade-offs

Render caches can consume a great deal of memory, but they are very useful for speeding up rendering. Using the AUTO (default) value for render caching allows Inventor to determine whether creating a render cache will save time.

Bounding-box caching is relatively inexpensive. Inventor uses bounding-box caching to speed up picking. If bounding-box caching is on and the user picks part of the graph that contains a separator group, the separator group can first check to see if the bounding box is picked. If not, it knows nothing under it is picked and does not need to traverse the subgraph.

Culling Part of the Scene

If you are dealing with a large scene and you know that the camera will frequently view only part of that scene, you may want to turn on render culling so that Inventor doesn't take time rendering parts of the scene that lie completely outside the camera's view. An **SoSeparator** node has two flags used for culling: **renderCulling** and **pickCulling**. By default, render culling is AUTO. By default, pick culling is ON.

This description deals with render culling. (Pick culling works in a similar manner and is relatively inexpensive; you will probably simply leave it ON.) Here's a brief summary of how render culling works:

1. The camera puts the world-space view volume into the traversal state when it is traversed.

2. During traversal, the separator node tests its **renderCulling** field. If it is ON, it culls the render area, as follows:

    a. It computes the bounding box for the separator, in object space. (This information may be cached already.)

    b. It transforms the bounding-box information into world space and compares it to the view volume in the state.

    c. If the bounding box is completely outside the current view volume, the separator does not traverse its children.

Since Step 2 (computing the bounding box and testing it) is fairly expensive in terms of time, render culling is off by default. You'll need to evaluate your scene graph to determine whether render culling will be efficient. For example, you could have a large scene graph with external walls, and detailed electrical and plumbing connections beneath them. Although the scene graph is complex, culling won't help because all elements would be in the camera's view at the same time. However, for scenes where objects are widely separated in space, such as a scene graph for a solar system, culling can be very useful.

❖ **Tip:** To facilitate culling, organize the database spatially so that objects that are close to each other in 3D space are under the same separator and objects far away from each other are under different separators. In the case of the scene graph with external walls, you could group the plumbing and electrical connections for *each* wall under a separator.

Guidelines for turning on render culling are as follows:

• In general, don't put a culling separator underneath a caching separator (that is, an **SoSeparator** with its **renderCaching** field set explicitly to ON). Use a culling separator under **SoSeparator** nodes with render caching set to OFF or AUTO.

    The reason for this guideline is that culling depends on the camera. If a separator makes a culling decision, any cache that it is part of will depend on the camera. Caches dependent on the camera will often be broken, because in most applications, the camera changes frequently.

    It's also efficient to turn on culling and caching at the *same* separator node (or turn on culling and leave caching at AUTO).

• Turn on culling only for objects that are separated in space.

- Turn on culling only for objects with a fairly large number of polygons, or deciding whether to cull might take longer than just drawing the object.

Calculating a Bounding Box

The bounding-box action computes a 3D bounding box that encloses the shapes in a subgraph under a node or defined by a path. This action also computes the center point of these shapes (see Example 9-3). **SoGet-BoundingBoxAction** is typically called on a path, which enables you to obtain a bounding box for a specific object in world coordinates. This action returns an **SbBox3f**, which specifies a 3D box aligned with the x-, y-, and z-axes in world coordinate space.

Create an Instance of the Action

An example of creating an instance of **SoGetBoundingBoxAction** is

```
SbViewportRegion vpReg;
vpReg.setWindowSize(300, 200);

SoGetBoundingBoxAction bboxAction (vpReg);
```

This constructor has one parameter, the viewport region. This information is needed for computing the bounding box of screen-aligned or screen-sized objects, such as **SoText2**.

Apply the Action

SoGetBoundingBoxAction can be applied to the root node of a subgraph, to a path, or to a path list.

Obtain Results

Three methods access the results of **SoGetBoundingBoxAction**:

getBoundingBox()
 returns an **SbBox3f** bounding box that encloses the shape or shapes

getCenter()	returns the computed center point for the shapes
getXfBoundingBox()	
	returns an **SbXfBox3f** bounding box

The center point returned by **getCenter()** is defined differently for different objects. For example, the center of an **SoFaceSet** is defined as the average of its vertices' coordinates. The center of a group is defined as the average of the centers of the objects in the group.

An **SbXfBox3f** stores the original bounding box for a shape and the matrix that transforms it to the correct world space. The advantage to using an **SbXfBox3f** instead of an **SbBox3f** is that the bounding box isn't enlarged unnecessarily. You may want to use this class if you need to perform additional transformations on the bounding box.

Example 9-3 shows using an **SoGetBoundingBoxAction** (*bboxAction*) to return the center of the graph rooted by a node so that rotations can be made around it.

Example 9-3   Setting the Center Field of a Transform Node

```
SbViewportRegion myViewport;
SoTransform *myTransform;

SoGetBoundingBoxAction bboxAction(myViewport);
bboxAction.apply(root);
myTransform->center = bboxAction.getCenter();
```

Accumulating a Transformation Matrix

The **SoGetMatrixAction** returns the current transformation matrix for any node derived from **SoTransformation** or for a path. When you apply this action to any **SoTransformation** node, it returns the transformation matrix for that node. When you apply it to a path, **SoGetMatrixAction** accumulates a transformation matrix for all the transformations in the subgraph defined by that path. This action enables you to convert from one coordinate space to another, typically from local space to world space (when you apply it to a path whose head node is the root of the scene graph).

An important distinction between **SoGetMatrixAction** and other actions is that **SoGetMatrixAction** does not traverse downward in the scene graph from the node or path to which it is applied. When applied to a node, it returns the current transformation matrix for that node only (and therefore makes sense only for transformation nodes, since all others return identity). When applied to a path, it collects transformation information for all nodes in the path but stops when it reaches the last node in the path chain.

Create an Instance of the Action

The constructor for **SoGetMatrixAction** has no parameters:

```
SoGetMatrixAction mtxAction;
```

Apply the Action

SoGetMatrixAction can be applied to a node or to a path.

Obtain Results

Two methods return the results of **SoGetMatrixAction**:

getMatrix()   returns an **SbMatrix** that is the cumulative transformation matrix for the node or path

getInverse()   returns an **SbMatrix** that is the inverse of the cumulative transformation matrix for the node or path

The **getInverse()** method enables you to take a point in world space and map it into an object's local coordinate space. See the *Open Inventor C++ Reference Manual* for a description of the many convenient methods available for **SbMatrix**. For example, you can use **multVecMatrix()** to transform a point by a matrix. Use **multDirMatrix()** to transform a direction vector by a matrix. (Inventor assumes row vectors.)

Tip: You can convert a point in one object's coordinate space into another ❖ object's space by applying a get-matrix action to the first object, transforming the point into world space using the matrix, applying a get-matrix action to the other object, and then transforming the world-space point by the inverse matrix of the second object.

As an example, assume that **SoGetMatrixAction** is applied to the path shown in Figure 9-5. The *xform1* node contains a translation of (0.0, 0.0, 1.0), and the *xform2* node contains a scale of (0.5, 0.5, 0.5).

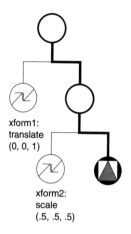

xform1:
translate
(0, 0, 1)

xform2:
scale
(.5, .5, .5)

— Path

Figure 9-5   Applying SoGetMatrixAction to a Path

Each new transformation is premultiplied onto the current transformation matrix. In this case, the matrix multiplication looks like this:

scale (*xform2*)   translate (*xform1*)

$$
\begin{bmatrix}
0.5 & 0 & 0 & 0 \\
0 & 0.5 & 0 & 0 \\
0 & 0 & 0.5 & 0 \\
0 & 0 & 0 & 1
\end{bmatrix}
\begin{bmatrix}
1 & 0 & 0 & 0 \\
0 & 1 & 0 & 0 \\
0 & 0 & 1 & 0 \\
0 & 0 & 1 & 1
\end{bmatrix}
$$

In this example, **getMatrix()** returns the following matrix:

$$
\begin{bmatrix}
0.5 & 0 & 0 & 0 \\
0 & 0.5 & 0 & 0 \\
0 & 0 & 0.5 & 0 \\
0 & 0 & 1 & 1
\end{bmatrix}
$$

For texture coordinates, use the **getTextureMatrix()** and **getTextureInverse()** methods. See Chapter 7 and the *Open Inventor C++ Reference Manual* for more information.

Writing to a File

Inventor scene graphs can be written to a file in either ASCII or binary format. **SoWriteAction** is used for writing scene graphs to files. An instance of this class contains an instance of **SoOutput**, which by default writes to **stdout** in ASCII format. The **getOutput()** method returns a pointer to the **SoOutput**. Other methods for **SoOutput** include the following:

openFile()   opens and writes to a file rather than to **stdout**.

setFilePointer() explicitly sets the pointer to the file to write to.

closeFile()   closes the file opened with **openFile()**. The file is closed automatically when the action is destroyed.

setBinary()   writes the file in binary format if TRUE; writes the file in ASCII if FALSE (the default).

setBuffer()   writes to a buffer in memory rather than to a file.

For example, to write in binary to an already open file pointed to by *fp*:

```
SoWriteAction myAction;
FILE *fp;

myAction.getOutput()->setBinary(TRUE);
myAction.getOutput()->setFilePointer(fp);
myAction.apply(root);
```

To write in ASCII to a named file:

```
SoWriteAction myAction;

myAction.getOutput()->openFile("myFile.iv");
myAction.getOutput()->setBinary(FALSE);
myAction.apply(root);
myAction.getOutput()->closeFile();
```

See Chapter 11 for a complete description of the Inventor file format. Here is an example of the output of **SoWriteAction** for a subgraph:

```
#Inventor V2.0 ascii

Separator {

   Separator {
      Transform {
         scaleFactor 1 2 1
      }
      Material {
         ambientColor .2 .2 .2
         diffuseColor .6 .6 .6
         specularColor .5 .5 .5
         shininess .5
      }
      Cube{
      }
   }
}
```

Searching for a Node

SoSearchAction searches through the scene graph for paths to specific nodes, types of nodes, or nodes with a given name. First, you initialize the action. Then, you specify the *node, node type,* or *name* to search for (or a combination of these elements). If you specify a *node type,* you can also specify whether to search for an exact type match, or to search for subclasses of the specified type as well.

Specify the Search Criteria

First, specify what you are searching for, whether you want to find all matches, and how to traverse the scene graph.

Searching for a Node

If you want to search for a particular node (by pointer), use the **setNode()** method. For example, you might use **setNode()** to search for a particular light-source node so that you can attach an editor to it.

Searching for a Node Type

Rather than searching for a specific node, you may want to search for a *type* of node (see Chapter 3). When searching for a node type, you then have the choice of searching for all nodes of a particular type, or for derivations of the given type (the default). The syntax for **setType()** is as follows:

setType(SoType *t*, int derivedIsOk = TRUE);

Searching for a Name

Use the **setName()** method to specify the name of the node to search for. (See Chapter 3 for more information on naming.)

Specify Whether to Find All Matches

Use the **setInterest()** method to specify which paths to return:

FIRST   returns only the first path found (the default)

LAST   returns only the last path found

ALL   returns all paths found

Specify the Type of Traversal

Use the **setSearchingAll()** method to specify whether to search using normal traversal (following traversal order for switches and separators) or to search every node in the scene graph, regardless of switch settings. The default is FALSE (search using normal traversal order).

Apply the Action

SoSearchAction is applied in the same manner as any other action.

Obtain the Results

To obtain the results of the search, use one of the following methods:

getPath()   returns the found path (if interest is FIRST or LAST)

getPaths()   returns the found path list (if interest is ALL)

See the *Open Inventor C++ Reference Manual* for a complete description of all methods available for **SoSearchAction**.

The following example searches a scene graph for any node derived from **SoLight**. If it does not find one, it creates and adds an **SoDirectionalLight**. This example searches for only the first match by calling **setInterest- (SoSearchAction::FIRST)**.

```
SoSearchAction mySearchAction;

// Look for first existing light derived from class SoLight
mySearchAction.setType(SoLight::getClassTypeId());
mySearchAction.setInterest(SoSearchAction::FIRST);

mySearchAction.apply(root);
if (mySearchAction.getPath() == NULL) { // No lights found

    // Add a default directional light to the scene
    SoDirectionalLight *myLight = new SoDirectionalLight;
    root->insertChild(myLight, 0);
}
```

Picking

SoRayPickAction finds objects along a ray from the camera through a point on the near plane of the view volume. This ray is typically specified by giving the coordinates of a window-space pixel through which it passes. **SoRayPickAction** traverses the scene graph you apply the action to and then returns the paths to all shapes along the picking ray, sorted from nearest to farthest. The picking action is primarily interested in geometry, transformation, and shape nodes.

❖ **Tip:** The **SoSelection** node picks objects automatically. You don't need to explicitly use the pick action to select objects. The **SoHandleEvent** action also performs picking automatically. In addition, the **SoEventCallback** node allows you to register a callback function that is invoked whenever a certain event (such as a mouse press) occurs over a specified object. See Chapter 10 for more information on **SoSelection**, **SoHandleEvent**, and **SoEventCallback**.

Picking Style

By default, all objects in the scene graph are pickable (even invisible and transparent objects). To make an object or group of objects invisible to the pick action, insert an **SoPickStyle** node in the scene graph and set its **style** field to UNPICKABLE. Anything that follows in the scene graph cannot be picked until the **SoPickStyle** node is reset to SHAPE (to pick points on the shape objects in the scene) or BOUNDING_BOX (to pick points on the bounding boxes for the objects in the scene). BOUNDING_BOX pick style is most often used for **SoText3** nodes. The pick style, like all other properties, is saved and restored by **SoSeparator** groups.

Create an Instance of the Action

The constructor for **SoRayPickAction** has one parameter, the viewport region (a required parameter).

An example of creating an instance of **SoRayPickAction** is

```
SbViewportRegion myViewport;
SoRayPickAction myPickAction(myViewport);
```

The viewport region is used to compute the bounding boxes for screen-aligned objects such as **SoText2**.

Set Parameters

Before you apply the picking action, you can set the following parameters:

- Ray to pick along
- Whether to return all objects along the ray, or only the closest one

The picking ray can be specified in one of two ways: either specify a window point and a radius, or specify a point and a direction in world space. The first method is the more typical for interactive programs, since you are generally most interested in the area underneath the cursor.

Specifying the Picking Ray with a Window Point

Before you apply the picking action, use the **setPoint()** and **setRadius()** methods to set the ray to be used for picking.

The ray to pick along is typically specified in *viewport coordinates*, where (0, 0) is the lower left corner of the viewport and (*vpWidth*–1, *vpHeight*–1) is the upper right corner (see Figure 9-6). In the figure, the viewport is 1000 by 1000. The near plane of the camera maps to the picking viewport.

To make it easier to pick lines and points, the ray can be augmented to be a cone (for a perspective camera; see Figure 9-6) or a cylinder (for an orthographic camera). Use the **setRadius()** method to control the size of this cone or cylinder where it intersects the near plane of the camera. (The default radius is 5 pixels.) Things that are picked must fall within this cone (or cylinder), as follows:

* For points and lines, if any part of the shape falls within this cone, it is picked. (A sphere drawn with LINES draw-style is still picked as a solid sphere.)

* For all other shapes, the ray itself must intersect the shape for it to be picked.

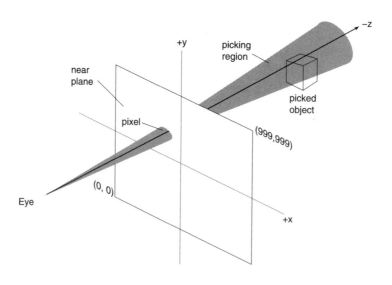

Figure 9-6   Cone Representing the Picking Ray for a Perspective Camera

Specifying the Picking Ray with a World-Space Ray

You can also specify the picking ray by specifying a world-space ray along which to pick. The ray is defined as a starting point, a direction vector, and a near distance and far distance for the picked objects. No radius is used. For example:

```
SbViewportRegion viewport(400, 300);
SbVec2s cursorPosition(250, 125);

SoRayPickAction myPickAction(viewport);

myPickAction.setRay(SbVec3f(0.0, 0.0, 0.0),  // starting point
                    SbVec3f(0.0, 0.0, -1.0); // direction vector
```

This example uses the default near and far distances, which disables clipping to the near and far planes.

Picking the Closest Object

Use the **setPickAll()** method to specify whether you want information returned for all objects picked (sorted from closest to farthest), or just the closest one. Specify TRUE for all objects, or FALSE (the default) for only the closest one.

Apply the Action

The picking action can be applied to either a node, a path, or a path list. To apply the picking action to the root node of a scene graph:

```
pickAction->apply(rootNode);
```

Obtain Results

The results of the pick are stored in an **SoPickedPoint** (for the first hit) or an **SoPickedPointList** (for information on all hit objects). Use the methods on **SoPickedPoint** to obtain this information.

SoPickedPoint

An **SoPickedPoint** represents a point on the surface of an object that was picked. The picked point contains the point of intersection, the surface normal and texture coordinates at that point, the index into the current set of materials, and the path to the object that was intersected. Use the following methods on **SoPickedPoint** to obtain this information:

getPoint()   returns the intersection point, in world space.

getNormal()   returns the surface normal at the intersected point, in world space.

getTextureCoords()

              returns the texture coordinates at the intersection point, in image space.

getMaterialIndex()

              returns the index into the current set of materials that is used at the intersection point. If the materials are interpolated between vertices, the index corresponds to the material at the closest vertex.

getPath()   returns the path to the object that was intersected.

For example:

```
SoPath *pathToPickedObject;

const SoPickedPoint *myPickedPoint =
        myPickAction.getPickedPoint();
if (myPickedPoint != NULL)
   pathToPickedObject = myPickedPoint->getPath();
```

Figure 9-7 shows the path returned by an **SoRayPickAction** (which can be obtained with the **getPath()** method on **SoPickedPoint**). This path contains a pointer to each node in the path to the picked object. Use the following methods on **SoPickedPoint** to obtain information about the pick in the *object space* of a particular node in the path chain. You pass in a pointer to the node you are interested in, or use the default (NULL) to obtain information about the tail of the path:

getObjectPoint()   returns the intersection point, in object space

getObjectNormal()

              returns the surface normal for the picked point

getObjectTextureCoords()

              returns the texture coordinates for the picked point

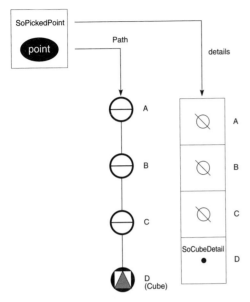

Figure 9-7   Path to Picked Point and Detail List

Using an SoDetail

Each node in the picked path may have an associated **SoDetail** in which it can store additional information about the pick. For some classes, this associated **SoDetail** is NULL. Table 9-2 shows the classes that store information in a subclass of **SoDetail**.

Figure 9-8 shows the class tree for **SoDetail**.

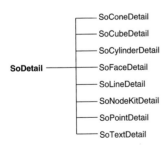

Figure 9-8   Detail Classes

Class Name	Type of Detail Added	Information Provided
SoCone	SoConeDetail	Contains information about which part of the cone was hit
SoCube	SoCubeDetail	Contains information about which face (part) of the cube was hit
SoCylinder	SoCylinderDetail	Contains information about which part of the cylinder was hit
SoText2, SoText3	SoTextDetail	Specifies the index of the string that was hit; the index of the character within the string that was hit; which part of the text was hit; the object-space bounding box of the character that was intersected
SoFaceSet; all vertex-based shapes except lines, points, and NURBS	SoFaceDetail	Specifies which face in the shape was hit
SoLineSet, SoIndexedLineSet	SoLineDetail	Specifies which line in the line set was hit
SoPointSet	SoPointDetail	Specifies which point in the point set was hit

Table 9-2   Classes That Store an SoDetail

Use the **getDetail()** method on **SoPickedPoint** to return the detail for a given node in the picked path. This method takes a pointer to a node in the picked path. It returns information for the tail of the path if NULL or no node is specified. For example, to determine whether a cylinder was hit and, if so, whether it was the top part of the cylinder, the code would be as follows:

```
const SoDetail *pickDetail = myPickedPoint->getDetail();
if (pickDetail != NULL && pickDetail->getTypeId() ==
                       SoCylinderDetail::getClassTypeId()) {
   // Picked object is a cylinder
   SoCylinderDetail *cylDetail =
           (SoCylinderDetail *) pickDetail;

   // See if top of the cylinder was hit
   if (cylDetail->getPart() == SoCylinder::TOP) {
      printf("Top of cylinder was hit\n");
   }
}
```

The following fragment shows how you could find the closest vertex to the hit point of a face-based shape using an **SoFaceDetail**. An **SoFaceDetail** contains an array of **SoPointDetails**. You can examine these details to find the coordinates of the point closest to the hit point by using the **getCoordinateIndex()** method on **SoPointDetail**. Finding the node that contains the coordinates is left to the application. (You can create a search action, apply it to the picked path, and ask for the last **SoCoordinate3** node in the path. But you also need to know something about the structure of your graph—for example, whether it contains Override flags or Ignore flags that may affect the search.)

```
//   This function finds the closest vertex to an intersection
//   point on a shape made of faces, passed in the
//   "pickedPoint" argument. It returns the SoCoordinate3 node
//   containing the vertex's coordinates in the "coordNode"
//   argument and the index of the vertex in that node in the
//   "closestIndex" argument. If the shape is not made of faces
//   or there were any other problems, this returns FALSE.

static SbBool
findClosestVertex(const SoPickedPoint *pickedPoint,
          SoCoordinate3 *&coordNode, int &closestIndex)
{
   const SoDetail *pickDetail = pickedPoint->getDetail();

   if (pickDetail != NULL && pickDetail->getTypeId() ==
                           SoFaceDetail::getClassTypeId()) {
      // Picked object is made of faces
      SoFaceDetail *faceDetail = (SoFaceDetail *) pickDetail;

      // Find the coordinate node that is used for the faces.
      // Assume that it's the last SoCoordinate3 node traversed
      // before the picked shape.
```

```
SoSearchAction  mySearchAction;
mySearchAction.setType(SoCoordinate3::getClassTypeId());
mySearchAction.setInterest(SoSearchAction::LAST);
mySearchAction.apply(pickedPoint->getPath());

if (mySearchAction.getPath() != NULL) {   // We found one
    coordNode = (SoCoordinate3 *)
               mySearchAction.getPath()->getTail();

    // Get the intersection point in the object space
    // of the picked shape
    SbVec3f objIntersect = pickedPoint->getObjectPoint();

    // See which of the points of the face is the closest
    // to the intersection point
    float minDistance = 1e12;
    closestIndex = -1;
    for (int i = 0; i < faceDetail->getNumPoints(); i++) {
        int pointIndex =
               faceDetail->getPoint(i)->getCoordinateIndex();
        float curDistance = (coordNode->point[pointIndex] -
            objIntersect).length();
        if (curDistance < minDistance) {
            closestIndex = pointIndex;
            minDistance = curDistance;
        }
    }

    if (closestIndex >= 0)
        return TRUE;
    }
}

return FALSE;
}
```

Using the Pick Action

Example 9-4 shows setting up the pick action and writing the path to the picked object to **stdout**.

Example 9-4   Writing the Path to the Picked Object

```
SbBool
writePickedPath (SoNode *root,
    const SbViewportRegion &viewport,
    const SbVec2s &cursorPosition)
{
    SoRayPickAction myPickAction(viewport);

    // Set an 8-pixel wide region around the pixel
    myPickAction.setPoint(cursorPosition);
    myPickAction.setRadius(8.0);

    // Start a pick traversal
    myPickAction.apply(root);
    const SoPickedPoint *myPickedPoint =
            myPickAction.getPickedPoint();
    if (myPickedPoint == NULL)
        return FALSE;           // no object was picked

    // Write out the path to the picked object
    SoWriteAction myWriteAction;
    myWriteAction.apply(myPickedPoint->getPath());

    return TRUE;
}
```

Calling Back to the Application

The **SoCallbackAction** allows you to traverse the scene graph and
accumulate state. It includes methods for calling back to application
functions whenever nodes of a specified type are encountered during the
traversal. At every node, the callback function has access to the entire
Inventor traversal state. It can thus query any element in the state, such as
the current coordinates, current normals, or current material binding. See
the *Open Inventor C++ Reference Manual* on **SoCallbackAction** for a
description of all state query functions.

The callback action also allows you to register callback functions that are
called whenever certain shape nodes are traversed. The primitives used to
draw the shape are passed to the callback function for use by the
application.

This action provides a convenient mechanism for adding your own action to Inventor without subclassing (see *The Inventor Toolmaker* for information on creating a new action). It is particularly useful for C programmers who want to add functionality to scene graph traversal.

Create an Instance of the Action

An example of creating an instance of **SoCallbackAction** is as follows:

```
SoCallbackAction cbAction;
```

Register Callback Functions

Inventor provides a number of methods for setting callback functions for a node. Each method takes a node type, a pointer to the user callback function, and a pointer to user data. The function is called whenever a node of the specified type or a subclass of that type, is encountered during traversal of the scene graph.

General-Purpose Callback Functions

The following functions are set for any type of node:

addPreCallback()
> adds a callback function that is called just before a node of a particular type is traversed

addPostCallback()
> adds a callback function that is called just after a node of a particular type is traversed

addPreTailCallback()
> adds a callback function that is called just before the last node in the path is traversed

addPostTailCallback()
> adds a callback function that is called just after the last node in the path is traversed

In the case of a separator node, the **addPreCallback()** method is called before the children are traversed, and the **addPostCallback()** method is called after the children are traversed but before the state is restored. The

addPreTailCallback() and **addPostTailCallback()** methods are used only when you apply the callback action to a path.

A general-purpose callback function must return one of three values:

SoCallbackAction::CONTINUE

                  continue traversal of the scene graph.

SoCallbackAction::PRUNE

                  do not go any lower in the scene graph; continue traversal of the rest of the scene graph above and to the right.

SoCallbackAction::ABORT

                  stop traversal of the scene graph and pop state back up to the root.

Primitive Generation

The following callback functions are set for a particular type of *shape* node. When these callback functions are set and the shape is traversed, primitives for the shape are generated, the callback function is invoked, and the primitives are passed to the callback function. You might use **addTriangleCallback()**, for example, if you are writing your own renderer and you want to tessellate all filled objects into triangles.

addTriangleCallback()

                  adds a callback function to a node that generates triangles, such as **SoFaceSet** or **SoNurbsSurface**

addLineSegmentCallback()

                  adds a callback function to a node that generates line segments, such as **SoLineSet** or **SoIndexedLineSet** (but not to **SoFaceSet** or related classes even when the draw-style is LINES)

addPointCallback()

                  adds a callback function to a node that generates points, such as **SoPointSet** (but not to **SoFaceSet** or **SoLineSet** even when the draw-style is POINTS)

For triangles, the associated callback is of the following form:

void **SoTriangleCB**(void *userData*, SoCallbackAction *action*,
                const SoPrimitiveVertex *v1*,
                const SoPrimitiveVertex *v2*,
                const SoPrimitiveVertex *v3*);

Here, the callback function is called once for each triangle the shape generates. An example of using this callback function would be if you are writing a ray tracer and want to deal with only one type of data structure for all polygonal shapes. A triangle callback function can be registered on spheres, cones, cylinders, and NURBS surfaces, as well as on face sets and quad meshes.

An **SoPrimitiveVertex** is a vertex of a primitive shape (triangle, line segment, or point) that is generated by a callback action. It contains an object-space point, normal, texture coordinate, material index, and a pointer to an instance of an **SoDetail** subclass. The detail may contain additional information about the vertex.

❖ **Tip:** Your callback function can use the value of the draw-style element from the state if you want to determine if the triangles would be rendered as points or lines. For example:

```
if(SoDrawStyleElement::get(action->getState())==
          SoDrawStyleElement::LINES)
...//do something
```

See *The Inventor Toolmaker* for more information on elements.

Apply the Action

SoCallbackAction can be applied to a node, a path, or a path list.

Using a Callback for Generated Primitives

Example 9-5 shows using the callback action to decompose a sphere into a set of triangle primitives.

Example 9-5   Using a Triangle Callback Function

```
...
SoSphere *mySphere = new SoSphere;
mySphere->ref();
printSpheres(mySphere);
...

void
printSpheres(SoNode *root)
{
```

```
   SoCallbackAction myAction;

   myAction.addPreCallback(SoSphere::getClassTypeId(),
           printHeaderCallback, NULL);
   myAction.addTriangleCallback(SoSphere::getClassTypeId(),
           printTriangleCallback, NULL);

   myAction.apply(root);
}

SoCallbackAction::Response
printHeaderCallback(void *, SoCallbackAction *,
     const SoNode *node)
{
   printf("\n Sphere ");
   // Print the node name (if it exists) and address
   if (! !node->getName())
      printf("named \"%s\" ", node->getName());
   printf("at address %#x\n", node);

   return SoCallbackAction::CONTINUE;
}

void
printTriangleCallback(void *, SoCallbackAction *,
   const SoPrimitiveVertex *vertex1,
   const SoPrimitiveVertex *vertex2,
   const SoPrimitiveVertex *vertex3)
{
   printf("Triangle:\n");
   printVertex(vertex1);
   printVertex(vertex2);
   printVertex(vertex3);
}

void
printVertex(const SoPrimitiveVertex *vertex)
{
   const SbVec3f &point = vertex->getPoint();
   printf("\tCoords      = (%g, %g, %g)\n",
             point[0], point[1], point[2]);

   const SbVec3f &normal = vertex->getNormal();
   printf("\tNormal      = (%g, %g, %g)\n",
             normal[0], normal[1], normal[2]);
}
```

## Chapter 10

Handling Events and Selection

Chapter Objectives

After reading this chapter, you'll be able to do the following:

- Explain how Open Inventor handles input events
- Select objects in the scene using one of Inventor's built-in selection policies
- Implement your own selection policy by creating an event callback node
- Highlight selected objects in the scene
- Write selection callback functions to allow the application to perform certain operations when the selection list changes

This chapter describes the Open Inventor event model, which provides a simple mechanism for passing events such as a key press or mouse movement to objects in the database for processing. In much the same way a window system passes events to its client windows, Inventor passes events to database objects that can handle them. Important concepts introduced in this chapter include the Inventor programming model for event handling and the use of the **SoXtRenderArea**, a widget that performs rendering and event handling on the Inventor database. The **SoHandleEventAction** is discussed in detail, as well as the concepts of *event callback functions*, the *selection node*, and *highlighting*.

Overview

When a user clicks a mouse button on a handle-box manipulator and drags the object to a new location on the screen, how does Inventor receive the user input from the mouse and translate the object accordingly? What happens if the user clicks the mouse on a space in the rendered image that doesn't contain any objects? How does Inventor keep track of several user-selected objects? These are all questions that need to be answered before you can write interactive Inventor applications.

This chapter begins by providing a brief description of how window-specific events are translated into Inventor events. It introduces you to the different kinds of Inventor events and the methods associated with them. You will learn how the scene manager finds the event handler for a specific event and how different nodes handle events.

General Programming Model for Event Handling

Inventor includes a built-in event model for the scene database. This model is not based on any specific window system or toolkit. When writing an Inventor program, you can select the X window programming model and use the tools provided by the window system to open windows and pass events into Inventor. Inventor provides event translation from X events into the Inventor event classes. Figure 10-1 shows how X events are passed to the render area and then translated into Inventor events that are handled by the Inventor scene manager. Since Inventor is independent of any window system, you can also choose a different window system and then write your own event translator.

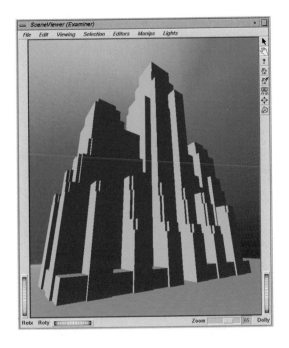

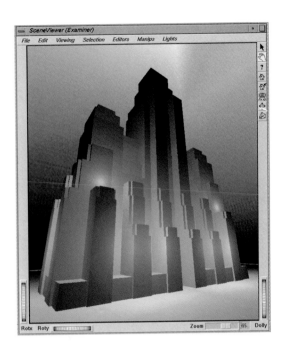

Plate 1. (top left) A scene showing the effects of directional lights. The scene contains blue and yellow directional lights; the building itself is white. (Images for Plates 1 through 21 by Paul Isaacs.)

Plate 2. (top right) The same scene, using purple point lights.

Plate 3. (left) The same scene, using spotlights for a dramatic effect. Gray icons show the placement and orientation of the spotlights. See Chapter 4.

Plate 4. (right) Scene rendered with a lighting model of BASE_COLOR.

Plate 5. (below) The same scene, with the lighting model changed to PHONG. See Chapter 5.

Plate 6. Scene showing the effects of an SoEnvironment node. The fog type is FOG, and the fog color is lavender. See Chapter 5.

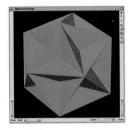

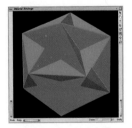

Plate 7. An indexed face set using per-face material binding.

Plate 8. The same face set using per-vertex-indexed material binding.

Plate 9. The same face set using per-face-indexed material binding. See Chapter 5.

Plate 10. Scene using nontextured surfaces, a white point light in the foreground, and orange point lights in the background.

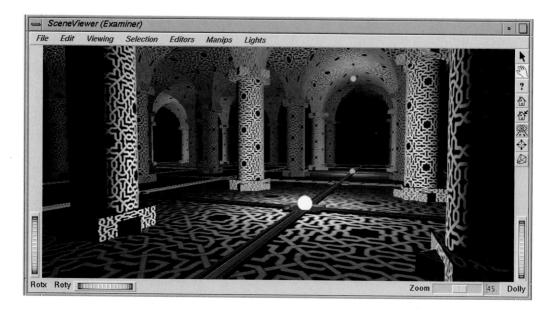

Plate 11. The same scene, with textures added using a MODULATE texture model.

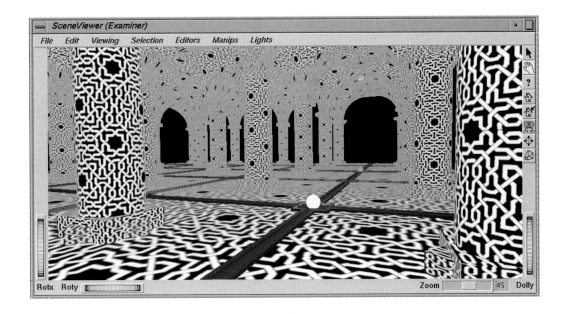

Plate 12. The same scene, using a DECAL texture model.

Plate 13. The same scene, using a BLEND texture model with a gold blend color to achieve a filigree effect. See Chapter 7.

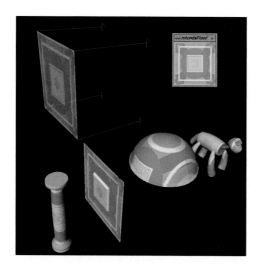

Plate 14. Texture mapping using SoTextureCoordinatePlane. The textured square at left (with arrows) is projected onto four different shapes.

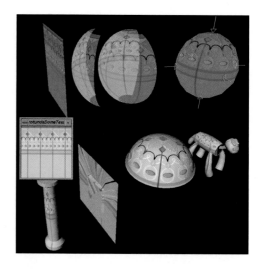

Plate 15. Texture mapping using a spherical projection. The textured sphere at right (with arrows) is projected onto four different shapes.

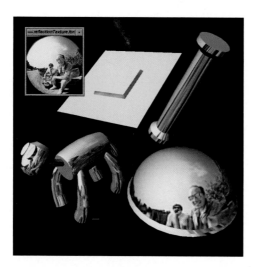

Plate 16. Texture mapping using SoTextureCoordinateEnvironment.

Plate 17. Scene using a variety of texture coordinate function nodes. See Chapter 7.

Plate 18. Scene using BLEND transparency type. The order of rendering is background, sphere, cone, black and gold buildings.

Plate 19. Scene using DELAYED_BLEND transparency type. Order of rendering is opaque objects (background, black and gold buildings), then transparent objects (sphere, cone).

Plate 20. Scene using SORTED_OBJECT_BLEND transparency type. Order of rendering is opaque objects (background, black and gold buildings), then transparent objects, sorted from back to front (cone, sphere). See Chapter 9.

Plate 21. Noodle, an object modeler. The user specifies a cross-section, spline, profile, and twist for each object. The gold airplane is made of Inventor NURBS surfaces. The purple airplane is made of face sets using the same data.

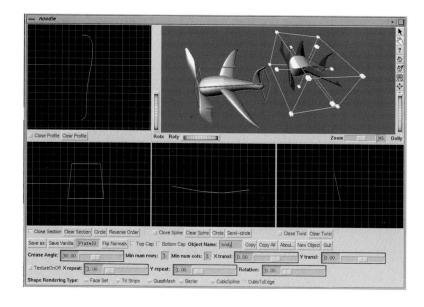

Plate 22. Movieola®, a modeling and animation system based on Inventor. This application makes extensive use of Inventor's 3D manipulators, components, and node kits to provide intuitive tools for creating complex shapes. (© 1993 Radiance Software International.)

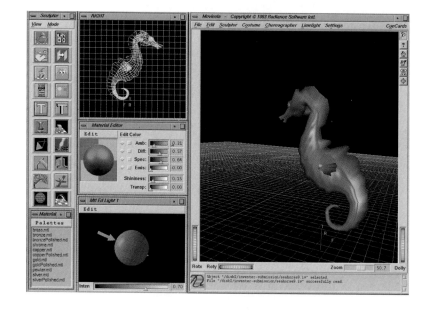

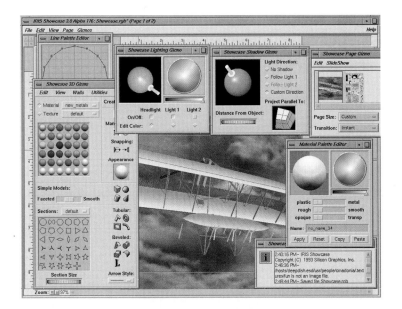

Plate 23. Showcase, an application for creating multimedia presentations. All 3D support, including rendering, interaction, and editing, is provided by Inventor. (Image by Rikk Carey.)

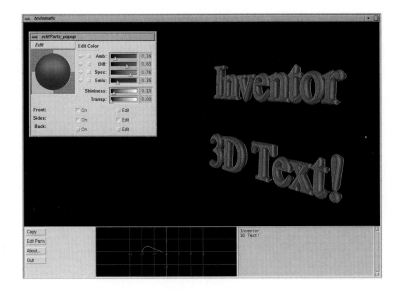

Plate 24. Textomatic, a simple Inventor application used for interactively defining profiles and materials for 3D text. (Image by Catherine Madonia.)

Plate 25. A hydrodynamics simulation created in Explorer, an application used for visualizing data. Inventor is used for the 3D rendering module. (Data courtesy of Drew Whitehouse and Gustav Meglicki, Australian National University Supercomputer Facility. Image by Roy Hashimoto.)

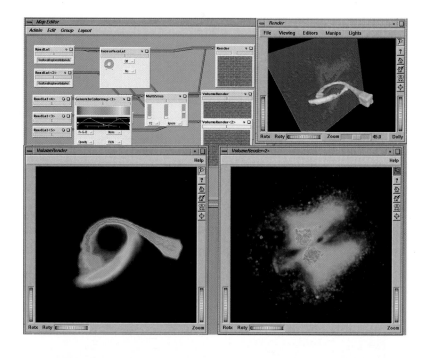

Plate 26. Five map layers showing the Mahantango Creek USDA Watershed in Pennsylvania. The layers show direction of steepest descent, slope, rainfall, soil saturation, and soil category. (Data courtesy of Dominique Thongs, Department of Civil Engineering; image courtesy of Interactive Computer Graphics Laboratory, Princeton University.)

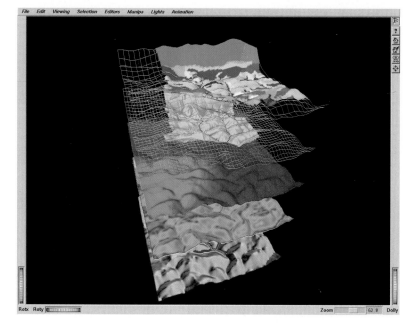

Plate 27. A multimedia repair manual and inventory database. The user can move the displayed object, zoom in on selected parts, view demonstration videos, and listen to voice annotations. (Image by Kevin Goldsmith.)

Plate 28. An application displaying radar coverage and status in 3D. Two new shape classes are used: a dome shape representing movable antenna radars and a pie shape representing phased-array radars. (Image courtesy of Decision-Science Applications, Inc.)

Plate 29. The Piero Project, an application for teaching art history using interactive 3D computer graphics. This image shows a reconstruction of the Church of San Francesco in Arezzo, Italy. Clicking on the pink box brings up the higher resolution image shown at right. Clicking on a white sphere allows the user to view the scene from that position. White spheres can be connected to create an animated tour of the church. (Image courtesy of Interactive Computer Graphics Laboratory, Princeton University, and The Piero Project by Kirk Alexander, Kevin Perry, and Marilyn Aronberg Lavin.)

Plate 30. An interactive art gallery tour. (Image by Gavin Bell and Kevin Goldsmith.)

Plate 31. Trenchmaster, an archaeological application. The main window contains shapes representing artifacts found in an excavation trench. Clicking on a shape brings up additional windows with text and photos. (Data courtesy of William Childs, Dept. of Art and Archaeology; image courtesy of Interactive Computer Graphics Laboratory, Princeton Univ.)

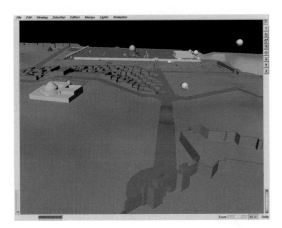

Plate 32. A reconstruction of early Islamic Jerusalem. The user can explore the city streets and then walk through the buildings. (Data for Plates 32 and 33 courtesy of Mohamed Alasad and Oleg Grabar, Institute for Advanced Study, Princeton, New Jersey.)

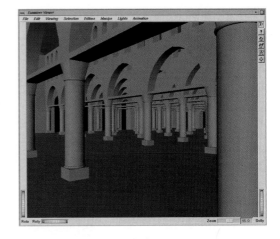

Plate 33. View inside a mosque, one of the buildings shown in Plate 32. (Images for Plates 32 and 33 courtesy of Interactive Computer Graphics Laboratory, Princeton Univ.)

Plate 34. Cuckoo clock. An engine connected to the real-time global field moves the hands of the clock. (Image by Rikk Carey.)

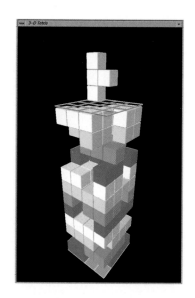

Plate 35. Tetris. A timer sensor animates the falling pieces. (Image by David Immel.)

Plate 36. Moxy Moto, a computer-generated character created using Alive, a real-time character animation program based on Inventor. (Moxy was created by (Colossal) Pictures and by the Cartoon Network. Alive is a product of deGraf/Associates.)

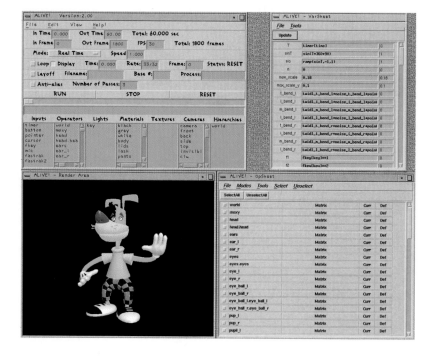

Plate 37. Scenes from the Out-of-Box Experience, an immersive multimedia presentation. This application adds multimedia nodes to the toolkit and the ability to synchronize Inventor objects with them. Clicking on one of the moving spheres sends the user to a new "room."

Plate 38. The Animations Room. Each animated object is surrounded by an invisible Inventor shape. When the user clicks on an object, a movie is played.

Plate 39. A live video window within the Stop-Motion Room. The control panel and background are built with Inventor objects.

Plate 40. The Earth Room. The user controls the spinning of the earth within its painted galaxy. When the user clicks on a pin on the globe, a video or audio clip for that geographical area is played. (Images by Kevin Goldsmith and (Colossal) Pictures.)

Plate 41. A lighting and shading editor that uses Inventor for OpenGL rendering, widget construction, file format, and user interaction. Data in other formats is brought into this Inventor-based application, where it is modified interactively. Inventor is used to render the dinosaur in the upper left window, and RenderMan™ is used in the lower right. (© 1993 Industrial Light & Magic.)

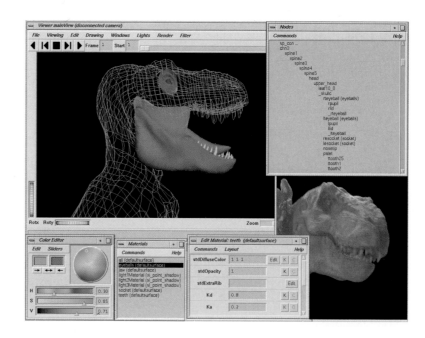

Plate 42. Scene from *Jurassic Park* showing the finished Tyrannosaurus rex in action. (© 1993 Universal Studios/Amblin Productions. Photograph courtesy of Industrial Light & Magic.)

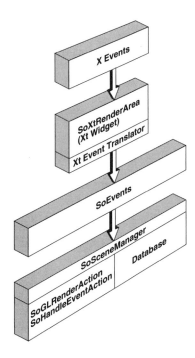

Figure 10-1 Event Processing in Inventor

Using the X Window System

Inventor provides a set of Xt utilities for use with the X Window System. This set of utilities contains the following:

- A render-area "widget"

- Main loop and initialization functions

- An event translator utility

In addition to these features, the Inventor Component Library also contains a set of Xt components. These components include viewers and editors with a user interface for modifying the scene database directly.

This chapter focuses on the aspects of Inventor that are independent of the window system:

- Events (derived from **SoEvent**)

- Scene manager

- Handle event action

- Event callback functions

- Selection node

Chapter 16 describes use of the Inventor Component Library in more detail. If you want to use Inventor viewers and editors, you must use an Xt render area (**SoXtRenderArea**) and the X Window System model. If you are not using these viewers and editors, you can choose a different window system and then implement your own render area, event loop, and event translator.

Render Area

The render-area widget provides a convenient object for creating a window and translating window-specific events into generic Inventor events. With the X Window System model, you create an **SoXtRenderArea** (see Figure 10-1). Window-specific events are passed into this render area and then automatically translated into a generic Inventor **SoEvent**.

The render area provides the following:

- Built-in sensors that redraw the window when the scene changes or when the window resizes or is exposed

- Built-in event processing

- Certain controls, such as the type of transparency and the amount of antialiasing

Inventor Events (SoEvent)

The class tree for **SoEvent** is shown in Figure 10-2.

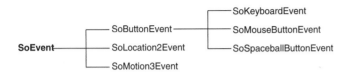

Figure 10-2   Event Classes

Each **SoEvent** instance contains the following information:

- Type identification (**SoType**)
- Time the event occurred
- Cursor position when the event occurred
- State of the modifier keys (Shift, Control, Alt) when the event occurred

Subclasses of **SoEvent** contain additional information. For example, **SoButtonEvent** contains information about whether the button was up or down when the event occurred. **SoMouseButtonEvent** contains information about which button was pressed (button 1, 2, or 3).

See the *Open Inventor C++ Reference Manual* entry on **SoEvent** for a list of methods available for querying the event. In addition, you can use the following macros:

- SO_MOUSE_PRESS_EVENT()—You pass in an **SoEvent** and a button number, and the macro returns TRUE if that button was pressed.
- SO_MOUSE_RELEASE_EVENT()—You pass in an **SoEvent** and a button number, and the macro returns TRUE if that button was released.

SoKeyboardEvent contains information on which key was pressed (but does not indicate uppercase or lowercase).

Tip: Using the **SoKeyboardEvent::getKey()** method is the same as
using XLookupKeysym() on an X key event.

An **SoLocation2Event** is generated whenever the cursor moves. This event contains the *absolute* location of the cursor in window coordinates. (Window coordinates begin with (0, 0) at the lower left corner of the window.) An **SoMotion3Event** is generated whenever a 3D input device, such as the spaceball, moves. This event contains the rotation and translation *relative to* the device's previous position.

❖ **Tip:** Inventor events are extensible. If you have a device that does not correspond to existing **SoEvent** classes, you can create your own. (See *The Inventor Toolmaker*, Chapter 11.)

Scene Manager

As shown in Figure 10-1, **SoSceneManager** is a common class used to tie window-system–dependent render areas (such as **SoXtRenderArea**) to Inventor. The render area employs the scene manager to handle the scene graph. The scene manager handles both rendering and event processing and is independent of any particular window system.

Inventor Event Handling

In Inventor, events are distributed to the 3D objects contained in the scene database. Manipulator and dragger objects, described in detail in Chapter 15, are the 3D objects in the Inventor scene graph that handle events. Shape objects (such as sphere, cylinder, quad mesh), property objects (such as material and draw style), transformation objects, light objects, and camera objects ignore events. Finding the node that handles an event is discussed in "How Nodes Handle Events: SoHandleEventAction" on page 257.

With Inventor, you can choose from one of four event-handling mechanisms:

1. You can use Inventor's automatic event-handling mechanism, provided by the scene manager, in which certain kinds of *nodes* handle events (see "How Nodes Handle Events: SoHandleEventAction" on page 257). This is probably the easiest mechanism to use. (Note that you can also create your own nodes to handle events. You might create your own node if you want to use it in several different applications or

give it to other programmers. You could also create a new manipulator to handle events. See *The Inventor Toolmaker* for more information on creating new nodes and manipulators.)

2. You can use Inventor's *event callback* mechanism, in which user-written callback nodes handle events (see "Using Event Callback Nodes" on page 264). This method handles events on a per-object basis and is fairly easy to implement. Its drawback is that, although the callback node does write to a file, it has no fields describing which path it is monitoring or which events it is interested in.

3. You can override Inventor's event-handling mechanisms entirely and pass all events directly to the application (see "Sending Events Directly to the Application" on page 266). Use this method if you prefer to work directly with X events and you do not need to handle events on a per-object basis. This method bypasses scene traversal and handles only window events.

4. You can use Inventor's generic callback mechanism in which user-written callback nodes handle all actions (see Chapter 17 for an example of an **SoCallback** node). Use this mechanism if you need to handle events and you want to implement another action, such as rendering. If you are only handling events, use Method 2 (the event callback node), because it does more work for you.

Methods 1, 2, and 4 are recommended because they are window-system–independent and therefore more flexible. Methods 1 and 2 are probably the easiest.

How Nodes Handle Events: SoHandleEventAction

Inventor provides a mechanism for automatic event handling by "smart" nodes, which can be summarized as follows:

1. The render area registers interest in particular events with its window system.

2. The render area receives an event from its window system. (**SoXtRenderArea** receives an X event.)

3. The render area translates the event into an **SoEvent**.

4. The **SoEvent** is sent to the scene manager, which creates an instance of the **SoHandleEventAction**.

5. The handle event action is applied to the top node of the scene graph. This action traverses the scene graph. Each node implements its own action behavior, as described in the following paragraphs. When a node is found to handle the event (typically a manipulator), the **SoHandleEventAction** stops traversing the scene graph and the node handles the event.

The following sections describe how different types of nodes implement **SoHandleEventAction**.

SoNode

SoNode, the base class for all nodes, does nothing for the handle event action. Therefore, all properties, transforms, shapes, cameras, and lights do nothing for this action.

SoGroup

When the handle event action is applied to an **SoGroup**, the group traverses its children from left to right, asking each child to handle the event. After each child, it checks to see if the event was handled. If it was, the handle event action ends its traversal of the scene graph. If the event was not handled, the **SoGroup** asks the next child to handle the event.

The **SoGroup** uses the **isHandled()** method of **SoHandleEventAction** to find out if an event has been handled. When a node handles an event, it calls **setHandled()** on the handle event action.

SoManipulator

Manipulators are the "smart" objects in the scene graph that handle certain kinds of events (see Chapter 15 for a more detailed discussion). Typically, a manipulator replaces a node in the scene graph with an editable version of that node. Using **SoHandleBoxManip**, you can change an object's size and position by replacing the transform node in the scene graph that affects the object with the handle-box manipulator. This manipulator then scales and translates itself in response to the user moving the mouse. Using **SoTrackballManip**, you can rotate an object around a center point by replacing the appropriate transform node in the scene graph with a trackball manipulator. This manipulator then changes its rotation field in response to the user moving the mouse.

Manipulators, such as the trackball and handle box, require picking information in addition to the event type. These manipulators call **getPickedPoint()** on **SoHandleEventAction** to see which object was picked. If the manipulator was picked, it handles the event. You can also create manipulators that do not require a hit on their geometry to be activated. (See *The Inventor Toolmaker*, Chapter 8, for information on creating your own manipulator.)

Grabbing

A node can request that all subsequent events be sent directly to it until further notice. This request is called *grabbing*. For example, after receiving a mouse-button-down event, a manipulator might grab all subsequent events until a mouse-button-up event occurs. The **setGrabber()** method is called on the handle event action, with a pointer to the manipulator (**this**):

```
handleEA->setGrabber(this);
```

The handle event action now applies the action directly to the grabbing node instead of to the scene graph root. To stop grabbing events, the manipulator uses the **releaseGrabber()** method:

```
handleEA->releaseGrabber();
```

If the node calls **releaseGrabber()** for an event but did not handle the event, the handle event action initiates a traversal at the root and passes the event to the entire scene graph. For example, manipulators grab after a mouse-press event. However, if a mouse release occurs with no mouse motion in between, the manipulator ungrabs and does not handle the event. The event is then passed to the scene graph for processing.

The **getGrabber()** method returns the node that is currently grabbing events. (See **SoHandleEventAction** in the *Open Inventor C++ Reference Manual*.)

Note: Grabbing events in the scene graph does not perform an X server grab.

SoSelection

An **SoSelection** node, derived from **SoGroup**, is typically inserted near the top of the scene graph, as shown in Figure 10-3. When the handle event action is applied to an **SoSelection** node, it traverses its children in the same way as **SoGroup**. However, if none of its children handles the event, the selection node itself handles it.

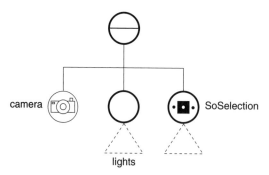

Figure 10-3   Inserting an SoSelection Node

Picking

When a left-mouse-button event occurs, the **SoSelection** object needs to know which node was picked. It calls the **getPickedPoint()** method on the handle event action. (**SoSelection** checks the picked object on both mouse-down and mouse-up events to make sure that both events occurred over the same object. Specify FALSE for the **setPickMatching()** method to disable this feature, and **SoSelection** will get the picked point only on mouse-up events.)

The handle event action performs the pick the first time a node in the scene graph requests information concerning the hit objects (picking is performed only when necessary). **SoHandleEventAction** caches this picking information so that any subsequent nodes encountered during traversal, such as manipulators and the selection object, can have access to this information quickly. Only one pick (at most) is performed during the traversal for **SoHandleEventAction**.

Selection Policy

After receiving the pick information, the **SoSelection** class implements the appropriate selection policy. Currently, you can choose one of three selection policies with the **policy** field. **SoSelection** keeps track of the selection list for you. Selected objects can be highlighted by the render area (see "Highlighting Selected Objects" on page 272). The default selection policy, **SoSelection::SHIFT**, is as follows:

- If the user clicks the left mouse button on a node, **SoSelection** clears the selection list and adds the node to the list.

- If the user clicks the left mouse button on a node while pressing the Shift key, **SoSelection** toggles the node's selection status (that is, if the node is currently in the selection list, it is removed from the list; if the node is not currently selected, it is added to the selection list).

- If the user clicks the left mouse button on nothing, **SoSelection** clears the selection list.

With the **SoSelection::SINGLE** policy, only one object can be selected at a time. This policy is as follows:

- If the user clicks the left mouse button on a node, **SoSelection** clears the selection list and adds the node to the list.

- If the user clicks the left mouse button on nothing, **SoSelection** clears the selection list.

With the **SoSelection::TOGGLE** policy, multiple objects can be selected at a time. This policy is as follows:

- If the user clicks the left mouse button on a node, **SoSelection** toggles that node's selection status (that is, it adds the node to the list if it was not previously selected, or it removes the node from the list if it was previously selected).

- If the user clicks the left mouse button on nothing, **SoSelection** does nothing.

Tip: Shift selection is the same as Single selection when the Shift key is not ❖ pressed, and Toggle selection when the Shift key is pressed.

If none of these selection policies meets your needs, you can implement your own custom selection policy by creating an event callback node and passing it a pointer to the **SoSelection** node. You can then call **select()**, **deselect()**, **toggle()**, and **deselectAll()** on the **SoSelection** node to implement your new selection policy. An additional alternative is to derive your own class from **SoSelection**.

See "Selection" on page 268 for more information on the selection list.

Finding the Event Handler

The following example illustrates the process of finding the event handler for a given event. Assume you have a scene graph containing several shape objects, with a handle-box manipulator that affects the transformation of an indexed face set. The scene graph also contains *yourManip*, a manipulator you've written that handles the middle mouse-button event. This scene graph is shown in Figure 10-4.

If the user clicks the left mouse button on the handle box surrounding the face-set object on the screen, the scene manager receives the event and sends it to the **SoHandleEventAction** with the **setEvent()** method. Here is how the nodes in Figure 10-4 respond during the handle event action traversal:

1. The **SoSeparator** group asks each child, from left to right in the scene graph, to handle the event.

2. The *yourManip* node does not handle the event, since it handles only middle mouse-button events.

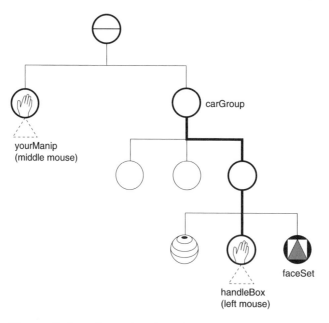

Figure 10-4   Scene Graph with Manipulators

3. The *carGroup* node traverses each of its children, from left to right, and asks them to handle the event. The third child, also a group, traverses its children from left to right.

4. The handle-box manipulator node, which handles left mouse events, needs to know if it is in the picked path. It calls **getPickedPoint()** on the **SoHandleEventAction**. Since it was hit, it then calls **setHandled()** and handles the event.

In Figure 10-5, the scene graph contains a new instance of a face set (*faceSet2*). Suppose the user clicks on this face set instead of the handle box surrounding *faceSet1*. Since the handle-box manipulator is not contained in the pick path and has no effect on the pick path, it does not handle the event. In this case, the **SoSelection** object handles the event.

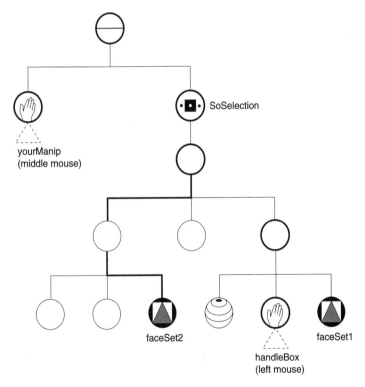

Figure 10-5   Picking a Shape Node

Using Event Callback Nodes

If you require an event-handling behavior that is not provided by Inventor manipulators, you can create your own manipulator, or you can write your own event handler using an *event callback node*. Creating new manipulators is discussed in *The Inventor Toolmaker*, Chapter 8. Using event callback nodes is discussed in this section.

An *event callback node* contains a user-written function that is invoked whenever an event of a specified type occurs, when the specified path is picked, and when the handle event action traverses the event callback node. If no path is specified (that is, NULL), the event callback function is invoked automatically every time an event of the specified type occurs and the node is traversed by the handle event action. You can write multiple event callback functions and add them to the list of callback functions maintained by the **SoEventCallback** node.

To specify which **SoEvents** the callback node is interested in and to specify the callback, use the **addEventCallback()** method:

```
SoEventCallback *eventCB = new SoEventCallback;
eventCB->addEventCallback(SoKeyboardEvent::getClassTypeId(),
        myCallbackFunc, userData);
```

To specify the path to be monitored, use the **setPath()** method.

When the callback function is invoked, it is passed the user data and a pointer to the instance of **SoEventCallback**. To remove a callback function from the event callback list, use the **removeEventCallback()** method.

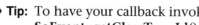 **Tip:** To have your callback invoked for every event type, pass **SoEvent::getClassTypeId()** as the type.

The **SoHandleEventAction**, discussed earlier in this chapter, does its work behind the scenes when you use event callback functions. It performs a pick when necessary and caches the pick information. The event callback function itself is responsible for setting whether the event was handled (with the **setHandled()** method). If there are multiple event callback functions in an event callback node, all of them are invoked, regardless of whether one of them has handled the event.

The event callback function can use any of the following methods on
SoEventCallback, which parallel those used in standard Inventor event
handling:

getAction()   returns the handle event action applied.

getEvent()   returns the Inventor event to handle.

getPickedPoint()   returns the object hit. The pick is performed
automatically by the **SoHandleEventAction**.

grabEvents()   tells the event callback node to grab events. However,
the event callback functions are still invoked only for
events of interest.

releaseEvents()   tells the event callback node to stop grabbing events.

setHandled()   tells the action that the event was handled.

isHandled()   returns whether the event has been handled.

Example 10-1 shows the use of event callback functions with the
SoEventCallback node. It creates an event callback node that is interested
in key-press events. The callback function, *myKeyPressCB*, is then registered
with the **addEventCallback()** method. The scene graph has four objects
that can be selected by picking with the left mouse button. (Use the Shift
key to extend the selection to more than one object.) When a key-press
occurs, it checks to see if the up or down arrow is pressed and scales the
picked object up or down accordingly.

Example 10-1   Using an Event Callback

```
// An event callback node so we can receive key press events
SoEventCallback *myEventCB = new SoEventCallback;
myEventCB->addEventCallback(
        SoKeyboardEvent::getClassTypeId(),
        myKeyPressCB, selectionRoot);
selectionRoot->addChild(myEventCB);


...


// userData is the selectionRoot from main().
void
myKeyPressCB(void *userData, SoEventCallback *eventCB)
{
   SoSelection *selection = (SoSelection *) userData;
   const SoEvent *event = eventCB->getEvent();
```

```
    // Check for the Up and Down arrow keys being pressed.
    if (SO_KEY_PRESS_EVENT(event, UP_ARROW)) {
       myScaleSelection(selection, 1.1);
       eventCB->setHandled();
    } else if (SO_KEY_PRESS_EVENT(event, DOWN_ARROW)) {
       myScaleSelection(selection, 1.0/1.1);
       eventCB->setHandled();
    }
}
```

 ## Sending Events Directly to the Application

In some cases, you may want to short-circuit Inventor event handling and send all events directly to the application. **SoXtRenderArea** contains a method that enables you to pass events to an application event handler. For example:

```
SoXtRenderArea *myRenderArea;
myRenderArea->setEventCallback(myEventCallback, userData);
```

When this method is passed a non-NULL user function, all events that come into the render area are passed to the user function. The callback function returns a Boolean value. If this value is TRUE, the callback function handled the event and the render area does not send the event to the scene manager for handling. If this value is FALSE, the event is sent to the scene graph for handling.

Note that the events sent to the event callback function are not Inventor events. For the **SoXtRenderArea**, X events are passed. The application is thus assured of receiving every event, even those that do not translate to Inventor events.

Example 10-2 demonstrates using **setEventCallback()**, which causes events to be sent directly to the application without being sent into the scene graph.

Example 10-2 Sending Events Directly to the Application

```
// Clicking the left mouse button and dragging will draw
// points in the xy plane beneath the mouse cursor.
// Clicking middle mouse and holding causes the point set
// to rotate about the Y axis.
// Clicking right mouse clears all points drawn so far out
// of the point set.
...
```

```
// Have render area send events to us instead of the scene
// graph.  We pass the render area as user data.
myRenderArea->setEventCallback(
            myAppEventHandler, myRenderArea);

SbBool
myAppEventHandler(void *userData, XAnyEvent *anyevent)
{
    SoXtRenderArea *myRenderArea = (SoXtRenderArea *) userData;
    XButtonEvent *myButtonEvent;
    XMotionEvent *myMotionEvent;
    SbVec3f vec;
    SbBool handled = TRUE;

    switch (anyevent->type) {

    case ButtonPress:
       myButtonEvent = (XButtonEvent *) anyevent;
       if (myButtonEvent->button == Button1) {
          myProjectPoint(myRenderArea,
                   myButtonEvent->x, myButtonEvent->y, vec);
          myAddPoint(myRenderArea, vec);
       } else if (myButtonEvent->button == Button2) {
          myTicker->schedule();  // start spinning the camera
       } else if (myButtonEvent->button == Button3) {
          myClearPoints(myRenderArea);  // clear the point set
       }
       break;

    case ButtonRelease:
       myButtonEvent = (XButtonEvent *) anyevent;
       if (myButtonEvent->button == Button2) {
          myTicker->unschedule();  // stop spinning the camera
       }
       break;

    case MotionNotify:
       myMotionEvent = (XMotionEvent *) anyevent;
       if (myMotionEvent->state & Button1Mask) {
          myProjectPoint(myRenderArea,
                   myMotionEvent->x, myMotionEvent->y, vec);
          myAddPoint(myRenderArea, vec);
       }
       break;

    default:
       handled = FALSE;
```

```
        break;
    }

    return handled;
}
```

Selection

The **SoSelection** node provides several additional features that relate to the topic of user interaction. These features include managing the selection list (introduced in "Selection Policy" on page 260), highlighting the selected objects, and the use of user-written callback functions that are invoked when the selection list changes. The following sections describe each of these features.

Managing the Selection List

The **SoSelection** node keeps a list of paths to objects that have been selected. This list is called the *selection list*. Typically, the user selects an object or objects and then performs an operation on the selected objects, such as copying them, deleting them, or setting their color.

Each path in the selection list begins with the selection node and ends with the selected object. Objects can be added to and removed from the selection list in one of two ways:

- By the event-processing mechanism of the selection object itself. This mechanism is based on the current selection policy.

- By methods on **SoSelection** that allow you to select, deselect, toggle, and clear objects from the selection list. You need to use these methods only if you want to manage the selection list directly.

The methods on **SoSelection** that are available for direct management of the selection list are as follows:

select(*path*)   adds a path to the selection list

deselect(*path*)   removes a path from the selection list

toggle(*path*)   toggles a path in the selection list (that is, adds the path if it is not already in the list, or removes the path if it is in the list)

deselectAll() removes all paths from the selection list

isSelected() returns TRUE if the passed path is in the selection list

getNumSelected() returns the length of the selection list

getList() returns the selection list

getPath(*index*) returns one item (*path*) in the selection list

For convenience, you can provide these methods with a node instead of a path. If the node is instanced multiple times in the scene graph, the path to the first instance of the node is used.

For example, suppose each of the objects in the scene graph has a name associated with it, such as a car part. The user selects the object by clicking on a name from a list displayed on the screen ("hubcap"). Your program then uses this name, finds the path to the selected object, and adds this path to the selection list. Example 10-3 shows using a Motif-style list to select objects in this manner. This example shows selecting and deselecting objects using a Motif-style list that contains names for four objects (cube, sphere, cone, cylinder).

Example 10-3   Using a Motif-Style List to Select Objects

```
//   The scene graph has 4 objects which may be
//   selected by picking with the left mouse button
//   (use shift key to extend the selection to more
//   than one object).
//
//   Hitting the up arrow key will increase the size of
//   each selected object; hitting down arrow will decrease
//   the size of each selected object.
//
//   This also demonstrates selecting objects from a Motif-style
//   list, and calling select/deselect functions on the
//   SoSelection node to change the selection. Use the Shift
//   key to extend the selection (i.e. pick more than one
//   item in the list.)
...
enum objects {
        CUBE,
        SPHERE,
        CONE,
        CYL,
        NUM_OBJECTS
};
```

```
static char *objectNames[] = {
        "Cube",
        "Sphere",
        "Cone",
        "Cylinder"
};
...
   cube->setName(objectNames[CUBE]);
   sphere->setName(objectNames[SPHERE]);
   cone->setName(objectNames[CONE]);
   cyl->setName(objectNames[CYL]);
...
   // Create a table of object names
   XmString *table = new XmString[NUM_OBJECTS];
   for (i=0; i<NUM_OBJECTS; i++) {
       table[i] = XmStringCreate(objectNames[i],
                                 XmSTRING_DEFAULT_CHARSET);
   }

   // Create the list widget
   n = 0;
   XtSetArg(args[n], XmNitems, table);
   n++;
   XtSetArg(args[n], XmNitemCount, NUM_OBJECTS);
   n++;
   XtSetArg(args[n], XmNselectionPolicy, XmEXTENDED_SELECT);
   n++;

   motifList = XmCreateScrolledList(shell, "funcList", args, n);
   XtAddCallback(motifList, XmNextendedSelectionCallback,
      (XtCallbackProc) myListPickCB, (XtPointer) selection);
...
   // Clear the selection node, then loop through the list
   // and reselect
   selection->deselectAll();

   // Update the SoSelection based on what is selected in
   // the list.  We do this by extracting the string
   // from the selected XmString, and searching for the
   // object of that name.
   for (int i = 0; i < listData->selected_item_count; i++) {
      mySearchAction.setName(
              SoXt::decodeString(listData->selected_items[i]));
      mySearchAction.apply(selection);
      selection->select(mySearchAction.getPath());
   }
```

Another example of how the selection list might be used is that the user selects several objects and wants to make all of them twice their original size. Here, you would call **getList()** or **getPath()** for each of the selected objects. Then you would find the appropriate **SoTransform** node in the path for each object and modify its **scaleFactor** field. Example 10-4 is an example of using the selection list in this way.

Example 10-4   Using the Selection List

```
// Scale each object in the selection list
void
myScaleSelection(SoSelection *selection, float sf)
{
    SoPath *selectedPath;
    SoTransform *xform;
    SbVec3f scaleFactor;
    int i,j;

    // Scale each object in the selection list

    for (i = 0; i < selection->getNumSelected(); i++) {
        selectedPath = selection->getPath(i);
        xform = NULL;

        // Look for the shape node, starting from the tail of the
        // path.  Once we know the type of shape, we know which
        // transform to modify
        for (j=0; j < selectedPath->getLength() &&
                (xform == NULL); j++) {
            SoNode *n = (SoNode *)selectedPath->getNodeFromTail(j);
            if (n->isOfType(SoCube::getClassTypeId())) {
                xform = cubeTransform;
            } else if (n->isOfType(SoCone::getClassTypeId())) {
                xform = coneTransform;
            } else if (n->isOfType(SoSphere::getClassTypeId())) {
                xform = sphereTransform;
            } else if (n->isOfType(SoCylinder::getClassTypeId())) {
                xform = cylTransform;
            }
        }
        // Apply the scale
        scaleFactor = xform->scaleFactor.getValue();
        scaleFactor *= sf;
        xform->scaleFactor.setValue(scaleFactor);
    }
}
```

Highlighting Selected Objects

Usually, when objects are selected, they are highlighted or treated in some other special way to distinguish them from unselected objects. With the **SoXtRenderArea**, Inventor provides two highlight styles. You can choose to have highlighted objects drawn in wireframe with a particular color, line pattern, and line width, or you can have selected objects drawn with a wireframe bounding box surrounding each object. The type of highlight can be set on **SoXtRenderArea**. The default highlight style is no highlight.

Figure 10-6 shows the class tree for the highlighting classes. Because highlighting objects are simply another way to render the scene, Inventor highlights are derived from the **SoGLRenderAction**. To create your own custom highlights, see *The Inventor Toolmaker*, Chapter 11.

Figure 10-6   Highlight Classes

To specify which highlight to use, pass a highlight to the **setGLRenderAction()** method on **SoXtRenderArea**. The action will render highlights for selected objects in the scene. Note that whenever you create a new highlight and pass it to the render area, you are responsible for deleting the highlight after the render area is destroyed. The render area will not delete it for you.

❖ **Tip:** The redraw sensor employed by the render area does not trigger a redraw when the selection changes. Use the **redrawOnSelectionChanges()** convenience method on **SoXtRenderArea** to ensure that a redraw occurs when the selection changes. Pass the selection node that should be monitored for changes.

How Highlighting Occurs

First, the highlight render action renders the scene graph. Then it renders the path for each object in the selection list. For **SoLineHighlightRender-Action**, the selected objects are drawn in wireframe, with the specified color, line pattern, and line width. The following methods are available for **SoLineHighlightRenderAction**:

setColor (*color*)   specifies the highlight color

setLinePattern (*pattern*)
    specifies the line pattern of the highlight

setLineWidth (*width*)
    specifies the line width of the highlight

For **SoBoxHighlightRenderAction**, the selected objects are drawn with a wireframe box surrounding them, using the specified color, line pattern, and line width. Methods for **SoBoxHighlightRenderAction** are the same as for **SoLineHighlightRenderAction**.

Custom Highlighting

If you want highlight styles other than the line and box highlight styles provided by Inventor, you can do either of the following:

- Create a new subclass from **SoGLRenderAction** and pass it to **renderArea->setGLRenderAction()**

- Specify NULL for **addSelectionHighlight()** and then use selection callback functions, described in the following section, to add geometry, draw-style, and other required nodes to the scene graph for highlighting selected objects. A common highlighting technique is to use selection callbacks to add a manipulator to selected objects.

See *The Inventor Toolmaker*, Chapter 10, for a detailed explanation of creating your own highlight.

Callback Functions for Selection Changes

The **SoSelection** class has several types of callback functions associated with it: selection callbacks, deselection callbacks, a pick filter callback, start callbacks, and finish callbacks. For example, you might write a callback function that puts a trackball around an object every time it is selected. This function would be a *selection callback* function. You would probably write a second callback function to remove the trackball when the object is deselected. This function would be a *deselection callback* function. The *pick filter callback* function is invoked whenever an object is picked and is about to be selected or deselected. This function allows you to truncate the selection path at a certain object type, such as a node kit (see Example 10-8).

A start callback function is called whenever the selection is about to change, and a finish callback function is called when the selection is finished changing. These functions are useful for implementing undo and redo features. When the selection is about to change, you can save the current selection in an undo buffer. To undo a change, you restore this saved information.

Another example of a user callback function for selected objects would be a function that checks to see if the material editor is on the screen when an object is selected. If it is, then the function finds the material node affecting the selected object and attaches the material editor to that node.

The following methods allow you to specify what happens when an object is selected and deselected:

addSelectionCallback(*functionName, userData*)
removeSelectionCallback(*functionName, userData*)
> are invoked whenever an object is selected.

addDeselectionCallback(*functionName, userData*)
removeDeselectionCallback(*functionName, userData*)
> are invoked whenever an object is deselected.

setPickFilterCallback(*functionName, userData*)
> is invoked whenever an object is picked and is about to be selected or deselected. This function allows you to truncate the selection path at a certain object type.

addStartCallback(*functionName, userData*)
removeStartCallback(*functionName, userData*)
> are invoked whenever the selection list is about to change.

addFinishCallback(*functionName, userData*)
removeFinishCallback(*functionName, userData*)
> are invoked when the selection list is finished changing.

These methods allow you to pass in a callback function and a pointer to user data. If you specify NULL for the pick filter callback function, whatever is picked will be selected and deselected.

Example 10-5 illustrates the use of selection callback functions. The scene graph in this example has a sphere and a 3D text object. A selection node is placed at the top of the scene graph. When an object is selected, a selection callback is invoked to change the material color of that object.

Example 10-5   Using Selection Callback Functions

```
#include <X11/Intrinsic.h>
#include <Inventor/Sb.h>
#include <Inventor/SoInput.h>
#include <Inventor/Xt/SoXt.h>
#include <Inventor/Xt/SoXtRenderArea.h>
#include <Inventor/nodes/SoDirectionalLight.h>
#include <Inventor/nodes/SoMaterial.h>
#include <Inventor/nodes/SoPerspectiveCamera.h>
#include <Inventor/nodes/SoPickStyle.h>
#include <Inventor/nodes/SoSelection.h>
#include <Inventor/nodes/SoSphere.h>
#include <Inventor/nodes/SoText3.h>
#include <Inventor/nodes/SoTransform.h>

// global data
SoMaterial *textMaterial, *sphereMaterial;
static float reddish[] = {1.0, 0.2, 0.2};
static float white[] = {0.8, 0.8, 0.8};

// This routine is called when an object gets selected.
// We determine which object was selected, and change
// that object's material color.
void
mySelectionCB(void *, SoPath *selectionPath)
{
   if (selectionPath->getTail()->
           isOfType(SoText3::getClassTypeId())) {
     textMaterial->diffuseColor.setValue(reddish);
   } else if (selectionPath->getTail()->
           isOfType(SoSphere::getClassTypeId())) {
     sphereMaterial->diffuseColor.setValue(reddish);
   }
}
```

```
// This routine is called whenever an object gets deselected.
// We determine which object was deselected, and reset
// that object's material color.
void
myDeselectionCB(void *, SoPath *deselectionPath)
{
   if (deselectionPath->getTail()->
           isOfType(SoText3::getClassTypeId())) {
      textMaterial->diffuseColor.setValue(white);
   } else if (deselectionPath->getTail()->
           isOfType(SoSphere::getClassTypeId())) {
      sphereMaterial->diffuseColor.setValue(white);
   }
}

void
main(int argc, char **argv)
{
   // Initialize Inventor and Xt
   Widget myWindow = SoXt::init(argv[0]);
   if (myWindow == NULL) exit(1);

   // Create and set up the selection node
   SoSelection *selectionRoot = new SoSelection;
   selectionRoot->ref();
   selectionRoot->policy = SoSelection::SINGLE;
   selectionRoot-> addSelectionCallback(mySelectionCB);
   selectionRoot-> addDeselectionCallback(myDeselectionCB);

   // Create the scene graph
   SoSeparator *root = new SoSeparator;
   selectionRoot->addChild(root);

   SoPerspectiveCamera *myCamera = new SoPerspectiveCamera;
   root->addChild(myCamera);
   root->addChild(new SoDirectionalLight);

   // Add a sphere node
   SoSeparator *sphereRoot = new SoSeparator;
   SoTransform *sphereTransform = new SoTransform;
   sphereTransform->translation.setValue(17., 17., 0.);
   sphereTransform->scaleFactor.setValue(8., 8., 8.);
   sphereRoot->addChild(sphereTransform);
```

```
sphereMaterial = new SoMaterial;
sphereMaterial->diffuseColor.setValue(.8, .8, .8);
sphereRoot->addChild(sphereMaterial);
sphereRoot->addChild(new SoSphere);
root->addChild(sphereRoot);

// Add a text node
SoSeparator *textRoot = new SoSeparator;
SoTransform *textTransform = new SoTransform;
textTransform->translation.setValue(0., -1., 0.);
textRoot->addChild(textTransform);

textMaterial = new SoMaterial;
textMaterial->diffuseColor.setValue(.8, .8, .8);
textRoot->addChild(textMaterial);
SoPickStyle *textPickStyle = new SoPickStyle;
textPickStyle->style.setValue(SoPickStyle::BOUNDING_BOX);
textRoot->addChild(textPickStyle);
SoText3 *myText = new SoText3;
myText->string = "rhubarb";
textRoot->addChild(myText);
root->addChild(textRoot);

SoXtRenderArea *myRenderArea = new SoXtRenderArea(myWindow);
myRenderArea->setSceneGraph(selectionRoot);
myRenderArea->setTitle("My Selection Callback");
myRenderArea->show();

// Make the camera see the whole scene
const SbViewportRegion myViewport =
        myRenderArea->getViewportRegion();
myCamera->viewAll(root, myViewport, 2.0);

SoXt::show(myWindow);
SoXt::mainLoop();
}
```

Pick Filter Callback

The pick filter callback returns a path for the new object to be selected, deselected, or toggled:

typedef SoPath *SoSelectionPickCB(void *userData, SoDetail *d);

void **setPickFilterCallback**(SoSelectionPickCB *f,
                void *userData = NULL,
                SbBool callOnlyIfSelectable = TRUE);

This callback can look at the picked point to see what was picked and return a path to whatever the selection policy is to be applied to. It can truncate the picked path so that it ends in a particular type of node. If an unselectable object is picked, the pick filter callback determines how that information is used. When the callback is set, the application passes in a Boolean value that specifies whether the callback is called only if the object is selectable, or is called for all objects. The pick filter callback can then return one of the following:

- NULL—the selection behaves as if nothing were picked (for SINGLE and SHIFT selection policies, this clears the selection list).

- Path—this path will be selected or deselected according to the selection policy. It must pass through the selection node.

- Path not passing through the selection node—the selection ignores this pick event and no change is made to the selection list.

- Path containing only the selection node—applies the selection policy as though nothing were picked, but continues traversal.

Examples 10-6 through 10-8 illustrate sample pick filter callbacks the application could use.

Example 10-6 shows the use of the pick filter callback to implement a top-level selection policy. Rather than selecting the actual node that was picked, it always selects the topmost group beneath the selection node. Figure 10-7 shows the two viewers created by this example.

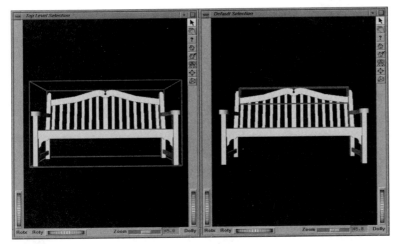

Figure 10-7 Top-Level Selection Policy (left) and Default Selection Policy (right)

Example 10-6 Creating a Top-Level Selection Policy

```
#include <X11/StringDefs.h>
#include <X11/Intrinsic.h>

#include <Inventor/SoDB.h>
#include <Inventor/SoInput.h>
#include <Inventor/SoPath.h>
#include <Inventor/Xt/SoXt.h>
#include <Inventor/Xt/viewers/SoXtExaminerViewer.h>
#include <Inventor/actions/SoBoxHighlightRenderAction.h>
#include <Inventor/misc/SoPickedPoint.h>
#include <Inventor/nodes/SoSelection.h>

// Pick the topmost node beneath the selection node
SoPath *
pickFilterCB(void *, const SoPickedPoint *pick)
{
   // See which child of selection got picked
   SoPath *p = pick->getPath();
   int i;
   for (i = 0; i < p->getLength() - 1; i++) {
      SoNode *n = p->getNode(i);
      if (n->isOfType(SoSelection::getClassTypeId()))
         break;
   }
```

```
   // Copy 2 nodes from the path:
   // selection and the picked child
   return p->copy(i, 2);
}


void
main(int argc, char *argv[])
{
   // Initialization
   Widget mainWindow = SoXt::init(argv[0]);

   // Open the data file
   SoInput in;
   char *datafile = "parkbench.iv";
   if (! in.openFile(datafile)) {
      fprintf(stderr, "Cannot open %s for reading.\n",
              datafile);
      return;
   }

   // Read the input file
   SoNode *n;
   SoSeparator *sep = new SoSeparator;
   while ((SoDB::read(&in, n) != FALSE) && (n != NULL))
      sep->addChild(n);

   // Create two selection roots - one will use the pick filter.
   SoSelection *topLevelSel = new SoSelection;
   topLevelSel->addChild(sep);
   topLevelSel->setPickFilterCallback(pickFilterCB);

   SoSelection *defaultSel = new SoSelection;
   defaultSel->addChild(sep);

   // Create two viewers, one to show the pick filter for top
   // level selection, the other to show default selection.
   SoXtExaminerViewer *viewer1 = new
            SoXtExaminerViewer(mainWindow);
   viewer1->setSceneGraph(topLevelSel);
   viewer1->setGLRenderAction(new SoBoxHighlightRenderAction());
   viewer1->redrawOnSelectionChange(topLevelSel);
   viewer1->setTitle("Top Level Selection");
```

```
SoXtExaminerViewer *viewer2 = new SoXtExaminerViewer();
viewer2->setSceneGraph(defaultSel);
viewer2->setGLRenderAction(new SoBoxHighlightRenderAction());
viewer2->redrawOnSelectionChange(defaultSel);
viewer2->setTitle("Default Selection");

viewer1->show();
viewer2->show();

SoXt::show(mainWindow);
SoXt::mainLoop();
}
```

Example 10-7 shows the use of the pick filter callback to pick through manipulators. In the complete example, the scene graph contains the text "Open Inventor." Clicking the left mouse on an object selects it and adds a manipulator to it. Clicking again deselects it and removes the manipulator. The pick filter is used to deselect the object rather than select the manipulator.

Example 10-7   Picking through Manipulators

```
SoPath *
pickFilterCB(void *, const SoPickedPoint *pick)
{
    SoPath *filteredPath = NULL;

    // See if the picked object is a manipulator.
    // If so, change the path so it points to the object the
    // manip is attached to.
    SoPath *p = pick->getPath();
    SoNode *n = p->getTail();
    if (n->isOfType(SoTransformManip::getClassTypeId())) {
        // Manip picked! We know the manip is attached
        // to its next sibling. Set up and return that path.
        int manipIndex = p->getIndex(p->getLength() - 1);
        filteredPath = p->copy(0, p->getLength() - 1);
        filteredPath->append(manipIndex + 1); // get next sibling
    }
    else filteredPath = p;

    return filteredPath;
}
```

Example 10-8 illustrates using the pick filter callback to truncate the pick path at a node kit. This filter facilitates editing the attributes of objects because the node kit takes care of the part creation details.

Example 10-8 Selecting Node Kits

```
// Truncate the pick path so a nodekit is selected
SoPath *
pickFilterCB(void *, const SoPickedPoint *pick)
{
    // See which child of selection got picked
    SoPath *p = pick->getPath();
    int i;
    for (i = p->getLength() - 1; i >= 0; i--) {
        SoNode *n = p->getNode(i);
        if (n->isOfType(SoShapeKit::getClassTypeId()))
            break;
    }

    // Copy the path down to the nodekit
    return p->copy(0, i+1);
}
```

## Chapter 11

File Format

Chapter Objectives

After reading this chapter, you'll be able to do the following:

- Write a scene graph to a file in ASCII or binary format
- Read a file into the Inventor database
- Use the Inventor file format as an alternative to creating scene graphs programmatically
- Read a scene graph from a buffer in memory

This chapter describes the Inventor ASCII file format. Whenever you apply a write action to a node, path, or path list, the output file is written in this format. You can read files that use this format into the Inventor scene database by using the read method on the database. The file format is also used for transferring 3D copy and paste data between processes.

Writing a Scene Graph

As described in Chapter 9, you can apply a write action to a node, path, or path list. When the write action is applied to a node, it writes the entire subgraph rooted at that node.

```
SoWriteAction writeAction;

writeAction.apply(root); //writes the entire scene graph to stdout
```

Reading a File into the Database

You can read a scene graph from a file into the scene database using the **readAll()** method on the Inventor database. This example reads a file with the given filename and returns a separator containing the file. It returns NULL if there is an error reading the file.

```
SoSeparator *
readFile(const char *filename)
{
   // Open the input file
   SoInput mySceneInput;
   if (!mySceneInput.openFile(filename)) {
      fprintf(stderr, "Cannot open file %s\n", filename);
      return NULL;
   }

   // Read the whole file into the database
   SoSeparator *myGraph = SoDB::readAll(&mySceneInput);
   if (myGraph == NULL) {
      fprintf(stderr, "Problem reading file\n");
      return NULL;
   }
   mySceneInput.closeFile();
   return myGraph;
}
```

There are two **read()** methods. One method reads a graph rooted by a node, returning a pointer to that node. The other reads a graph defined by a path. You must call the correct method, based on the contents of the input. When you read in a model, you usually read a node. If you are cutting and pasting with paths, you will need to read a path.

SoDB uses the **SoInput** class when reading Inventor data files. This class can also be used to read from a buffer in memory. By default, **SoInput** looks for a specified file in the current directory (unless the specification begins with /). You can add directories to the search path with the **addDirectory-First()** and **addDirectoryLast()** methods (see the *Open Inventor C++ Reference Manual* on **SoInput**). Use the **clearDirectories()** method to clear the directory list.

You can also add a list of directories that is specified as the value of an environment variable. Use the following methods on **SoInput**:

addEnvDirectoriesFirst()

addEnvDirectoriesLast()

File Format Syntax

The following sections outline the syntax for the Inventor ASCII file format. In this file format, extra white space created by spaces, tabs, and new lines is ignored. Comments begin with a number sign (#) anywhere on a line and continue to the end of the line:

```
# this is a comment in the Inventor file format
```

For simplicity, this discussion focuses on *writing* a scene graph to a file. This same format applies to files you create that will be *read* into the Inventor database.

See the *Open Inventor C++ Reference Manual* for descriptions of the file format for each Inventor class.

File Header

Every Inventor data file must have a standard header to identify it. This header is the first line of the file and has the following form:

```
#Inventor V2.0 ascii
```

or

```
#Inventor V2.0 binary
```

To determine whether a random file is an Inventor file, use the **SoDB::isValidHeader()** method and pass in the beginning of the file in question. Although the header may change from version to version (V2.0 is the current version), it is guaranteed to begin with a # sign, be no more than 80 characters, and end at a newline. Therefore, the C **fgets()** routine can be used. The **isValidHeader()** method returns TRUE if the file contains an Inventor header. Inventor also reads older (V1.0) files and converts them.

Writing a Node

A node is written with the following elements:

- Name of the node (without the **So** prefix)
- Open brace ({)
- *Fields* within the node (if any), followed by *children* of the node (if any)
- Close brace (})

For example:

```
DrawStyle {
    style       LINES
    lineWidth   3
    linePattern 255
}
```

Writing Values within a Field

Fields within a node are written as the name of the field, followed by the value or values contained in the field. If the field value has not been changed from its default value, that field is not written out. Fields within a node can be written in any order. An example of writing field values is as follows:

```
Transform {
    translation    0 -4 0.2
}

LightModel {
    model          BASE_COLOR
}

Material {
    ambientColor   .3 .1 .1
    diffuseColor   [.8 .7 .2,
                    1 .2 .2,
                    .2  1 .2,
                    .2 .2  1]
    specularColor  .4 .3 .1
    emissiveColor  .1  0 .1
}
```

Brackets surround multiple-value fields, with commas separating the values, as shown for the **diffuseColor** field in the preceding example. It's all right to have a comma after the last value as well:

[*value1, value2, value3,*]

Single-value (**SF**) fields do not contain any brackets or commas. Multiple-value (**MF**) fields usually have brackets, but they are not necessary if only one value is present:

```
specularColor   .4 .3 .1
```

or

```
specularColor   [.4 .3 .1]
```

The value that is written depends on the type of the field, as described in the following list.

Type of Field	Acceptable Formats
longs, shorts, unsigned shorts	integers, in decimal, hexadecimal, or octal; For example:

```
255
0xff
0177
```

floats	integer or floating point number. For example:

```
13
13.0
13.123
1.3e-2
```

names, strings	double quotation marks (" ") around the name if it is more than one word, or just the name (with no white space) if it is a single word (quotation marks are optional). For example:

```
label    " front left leg "
label    car
```

You can have any ASCII character in the string, including newlines and backslashes, except for double quotation marks. To include a double quotation mark in the string, precede it with a backslash (\ ").

enums	either the mnemonic form of the enum or the integer form. (The mnemonic form is recommended, both for portability and readability of code.) For example:

```
MaterialBinding {
   value    PER_FACE
}
```

Type of Field	Acceptable Formats (cont.)
bit mask	one or more mnemonic flags, separated by a vertical bar (|) if there are multiple flags. When more than one flag is used, parentheses are required:

```
Cylinder {
    parts    SIDES
}

Cylinder {
    parts    (SIDES | TOP)
}
```

vectors (SbVec*n*f, where *n* is the number of components of the vector)	*n* floats separated by white space:

```
PerspectiveCamera {
    position    0 0 9.5
}
```

colors	3 floats (RGB) separated by white space:

```
BaseColor {
    rgb    0.3 0.2 0.6
}
```

rotation	a 3-vector for the axis, followed by a float for the angle (in radians), separated by white space:

```
Transform {
    rotation    0 1 0 1.5708
    # y axis ... pi /2 radians
}
```

matrix	16 floats, separated by white space
path	an **SFPath** has one value, a pointer to a path. To write this value, write the path (see "Writing a Path" on page 292). An **MFPath** has multiple values, which are all pointers to paths. To write this value, enclose the path list in brackets, and use commas to separate each path:

[*first_path, second_path, ... nth_path*]

Type of Field	Acceptable Formats (cont.)
node	an **SFNode** has one value, a pointer to a node. To write this value, write the node. An **MFNode** has multiple values, which are all pointers to nodes. To write this value, enclose the node list in brackets, and use commas to separate each node: [*node1, node2, ... noden*]
Boolean	TRUE, FALSE or 0, 1:

```
SoFile {
    isWriteBack    FALSE
}
```

Ignore Flag

The Ignore flag for a field (see Chapter 3) is written as a tilde (~), either after or in place of the field value or values. For example:

```
transparency [ .9, .1 ] ~
```

or

```
transparency ~
```

The first case preserves the values even though the field is ignored. The second case uses the default value but ignores the field.

 Tip: The Ignore flag applies only to properties. It is not used for cameras, lights, and shapes.

Field Connections

Connections are written as the object containing the field or output connected to the field, followed by a period (.) and then the name of the field or output. For example:

```
Separator {
    DEF Trans Translation { translation  1 2 3 }
    Cube {}
}
Separator {
    Translation { translation 0 0 0 = USE Trans.translation }
    Cone {}
}
```

The value of a connected field (0 0 0 in this case) is optional, so the second **Translation** node could be written as

```
Translation { translation = USE Trans.translation }
```

If an ignored field is connected, the connection specification follows the Ignore flag:

```
translation 000 ~ = USE Trans.translation
#or
translation ~ = USE Trans.translation
```

If a value is given as well as a connection, the value is used for the field. If a value is sent along the connection later, it will override the value.

Global Fields

A global field needs to have at least one connection in order for it to be written out. It is written out in this format:

GlobalField {
  type
  value
}

The braces contain the type and value of the field. The name of the global field is stored as the name of the value field. For example, the **Text3** node could be connected to a global field (here, **currentFile**) that stores the current file name an application is working on. The **Text3** node would then always display that current file name. Here is the ASCII file format for that connection:

```
Text3 {
    string "" = GlobalField {
        type SFString
        currentFile "aircar.iv"
    } . currentFile
}
```

Writing an Engine

The syntax for an engine definition is the same as that of a nongroup node:

EngineType {
   input_fields
}

Engines can't be written on their own; they must be connected to at least one part of the scene graph. A field-to-engine connection is specified as follows:

fieldname value = engine . outputname

Here is an example of changing a sphere's radius using an **SoOneShot** engine:

```
Sphere {
    radius 0.5 = OneShot { duration 3.0 } . ramp
}
```

For a more complex example, see "Defining and Using Shared Instances of Nodes" on page 297.

Writing a Path

A path (see Chapter 3) is written with the following elements:

- The word **Path**
- Open brace (**{**)
- The entire subgraph that is rooted on the head node for the path
- Number of indices in the rest of the path chain
- The indices themselves
- Close brace (**}**)

When Inventor encounters separator groups within the subgraph, it ignores them if they do not affect the nodes in the path chain. Written indices for the children within a group are adjusted to account for the skipped separator groups. For example, in Figure 11-1, node *N* is counted as child index 1 when written, since the two previous children are separator groups that do not affect this node at all. (The indices in the path itself remain unchanged.)

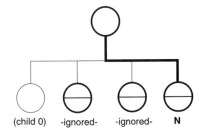

(child 0)   -ignored-   -ignored-   **N**

━━━ Path

Figure 11-1   Adjusting Path Indices to Account for Separator Groups

Note: If a path contains connections to nodes that are not part of the path, these nodes are not written out. For example, if a path contains an engine connected to a node outside the path, the engine will be written, but the node will not be.

Example 11-1 illustrates the process of writing a path to a file. First, here is the file for the scene graph, which creates chartreuse, rust, and violet spheres.

```
Separator {
   PerspectiveCamera {
      position 0 0 9.53374
      aspectRatio 1.09446
      nearDistance 0.0953375
      farDistance 19.0675
      focalDistance 9.53374
   }

   DirectionalLight {
   }

   Transform {
      rotation -0.189479 0.981839 -0.00950093 0.102051
      center 0 0 0
   }

   DrawStyle {
   }
```

```
Separator {
    LightModel {
        model    BASE_COLOR
    }
    Separator {
        Transform {
            translation -2.2 0 0
        }
        BaseColor {
            rgb .2 .6 .3    # chartreuse
        }
        Sphere { }
    }
    Separator {
        BaseColor {
            rgb .6 .3 .2    # rust
        }
        Sphere { }
    }
    Separator {
        Transform {
            translation 2.2 0 0
        }
        BaseColor {
            rgb .3 .2 .6    # violet
        }
        Sphere { }
    }
}
```

Figure 11-2 shows the scene graph for this file.

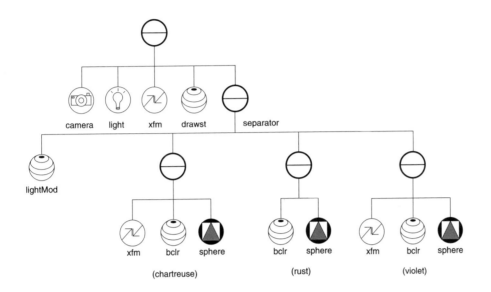

Figure 11-2   Scene Graph for a Scene with Three Spheres

If you pick the third sphere (the violet one), the pick path could be written to a file as shown in Example 11-1. First, the subgraph under the root node is written. This description is followed by the number of indices in the path (3), and the indices themselves (4, 1, 2), as shown in Figure 11-3.

Example 11-1   Writing a Path

```
Path {
    Separator {
        PerspectiveCamera {
            position 0 0 9.53374
            aspectRatio 1.09446
            nearDistance 0.0953375
            farDistance 19.0675
            focalDistance 9.53374
        }
        DirectionalLight {
        }
        Transform {
            rotation -0.189479 0.981839 -0.00950093 0.102051
        }
        DrawStyle {
        }
```

```
Separator {
   LightModel {
      model BASE_COLOR
   }
   Separator {
      Transform {
         translation 2.2 0 0
      }
      BaseColor {
         rgb 0.3 0.2 0.6
      }
      Sphere {
      }
   }
}
}
3
4
1
2
}
```

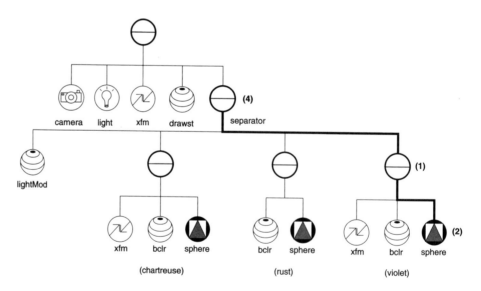

—— Path (x)

Figure 11-3   Pick Path for Violet Sphere

Defining and Using Shared Instances of Nodes

In the file format, the keyword DEF introduces a named instance of a node, path, or engine. It can be referenced later with the USE keyword. For example:

```
// This example shows keeping a cone between two cubes using an
// InterpolateVec3f engine.

Separator {
    DEF A Translation { translation -4 0 0 }
    Cube { }
}
Separator {
    DEF B Translation { translation 4 5 6 }
    Cube { }
}
Separator {
    Translation { translation 0 0 0 =
                  InterpolateVec3f {
                      input0 0 0 0 = USE A.translation
                      input1 0 0 0 = USE B.translation
                      alpha 0.5
                  } . output
              }
    Cone { }
}
```

The name can be any valid **SbName**. In certain cases, Inventor adds some extra characters to the name when the file is written out. For example, consider the somewhat unusual scene graph shown in Figure 11-4. To indicate which instance of the beachball node is used by node B, the scene graph is written out as follows:

```
Separator{
    Separator{
        DEF beachball+0
        DEF beachball+1
    }
    Separator{
        USE beachball+0
        USE beachball+1
    }
}
```

When the scene graph is read back in, the original names are preserved, but the +*n* notations are discarded.

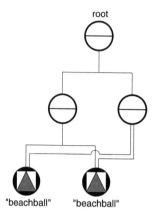

Figure 11-4   Shared Instances of Nodes

Writing a Node Kit

When a node kit is written, it includes one field for each part. For example:

```
AppearanceKit {
    lightModel    LightModel { model PHONG }
    drawStyle     DrawStyle  { style LINES }
    material      Material   { diffuseColor .5 .5 .5 }
    complexity    Complexity { value .5 }
}
```

In this format, the name of the field (**lightModel**) is followed by the name of the node (**LightModel**), and then the node's fields and values (each part is contained in an **SoSFNode** field). If the part has not been created, or if it is NULL, it is not written out. However, if a part is created by default (such as the shape part in the **SoShapeKit**), and if the part is explicitly set to NULL, it is written out.

This example shows nesting node kits. Here, the appearance kit is the value for the **appearance** field. The appearance kit, in turn, has a **material** field.

```
SeparatorKit {
    appearance      AppearanceKit {
       material     Material { diffuseColor   1 1 1 }
    }
}
```

When Inventor writes out a node kit, it writes out the intermediate parts. When you enter the information yourself, you can use a shorthand method and omit the intermediate parts. For example, if you omit the **AppearanceKit**, the **SeparatorKit** knows to add an **AppearanceKit** and put the **Material** node inside. So, you could simply enter this:

```
SeparatorKit {
    material    Material { diffuseColor    1 1 1 }
}
```

The file format for list parts within node kits is a bit more specialized. Each list part has three standard fields:

containerTypeName
for example, separator or switch; in string format

childTypeName   an **SoMFString** that lists the types of children that this node is allowed to contain

containerNode   the node that contains the children

For example, here is the **childList** part of an instance of **SoSeparatorKit**:

```
SeparatorKit {
    childList       NodeKitListPart {
        containerTypeName    "Separator"
        childTypeNames       "SeparatorKit"
        containerNode        Separator {
           SeparatorKit {
              transform      Transform { translation 1 0 0 }
           }
           SeparatorKit {
              transform      Transform { translation 0 1 0 }
           }
           SeparatorKit {
              transform      Transform { translation 0 0 1 }
           }
        }
    }
}
```

By default, Inventor does not write out the internal parts, such as separators and groups, or fields with default values. But if the node kit is in a path, everything is written out, as the following example shows. Generally, it writes out the parts in the reverse order they are defined in the catalog, with the leaf nodes first:

```
#Inventor V2.0 ascii

SeparatorKit {
    appearance      DEF +0 AppearanceKit {
        material    DEF +1 Material {
            diffuseColor    1 0 1
        }
    }
    childList       DEF +2 NodeKitListPart {
        containerTypeName    "Separator"
        childTypeNames        "SeparatorKit"
        containerNode         DEF +3 Separator {
            ShapeKit {
                appearance      DEF +4 AppearanceKit {
                    material    DEF +5 Material {}
                }
                transform    DEF +6 Transform {}
                shape    DEF +7 Cube {}
                topSeparator    Separator {
                    USE +4
                    USE +6
                    DEF +8 Separator {
                        USE +7
                    }
                }

                shapeSeparator    USE +8
            }
        }
    }
    topSeparator      Separator {
        USE +0
        USE +2
    }
}
```

Including Other Files

To include a file within another file, use an **SoFile** node. This node is useful when you are building scene graphs that include many objects. The objects can reside in their own files, and **SoFile** nodes can be used to refer to them without copying them directly into the new file. The **SoFile** node is written as

```
File {
    name "myFile.iv"
}
```

where the **name** field is the name of the file to be included. On read, the contents of the file myFile.iv are added as hidden children of **SoFile**. On write, Inventor just writes the filename (but not the children).

The objects within an **SoFile** node are not editable. You can copy the contents of an **SoFile** node using the method

```
SoFile::copyChildren()
```

or you can modify the **name** field of the **SoFile** node. Whenever the value of the **name** field changes, the new file is read in. If the name is not an absolute path name, the list of directories set on **SoInput** is used to search for the file (see "Reading a File into the Database" on page 284). **SoDB::read** automatically adds the directory of the file being read to **SoInput**'s list of directories to search.

For example, suppose you have myFile.iv, which contains windmill.iv.

Contents of /usr/tmp/myFile.iv:

```
#Inventor V2.0 ascii
File { name "myObjects/windmill.iv" }
```

Contents of /usr/tmp/myObjects/windmill.iv:

```
#Inventor V2.0 ascii
//format to make the windmill
```

When /usr/tmp/myFile.iv is read in, /usr/tmp is added to the directory search list. When the **SoFile** node in myFile.iv calls **SoDB::read**, **SoInput** will find /usr/tmp/myObjects/windmill.iv, and it will be read (the directory /usr/tmp/myObjects will also be added to the list of search directories). When reading finishes, /usr/tmp/myObjects and /usr/tmp will be removed from the search directories list.

ASCII and Binary Versions

The **SoOutput** object in an **SoWriteAction** has a **setBinary()** method, which sets whether the output should be in ASCII (default) or binary format (see Chapter 9). The **getOutput()** method returns a pointer to the **SoOutput**. When a file is written, Inventor inserts a header line that indicates whether the file is in ASCII or binary format, as well as the Inventor version number (see "File Header" on page 286).

Reading in Extender Nodes and Engines

As described in *The Inventor Toolmaker*, developers can create their own nodes or engines and use them in new applications. This section describes what happens if you read in a file with references to extender nodes and engines whose code may or may not be accessible to your program. (In most cases, nodes and engines are interchangeable, so the discussion refers only to nodes for simplicity. In cases where engines differ slightly from nodes, those differences are called out explicitly.)

When an Inventor node is read from a file, Inventor first checks to see if the node's type has been registered. If the name is found, an instance of that node is created and the fields for the node are read in. This situation occurs if your program is linked with the code for the new node.

However, if your program is not linked with the code for the new node, things become slightly more interesting. If your system supports dynamic loading of compiled objects, Inventor can find the compiled object and recognize the new node. In this case, the author of the new node supplies the compiled object for the node and places it in a directory that can be found by the system. (Check your release notes for information on whether your system supports dynamic loading of shared objects and how it implements searching directories for the objects.)

File Format for Unknown Nodes and Engines

If Inventor is unable to locate the code for the new node or engine, it creates an instance of the class **SoUnknownNode** or **SoUnknownEngine**. The first keyword in the file format for all new nodes is named **fields**, and it is followed by the field type and name of all fields defined within the node. For example:

```
WeirdNode {
    fields [ SFFloat length, SFLong data ]
    length 5.3
    Material {}
    Cube {}
}
```

This unknown node has two fields, **length** and **data**. Because the **data** field uses its default value, it is not written out. The node also has two children, an **SoMaterial** and an **SoCube**, which are listed after the fields of **WeirdNode**. These nodes are treated as hidden children and are not used for rendering, picking, or searching. They are only used by the write action.

The file format for new engines contains descriptions of both the inputs and outputs for the engine, as follows:

```
WeirdEngine {
    inputs [ SFFloat factor, SFFloat seed ]
    factor 100
    seed 0.5
    outputs [ SFFloat result ]
}
```

Since no code accompanies the node, most operations on the unknown node will not function. However, reading, writing, and searching can still be performed on this node (but not on its children).

Alternate Representation

The author of a new node class may also provide an alternate representation for the node, to be used in cases where the node is treated as an unknown node. This representation is specified in the **alternateRep** field for the node, which contains the complete scene graph for the alternate representation. This scene graph will be used in place of the actual node for picking, rendering, and bounding-box actions.

The following node kit provides an alternate representation:

```
Airplane {
    fields [ SFNode wing, SFNode fuselage, SFNode alternateRep ]
    wing Separator { ... the wing scene graph ... }
    fuselage Separator { ... the fuselage scene graph ... }
    alternateRep Separator {
        Cube {}
        Transform { translation 10 0 0 }
        Cone {}
    }
}
```

Reading from a String

"Reading a File into the Database" on page 284 showed you how to read from a file. Example 11-2 shows how you can read from a string stored in memory. Note that when a graph is read from a buffer, you do not need the file-header string. This example creates a dodecahedron from an indexed face set.

Example 11-2   Reading from a String

```
// Reads a dodecahedron from the following string:
// (Note: ANSI compilers automatically concatenate
// adjacent string literals together, so the compiler sees
// this as one big string)

static char *dodecahedron =
    "Separator { "
    "    Material { "
    "       diffuseColor [ "
    "           1  0  0,    0 1  0,    0  0 1,    0  1  1, "
    "           1  0  1,   .5 1  0,   .5  0 1,   .5  1  1, "
    "           1 .3 .7,   .3 1 .7,   .3 .7 1,   .5 .5 .8 "
    "       ] "
    "    } "
    "    MaterialBinding { value PER_FACE } "
    "    Coordinate3 { "
    "       point [ "
    "           1.7265 0 0.618,    1 1 1, "
    "           0 0.618 1.7265,    0 -0.618 1.7265, "
    "           1 -1 1,    -1 -1 1, "
    "           -0.618 -1.7265 0,    0.618 -1.7265 0, "
    "           1 -1 -1,    1.7265 0 -0.618, "
```

```
"         1 1 -1,     0.618 1.7265 0, "
"         -0.618 1.7265 0,     -1 1 1, "
"         -1.7265 0 0.618,     -1.7265 0 -0.618, "
"         -1 -1 -1,     0 -0.618 -1.7265, "
"         0 0.618 -1.7265,     -1 1 -1 "
"      ] "
"   } "
"   IndexedFaceSet { "
"      coordIndex [ "
"         1, 2, 3, 4, 0, -1,  0, 9, 10, 11, 1, -1, "
"         4, 7, 8, 9, 0, -1,  3, 5, 6, 7, 4, -1, "
"         2, 13, 14, 5, 3, -1,  1, 11, 12, 13, 2, -1, "
"         10, 18, 19, 12, 11, -1,  19, 15, 14, 13, 12, -1, "
"         15, 16, 6, 5, 14, -1,  8, 7, 6, 16, 17, -1, "
"         9, 8, 17, 18, 10, -1,  18, 17, 16, 15, 19, -1, "
"      ] "
"   } "
"}";

// Routine to create a scene graph representing a dodecahedron
SoNode *
makeDodecahedron()
{
   // Read from the string.
   SoInput in;
   in.setBuffer(dodecahedron, strlen(dodecahedron));

   SoNode *result;
   SoDB::read(&in, result);

   return result;
}
```

Part V

Application Tools

## Chapter 12

Sensors

Chapter Objectives

After reading this chapter, you'll be able to do the following:

- Describe the different types of sensors that can be used in a scene graph and give possible uses for each type

- Understand how sensors are scheduled in the delay queue and the timer queue and when they are processed

- Write callback functions for use by data and timer sensors

- Set the priority of a delay-queue sensor

This chapter describes how to add sensors to the scene graph. A sensor is an Inventor object that watches for various types of events and invokes a user-supplied callback function when these events occur. Sensors fall into two general categories: *data sensors*, which respond to changes in the data contained in a node's fields, in a node's children, or in a path; and *timer sensors*, which respond to certain scheduling conditions.

Introduction to Sensors

Sensors are a special class of objects that can be attached to the database. They respond to database changes or to certain timer events by invoking a user-supplied callback function. Data sensors (derived from **SoDataSensor**) monitor part of the database and inform the application when that part changes. Timer sensors (such as **SoAlarmSensor** and **SoTimerSensor**) notify the application when certain types of timer events occur. Note that timer "events" occur within Inventor and are not part of the event model described in Chapter 10. See Figure 12-1 for a diagram of the portion of the class tree that includes sensors.

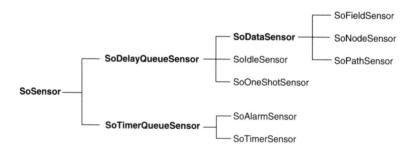

Figure 12-1   Sensor Classes

Sensor Queues

As the class tree in Figure 12-1 suggests, sensors are placed in one of two queues:

- *Timer queue*, which is called when an alarm or timer sensor is scheduled to go off

- *Delay queue*, which is called whenever the CPU is idle (that is, there are no events or timer sensors to handle) or after a user-specifiable time-out

When processing of either queue begins, all sensors in that queue are processed once, in order (see "Using a Field Sensor" on page 314).

Key Terms

The following discussion of data and timer sensors uses a few new terms.

- *Triggering* a sensor means calling its user-defined callback function and removing it from the queue.

- *Scheduling* a sensor means adding it to a queue so that it can be triggered at some future time. If a sensor is already scheduled, scheduling it again has no effect. *Unscheduling* a sensor means removing it from the queue without processing it.

- *Notifying* a data sensor means letting it know that the node (or field or path) to which it is attached has changed. A data sensor automatically schedules itself when it is notified of a change.

Data Sensors

There are three types of data sensors:

- **SoFieldSensor**, which is attached to a field

- **SoNodeSensor**, which is attached to a node

- **SoPathSensor**, which is attached to a path

An **SoFieldSensor** is notified whenever data in a particular field changes. An **SoNodeSensor** is notified when data changes within a certain node, when data changes within any of the child nodes underneath that node, or when the graph topology changes under the node. An **SoPathSensor** is notified whenever data within any of the nodes in a certain path changes, or when nodes are added to or deleted from that path. A node is considered to be *in the path* if traversing the path would cause the node to be traversed.

❖ **Tip:** Setting the value of a field to the same value it had before (for example,

```
field.setValue(field.getValue()))
```

is considered a change. Calling the **touch()** method of a field or node is also considered a change.

A render area attaches a node sensor to the root of the scene graph so that it can detect when you make any changes to the scene. It then automatically renders the scene again.

Data sensors are also useful if you want to monitor changes in part of a scene and communicate them to another element in the scene. For example, suppose you have a material in the scene graph with an editor attached to it. If the material changes, the editor needs to change the values of its sliders to reflect the new material. An **SoNodeSensor** supplies this feedback to the material editor.

❖ **Tip:** Field-to-field connections are another way of keeping different parts of the scene graph in sync. See Chapter 13.

General Sequence for Data Sensors

The following sequence describes the necessary steps for setting up a data sensor:

1. Construct the sensor.

2. Set the callback function (see the next section).

3. Set the priority of the sensor (see "Priorities" on page 313).

4. Attach the sensor to a field, node, or path.

5. When you are finished with the sensor, delete it.

Callback Function

Callback functions, as their name suggests, allow Inventor to call back to the application when some predefined event occurs. A callback function usually takes a single argument of type **void*** that can be used to pass extra user-defined data to the function. Callback functions used by sensors also have a second argument of type **SoSensor***. This argument is useful if the same callback function is used by more than one sensor. The argument is filled with a pointer to the sensor that caused the callback.

In C++, a sensor callback function can be declared as a static member function of a class. In this case, because static functions have no concept of **this**, you need to explicitly pass an instance of the class you want to modify as user data:

```
colorSensor->setData(this);
```

Nonstatic C++ member functions are not suitable for use as callback functions.

Priorities

Classes derived from **SoDelayQueueSensor** use priorities to maintain sorting in the delay queue. The following methods are used to set and obtain the priority of a given sensor:

setPriority(*priority*)
> assigns a priority to the sensor. All delay queue sensors have a default priority of 100. Sensors are sorted in the queue in order of their priority, with lower numbers first.

getPriority()   obtains the priority of a given sensor.

getDefaultPriority()
> obtains the default priority (100) for a sensor.

A sensor with a priority of 0 has the highest priority. It triggers as soon as the change to the scene graph is complete. If two sensors have the same priority, there is no guarantee about which sensor will trigger first.

The **SoXtRenderArea** has a redraw data sensor with a default priority of 10000. You can schedule other sensors before or after the redraw by choosing appropriate priorities.

For example, to set the priority of a sensor so that it is triggered right before redraw:

```
SoNodeSensor    *s;
SoRenderArea    *renderArea;

s->setPriority(renderArea->getRedrawPriority() - 1);
```

Triggering a Data Sensor

When data in the sensor's field, node, or path changes, the following things happen:

1. The sensor is notified that the data changed.

2. The sensor is *scheduled*—that is, it is added to the delay queue, according to its priority.

3. At some future time, the queue is processed and all sensors in it are triggered.

4. When triggered, the sensor is removed from the queue, and it invokes its callback function.

5. The callback function executes. This function can access the trigger field, trigger node, or trigger path responsible for the original notification (see "Using the Trigger Node and Field" on page 316).

Using a Field Sensor

Example 12-1 shows attaching a field sensor to the **position** field of a viewer's camera. A callback function reports each new camera position.

Example 12-1   Attaching a Field Sensor

```
#include <Inventor/SoDB.h>
#include <Inventor/Xt/SoXt.h>
#include <Inventor/Xt/viewers/SoXtExaminerViewer.h>
#include <Inventor/nodes/SoCamera.h>
#include <Inventor/nodes/SoSeparator.h>
#include <Inventor/sensors/SoFieldSensor.h>
```

```
// Callback that reports whenever the viewer's position changes.
static void
cameraChangedCB(void *data, SoSensor *)
{
    SoCamera *viewerCamera = (SoCamera *)data;

    SbVec3f cameraPosition = viewerCamera->position.getValue();
    printf("Camera position: (%g,%g,%g)\n",
            cameraPosition[0], cameraPosition[1],
            cameraPosition[2]);
}

main(int argc, char **argv)
{
    if (argc != 2) {
        fprintf(stderr, "Usage: %s filename.iv\n", argv[0]);
        exit(1);
    }

    Widget myWindow = SoXt::init(argv[0]);
    if (myWindow == NULL) exit(1);

    SoInput inputFile;
    if (inputFile.openFile(argv[1]) == FALSE) {
        fprintf(stderr, "Could not open file %s\n", argv[1]);
        exit(1);
    }

    SoSeparator *root = SoDB::readAll(&inputFile);
    root->ref();

    SoXtExaminerViewer *myViewer =
            new SoXtExaminerViewer(myWindow);
    myViewer->setSceneGraph(root);
    myViewer->setTitle("Camera Sensor");
    myViewer->show();

    // Get the camera from the viewer, and attach a
    // field sensor to its position field:
    SoCamera *camera = myViewer->getCamera();
    SoFieldSensor *mySensor =
            new SoFieldSensor(cameraChangedCB, camera);
    mySensor->attach(&camera->position);

    SoXt::show(myWindow);
    SoXt::mainLoop();
}
```

Using the Trigger Node and Field

You can use one of the following methods to obtain the field, node, or path that initiated the notification of any data sensor:

- getTriggerField()
- getTriggerNode()
- getTriggerPath()

These methods work only for immediate (priority 0) sensors.

The *trigger path* is the chain of nodes from the last node notified down to the node that initiated notification. To obtain the trigger path, you must first use **setTriggerPathFlag()** to set the trigger-path flag to TRUE since it's expensive to save the path information. You must make this call before the sensor is notified. Otherwise, information on the trigger path is not saved and **getTriggerPath()** always returns NULL. (By default, this flag is set to FALSE.) The trigger field and trigger node are always available. Note that **getTriggerField()** returns NULL if the change was not to a field (for example, **addChild()** or **touch()** was called).

Example 12-2 shows using **getTriggerNode()** and **getTriggerField()** in a sensor callback function that prints a message whenever changes are made to the scene graph.

Example 12-2 Using the Trigger Node and Field

```
#include <Inventor/SoDB.h>
#include <Inventor/nodes/SoCube.h>
#include <Inventor/nodes/SoSeparator.h>
#include <Inventor/nodes/SoSphere.h>
#include <Inventor/sensors/SoNodeSensor.h>

// Sensor callback function:
static void
rootChangedCB(void *, SoSensor *s)
{
    // We know the sensor is really a data sensor:
    SoDataSensor *mySensor = (SoDataSensor *)s;

    SoNode *changedNode = mySensor->getTriggerNode();
    SoField *changedField = mySensor->getTriggerField();

    printf("The node named '%s' changed\n",
            changedNode->getName().getString());
```

```
   if (changedField != NULL) {
      SbName fieldName;
      changedNode->getFieldName(changedField, fieldName);
      printf(" (field %s)\n", fieldName.getString());
   }
   else
      printf(" (no fields changed)\n");
}

main(int, char **)
{
   SoDB::init();

   SoSeparator *root = new SoSeparator;
   root->ref();
   root->setName("Root");

   SoCube *myCube = new SoCube;
   root->addChild(myCube);
   myCube->setName("MyCube");

   SoSphere *mySphere = new SoSphere;
   root->addChild(mySphere);
   mySphere->setName("MySphere");

   SoNodeSensor *mySensor = new SoNodeSensor;

   mySensor->setPriority(0);
   mySensor->setFunction(rootChangedCB);
   mySensor->attach(root);

   // Now, make a few changes to the scene graph; the sensor's
   // callback function will be called immediately after each
   // change.
   myCube->width = 1.0;
   myCube->height = 2.0;
   mySphere->radius = 3.0;
   root->removeChild(mySphere);
}
```

Other Delay-Queue Sensors

In addition to data sensors, two other types of sensors are added to the delay queue: the **SoOneShotSensor** and the **SoIdleSensor**.

General Sequence for One-Shot and Idle Sensors

The following sequence describes the necessary steps for setting up one-shot and idle sensors:

1. Construct the sensor.
2. Set the callback function (see "Callback Function" on page 313).
3. Set the priority of the sensor (see "Priorities" on page 313).
4. Schedule the sensor using the **schedule()** method.
5. When you are finished with the sensor, delete it.

Note that these sensors must be scheduled explicitly. Use the **unschedule()** method to remove a sensor from the queue.

SoOneShotSensor

An **SoOneShotSensor** invokes its callback once whenever the delayed sensor queue is processed. This sensor is useful for a task that does not need to be performed immediately or for tasks that *should* not be performed immediately (possibly because they are time-consuming). For example, when handling events for a device that generates events quickly (such as the mouse), you want to be able to process each event quickly so that events don't clog up the event queue. If you know that a certain type of event is time-consuming, you can schedule it with a one-shot sensor. For example:

```
handleEvent(SoHandleEventAction *action)
{
    //Check for correct event type ...
    .
    .
    .
    // Remember information from event for later processing
    currentMousePosition = event->getPosition();
```

```
    // Schedule a one-shot sensor to do hard work later
    SoOneShotSensor oneShot = new SoOneShotSensor(
         OneShotTriggerCallback, NULL);
    oneShot->schedule();
}
void OneShotTriggerCallback(void *userData, SoSensor *)
{
    // Do lengthy operation based on current mouse position;
}
```

Note that sensors that invoke their callback one time only, such as **SoOneShotSensor**, **SoIdleSensor**, and **SoAlarmSensor**, continue to exist after their callback has been executed, but they do not trigger again unless they are rescheduled. Use the **unschedule()** method to stop any sensor from invoking its callback when it is scheduled.

The following example uses an **SoOneShotSensor** to delay rendering until the CPU is idle.

```
SoOneShotSensor *renderTask;

main() {
    ...
    renderTask = new SoOneShotSensor(doRenderCallback, NULL);
    // ... set up events, UI, which will call changeScene()
    // routine.
}

void
changeScene()
{
    // ... change scene graph ...
    renderTask->schedule();
}

void
doRenderCallback(void *userData, SoSensor *)
{
    // ... does rendering ...
}
```

SoIdleSensor

An **SoIdleSensor** invokes its callback once whenever the application is idle (there are no events or timers waiting to be processed). Use an idle sensor for low-priority tasks that should be done only when there is nothing else to do. Call the sensor's **schedule()** method in its callback function if you want it to go off repeatedly (but beware, since this keeps the CPU constantly busy). Note that idle sensors may never be processed if events or timers happen so often that there is no idle time; see "Processing the Sensor Queues" on page 323 for details.

Timer-Queue Sensors

Timer-queue sensors, like data sensors, can be used to invoke user-specified callbacks. Instead of attaching a timer-queue sensor to a node or path in the scene graph, however, you simply *schedule* it, so that its callback is invoked at a specific time. (Timer-queue sensors are sorted within the timer queue by time rather than by priority.) Inventor includes two types of timer-queue sensors: **SoAlarmSensor** and **SoTimerSensor**.

General Sequence for Timer-Queue Sensors

The following sequence describes the necessary steps for setting up timer-queue sensors:

1. Construct the sensor.
2. Set the callback function (see "Callback Function" on page 313).
3. Set the timing parameters for the sensor.
4. Schedule the sensor using the **schedule()** method.
5. When you are finished with the sensor, delete it.

Timing parameters (when and how often the sensor is triggered) should not be changed while a sensor is scheduled. Use the **unschedule()** method to remove a sensor from the queue, change the parameter(s), and then schedule the sensor again.

SoAlarmSensor

An **SoAlarmSensor**, like an alarm clock, is set to go off at a specified time. When that time is reached or passed, the sensor's callback function is invoked. A calendar program might use an **SoAlarmSensor**, for example, to put a flag on the screen to indicate that it's time for your scheduled 2 o'clock meeting.

Use one of the following methods to set the time for this sensor:

setTime(*time*)   schedules a sensor to occur at *time*

setTimeFromNow(*time*)
                schedules a sensor to occur at a certain amount of *time* from now

The time is specified using the **SbTime** class, which provides several different formats for time. Use the **getTime()** method of **SoAlarmSensor** to obtain the scheduled time for an alarm sensor.

Example 12-3 shows using an **SoAlarmSensor** to raise a flag on the screen when one minute has passed.

Example 12-3   Using an Alarm Sensor

```
static void
raiseFlagCallback(void *data, SoSensor *)
{
   // We know data is really a SoTransform node:
   SoTransform *flagAngleXform = (SoTransform *)data;

   // Rotate flag by 90 degrees about the z axis:
   flagAngleXform->rotation.setValue(SbVec3f(0,0,1), M_PI/2);
}


{
   ...

   SoTransform *flagXform = new SoTransform;

   // Create an alarm that will call the flag-raising callback:
   SoAlarmSensor *myAlarm =
      new SoAlarmSensor(raiseFlagCallback, flagXform);
   myAlarm->setTimeFromNow(60.0);
   myAlarm->schedule();
}
```

SoTimerSensor

An **SoTimerSensor** is similar to an **SoAlarmSensor**, except that it is set to go off at regular intervals—like the snooze button on your alarm clock. You might use an **SoTimerSensor** for certain types of animation, for example, to move the second hand of an animated clock on the screen. You can set the interval and the base time for an **SoTimerSensor** using these methods:

setInterval(*interval*)

> schedules a sensor to occur at a given *interval*, for example, every minute. The default interval is 1/30 of a second.

setBaseTime(*time*)

> schedules a sensor to occur starting at a given *time*. The default base time is right now—that is, when the sensor is first scheduled.

Before changing either the interval or the base time, you must first unschedule the sensor, as shown in Example 12-4.

Example 12-4 creates two timer sensors. The first sensor rotates an object. The second sensor goes off every 5 seconds and changes the interval of the rotating sensor. The rotating sensor alternates between once per second and ten times per second. (This example is provided mainly for illustration purposes. It would be better (and easier) to use two engines to do the same thing (see Chapter 13).

Example 12-4   Using a Timer Sensor

```
// This function is called either 10 times/second or once every
// second; the scheduling changes every 5 seconds (see below):
static void
rotatingSensorCallback(void *data, SoSensor *)
{
   // Rotate an object...
   SoRotation *myRotation = (SoRotation *)data;
   SbRotation currentRotation = myRotation->rotation.getValue();
   currentRotation = SbRotation(SbVec3f(0,0,1), M_PI/90.0) *
           currentRotation;
   myRotation->rotation.setValue(currentRotation);
}
```

```
// This function is called once every 5 seconds, and
// reschedules the other sensor.
static void
schedulingSensorCallback(void *data, SoSensor *)
{
   SoTimerSensor *rotatingSensor = (SoTimerSensor *)data;
   rotatingSensor->unschedule();
   if (rotatingSensor->getInterval() == 1.0)
      rotatingSensor->setInterval(1.0/10.0);
   else
      rotatingSensor->setInterval(1.0);
      rotatingSensor->schedule();
}


{

   ...

   SoRotation *myRotation = new SoRotation;
   root->addChild(myRotation);

   SoTimerSensor *rotatingSensor =
      new SoTimerSensor(rotatingSensorCallback, myRotation);
   rotatingSensor->setInterval(1.0); //scheduled once per second
   rotatingSensor->schedule();

   SoTimerSensor *schedulingSensor =
   new SoTimerSensor(schedulingSensorCallback, rotatingSensor);
   schedulingSensor->setInterval(5.0); // once per 5 seconds
   schedulingSensor->schedule();
}
```

Processing the Sensor Queues

The following descriptions apply only to applications using the Inventor
Component Library with the Xt toolkit. Other window system toolkits may
have a different relationship between processing of the different queues. If
you aren't interested in the details of how timers are scheduled, you can
skip this section.

The general order of processing is event queue, timer queue, delay queue. A slight deviation from this order arises because the delay queue is also processed at regular intervals, whether or not there are timers or events pending. The sequence can be described as follows:

SoXt main loop calls XtAppMainLoop:

```
BEGIN:
If there's an event waiting:
   Process all pending timers.
   Process the delay queue if the delay queue time-out is
            reached.
   Process the event.
   Go back to BEGIN.
else (no event waiting)
   if there are timers,
      Process timers.
      Go back to BEGIN.
else (no timers or events pending)
   Process delay queue.
   Go back to BEGIN.
```

When the timer queue is processed, the following conditions are guaranteed:

- All timer or alarm sensors that are scheduled to go off before or at the time processing of the queue ends are triggered, in order.

- When timer sensors are rescheduled, they are all rescheduled at the same time, after they have all been triggered.

For example, in Figure 12-2, at time A after the redraw, the timer queue is processed. Three timers have been scheduled in the queue (timers 0, 1, and 2). Timers 0 and 1 are ready to go off (their trigger time has already passed). Timer 2 is set to go off sometime in the future. The sequence is as follows:

1. Timer 0 is triggered.

2. Timer 1 is triggered.

3. The scheduler checks the timer queue (the time is now B) and notices that timer 2's time has passed as well , so it triggers timer 2.

4. Timers 0, 1, and 2 are rescheduled at time C.

5. The scheduler returns to the main event loop to check for pending events.

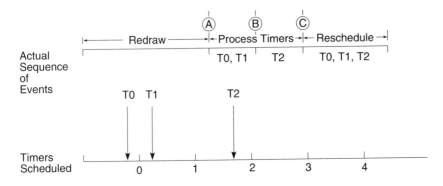

Figure 12-2   Triggering and Rescheduling Timers

The delay queue is processed when there are no events or timer sensors pending or when the delay queue's time-out interval elapses. By default, the delay queue times out 30 times a second. You can change this interval with the **SoDB::setDelaySensorTimeout()** method. Idle sensors are ignored when the delay sensor causes processing of the delay queue (because the CPU is not really idle under this condition).

When the delay queue is processed, the following conditions are guaranteed:

* All sensors in the delay queue are triggered, in order of priority.

* Each sensor is triggered once and only once, regardless of whether the sensor reschedules itself.

## Chapter 13

Engines

Chapter Objectives

After reading this chapter, you'll be able to do the following:

- Connect fields in a scene graph to each other
- Create and use global fields in the database
- Connect a variety of engines to fields and other engines in a scene graph
- Disable engine connections temporarily
- Create a simple engine network
- Animate parts of a scene using engines
- Use the rotor, blinker, shutter, and pendulum nodes to animate parts of a scene graph

This chapter describes *engines*, classes of Inventor objects that can be connected to fields in the scene graph and used to *animate* parts of the scene or to *constrain* certain elements of the scene to each other. It also describes how fields can be connected to engines and to other fields, and how to use and create *global fields* in the database.

Introduction to Engines

In earlier chapters, you've created scene graphs with 3D objects that responded to user events. The 3D objects themselves were fixed, and they moved only in response to user interaction or to sensor activity. In this chapter, you'll learn about a new class of object, called *engines*, that allows you to encapsulate both motion and geometry into a single scene graph. Just as you would connect a real-world engine to other equipment to spin a flywheel or turn a fan belt, you "wire" engine objects into the scene database to cause animated movement or other complex behavior in the scene graph. Engines can also be connected to other engines so that they move or react in relation to each other, and eventually make changes to the Inventor database.

As a simple example, consider a scene graph that describes the geometry for a windmill. You can attach an engine object that describes the rotation of the windmill blades and performs an incremental rotation of the blades in response to time. This scene graph, including the engine, can be saved in an Inventor file. Whenever the scene graph is read in, the windmill is displayed *and* the blades animate. Both the geometry and the behavior are described by the nodes and engines in the scene graph.

A more complex example would involve wiring two objects together. For example, you might create a scene with a car whose motion is based on an engine object. A second engine could look at the car's motion and turn that information into camera motion so that the camera could follow the moving car. Or you might wire two engines together so that one engine affects the activity of the other engine. In the case of the windmill, you could connect a second engine in front of the rotation engine to filter time so that the windmill blades rotate only between the hours of nine in the morning and five at night.

In some cases, you could use either a sensor or an engine to create a certain effect. Table 13-1 compares sensors and engines to help you weigh the trade-offs between the two.

Sensors	Engines
Are part of the application (are not written to file)	Are part of the scene graph (can be read from file and written to file)
Have user-defined callback functions	Have built-in functions
Allow explicit control over order of firing	Are evaluated automatically
Can be attached to any kind of field (field data sensors)	Have inputs and outputs of a fixed type
Can affect objects outside the scene graph	Can affect only other nodes or engines in a scene graph

Table 13-1   Comparison of Sensors and Engines

General Uses of Engines

Engines are generally used in two different ways:

- To animate parts of a scene

- To constrain one part of a scene in relation to some other part of the scene

Figures 13-1 and 13-2 show applications that use engines. In Figure 13-1, four different classes of links are created—struts, hinges, cranks, and double struts. Engines are used to connect links end-to-end. The objects in Figure 13-2 use engines to edit transform nodes that animate the animals and objects in the scene.

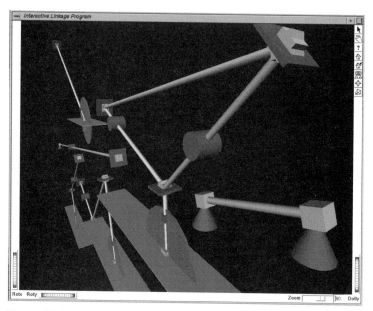

Figure 13-1　Mechanisms Made from a Set of Link Classes

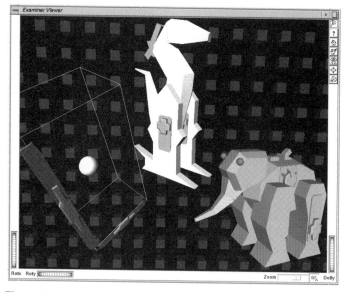

Figure 13-2　Objects That Use Engines for Animation and Placement

As shown in Example 13-1 later in this chapter, you can connect parts of a scene to a clock so that animation in the scene occurs in relation to changes in time. Example 13-6 shows an example of constraints, where the movement of an object is constrained to a set path.

You can think of an engine as a black box that receives input values, performs some operation on them, and then copies the results into one or more outputs. Both the inputs and the outputs of the engine can be connected to other fields or engines in the scene graph. When an engine's output values change, those new values are sent to any fields or engines connected to them.

An engine, shown in Figure 13-3, has inputs derived from **SoField** and outputs derived from **SoEngineOutput**. Each engine evaluates a built-in function when its input values change. The resulting output values are then sent to all fields and engines connected to that engine. Because **SoEngine** is derived from the **SoBase** class, it includes methods for reading and writing to files.

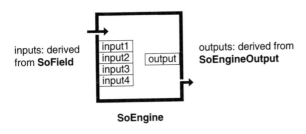

Figure 13-3   Anatomy of an Engine

For example, the engine shown in Figure 13-3 could represent **SoComposeVec4f**, an engine that creates an **SoMFVec4f** object. It has four inputs of type **SoMFFloat** and one output of type **SoMFVec4f**. This engine composes the four inputs into one **SoMFVec4f** output.

Types of Engines

Figure 13-4 shows the class tree for engines, which can be grouped according to the kinds of operations they perform.

Arithmetic engines are as follows:

- SoCalculator

- SoBoolOperation

- SoInterpolateFloat, SoInterpolateRotation, SoInterpolateVec2f, SoInterpolateVec3f, SoInterpolateVec4f

- SoTransformVec3f

- SoComposeVec2f, SoDecomposeVec2f
  SoComposeVec3f, SoDecomposeVec3f
  SoComposeVec4f, SoDecomposeVec4f
  SoComposeRotation, SoDecomposeRotation
  SoComposeMatrix, SoDecomposeMatrix

- SoComputeBoundingBox

Animation engines are as follows:

- SoElapsedTime

- SoOneShot

- SoTimeCounter

Triggered engines are as follows:

- SoCounter

- SoOnOff

- SoTriggerAny

- SoGate

Engines used for array manipulation are as follows:

- SoSelectOne

- SoConcatenate

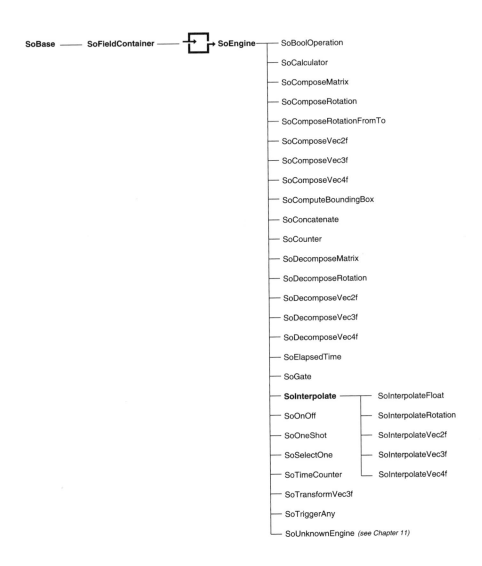

Figure 13-4   Engine Class Tree

Making Field Connections

Use the **connectFrom()** method on **SoField** to connect a field to another field or engine. When you connect fields of different types, the value of the input field is automatically converted to the new output field type. The syntax for connecting a field is as follows:

void **connectFrom**(SoField *field);

void **connectFrom**(SoEngineOutput *engineOutput);

For example, to connect the **orientation** field in an **SoPerspective** camera to the **rotation** field of an **SoTransform**:

```
xform->rotation.connectFrom(&pCamera->orientation);
```

To connect the **SoElapsedTime** engine to the **string** field of an **SoText3** node:

```
yourText->string.connectFrom(&elapsedTime->timeOut);
```

Suppose you connect two fields as shown in Figure 13-5. In this example, the top arrow indicates that *fieldA* is the source field and *fieldB* is the destination field. The bottom arrow indicates that *fieldB* is the source field and *fieldA* is the destination field. Once you have set up this connection, whenever you change *fieldA*, *fieldB* changes. When you change *fieldB*, *fieldA* changes. You may be concerned that you've set up an infinite loop where the two fields continuously update each other. Actually, when the value in *fieldA* changes, *fieldB* changes. At this point, *fieldA* knows that it has already been changed and does not change again.

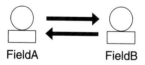

FieldA   FieldB

Figure 13-5   Field-to-Field Connections

Use the **disconnect()** method to break a field connection (on the destination field), and use the **isConnected()** method to query whether a connection exists. Methods such as **setValue()** can also be called on a field that is connected from another field or engine. Whoever sets the field value last, wins.

Multiple Connections

The term *engine network* refers to the collection of engines and fields that are "wired together" in the scene graph. When planning larger engine networks, you may sometimes consider having multiple connections to a field or engine. The rule to follow is that a given field or engine can have only one incoming connection, but it can have multiple outgoing connections. Figure 13-6 illustrates this principle.

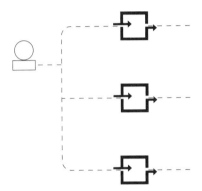

Figure 13-6   Multiple Outputs Are Allowed

If you call **connectFrom()** on a field or engine that has already been connected from a different source, the original connection is broken and the new connection is made.

Field Conversion

When you connect fields of different types, Inventor automatically converts values from one type to another. It performs the following conversions when necessary:

- Any field type to **String**
- **String** to any field type
- Between any two of **Bool, Float, Long, Short, ULong, UShort**
- Between **Color** and **Vec3f**
- Between **Float** and **Time**
- Between **Matrix** and **Rotation**

- Between **Name** and **Enum**

- Between **Rotation** and **Vec4f** (quaternion)

- From an **MF** field to its **SF** version, and from an **SF** field to its **MF** version

Multiple-step conversions are not supported—that is, although you can convert directly from a **Vec4f** to a **Rotation** and a **Rotation** to a **Matrix**, you cannot convert from a **Vec4f** to a **Matrix**.

If your program tries to connect a field to a field or engine output of a different type and no conversion between the types exists, the connection will not be made and a debugging error will occur. See *The Inventor Toolmaker* for details on how to create your own field converter.

Reference Counting

Reference counting for engines is similar to that for nodes. Field-to-field connections, including connections from an engine's input to a field, do not increment any reference counts. Each engine-output-to-field connection increments the engine's reference count by 1. Similarly, removing an engine output's field connection decrements its reference count. If the last connection is removed, the reference count for that engine goes to 0 and it is deleted. To preserve the engine when you are disconnecting it, reference it. Also, be aware that field connections are broken when the node or engine containing the field is deleted. This, in turn, could cause a connected engine to be deleted as well.

Disabling a Connection

To temporarily disable a field connection, call **enableConnection**(FALSE) on the destination field or call **enable**(FALSE) on the engine output.

This method is useful when you want to temporarily disable a large engine network. If you disconnect the field from the engine, that engine might be unreferenced to 0, and then mistakenly deleted. Disabling a field connection does not affect the engine's reference count. Use the **isConnectionEnabled**() method to query whether a connection has been enabled.

Updating Values

When you change one value in an engine network, you can assume that all other values that depend on this value are updated at once. In fact, for efficiency, fields and inputs are marked when they are out of date, but they are updated only when their values are used. A complicated engine network, for example, could be connected to an unselected child of a switch group and never used. In this case, its values could be marked as needing to be updated but never actually reevaluated because the engine network is never traversed.

Some engines, such as the gate and animation engines, can selectively control when their values are updated. Many of these engines use a field of type **SoSFTrigger** that updates the output value one time only when the field is touched. See "Gate Engine" on page 344 for more information.

Global Fields

Global fields are fields in the Inventor database that you can access by name and that are not contained in any specific node or engine. One built-in global field is provided: the **realTime** global field, which is of type **SoSFTime**. This field contains the current real-clock time and can be connected to fields or engines to create clock-based animation. You can create additional global fields as required. If you were creating a key-frame animation editor, for example, you might want to create a "current frame" field that could be connected to various engines. Once the field is created, you use the standard field methods to connect it to other parts of the scene graph.

Use the **createGlobalField()** method of **SoDB** to create a global field:

static SoField ***SoDB::createGlobalField**(const SbName &*name*,
                                     SoType *type*);

There can be only one global field with a given name. If there is already a field with the given name and type, it is returned. If there is already a field with the given name, but it is of an incompatible type, NULL is returned.

The **getGlobalField()** method returns the global field with the given name:

static SoField *SoDB::getGlobalField(const SbName &*name*);

The type of the returned field can be checked using the field class's **getTypeId()** method. For example,

```
if (globalField->isOfType(SoSFFloat::getClassTypeId())) ...
```

An example of using the **realTime** global field is

```
engineA->input1.connectFrom(SoDB::getGlobalField("realTime"));
```

Example 13-1 creates a digital clock that connects an **SoText3** string to the **realTime** global field. Figure 13-7 shows the scene graph for this example. Figure 13-8 shows the digital clock.

Example 13-1   Using the Real-Time Global Field

```
#include <Inventor/SoDB.h>
#include <Inventor/Xt/SoXt.h>
#include <Inventor/Xt/SoXtRenderArea.h>
#include <Inventor/nodes/SoDirectionalLight.h>
#include <Inventor/nodes/SoMaterial.h>
#include <Inventor/nodes/SoPerspectiveCamera.h>
#include <Inventor/nodes/SoSeparator.h>
#include <Inventor/nodes/SoText3.h>
```

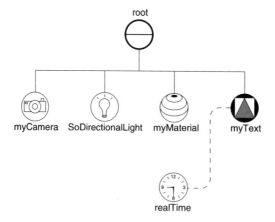

Figure 13-7   Scene Graph for the Digital Clock Example

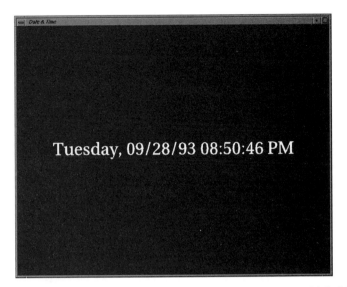

Tuesday, 09/28/93 08:50:46 PM

Figure 13-8   Digital Clock That Uses the Real-Time Global Field

```
main(int , char **argv)
{
   // Initialize Inventor and Xt
   Widget myWindow = SoXt::init(argv[0]);
   if (myWindow == NULL)
      exit(1);

   SoSeparator *root = new SoSeparator;
   root->ref();

   // Add a camera, light, and material
   SoPerspectiveCamera *myCamera = new SoPerspectiveCamera;
   root->addChild(myCamera);
   root->addChild(new SoDirectionalLight);
   SoMaterial *myMaterial = new SoMaterial;
   myMaterial->diffuseColor.setValue(1.0, 0.0, 0.0);
   root->addChild(myMaterial);

   // Create a Text3 object, and connect to the realTime field
   SoText3 *myText = new SoText3;
   root->addChild(myText);
   myText->string.connectFrom(SoDB::getGlobalField("realTime"));

   SoXtRenderArea *myRenderArea = new SoXtRenderArea(myWindow);
   myCamera->viewAll(root, myRenderArea->getSize());
```

```
myRenderArea->setSceneGraph(root);
myRenderArea->setTitle("Date & Time");
myRenderArea->show();

SoXt::show(myWindow);
SoXt::mainLoop();
}
```

Animation Engines

The following engines can be used to animate objects in the scene graph.
Each of these engines has a **timeIn** field, which is connected automatically
to the **realTime** global field when the engine is constructed. This field can,
however, be connected to any other time source.

- **SoElapsedTime**—functions as a stopwatch; outputs the time that has
  elapsed since it started running.

- **SoOneShot**—runs for a preset amount of time, then stops.

- **SoTimeCounter**—cycles from a minimum count to a maximum count
  at a given frequency.

Elapsed-Time Engine

The elapsed-time engine is a basic controllable time source. You can start,
stop, reset, pause, and control the speed of this engine. If you pause it (by
setting the **pause** field to TRUE), it stops updating its **timeOut** field, but it
keeps counting internally. When you turn off the pause, it jumps to its
current position without losing time.

Example 13-2 uses the output from an elapsed time engine to control the
translation of a figure. The resulting effect is that the figure slides across the
scene. Figure 13-9 shows the scene graph for this example. The **timeOut**
output of the elapsed time engine (*myCounter*) is connected to an
SoComposeVec3f engine (*slideDistance*). This second engine inserts the
timeOut value into the x slot of a vector. Once the value is in vector format,
it can be connected to the **translation** field of the *slideTranslation* node.

Note that the **timeOut** value is an **SoSFTime**, but the **SoComposeVec3f**
engine requires inputs of type **SoSFFloat**. Inventor performs this
conversion automatically for you, converting the time to a number of
seconds.

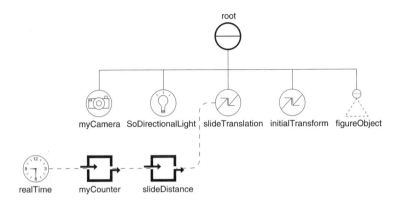

Figure 13-9   Scene Graph for Elapsed-Time Engine Example

Example 13-2   Using an Elapsed-Time Engine

```
// Set up transformations
SoTranslation *slideTranslation = new SoTranslation;
root->addChild(slideTranslation);
SoTransform *initialTransform = new SoTransform;
initialTransform->translation.setValue(-5., 0., 0.);
initialTransform->scaleFactor.setValue(10., 10., 10.);
initialTransform->rotation.setValue(SbVec3f(1,0,0), M_PI/2.);
root->addChild(initialTransform);

// Read the figure object from a file and add to the scene
SoInput myInput;
if (!myInput.openFile("jumpyMan.iv"))
   return (1);
SoSeparator *figureObject = SoDB::readAll(&myInput);
if (figureObject == NULL)
   return (1);
root->addChild(figureObject);

// Make the X translation value change over time.
SoElapsedTime *myCounter = new SoElapsedTime;
SoComposeVec3f *slideDistance = new SoComposeVec3f;
slideDistance->x.connectFrom(&myCounter->timeOut);
slideTranslation->translation.connectFrom(
        &slideDistance->vector);
```

One-Shot Engine

The **SoOneShot** engine is started when its **trigger** input is touched (with either **touch()** or **setValue()**). It runs for the specified **duration**, updating its **timeOut** field until it reaches the duration time. The **ramp** output, a float value from 0.0 (when the trigger starts) to 1.0 (when the duration is reached), is provided as a convenience. For example, the **ramp** output of a one-shot engine could be connected to the **alpha** input of a rotation interpolation to make a door open.

This engine has two flags stored in an **SoSFBitMask** field. The Retriggerable flag specifies whether to start the cycle over if a trigger occurs in the middle of a cycle. If this flag is not set (the default), the trigger is ignored and the cycle is finished. If this flag is set, the cycle restarts when a trigger occurs.

The Hold_Final flag specifies what happens at the end of the cycle. If this flag is not set (the default), all outputs return to 0 when the cycle finishes. If this flag is set, the **isActive** output returns to 0, but **ramp** and **timeOut** stay at their final values.

Time-Counter Engine

The **SoTimeCounter** engine counts from a minimum count (**min**) to a maximum count (**max**). The value for **step** indicates how the timer counts (the default is in increments of 1). The **frequency** input specifies the number of min-to-max cycles per second.

Unlike the one-shot and elapsed-time engines, the time-counter engine does not output a time; it outputs the current *count*. Each time the time counter starts a cycle, it triggers its **syncOut** output. This output can be used to synchronize one of the triggered engines with some other event.

Example 13-3 uses the output from two time-counter engines to control the horizontal and vertical motion of a figure. The resulting effect is that the figure jumps across the screen.

This example creates three engines, as shown in Figure 13-10. The output of the *jumpWidthCounter* (a time counter engine) is connected to the *x* input of the *jump* engine (an **SoComposeVec3f** engine). The output of the *jumpHeightCounter* (another time counter engine) is connected to the *y* input of the *jump* engine. The *jump* engine composes a vector using the *x* and *y* inputs, and then feeds this vector into the **translation** field of the *jumpTranslation* node. Figure 13-11 shows scenes from this example.

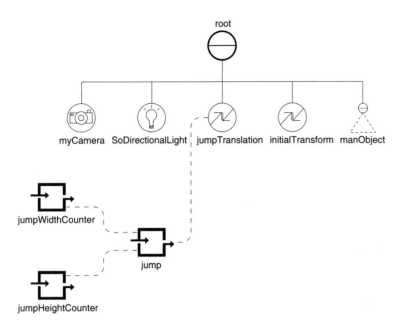

Figure 13-10   Scene Graph for the Time-Counter Example

Example 13-3   Using Time-Counter Engines

```
// Set up transformations
SoTranslation *jumpTranslation = new SoTranslation;
root->addChild(jumpTranslation);
SoTransform *initialTransform = new SoTransform;
initialTransform->translation.setValue(-20., 0., 0.);
initialTransform->scaleFactor.setValue(40., 40., 40.);
initialTransform->rotation.setValue(SbVec3f(1,0,0), M_PI/2.);
root->addChild(initialTransform);

// Read the man object from a file and add to the scene
SoInput myInput;
if (!myInput.openFile("jumpyMan.iv"))
   return (1);
SoSeparator *manObject = SoDB::readAll(&myInput);
if (manObject == NULL)
   return (1);
root->addChild(manObject);
```

Figure 13-11 Controlling an Object's Movement Using Time-Counter Engines

```
// Create two counters, and connect to X and Y translations.
// The Y counter is small and high frequency.
// The X counter is large and low frequency.
// This results in small jumps across the screen,
// left to right, again and again and again.
SoTimeCounter *jumpHeightCounter = new SoTimeCounter;
SoTimeCounter *jumpWidthCounter = new SoTimeCounter;
SoComposeVec3f *jump = new SoComposeVec3f;

jumpHeightCounter->max = 4;
jumpHeightCounter->frequency = 1.5;
jumpWidthCounter->max = 40;
jumpWidthCounter->frequency = 0.15;

jump->x.connectFrom(&jumpWidthCounter->output);
jump->y.connectFrom(&jumpHeightCounter->output);
jumpTranslation->translation.connectFrom(&jump->vector);
```

Gate Engine

This section discusses the *gate engine*, which provides a convenient mechanism for selectively copying values from input to output. It also introduces the *enable* field and the *trigger* field, used by other engines.

By default, each time a value in an engine network changes, the new value propagates through the network. If a value is constantly changing, however, you may not want this change to propagate continuously through the scene graph. In this case, you might want to sample the value at regular intervals, or update the value only when a certain event occurs. Use the gate engine to control when such values are sent to the rest of the scene graph.

When you construct the gate engine, you pass in the type of its input and output fields. This type must be the type of a multiple-value field. (If you want to gate a single-value field, just pass in the corresponding multiple-value type and Inventor will automatically convert it.) Other engines with similar constructors are **SoSelectOne** and **SoConcatenate**.

SoGate has these two inputs:

enable (SoSFBool) allows continuous flow of updated values

trigger (SoSFTrigger)
                    copies a single value

When the **enable** field is TRUE, data is allowed to be copied to the engine output each time a new value is received as input. To send only one value to the engine output, set the **enable** field to FALSE and use the **trigger** field to send the value. When the **trigger** field is touched, one value is sent. The **trigger** field is touched by calling either **touch()** or **setValue()** on it. Example 13-4 connects an elapsed time engine (*myCounter*) to a gate engine (*myGate*). Pressing the mouse button enables and disables the gate engine, which in turn controls the motion of a duck in the scene. The scene graph for this example is shown in Figure 13-12.

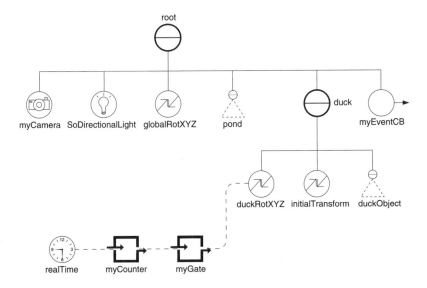

Figure 13-12   Scene Graph for Gate Engine Example

Example 13-4   Using a Gate Engine

```
// Duck group
SoSeparator *duck = new SoSeparator;
root->addChild(duck);

// Read the duck object from a file and add to the group
SoInput myInput;
if (!myInput.openFile("duck.iv"))
   return (1);
SoSeparator *duckObject = SoDB::readAll(&myInput);
if (duckObject == NULL)
   return (1);

// Set up the duck transformations
SoRotationXYZ *duckRotXYZ = new SoRotationXYZ;
duck->addChild(duckRotXYZ);
SoTransform *initialTransform = new SoTransform;
initialTransform->translation.setValue(0., 0., 3.);
initialTransform->scaleFactor.setValue(6., 6., 6.);
duck->addChild(initialTransform);

duck->addChild(duckObject);

// Update the rotation value if the gate is enabled.
SoGate *myGate = new SoGate(SoMFFloat::getClassTypeId());
SoElapsedTime *myCounter = new SoElapsedTime;
myGate->input->connectFrom(&myCounter->timeOut);
duckRotXYZ->axis = SoRotationXYZ::Y;  // rotate about Y axis
duckRotXYZ->angle.connectFrom(myGate->output);

// Add an event callback to catch mouse button presses.
// Each button press will enable or disable the duck motion.
SoEventCallback *myEventCB = new SoEventCallback;
myEventCB->addEventCallback(
        SoMouseButtonEvent::getClassTypeId(),
        myMousePressCB, myGate);
root->addChild(myEventCB);

...

// This routine is called for every mouse button event.
void
myMousePressCB(void *userData, SoEventCallback *eventCB)
{
   SoGate *gate = (SoGate *) userData;
   const SoEvent *event = eventCB->getEvent();
```

```
    // Check for mouse button being pressed
    if (SO_MOUSE_PRESS_EVENT(event, ANY)) {

        // Toggle the gate that controls the duck motion
        if (gate->enable.getValue())
            gate->enable.setValue(FALSE);
        else
            gate->enable.setValue(TRUE);

        eventCB->setHandled();
    }
}
```

Arithmetic Engines

By convention, all inputs and outputs for the arithmetic engines in
Inventor are multiple-value (**MF**) fields. If you supply a value of type **SoSF**,
it is automatically converted to an **MF** field. Another important feature is
that if you supply an array of values for one of the inputs, the output will
also be an array (an **MF** value). If an engine has more than one input, some
inputs may have more values than others. For example, **input1** might have
five values and **input2** might have only three values. In such cases, the last
value of the field with fewer values is repeated as necessary to fill out the
array. (Here, the third value of **input2** would be repeated two more times.)

Boolean Engine

As shown in Figure 13-13, the Boolean engine, **SoBoolOperation**, has two
Boolean inputs (**a** and **b**) and one **SoSFEnum** input (**operation**) that
describes the operation to be performed.

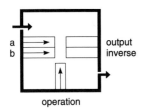

Figure 13-13   SoBoolOperation Engine

The value for **operation** can be one of the following:

Operation	Output Is TRUE If
CLEAR	never TRUE
SET	always TRUE
A	A is TRUE
NOT_A	A is FALSE
B	B is TRUE
NOT_B	B is FALSE
A_OR_B	A is TRUE or B is TRUE
NOT_A_OR_B	A is FALSE or B is TRUE
A_OR_NOT_B	A is TRUE or B is FALSE
NOT_A_OR_NOT_B	A is FALSE or B is FALSE
A_AND_B	A and B are TRUE
NOT_A_AND_B	A is FALSE and B is TRUE
A_AND_NOT_B	A is TRUE and B is FALSE
NOT_A_AND_NOT_B	A and B are FALSE
A_EQUALS_B	A equals B
A_NOT_EQUALS_B	A does not equal B

This engine has two outputs, **output** and **inverse**. The **inverse** field is TRUE if **output** is FALSE, and vice versa. If either of the inputs contains an array of values (they are of type **SoMFBool**), the output will also contain an array of values.

Example 13-5 modifies Example 13-4 and adds a Boolean engine to make the motion of the smaller duck depend on the motion of the larger duck. The smaller duck moves when the larger duck is still. Figure 13-14 shows an image created by this example.

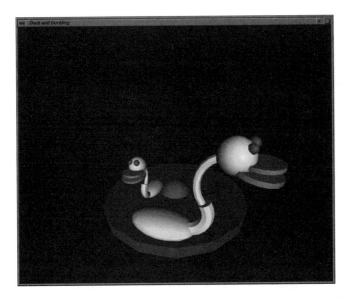

Figure 13-14   Swimming Ducks Controlled by a Boolean Engine

Example 13-5   Using a Boolean Engine

```
// Bigger duck group
SoSeparator *bigDuck = new SoSeparator;
root->addChild(bigDuck);
SoRotationXYZ *bigDuckRotXYZ = new SoRotationXYZ;
bigDuck->addChild(bigDuckRotXYZ);
SoTransform *bigInitialTransform = new SoTransform;
bigInitialTransform->translation.setValue(0., 0., 3.5);
bigInitialTransform->scaleFactor.setValue(6., 6., 6.);
bigDuck->addChild(bigInitialTransform);
bigDuck->addChild(duckObject);

// Smaller duck group
SoSeparator *smallDuck = new SoSeparator;
root->addChild(smallDuck);
SoRotationXYZ *smallDuckRotXYZ = new SoRotationXYZ;
smallDuck->addChild(smallDuckRotXYZ);
SoTransform *smallInitialTransform = new SoTransform;
smallInitialTransform->translation.setValue(0., -2.24, 1.5);
smallInitialTransform->scaleFactor.setValue(4., 4., 4.);
smallDuck->addChild(smallInitialTransform);
smallDuck->addChild(duckObject);
```

```
// Use a gate engine to start/stop the rotation of
// the bigger duck.
SoGate *bigDuckGate =
        new SoGate(SoMFFloat::getClassTypeId());
SoElapsedTime *bigDuckTime = new SoElapsedTime;
bigDuckGate->input->connectFrom(&bigDuckTime->timeOut);
bigDuckRotXYZ->axis = SoRotationXYZ::Y;
bigDuckRotXYZ->angle.connectFrom(bigDuckGate->output);

// Each mouse button press will enable/disable the gate
// controlling the bigger duck.
SoEventCallback *myEventCB = new SoEventCallback;
myEventCB->addEventCallback(
        SoMouseButtonEvent::getClassTypeId(),
        myMousePressCB, bigDuckGate);
root->addChild(myEventCB);

// Use a Boolean engine to make the rotation of the smaller
// duck depend on the bigger duck.  The smaller duck moves
// only when the bigger duck is still.
SoBoolOperation *myBoolean = new SoBoolOperation;
myBoolean->a.connectFrom(&bigDuckGate->enable);
myBoolean->operation = SoBoolOperation::NOT_A;

SoGate *smallDuckGate = new
        SoGate(SoMFFloat::getClassTypeId());
SoElapsedTime *smallDuckTime = new SoElapsedTime;
smallDuckGate->input->connectFrom(&smallDuckTime->timeOut);
smallDuckGate->enable.connectFrom(&myBoolean->output);
smallDuckRotXYZ->axis = SoRotationXYZ::Y;
smallDuckRotXYZ->angle.connectFrom(smallDuckGate->output);
```

Calculator Engine

The calculator engine, **SoCalculator**, is similar to the Boolean engine, but it handles a wider range of operations and has more inputs and outputs. As shown in Figure 13-15, this engine has the following inputs and outputs:

Inputs	SoMFFloat	a, b, c, d, e, f, g, h
	SoMFVec3f	A, B, C, D, E, F, G, H
	SoMFString	expression
Outputs	SoEngineOutput	oa, ob, oc, od (SoMFFloat)
	SoEngineOutput	oA, oB, oC, oD (SoMFVec3f)

The **expression** input, shown at the bottom of the engine, is of type
SoMFString and is of the form:

"lhs = rhs"

lhs (lefthand side) can be any one of the outputs or a temporary variable.
This engine provides eight temporary floating-point variables (ta – th) and
eight temporary vector variables (tA – tH).

rhs (righthand side) supports the following operators:

Type of Operator	Example
Binary operators	+ – * / < > >= <= == != && ||
Unary operators	– !
Ternary operator	*cond* ? *trueexpr* : *falseexpr*
Parentheses	(*expr*)
Vector indexing	*vec* [*int*]
Functions	func(*expr*, ...)
Terms	integer or floating-point constants; named constants such as MAXFLOAT, MINFLOAT, M_LOG2E, M_PI; the names of the calculator engine's inputs, outputs, and temporary variables (a, b, A, B, oa, ob, ta, tb, tA, tB, and so on)

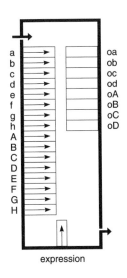

Figure 13-15   SoCalculator Engine

See the *Open Inventor C++ Reference Manual* for detailed information on using these operators.

Here is a simple example of using the calculator engine. It uses the following inputs and outputs:

Inputs	Outputs
2 vectors (A, B)	oA (f times the negation of the cross product of A and B)
2 scalars (a, f)	oa (convert a from degrees to radians)

To specify the expression for a calculator engine called *calc*, the code would be

```
calc->expression.set1Value(0, "oa = a * M_PI / 180");
calc->expression.set1Value(1, "oA = -f * cross(A, B)");
```

Multiple expressions are evaluated in order, so a variable assigned a value in an earlier expression can be used in the righthand side of a later expression. Several expressions can be specified in one string, separated by semicolons.

The expressions can also operate on arrays. If one input contains fewer values than another input, the last value is replicated as necessary to fill out the array. All the expressions will be applied to all elements of the arrays. For example, if input *a* contains multiple values and input *b* contains the value 1.0, then the expression "oa = a + b" will add 1 to all of the elements in *a*.

Using the Calculator to Constrain Object Behavior

Example 13-6 shows using the calculator engine to move a flower along a path. The calculator engine computes a closed, planar curve. The output of the engine is connected to the translation applied to a flower object, which then moves along the path of the curve. Figure 13-16 shows the scene graph for this example. The dancing flower is shown in Figure 13-17.

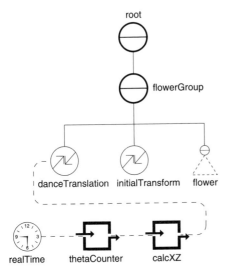

Figure 13-16   Scene Graph for Calculator Engine Example

Example 13-6   Using a Calculator Engine

```
// Flower group
SoSeparator *flowerGroup = new SoSeparator;
root->addChild(flowerGroup);

// Read the flower object from a file and add to the group
if (!myInput.openFile("flower.iv"))
   exit(1);
SoSeparator *flower= SoDB::readAll(&myInput);
if (flower == NULL)
   exit(1);

// Set up the flower transformations
SoTranslation *danceTranslation = new SoTranslation;
SoTransform *initialTransform = new SoTransform;
flowerGroup->addChild(danceTranslation);
initialTransform->scaleFactor.setValue(10., 10., 10.);
initialTransform->translation.setValue(0., 0., 5.);
flowerGroup->addChild(initialTransform);
flowerGroup->addChild(flower);
```

Figure 13-17   Using a Calculator Engine to Constrain an Object's Movement

```
// Set up an engine to calculate the motion path:
// r = 5*cos(5*theta); x = r*cos(theta); z = r*sin(theta)
// Theta is incremented using a time counter engine,
// and converted to radians using an expression in
// the calculator engine.
SoCalculator *calcXZ = new SoCalculator;
SoTimeCounter *thetaCounter = new SoTimeCounter;

thetaCounter->max = 360;
thetaCounter->step = 4;
thetaCounter->frequency = 0.075;

calcXZ->a.connectFrom(&thetaCounter->output);
calcXZ->expression.set1Value(0, "ta=a*M_PI/180");   // theta
calcXZ->expression.set1Value(1, "tb=5*cos(5*ta)");  // r
calcXZ->expression.set1Value(2, "td=tb*cos(ta)");   // x
calcXZ->expression.set1Value(3, "te=tb*sin(ta)");   // z
calcXZ->expression.set1Value(4, "oA=vec3f(td,0,te)");
danceTranslation->translation.connectFrom(&calcXZ->oA);
```

Nodes Used for Animation

Engines are usually connected to nodes. You can, though, create a node
class that has built-in engines automatically connected to it. Here are some
examples that Inventor provides. These nodes provide a convenient
mechanism for adding animation to a scene graph:

- **SoRotor** is a transformation node that spins the rotation angle while
  keeping the axis constant.

- **SoPendulum** is a transformation node that oscillates between two
  rotations.

- **SoShuttle** is a transformation node that oscillates between two translations.

- **SoBlinker** is a switch node that cycles through its children.

Let's look at examples of rotor and blinker nodes.

Rotor Node

The **SoRotor** node, derived from **SoRotation**, changes the angle of rotation at a specified speed. You can use an **SoRotor** node any place you would use an **SoRotation**. It has these fields:

rotation (SoSFRotation)
        specifies the rotation (axis and initial angle). The angle changes when the rotor spins.

speed (SoSFFloat)   specifies the number of cycles per second.

on (SoSFBool)   TRUE to run, FALSE to stop. The default is TRUE.

The number of times a second it is updated depends on the application. This node contains an engine that is connected to the real-time global field. Example 13-7 illustrates how you could use this node to rotate the vanes of a windmill. It specifies the rotation and speed for the rotor node and adds it to the scene graph before the windmill vanes, as shown in Figure 13-18. The rotation axis of the windmill vanes is (0.0, 0.0, 1.0) and the initial angle is 0.0. This rotation angle is updated automatically by the rotor node.

Example 13-7   A Spinning Windmill Using an SoRotor Node

```
#include <Inventor/SoDB.h>
#include <Inventor/SoInput.h>
#include <Inventor/Xt/SoXt.h>
#include <Inventor/Xt/viewers/SoXtExaminerViewer.h>
#include <Inventor/nodes/SoSeparator.h>
#include <Inventor/nodes/SoRotor.h>

SoSeparator *
readFile(const char *filename)
{
   // Open the input file
   SoInput mySceneInput;
   if (!mySceneInput.openFile(filename)) {
      fprintf(stderr, "Cannot open file %s\n", filename);
      return NULL;
   }
```

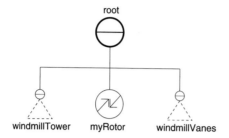

root

windmillTower   myRotor   windmillVanes

Figure 13-18   Scene Graph for Rotor Node Example

```
   // Read the whole file into the database
   SoSeparator *myGraph = SoDB::readAll(&mySceneInput);
   if (myGraph == NULL) {
      fprintf(stderr, "Problem reading file\n");
      return NULL;
   }

   mySceneInput.closeFile();
   return myGraph;
}

main(int, char **argv)
{
   // Initialize Inventor and Xt
   Widget myWindow = SoXt::init(argv[0]);

   SoSeparator *root = new SoSeparator;
   root->ref();

   // Read in the data for the windmill tower
   SoSeparator *windmillTower =
            readFile("windmillTower.iv");
   root->addChild(windmillTower);

   // Add a rotor node to spin the vanes
   SoRotor *myRotor = new SoRotor;
   myRotor->rotation.setValue(SbVec3f(0, 0, 1), 0); // z axis
   myRotor->speed = 0.2;
   root->addChild(myRotor);
```

```
// Read in the data for the windmill vanes
SoSeparator *windmillVanes =
        readFile("windmillVanes.iv");
root->addChild(windmillVanes);

// Create a viewer
SoXtExaminerViewer *myViewer =
        new SoXtExaminerViewer(myWindow);

// Attach and show viewer
myViewer->setSceneGraph(root);
myViewer->setTitle("Windmill");
myViewer->show();

// Loop forever
SoXt::show(myWindow);
SoXt::mainLoop();
}
```

Blinker Node

The **SoBlinker** node, derived from **SoSwitch**, cycles among its children by changing the value of the **whichChild** field. This node has the following fields:

whichChild (SoSFLong)
                index of the child to be traversed.

speed (SoSFFloat)   cycles per second.

on (SoSFBool)   TRUE to run, FALSE to stop. The default is TRUE.

When it has only one child, **SoBlinker** cycles between that child (0) and SO_SWITCH_NONE. Example 13-8 shows how you could make the text string "Eat at Josie's" flash on and off.

Figure 13-19   Flashing Sign Controlled by a Blinker Node

Example 13-8   Using a Blinker Node to Make a Sign Flash

```
// Add the non-blinking part of the sign to the root
root->addChild(eatAt);

// Add the fast-blinking part to a blinker node
SoBlinker *fastBlinker = new SoBlinker;
root->addChild(fastBlinker);
fastBlinker->speed = 2;  // blinks 2 times a second
fastBlinker->addChild(josie);

// Add the slow-blinking part to another blinker node
SoBlinker *slowBlinker = new SoBlinker;
root->addChild(slowBlinker);
slowBlinker->speed = 0.5;  // 2 secs per cycle; 1 on, 1 off
slowBlinker->addChild(frame);
```

Chapter 14

Node Kits

Chapter Objectives

After reading this chapter, you'll be able to do the following:

- Use node kits in a scene graph, selecting the required parts and setting their values

- Explain the difference between a path, a full path, and a node-kit path

- Create a simple motion hierarchy using node kits

This chapter describes node kits, which are a convenient mechanism for creating groupings of Inventor nodes. When you create a shape node such as an indexed triangle strip set, you usually also need at least a coordinate node, a material node, and a transform node. You may also want to specify drawing style and a material binding. Instead of creating each of these nodes individually, specifying values for their fields, and then arranging them into a subgraph, you can simply use an **SoShapeKit**, which already contains information on how these nodes should be arranged in the subgraph. You then use a special set of convenience methods to specify which nodes you want to use and to set and get the values of these nodes. This chapter introduces the concepts of *node kits*, *node-kit catalogs*, *catalog entries*, and *hidden children*.

Why Node Kits?

Node kits offer a convenient way to create both simple and complex graphs of nodes. Node kits can contain other node kits, a feature that allows you to build hierarchies of kits relative to each other. Some of the advantages of node kits include the following:

- Node kits organize a number of Inventor nodes into a subgraph that has a higher-level meaning for you. An **SoShapeKit**, for example, can describe a shape that can move and has a particular appearance. The shape and its properties are all packaged into one node kit. You do not need to worry about how the nodes are placed into the graph because the node kit takes care of this organization for you.

- Node kits are flexible, allowing you to create complex subgraphs that use many Inventor features, or simple subgraphs that use only a few features.

- Node kits create collections of nodes efficiently. They create only the nodes needed for a particular instance.

- Node kits provide shortcut routines for creating nodes and setting values in them. Your code is short and easy to read.

- Through subclassing, you can design your own node kits that are tailored to the kinds of groupings used in your particular application. (See *The Inventor Toolmaker*, Chapter 7.)

Hidden Children and SoNodeKitPath

A node kit contains a collection of nodes. The node kit manages these nodes and how they are arranged in its subgraph. You can create and remove these nodes, or *parts*, of the node kit. But, because the node kit is actually managing these parts, you do not have direct access to them. These parts are referred to as the *hidden children* of the node kit. Although a node kit is a grouping of nodes, it is not subclassed from **SoGroup**; methods such as **addChild()** do not exist for node kits.

Whenever you perform a pick or a search action, a path may be returned. The default path returned, **SoPath**, stops at the first node in the path that has hidden children (often a node kit). If you need more detailed information about what is in the path underneath the node kit, you can cast the **SoPath** to an **SoFullPath**, which includes hidden children as well as public children. If, for example, you search for spheres in a given scene graph, you may get a path to a node kit with hidden children, one of which is a sphere. The **SoPath** returned by the search action ends in the node kit. In most cases, you can probably ignore the hidden children. But if you need information about them, you can cast this path to an **SoFullPath**.

You will probably use node kit paths more often than you use full paths. If you use full paths with node kits, take care not to change the node kit's structure.

Tip: When you cast a path (not a pointer) to a full path, be sure to cast a ❖ pointer; otherwise a new instance of the path is created. For example, you can do this:

```
SoPath &pathRef;
((SoFullPath *) &pathRef)->getLength();
```

But don't do this:
```
length = ((SoFullPath) pathRef).getLength();
```

Another kind of path is the **SoNodeKitPath**, which contains only the node kits and leaves out the intermediate nodes in the path. You might use a node-kit path if you are looking at a motion hierarchy (see Example 14-3) and you want to think of each kit as an object. Figure 14-1 shows a path, a full path, and a node-kit path for the same subgraph. The shaded circles are node kits, and the light circles are not.

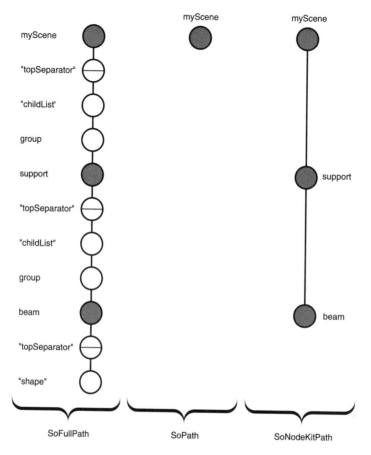

Figure 14-1   Different Types of Paths

Node-Kit Classes

Figure 14-2 shows the class tree for node kits, which are all derived from **SoBaseKit**.

See the entry for **SoBaseKit** in the *Open Inventor C++ Reference Manual* for a complete list of the methods for getting and setting parts in node kits.

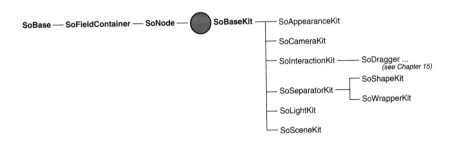

Figure 14-2   Node-Kit Classes

Node-Kit Catalog

Each node-kit class shown in Figure 14-2 has an associated *catalog*. The catalog lists all the parts (nodes) available in this kit, in the same way as an electronics or software catalog lists all the items available for sale. Just as you order items selectively from a software catalog, you can choose nodes selectively from a node-kit catalog. In addition to simply listing the available parts, a node-kit catalog also describes how the nodes are arranged into a subgraph when you select them.

For example, the catalog for an **SoShapeKit** is shown in Figure 14-3.

When you first create an **SoShapeKit**, you get the "base model," shown in Figure 14-4. By default, the "shape" part is a cube. You can change this shape and also add options as you need them.

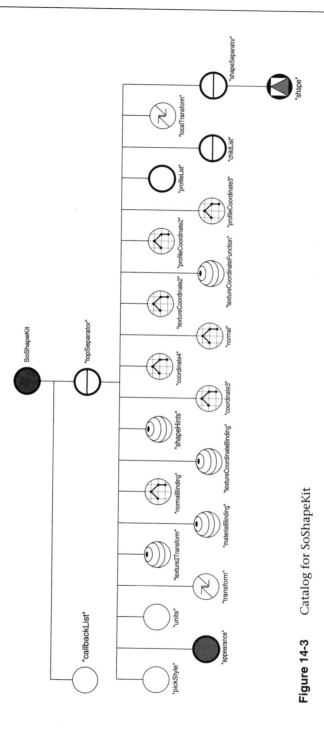

Figure 14-3   Catalog for SoShapeKit

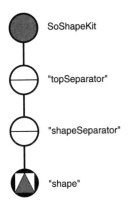

SoShapeKit

"topSeparator"

"shapeSeparator"

"shape"

Figure 14-4   Basic Version of an SoShapeKit

A node-kit catalog contains a separate entry to describe each part. The **SoShapeKit** catalog shown in Figure 14-3 has 24 entries. Each catalog entry contains the following pieces of information:

- *Name* of the part
- *Type* of node
- *Default* type (used if *Type* is an abstract class)
- Whether this part is *created by default*
- Name of this part's *parent*
- Name of the *right sibling* of this part
- Whether this part is a *list*
- If the part is a list, the *type of group node* that is used to contain the list items
- If the part is a list, the permissible *node types* for entries in this list
- Whether this part is *public*

The following list shows several sample catalog entries from **SoShapeKit**.

Information	Sample Entry 1	Sample Entry 2
Name	"callbackList"	"transform"
Type	SoNodeKitListPart	SoTransform
Default Type	(Not Applicable)	(Not Applicable)
Created by Default?	FALSE	FALSE
Parent Name	"this"	"topSeparator"
Right Sibling	"topSeparator"	"texture2Transform"
Is It a List?	TRUE	FALSE
List Container Type	SoSeparator	(Not Applicable)
List Element Type	SoCallback SoEventCallback	(Not Applicable)
Is It Public?	TRUE	TRUE

An **SoShapeKit** contains another node kit, "appearance," which is an **SoAppearanceKit**. The catalog for **SoAppearanceKit** is shown in Figure 14-5.

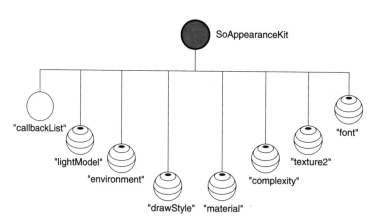

Figure 14-5   Catalog for SoAppearanceKit

Parts Created by Default

The following constructor creates an instance of an **SoShapeKit**:

```
SoShapeKit *myShapeKit = new SoShapeKit();
```

When an instance of a node kit is created, certain nodes are created by default. In the kits provided, the **SoShapeKit**, **SoLightKit**, and **SoCameraKit** create the parts "shape," "light," and "camera," respectively. The default types for these parts are **SoCube**, **SoDirectionalLight**, and **SoPerspectiveCamera**.

When the shape kit is constructed, it automatically creates the cube node as well as the top separator and shape separator nodes for the group. (Internal nodes, such as the separator node, are automatically created when you add a node lower in the node kit structure.) At this point, the scene graph would look like Figure 14-6. The shape kit now consists of four nodes: the **SoShapeKit** node itself, the top separator node, the shape separator (used for caching even when the transform or material is changing) and the cube node. The other nodes in the shape-kit catalog are not created until you explicitly request them, as described below.

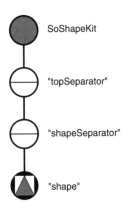

Figure 14-6   Creating an Instance of SoShapeKit

Selecting Parts and Setting Values

Next you can use the **set()** method, a method for **SoBaseKit** that is inherited by all node kits. Use the **set()** method to create a part *and* specify field values in the new node. This method has two different forms:

set(*nameValuePairListString*);   // uses braces to separate
                                               // part names from value pairs

or

set(*partNameString, parameterString*);   // does not use braces

An example of the first form of **set()**, which makes a material node and sets the diffuse color field to purple is as follows:

```
myShape->set("material { diffuseColor 1 0 1 }");
```

An example of the second form of **set()**, which does the same thing, is as follows:

```
myShape->set("material", "diffuseColor 1 0 1");
```

The scene graph for this instance of the shape kit now looks like Figure 14-7. Note that the **SoAppearanceKit** node is created automatically when you request the material node. Also note that the node is created only if it does not yet exist. Subsequent calls to **set()** edit the fields of the material node rather than recreate it.

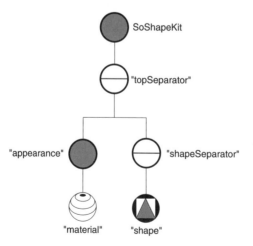

Figure 14-7   Adding the Material Node

Now suppose you want to make the cube wireframe rather than solid, and twice its original size:

```
myShape->set("drawStyle { style LINES }
             transform { scaleFactor 2.0 2.0 2.0 } ");
```

The scene graph now looks like Figure 14-8.

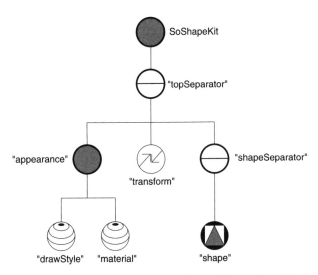

Figure 14-8 Adding Draw-Style and Transform Nodes

Note that you can use the **set**() method to create the nodes in any order. The node kit automatically inserts the nodes in their correct positions in the scene graph, as specified by the node-kit catalog.

This instance of the shape kit now contains eight nodes, as shown in Figure 14-8.

Other Methods: getPart() and setPart()

Two other useful methods of **SoBaseKit**() are **getPart**() and **setPart**().

The getPart() Method

The **getPart**() method returns the requested node (part):

getPart(*partName, makeIfNeeded*);

If *makeIfNeeded* is TRUE and no node is present, the node is created. In addition, if any extra nodes are needed to connect the node to the top node ("this") of the node kit, those nodes are created as well.

For example:

```
xf = (SoTransform *) myKit->getPart("transform", TRUE);
```

looks for "transform" and either returns it (if found) or makes it (if not found). It then assigns this node to *xf*. If you specify FALSE for *makeIfNeeded* and the node kit has no "transform" yet, the method returns NULL without creating the node. If the catalog for the type of node kit you are using does not have an entry for a part named "transform," the **getPart()** method returns NULL.

The setPart() Method

The **setPart()** method inserts the given node as a new part in the node kit:

setPart(*partName*, *node*);

If extra nodes are required to connect the part into the node-kit structure, those nodes are created as well. For example, suppose you want another node kit to share the transform node (*xf*) created in the previous example:

```
myOtherKit->setPart("transform", xf);
```

If the given node is not derived from the type of that part, as described in the node-kit catalog, the part will not be set. If you have linked with the debugging library, an error message will print.

To delete the transform node entirely, use a NULL argument for the node pointer:

```
myOtherKit->setPart("transform", NULL);
```

To change the "shape" in **SoShapeKit** from the default cube to a cone:

```
myShape->setPart("shape", new SoCone);
```

And, of course, **setPart()** will do nothing if there is no part with the specified name in the catalog.

Macros for Getting Parts

Instead of using the **getPart()** method, you can use the macros SO_GET_PART() and SO_CHECK_PART(). If you compile with the debugging version of the Inventor library, these macros perform casting and type check the result for you. (If you link with the optimized version of Inventor, no type-checking is performed.)

The SO_GET_PART() Macro

The syntax for SO_GET_PART() is as follows:

SO_GET_PART(*kitContainingPart, partName, partClassName*);

This macro does the type-casting for you and is equivalent to

(*partClassName* *) *kitContainingPart*->**getPart**(*partName*, TRUE);

Since the *makeIfNeeded* argument is TRUE in this macro, the part is created if it is not already in the node kit.

For example:

```
xf = SO_GET_PART(myKit, "transform", SoTransform);
```

The SO_CHECK_PART() Macro

The syntax for SO_CHECK_PART() is as follows:

SO_CHECK_PART(*kitContainingPart, partName, partClassName*);

This macro does the type-casting for you and is equivalent to

(*partClassName* *) *kitContainingPart*->**getPart**(*partName*, FALSE);

Since the *makeIfNeeded* argument is FALSE in this macro, the part is *not* created if it is not already in the node kit.

For example:

```
xf = SO_CHECK_PART(myKit, "transform", SoTransform);
if (xf == NULL)
   printf("Transform does not exist in myKit.");
else
   printf("Got it!");
```

Specifying Part Names

Suppose you have created the three node-kit classes shown in Figure 14-9 (see *The Inventor Toolmaker*, Chapter 7, for information on how to subclass node kits):

- An **SoGoonKit**, which defines the complete creature, a goon. This goon consists of an **SoAppearanceKit**, two instances of **SoLegKit** for *leg1* and *leg2*, and an **SoCone** for *body*.

- An **SoLegKit**, which defines a leg for a goon. This class contains an **SoAppearanceKit**, an **SoFootKit**, and an **SoCylinder** for *thigh*.

- An **SoFootKit**, which defines a foot for a goon. This class contains an **SoAppearanceKit**, an **SoCube** for *toe1*, and an **SoCube** for *toe2*.

After creating an instance of **SoGoonKit** (*myGoon*), you can be very specific when asking for the parts. For example:

```
myCube = SO_GET_PART(myGoon, "toe1", SoCube);
```

first looks in the catalog of *myGoon* for *toe1*. If it doesn't find *toe1* and some children in the catalog are node kits, it looks inside the leaf node kits for *toe1* and uses the first match it finds. Here, the match would be found in the foot of *leg1*. But what if you really want *toe1* in *leg2*? In that case, you may specify:

```
myCube = SO_GET_PART(myGoon, "leg2.toe1", SoCube);
```

which returns *toe1* in *leg2*. This is equivalent to *leg2.foot.toe1*.

You can also refer to parts by indexing into any part that is defined as a list in the catalog—for example, "childList[0]" or "callbackList[2]."

The following excerpts illustrate three different ways to create node-kit parts and set their values. These excerpts assume you have subclassed to create your own class, derived from **SoBaseKit**, an **SoGoonKit** (see *The Inventor Toolmaker*, Chapter 7). This goon has a body, legs, and feet, as described earlier.

This fragment shows setting each part individually:

```
SoGoonKit *myGoon = new SoGoonKit();

myGoon->set("body.material", "diffuseColor [1 0 0 ]");
// makes body red
myGoon->set("leg2.toe1", "width 2 height 3 depth 1");
// creates toe with proper dimensions
```

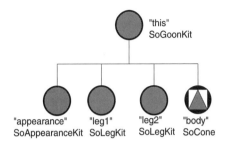

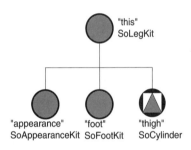

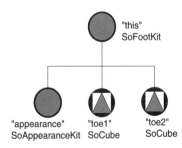

Figure 14-9   Three Node-Kit Classes for Making "Goons"

This fragment shows getting parts and editing them:

```
SoGoonKit *myGoon = new SoGoonKit();
SoMaterial *bodyMtl;
SoCube     *toe;

bodyMtl = SO_GET_PART(myGoon, "body.material", SoMaterial);
bodyMtl->diffuseColor.setValue(1, 0, 0);
toe = SO_GET_PART(myGoon, "leg2.toe1", SoCube);
toe->width.setValue(2);
toe->height.setValue(3);
toe->depth.setValue(1);
```

This fragment shows setting both parts in one command:

```
SoGoonKit *myGoon = new SoGoonKit();

myGoon->set("body.material { diffuseColor [ 1 0 0 ] }
            leg2.toe1      { width 2
                             height 3
                             depth 1 }");
```

Creating Paths to Parts

Sometimes you will need a path down to one of the node kit parts—for instance, to replace a part with a manipulator as described in Chapter 15. Use the **createPathToPart()** method to obtain the path to the desired node for the manipulator.

createPathToPart(*partName, makeIfNeeded, pathToExtend*);

For example, after picking a node kit, replace the transform part with a trackball manipulator:

```
SoPath *pickPath = myPickAction->getPath();

if((pickPath != NULL) &&
(pickPath->getTail()->isOfType(SoBaseKit::getClassTypeId()))){
SoTrackballManip *tb = new SoTrackball;
SoBaseKit *kit = (SoBaseKit *) pickPath->getTail();
   // extends the pick path all the way down
   // to the transform node
SoPath *attachPath = kit->createPathToPart("transform",
                TRUE, pickPath);
tb->replaceNode(attachPath);
```

Note that using **replaceNode()** does more work for you than simply calling

```
setPart("transform", tb)
```

Field values are copied from the existing "transform" part into the trackball manipulator's fields.

If the *pathToExtend* parameter is NULL or missing, **createPathToPart()** simply returns the path from the top of the node kit to the specified part (see Figure 14-10):

```
SoPath *littlePath;

littlePath = myKit->createPathToPart("transform", TRUE);
```

Since *makeIfNeeded* is TRUE, the "transform" part will be created if it does not already exist. However, if *makeIfNeeded* is FALSE and the part does not exist, *createPathToPart* returns NULL.

Tip: If you want to view the full path, including hidden children, be sure to ❖ cast the **SoPath** to an **SoFullPath**.

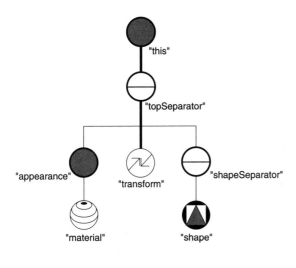

— littlePath

Figure 14-10   Obtaining the Path to a Given Part

If the *pathToExtend* parameter is used, **createPathToPart()** extends the path provided all the way down to the specified part within the node kit (here, the "transform" node). (See Figure 14-11.) If the path provided as input (in this case, *pickPath*) does not include the specified node kit, *bigPath* equals NULL. If the path given as input extends past the specified node kit, the path will first be truncated at the node kit before extending it to reach the part.

```
bigPath = myKit->createPathToPart("transform", TRUE, pickPath);
```

To create a path to a child within a list part, use the same indexing notation as you would for **setPart()** or **getPart()**:

```
pathToListElement = createPathToPart("callbackList[0]", TRUE);
```

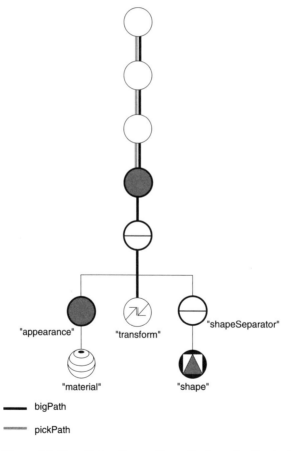

Figure 14-11   Extending a Given Path to the Desired Part

Using List Parts

Some node-kit parts are actually *lists* of parts. These lists, of type **SoNodeKitListPart**, are a special type of group that restricts its children to certain classes of nodes. Examples are "childList" (found in **SoSeparatorKit** and **SoSceneKit**) and "cameraList" and "lightList" (both found in **SoSceneKit**). Whenever you add a child to a node-kit list, the group checks to see if that child is legitimate. If the child is not legitimate, it is not added (and if you are using the debugging library, an error is printed).

Use **getPart**() to obtain the requested list, then use any of the standard group methods for adding, removing, replacing, and inserting children in the parts list. (But remember that each of these methods is redefined to check the types of children before adding them.) For example:

```
SoPointLight *myLight = new SoPointLight;

ls = (SoNodeKitListPart *) k->getPart("lightList", TRUE);

ls->addChild(myLight);
```

Using Separator Kits to Create Motion Hierarchies

SoSeparatorKit is a class of node kit. All classes derived from separator kit inherit a part called "childList," of type **SoNodeKitListPart**. Through use of the "childList," separator kits allow you to think in terms of how parts of an object move relative to each other. Each element of the child list is, in turn, an **SoSeparatorKit** and may contain its own transform node. By nesting separator kits, multiple levels of relative motion can be achieved.

Figure 14-12 shows how you might group individual parts that move together. Assume you have already made an individual **SoSeparatorKit** for each part in a balance scale, shown in Figure 14-12. You want *tray1* and *string1* to move as a unit, and *tray2* and *string2* to move as a unit. But when the beam moves, both trays and both strings move with it.

As you arrange these group kits into a hierarchy, you don't need to think in terms of the individual parts each group kit contains ("material," "complexity," and so on). You can think of the objects themselves (beam, strings, trays) and how they move relative to each other. The **childList** for **SoSeparatorKit** can contain any node derived from **SoSeparatorKit**, so any type of separator kit is permissible as an entry in this list.

The following code constructs the hierarchy shown in Figure 14-12. A working version of this model is provided in Example 14-3 at the end of this chapter.

```
scale->setPart("childList[0]", support);
scale->setPart("childList[1]", beam);
beam->setPart("childList[0]", string1);
beam->setPart("childList[1]", string2);
string1->setPart("childList[0]", tray1);
string2->setPart("childList[0]", tray2);
```

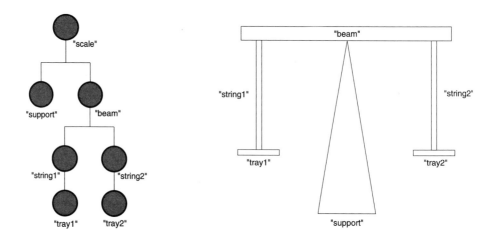

Figure 14-12   Hierarchical Motion Relationships

Examples

This section includes three examples of node kits. The first example uses two **SoShapeKits**. The second example, with detailed comments, uses an **SoWrapperKit** and an **SoSceneKit** that contains an **SoLightKit** and an **SoCameraKit**. The third example uses various node kits as well as an **SoEventCallback** with an associated function for animating the balance scale.

Simple Use of Node Kits

Example 14-1 uses node kits to create two 3D words and shows use of node kit methods to access the fields of the "material" and "transform" parts of the shape kits. It uses a calculator engine and an elapsed time engine to make the words change color and fly around the screen. Figure 14-13 shows two images from this example.

Example 14-1   Simple Use of Node Kits

```
#include <Inventor/engines/SoCalculator.h>
#include <Inventor/engines/SoElapsedTime.h>
#include <Inventor/nodekits/SoShapeKit.h>
#include <Inventor/nodes/SoMaterial.h>
#include <Inventor/nodes/SoSeparator.h>
#include <Inventor/nodes/SoText3.h>
#include <Inventor/nodes/SoTransform.h>

#include <Inventor/Xt/SoXt.h>
#include <Inventor/Xt/viewers/SoXtExaminerViewer.h>

main(int , char **argv)
{
   Widget myWindow = SoXt::init(argv[0]);
   if (myWindow == NULL) exit(1);

   SoSeparator *root = new SoSeparator;
   root->ref();

   // Create shape kits with the words "HAPPY" and "NICE"
   SoShapeKit *happyKit = new SoShapeKit;
   root->addChild(happyKit);
   happyKit->setPart("shape", new SoText3);
   happyKit->set("shape { parts ALL string \"HAPPY\"}");
   happyKit->set("font { size 2}");

   SoShapeKit *niceKit = new SoShapeKit;
   root->addChild(niceKit);
   niceKit->setPart("shape", new SoText3);
   niceKit->set("shape { parts ALL string \"NICE\"}");
   niceKit->set("font { size 2}");

   // Create the Elapsed Time engine
   SoElapsedTime *myTimer = new SoElapsedTime;
   myTimer->ref();
```

Figure 14-13　　Using an SoShapeKit with Engines

```
// Create two calculators - one for HAPPY, one for NICE.
SoCalculator *happyCalc = new SoCalculator;
happyCalc->ref();
happyCalc->a.connectFrom(&myTimer->timeOut);
happyCalc->expression = "ta=cos(2*a); tb=sin(2*a);\
    oA = vec3f(3*pow(ta,3),3*pow(tb,3),1);              \
    oB = vec3f(fabs(ta)+.1,fabs(.5*fabs(tb))+.1,1);\
    oC = vec3f(fabs(ta),fabs(tb),.5)";

// The second calculator uses different arguments to
// sin() and cos(), so it moves out of phase.
SoCalculator *niceCalc = new SoCalculator;
niceCalc->ref();
niceCalc->a.connectFrom(&myTimer->timeOut);
niceCalc->expression = "ta=cos(2*a+2); tb=sin(2*a+2);\
    oA = vec3f(3*pow(ta,3),3*pow(tb,3),1);              \
    oB = vec3f(fabs(ta)+.1,fabs(.5*fabs(tb))+.1,1);   \
    oC = vec3f(fabs(ta),fabs(tb),.5)";

// Connect the transforms from the calculators...
SoTransform *happyXf
    = (SoTransform *) happyKit->getPart("transform",TRUE);
happyXf->translation.connectFrom(&happyCalc->oA);
happyXf->scaleFactor.connectFrom(&happyCalc->oB);
SoTransform *niceXf
    = (SoTransform *) niceKit->getPart("transform",TRUE);
niceXf->translation.connectFrom(&niceCalc->oA);
niceXf->scaleFactor.connectFrom(&niceCalc->oB);
```

```
// Connect the materials from the calculators...
SoMaterial *happyMtl
   = (SoMaterial *) happyKit->getPart("material",TRUE);
happyMtl->diffuseColor.connectFrom(&happyCalc->oC);
SoMaterial *niceMtl
   = (SoMaterial *) niceKit->getPart("material",TRUE);
niceMtl->diffuseColor.connectFrom(&niceCalc->oC);

SoXtExaminerViewer *myViewer = new
         SoXtExaminerViewer(myWindow);
myViewer->setSceneGraph(root);
myViewer->setTitle("Frolicking Words");
myViewer->viewAll();
myViewer->show();

SoXt::show(myWindow);
SoXt::mainLoop();
}
```

Using Node Kits with Editors

Example 14-2 reads in a desk from a file and puts it in the "contents" part of an **SoWrapperKit**. It adds a directional light editor to the light in the scene and a material editor to the desk, as shown in Figure 14-14. The scene is organized using an **SoSceneKit**, which contains lists for grouping lights ("lightList"), cameras ("cameraList"), and objects ("childList") in a scene.

Example 14-2   Using Node Kits and Editors

```
#include <Inventor/SoDB.h>
#include <Inventor/SoInput.h>
#include <Inventor/nodekits/SoCameraKit.h>
#include <Inventor/nodekits/SoLightKit.h>
#include <Inventor/nodekits/SoSceneKit.h>
#include <Inventor/nodekits/SoWrapperKit.h>
#include <Inventor/nodes/SoMaterial.h>
#include <Inventor/nodes/SoPerspectiveCamera.h>
#include <Inventor/nodes/SoSeparator.h>

#include <Inventor/Xt/SoXt.h>
#include <Inventor/Xt/SoXtDirectionalLightEditor.h>
#include <Inventor/Xt/SoXtMaterialEditor.h>
#include <Inventor/Xt/SoXtRenderArea.h>
```

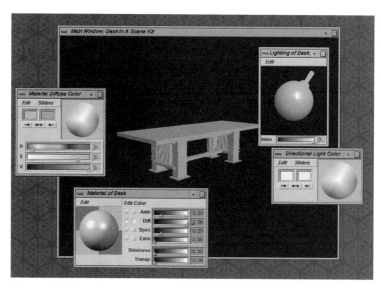

Figure 14-14 Using an SoSceneKit with Directional Light and Material Editors

```
main(int , char **argv)
{
   // Initialize Inventor and Xt
   Widget myWindow = SoXt::init(argv[0]);
   if (myWindow == NULL) exit(1);

   // SCENE!
   SoSceneKit *myScene = new SoSceneKit;
   myScene->ref();

   // LIGHTS! Add an SoLightKit to the "lightList." The
   // SoLightKit creates an SoDirectionalLight by default.
   myScene->setPart("lightList[0]", new SoLightKit);

   // CAMERA!! Add an SoCameraKit to the "cameraList." The
   // SoCameraKit creates an SoPerspectiveCamera by default.
   myScene->setPart("cameraList[0]", new SoCameraKit);
   myScene->setCameraNumber(0);

   // Read an object from file.
   SoInput myInput;
   if (!myInput.openFile("desk.iv"))
      return (1);
   SoSeparator *fileContents = SoDB::readAll(&myInput);
   if (fileContents == NULL) return (1);
```

```
// OBJECT!! Create an SoWrapperKit and set its contents to
// be what you read from file.
SoWrapperKit *myDesk = new SoWrapperKit();
myDesk->setPart("contents", fileContents);
myScene->setPart("childList[0]", myDesk);
// Give the desk a good starting color
myDesk->set("material { diffuseColor .8 .3 .1 }");

// MATERIAL EDITOR!!  Attach it to myDesk's material node.
// Use the SO_GET_PART macro to get this part from myDesk.
SoXtMaterialEditor *mtlEditor = new SoXtMaterialEditor();
SoMaterial *mtl = SO_GET_PART(myDesk,"material",SoMaterial);
mtlEditor->attach(mtl);
mtlEditor->setTitle("Material of Desk");
mtlEditor->show();

// DIRECTIONAL LIGHT EDITOR!! Attach it to the
// SoDirectionalLight node within the SoLightKit we made.
SoXtDirectionalLightEditor *ltEditor =
            new SoXtDirectionalLightEditor();
SoPath *ltPath = myScene->createPathToPart(
   "lightList[0].light", TRUE);
ltEditor->attach(ltPath);
ltEditor->setTitle("Lighting of Desk");
ltEditor->show();

SoXtRenderArea *myRenderArea = new SoXtRenderArea(myWindow);

// Set up Camera with ViewAll...
// -- use the SO_GET_PART macro to get the camera node.
// -- viewall is a method on the 'camera' part of
//    the cameraKit, not on the cameraKit itself.  So the part
//    we ask for is not 'cameraList[0]' (which is of type
//    SoPerspectiveCameraKit), but
//    'cameraList[0].camera' (which is of type
//    SoPerspectiveCamera).
SoPerspectiveCamera *myCamera = SO_GET_PART(myScene,
   "cameraList[0].camera", SoPerspectiveCamera);
SbViewportRegion myRegion(myRenderArea->getSize());
myCamera->viewAll(myScene, myRegion);
myRenderArea->setSceneGraph(myScene);
myRenderArea->setTitle("Main Window: Desk In A Scene Kit");
myRenderArea->show();

SoXt::show(myWindow);
SoXt::mainLoop();
}
```

Creating a Motion Hierarchy

Example 14-3 creates a balance scale using node kits and their motion hierarchies. Figure 14-15 shows the balance scale created by this example.

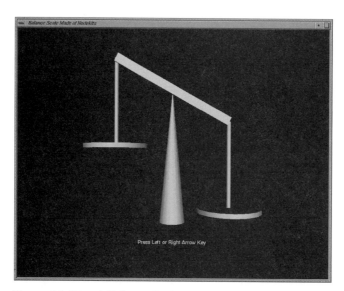

Figure 14-15   A Balance Scale Created with Node Kits

Example 14-3   Using Node Kits to Create a Motion Hierarchy

```
// This example illustrates the creation of motion hierarchies
// using nodekits by creating a model of a balance-style scale.

// It adds an SoEventCallback to the "callback" list in the
// nodekit called 'support.'
// The callback will have the following response to events:
// Pressing right arrow key == lower the right pan
// Pressing left arrow key  == lower the left pan
// The pans are lowered by animating three rotations in the
// motion hierarchy.
// Use an SoText2Kit to print instructions to the user as part
// of the scene.

#include <Inventor/events/SoKeyboardEvent.h>
#include <Inventor/nodekits/SoCameraKit.h>
#include <Inventor/nodekits/SoLightKit.h>
```

```
#include <Inventor/nodekits/SoSceneKit.h>
#include <Inventor/nodekits/SoShapeKit.h>
#include <Inventor/nodes/SoCone.h>
#include <Inventor/nodes/SoCube.h>
#include <Inventor/nodes/SoCylinder.h>
#include <Inventor/nodes/SoEventCallback.h>
#include <Inventor/nodes/SoText2.h>
#include <Inventor/nodes/SoTransform.h>
#include <Inventor/nodes/SoPerspectiveCamera.h>

#include <Inventor/Xt/SoXt.h>
#include <Inventor/Xt/SoXtRenderArea.h>

// Callback Function for Animating the Balance Scale.
// --used to make the balance tip back and forth
// --Note: this routine is only called in response to KeyPress
//    events since the call 'setEventInterest(KeyPressMask)' is
//    made on the SoEventCallback node that uses it.
// --The routine checks if the key pressed was left arrow (which
//    is XK_Left in X-windows talk), or right arrow (which is
//    XK_Right)
// --The balance is made to tip by rotating the beam part of the
//    scale (to tip it) and then compensating (making the strings
//    vertical again) by rotating the string parts in the opposite
//    direction.
void
tipTheBalance(
   void *userData, // The nodekit representing 'support', the
                   // fulcrum of the balance. Passed in during
                   // main routine, below.
   SoEventCallback *eventCB)
{
   const SoEvent *ev = eventCB->getEvent();

   // Which Key was pressed?
   // If Right or Left Arrow key, then continue...
   if (SO_KEY_PRESS_EVENT(ev, RIGHT_ARROW) ||
       SO_KEY_PRESS_EVENT(ev, LEFT_ARROW)) {
      SoShapeKit  *support, *beam1, *string1, *string2;
      SbRotation  startRot, beamIncrement, stringIncrement;

      // Get the different nodekits from the userData.
      support = (SoShapeKit *) userData;
```

```
    // These three parts are extracted based on knowledge of
    // the motion hierarchy (see the diagram in the main
    // routine.
    beam1   = (SoShapeKit *)support->getPart("childList[0]",TRUE);
    string1 = (SoShapeKit *) beam1->getPart("childList[0]",TRUE);
    string2 = (SoShapeKit *) beam1->getPart("childList[1]",TRUE);

       //Set angular increments to be .1 Radians about the Z-Axis
       //The strings rotate opposite the beam, and the two types
       //of key press produce opposite effects.
       if (SO_KEY_PRESS_EVENT(ev, RIGHT_ARROW)) {
          beamIncrement.setValue(SbVec3f(0, 0, 1), -.1);
          stringIncrement.setValue(SbVec3f(0, 0, 1), .1);
       }
       else {
          beamIncrement.setValue(SbVec3f(0, 0, 1), .1);
          stringIncrement.setValue(SbVec3f(0, 0, 1), -.1);
       }

       // Use SO_GET_PART to find the transform for each of the
       // rotating parts and modify their rotations.

       SoTransform *xf;
       xf = SO_GET_PART(beam1, "transform", SoTransform);
       startRot = xf->rotation.getValue();
       xf->rotation.setValue(startRot *  beamIncrement);

       xf = SO_GET_PART(string1, "transform", SoTransform);
       startRot = xf->rotation.getValue();
       xf->rotation.setValue(startRot *  stringIncrement);

       xf = SO_GET_PART(string2, "transform", SoTransform);
       startRot = xf->rotation.getValue();
       xf->rotation.setValue(startRot *  stringIncrement);

       eventCB->setHandled();
    }
}

main(int , char **argv)
{
    Widget myWindow = SoXt::init(argv[0]);
    if (myWindow == NULL) exit(1);

    SoSceneKit *myScene = new SoSceneKit;
    myScene->ref();
```

```
myScene->setPart("lightList[0]", new SoLightKit);
myScene->setPart("cameraList[0]", new SoCameraKit);
myScene->setCameraNumber(0);

// Create the Balance Scale -- put each part in the
// childList of its parent, to build up this hierarchy:
//
//                      myScene
//                         |
//                      support
//                         |
//                       beam
//                         |
//                     --------
//                     |       |
//                  string1  string2
//                     |       |
//                  tray1     tray2

SoShapeKit *support = new SoShapeKit();
support->setPart("shape", new SoCone);
support->set("shape { height 3 bottomRadius .3 }");
myScene->setPart("childList[0]", support);

SoShapeKit *beam = new SoShapeKit();
beam->setPart("shape", new SoCube);
beam->set("shape { width 3 height .2 depth .2 }");
beam->set("transform { translation 0 1.5 0 } ");
support->setPart("childList[0]", beam);

SoShapeKit *string1 = new SoShapeKit;
string1->setPart("shape", new SoCylinder);
string1->set("shape { radius .05 height 2}");
string1->set("transform { translation -1.5 -1 0 }");
string1->set("transform { center 0 1 0 }");
beam->setPart("childList[0]", string1);

SoShapeKit *string2 = new SoShapeKit;
string2->setPart("shape", new SoCylinder);
string2->set("shape { radius .05 height 2}");
string2->set("transform { translation 1.5 -1 0 } ");
string2->set("transform { center 0 1 0 } ");
beam->setPart("childList[1]", string2);
```

```
SoShapeKit *tray1 = new SoShapeKit;
tray1->setPart("shape", new SoCylinder);
tray1->set("shape { radius .75 height .1 }");
tray1->set("transform { translation 0 -1 0 } ");
string1->setPart("childList[0]", tray1);

SoShapeKit *tray2 = new SoShapeKit;
tray2->setPart("shape", new SoCylinder);
tray2->set("shape { radius .75 height .1 }");
tray2->set("transform { translation 0 -1 0 } ");
string2->setPart("childList[0]", tray2);

// Add EventCallback so Balance Responds to Events
SoEventCallback *myCallbackNode = new SoEventCallback;
myCallbackNode->addEventCallback(
    SoKeyboardEvent::getClassTypeId(),
        tipTheBalance, support);
support->setPart("callbackList[0]", myCallbackNode);

// Add Instructions as Text in the Scene...
SoShapeKit *myText = new SoShapeKit;
myText->setPart("shape", new SoText2);
myText->set("shape { string \"Press Left or Right Arrow Key\" }");
myText->set("shape { justification CENTER }");
myText->set("font { name \"Helvetica-Bold\" }");
myText->set("font { size 16.0 }");
myText->set("transform { translation 0 -2 0 }");
myScene->setPart("childList[1]", myText);

SoXtRenderArea *myRenderArea = new SoXtRenderArea(myWindow);

// Get camera from scene and tell it to viewAll...
SbViewportRegion myRegion(myRenderArea->getSize());
SoPerspectiveCamera *myCamera = SO_GET_PART(myScene,
    "cameraList[0].camera", SoPerspectiveCamera);
myCamera->viewAll(myScene, myRegion);

myRenderArea->setSceneGraph(myScene);
myRenderArea->setTitle("Balance Scale Made of Nodekits");
myRenderArea->show();

SoXt::show(myWindow);
SoXt::mainLoop();
}
```

## Chapter 15

Draggers and Manipulators

Chapter Objectives

After reading this chapter, you'll be able to do the following:

- Connect draggers to fields or engines in the scene graph

- Explain the difference between a dragger and a manipulator

- Write callback functions that are performed when interaction starts or finishes, when the mouse moves, or when the value in a dragger's field changes

- Use manipulators in your application to allow the user to edit nodes in the scene graph directly

- Customize the appearance of a dragger

This chapter describes how to use *draggers* and *manipulators*, which are special objects in the scene graph that have a user interface and respond to events. Manipulators, such as the handle box, trackball, and directional light manipulator, are nodes that employ draggers to enable the user to interact with them and edit them. For information on how draggers receive and respond to events, see Chapter 10.

What Is a Dragger?

A dragger is a node in the scene graph with specialized behavior that enables it to respond to user events. All Inventor draggers have a built-in user interface, and they insert geometry into the scene graph that is used for picking and user feedback. Figure 15-1 shows the class tree for dragger classes.

Types of Draggers

For all draggers subclassed from **SoDragger**, the user employs a click-drag-release motion with the mouse. Table 15-1 indicates the use of each dragger subclassed from **SoDragger**. For example, the drag-point dragger responds to dragging by translating in three dimensions.

Subclasses of **SoDragger** fall into two general categories: *simple* draggers and *compound* draggers. In general, simple draggers perform only one operation, such as a scale or a translation. Compound draggers perform several operations and are composed of multiple simple draggers. Simple draggers can be used in three ways:

- You can *connect the field* of a simple dragger to other fields or to engines in the scene graph. This is a simple way to set up dependencies within the scene graph.

- You can write *callback functions* that are performed when interaction starts or finishes, whenever the mouse moves, or when the value in the dragger's field changes.

- You can use the simple draggers as *building blocks* to create more complex draggers.

Compound draggers are similar to simple draggers, except that they have more parts because they are comprised of two or more draggers. The **SoTransformBoxDragger**, for example, uses a scale dragger, three rotators, and six translators.

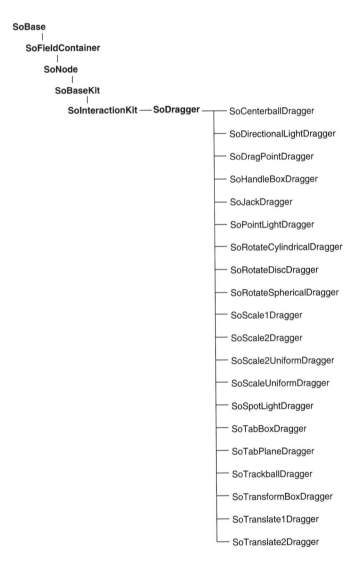

SoBase
|
SoFieldContainer
|
SoNode
|
SoBaseKit
|
SoInteractionKit — **SoDragger** —
- SoCenterballDragger
- SoDirectionalLightDragger
- SoDragPointDragger
- SoHandleBoxDragger
- SoJackDragger
- SoPointLightDragger
- SoRotateCylindricalDragger
- SoRotateDiscDragger
- SoRotateSphericalDragger
- SoScale1Dragger
- SoScale2Dragger
- SoScale2UniformDragger
- SoScaleUniformDragger
- SoSpotLightDragger
- SoTabBoxDragger
- SoTabPlaneDragger
- SoTrackballDragger
- SoTransformBoxDragger
- SoTranslate1Dragger
- SoTranslate2Dragger

Figure 15-1   Dragger Classes

Dragger	Use
SoCenterballDragger	rotation, center
SoDirectionalLightDragger	rotation
SoDragPointDragger	translation
SoHandleBoxDragger	translation, scale
SoJackDragger	rotation, translation, uniform scale (three dimensions)
SoPointLightDragger	translation
SoRotateCylindricalDragger	rotation
SoRotateDiscDragger	rotation
SoRotateSphericalDragger	rotation
SoScale1Dragger	scale (one dimension)
SoScale2Dragger	scale (two dimensions)
SoScaleUniformDragger	uniform scale (three dimensions)
SoScale2UniformDragger	uniform scale (two dimensions)
SoSpotLightDragger	translation, rotation, cone angle
SoTabBoxDragger	scale, translation
SoTabPlaneDragger	scale (two dimensions), translation (two dimensions)
SoTrackballDragger	rotation, scale
SoTransformBoxDragger	rotation, translation, scale
SoTranslate1Dragger	translation (one dimension)
SoTranslate2Dragger	translation (two dimensions)

Table 15-1   Uses of Draggers

Manipulators versus Draggers

Manipulators are subclasses of other nodes (such as **SoTransform** or **SoDirectionalLight**) that employ draggers (as hidden children) to respond to user events and edit themselves. Figure 15-2 shows the portions of the class tree that contain manipulator classes. Each manipulator *contains* a dragger that responds directly to user events and in turn modifies the fields of the manipulator. A manipulator inserts geometry into the scene that provides feedback to the user; this geometry is provided by the manipulator's dragger. An **SoHandleBoxManip**, for example, inserts cubes and lines into the scene that allow the user to edit the scale and translate fields of an **SoTransform** node by moving the mouse in various ways (see Figure 15-3). This geometry is part of the **SoHandleBoxDragger** contained within the **SoHandleBoxManip** manipulator. An **SoTrackballManip** allows the user to edit the rotation field of an **SoTransform** node by inserting a sphere surrounded by three ribbons into the scene (see Figure 15-4). The user can then rotate or scale the object inside this trackball.

A dragger moves only itself when it responds to user events. A manipulator, on the other hand, moves itself and affects other objects in the scene graph because, as a subclass of **SoTransform** or **SoLight**, it functions as a transform or light node and modifies the traversal state. A dragger supplies geometry and a user interface for a manipulator. A manipulator uses the values it receives from the dragger and copies them into its own fields. When interaction finishes and the manipulator is removed from the scene graph, it copies its values into the transform or light node it was replacing.

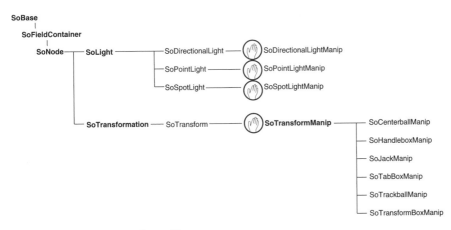

Figure 15-2   Manipulator Classes

A manipulator replaces a node in the scene graph, substituting an editable version of that node for the original. When interaction finishes, the original (non-editable) node can be restored. Each manipulator contains a dragger that allows the user to edit its fields. Manipulators derived from **SoTransform** are as follows:

SoCenterBallManip

SoHandleBoxManip

SoJackManip

SoTabBoxManip

SoTrackballManip

SoTransformBoxManip

Other manipulators include the **SoPointLightManip**, derived from **SoPointLight**, and the **SoDirectionalLightManip**, derived from **SoDirectionalLight**.

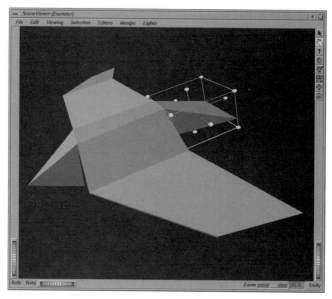

Figure 15-3   Handle-Box Manipulator

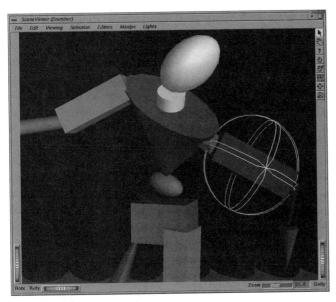

Figure 15-4   Trackball Manipulator

Simple Draggers

A simple dragger moves in 3D space in response to click-drag-release mouse events. Its position in space is determined by its position in the scene graph. Each simple dragger has a field that reflects the current state of the dragger. For example, the **SoRotateDiscDragger** has a rotation field that indicates its current rotation value. This field can be connected to other fields in the scene graph or to the input field of an engine (see the following section). Callback functions can also be used with simple draggers, as described in "Callback Functions" on page 397.

Field Connections

A convenient way to use a dragger is to connect its fields to other fields or engines in the scene graph. For example, the **SoTranslate1Dragger** has a **translation** field that could be used in a variety of ways. Figure 15-5 shows how this field could be used to edit the radius of a cone node. Since the dragger's **translation** field is an **SoSFVec3f**, you need to use an **SoDecomposeVec3f** engine to extract the *x* value of the dragger's translation. This *x* value is then fed into the **bottomRadius** field of the cone node. Now, whenever the dragger is translated, the radius of the cone changes.

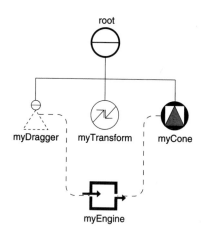

Figure 15-5   Connecting a Dragger's Field to Another Field in the Scene Graph

Example 15-1 shows the code for connecting these fields and engines. Figure 15-6 shows an image created by this example.

Example 15-1   Using a Simple Dragger

```
// Create myDragger with an initial translation of (1,0,0)
SoTranslate1Dragger *myDragger = new SoTranslate1Dragger;
root->addChild(myDragger);
myDragger->translation.setValue(1,0,0);

// Place an SoCone below myDragger
SoTransform *myTransform = new SoTransform;
SoCone *myCone = new SoCone;
root->addChild(myTransform);
root->addChild(myCone);
myTransform->translation.setValue(0,3,0);

// SoDecomposeVec3f engine extracts myDragger's x-component
// The result is connected to myCone's bottomRadius.
SoDecomposeVec3f *myEngine = new SoDecomposeVec3f;
myEngine->vector.connectFrom(&myDragger->translation);
myCone->bottomRadius.connectFrom(&myEngine->x);
```

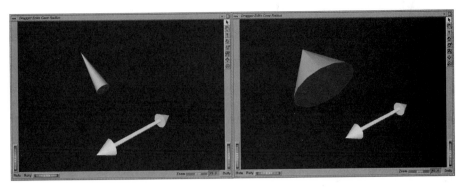

Figure 15-6   Using a Dragger and Engine to Edit the Radius of a Cone

Callback Functions

Any dragger or manipulator can use callback functions to pass data back to the application. This callback mechanism can be used to augment the default functionality of the dragger or manipulator. Several lists of callback functions and associated data, of class **SoCallbackList**, are automatically created when a dragger is constructed. You can add functions to and remove functions from these lists and pass a pointer to the user callback data. Draggers use these lists of callback functions:

- *Start callbacks*—called when manipulation starts

- *Motion callbacks*—called after each mouse movement during manipulation

- *Value-changed callbacks*—called when any of the dragger's fields change

- *Finish callbacks*—called when manipulation finishes

The following methods add functions to and remove functions from these callback lists:

addStartCallback(*functionName, userData*)
removeStartCallback(*functionName, userData*)

addMotionCallback(*functionName, userData*)
removeMotionCallback(*functionName, userData*)

addValueChangedCallback(*functionName, userData*)
removeValueChangedCallback(*functionName, userData*)

addFinishCallback(*functionName, userData*)
removeFinishCallback(*functionName, userData*)

These methods are called on **SoDragger**. To call one of these methods on the manipulator, call **getDragger()** first, then call the callback list method.

For example, you could write a start callback function that would turn an object to wireframe during manipulation and a finish callback function that would turn it back to filled drawing style when manipulation finishes. You could write a value-changed callback to find out when the value being manipulated has changed, and then use the **getValue()** method to obtain the field's new value.

Using Multiple Draggers

Example 15-2 uses three **translate1Draggers** to change the *x*, *y*, and *z* components of a translation that affects some 3D text. Figure 15-7 shows two images created by this program.

Figure 15-7   A Slider Box That Uses Draggers and Engines to Move Text

Example 15-2   Using Multiple Draggers

```
//  Uses 3 translate1Draggers to change the x, y, and z
//  components of a translation. A calculator engine assembles
//  the components.
//  Arranges these draggers along edges of a box containing the
//  3D text to be moved.
//  The 3D text and the box are made with SoShapeKits

#include <Inventor/engines/SoCalculator.h>
#include <Inventor/nodekits/SoShapeKit.h>
```

```
#include <Inventor/nodes/SoCube.h>
#include <Inventor/nodes/SoSeparator.h>
#include <Inventor/nodes/SoText3.h>
#include <Inventor/nodes/SoTransform.h>

#include <Inventor/Xt/SoXt.h>
#include <Inventor/Xt/viewers/SoXtExaminerViewer.h>

#include <Inventor/draggers/SoTranslate1Dragger.h>

main(int , char **argv)
{
   Widget myWindow = SoXt::init(argv[0]);
   if (myWindow == NULL) exit(1);

   SoSeparator *root = new SoSeparator;
   root->ref();

   // Create 3 translate1Draggers and place them in space.
   SoSeparator *xDragSep = new SoSeparator;
   SoSeparator *yDragSep = new SoSeparator;
   SoSeparator *zDragSep = new SoSeparator;
   root->addChild(xDragSep);
   root->addChild(yDragSep);
   root->addChild(zDragSep);
   // Separators will each hold a different transform
   SoTransform *xDragXf = new SoTransform;
   SoTransform *yDragXf = new SoTransform;
   SoTransform *zDragXf = new SoTransform;
   xDragXf->set("translation 0 -4 8");
   yDragXf->set("translation -8 0 8 rotation 0 0 1 1.57");
   zDragXf->set("translation -8 -4 0 rotation 0 1 0 -1.57");
   xDragSep->addChild(xDragXf);
   yDragSep->addChild(yDragXf);
   zDragSep->addChild(zDragXf);

   // Add the draggers under the separators, after transforms
   SoTranslate1Dragger *xDragger = new SoTranslate1Dragger;
   SoTranslate1Dragger *yDragger = new SoTranslate1Dragger;
   SoTranslate1Dragger *zDragger = new SoTranslate1Dragger;
   xDragSep->addChild(xDragger);
   yDragSep->addChild(yDragger);
   zDragSep->addChild(zDragger);

   // Create shape kit for the 3D text
   // The text says 'Slide Arrows To Move Me'
   SoShapeKit *textKit = new SoShapeKit;
```

```
root->addChild(textKit);
SoText3 *myText3 = new SoText3;
textKit->setPart("shape", myText3);
myText3->justification = SoText3::CENTER;
myText3->string.set1Value(0,"Slide Arrows");
myText3->string.set1Value(1,"To");
myText3->string.set1Value(2,"Move Me");
textKit->set("font { size 2}");
textKit->set("material { diffuseColor 1 1 0}");

// Create shape kit for surrounding box.
// It's an unpickable cube, sized as (16,8,16)
SoShapeKit *boxKit = new SoShapeKit;
root->addChild(boxKit);
boxKit->setPart("shape", new SoCube);
boxKit->set("drawStyle { style LINES }");
boxKit->set("pickStyle { style UNPICKABLE }");
boxKit->set("material { emissiveColor 1 0 1 }");
boxKit->set("shape { width 16 height 8 depth 16 }");

// Create the calculator to make a translation
// for the text. The x component of a translate1Dragger's
// translation field shows how far it moved in that
// direction. So our text's translation is:
// (xDragTranslate[0],yDragTranslate[0],zDragTranslate[0])
SoCalculator *myCalc = new SoCalculator;
myCalc->ref();
myCalc->A.connectFrom(&xDragger->translation);
myCalc->B.connectFrom(&yDragger->translation);
myCalc->C.connectFrom(&zDragger->translation);
myCalc->expression = "oA = vec3f(A[0],B[0],C[0])";

// Connect the the translation in textKit from myCalc
SoTransform *textXf = (SoTransform *)
        textKit->getPart("transform",TRUE);
textXf->translation.connectFrom(&myCalc->oA);

SoXtExaminerViewer *myViewer = new
        SoXtExaminerViewer(myWindow);
myViewer->setSceneGraph(root);
myViewer->setTitle("Slider Box");
myViewer->viewAll();
myViewer->show();

SoXt::show(myWindow);
SoXt::mainLoop();
}
```

Manipulators

You can use manipulators in your application in various ways:

- You can use the **replaceNode()** method to replace certain kinds of nodes in the scene graph with an editable version. When the user is finished manipulating the node, use the **replaceManip()** method to restore the original node to the scene graph.

- You can write your own callback functions to use the field values of the manipulator. The callback functions described in "Callback Functions" on page 397 can be used for any manipulator. (Recall that these functions belong to the dragger, so you need to call **getDragger()** before using them.)

You can also combine use of these two techniques. For example, you can use **replaceNode()** to replace an **SoTransform** with a manipulator. Then you can use a value-changed callback to notify the application when any of the manipulator's dragger fields changes, and the application can use this new value, if desired.

The following sections describe both of these techniques in more detail.

Replacing a Node with a Manipulator

To use any manipulator in an application, follow these basic steps:

1. Construct the manipulator.

2. Reference it if you plan on reusing it.

3. Replace the node in the scene graph with the manipulator. Manipulators derived from **SoTransform**, such as the handle box and trackball, replace an **SoTransform** node. An **SoDirectionalLight-Manip** replaces an **SoDirectionalLight** node, an **SoPointLightManip** replaces an **SoPointLight** node, and so on.

Replacing a Node

The **replaceNode()** method takes a path as an argument:

replaceNode(SoPath *p)

The path is supplied by the application. For example, Figure 15-8 shows the path to a target **SoTransform** node. When a transform manipulator replaces this node, editing the manipulator will affect *cube2* in the scene graph.

Manipulators subclassed from **SoTransformManip** use special nodes to maintain their shape (so that the trackball remains spherical, for example) and to ensure that they surround the shape objects they affect. These nodes are described in *The Inventor Toolmaker*.

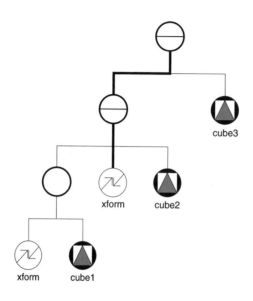

Figure 15-8   Specifying the Path to the Target Node

Removing the Manipulator

To remove the manipulator from the scene graph:

1. Use the **replaceManip()** method to restore the original node to the scene graph. In the example, the field values from the manipulator are copied into the transform node.

2. Use **unref()** on the manipulator so that it will be deleted.

Because the manipulator methods **replaceManip()** and **replaceNode()** exchange the new node for the tail of the given path, you can reuse the path for subsequent calls to these methods.

For example, if we begin with:

```
myManip = new SoTrackballManip;
myPathToTransform = createPathtoTransform(pickPath);
```

Then we can call:

```
myManip->replaceNode(myPathToTransform);
```

to put the manipulator at the end of the path.

Later, we can call

```
myManip->replaceManip(myPathToTransform, new SoTransform);
```

to remove the manipulator and replace it with a transform.

Using the replaceNode() Method

Example 15-3 displays a cube, a sphere, and a lamp. The lamp is read from a file and inserted as the "contents" part of an **SoWrapperKit**. When the user picks the cube, a trackball replaces the transform node that affects the cube. When the user picks the sphere, a handle box replaces the transform node that affects the sphere. When the user picks the lamp, a transform box replaces the "transform" part of the wrapper kit containing the lamp. Figure 15-9 shows an image created by this program. This example shows the following techniques:

- Using **replaceNode()** and **replaceManip()** to make certain nodes in the scene graph editable and to restore the original nodes when manipulation finishes

- Using selection callbacks (see Chapter 10)

Example 15-3   Using Manipulators to Transform Objects

```
// Note that for illustration purposes, the
// cube and SoWrapperKit already have transform nodes
// associated with them; the sphere does not. In all cases,
// the routine createTransformPath() is used to find the
// transform node that affects the picked object.

#include <Inventor/SoDB.h>
#include <Inventor/SoInput.h>
#include <Inventor/manips/SoHandleBoxManip.h>
#include <Inventor/manips/SoTrackballManip.h>
#include <Inventor/manips/SoTransformBoxManip.h>
#include <Inventor/nodekits/SoWrapperKit.h>
#include <Inventor/nodes/SoCamera.h>
#include <Inventor/nodes/SoCube.h>
#include <Inventor/nodes/SoGroup.h>
#include <Inventor/nodes/SoLight.h>
```

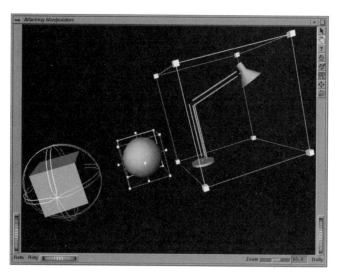

Figure 15-9   Adding Manipulators to a Scene

```
#include <Inventor/nodes/SoMaterial.h>
#include <Inventor/nodes/SoSelection.h>
#include <Inventor/nodes/SoSphere.h>
#include <Inventor/nodes/SoTransform.h>

#include <Inventor/Xt/SoXt.h>
#include <Inventor/Xt/viewers/SoXtExaminerViewer.h>

// function prototypes
void selectionCallback(void *, SoPath *);
void deselectionCallback(void *, SoPath *);
void dragStartCallback(void *, SoDragger *);
void dragFinishCallback(void *, SoDragger *);

// global data
SoSeparator *root;
SoHandleBoxManip    *myHandleBox;
SoTrackballManip    *myTrackball;
SoTransformBoxManip *myTransformBox;
SoPath *handleBoxPath    = NULL;
SoPath *trackballPath    = NULL;
SoPath *transformBoxPath = NULL;
```

```
main(int, char **argv)
{
   // Initialize Inventor and Xt
   Widget myWindow = SoXt::init(argv[0]);
   if (myWindow == NULL) exit(1);

   // Create and set up the selection node
   SoSelection *selectionRoot = new SoSelection;
   selectionRoot->ref();
   selectionRoot->
      addSelectionCallback(selectionCallback, NULL);
   selectionRoot->
      addDeselectionCallback(deselectionCallback, NULL);

   // Create the scene graph
   root = new SoSeparator;
   selectionRoot->addChild(root);

   // Read a file into contents of SoWrapperKit
   // Translate it to the right.
   SoWrapperKit *myWrapperKit = new SoWrapperKit;
   root->addChild(myWrapperKit);
   SoInput myInput;
   if (!myInput.openFile("luxo.iv"))
      return (1);
   SoSeparator *objectFromFile = SoDB::readAll(&myInput);
   if (objectFromFile == NULL) return (1);
   myWrapperKit->setPart("contents",objectFromFile);
   myWrapperKit->set("transform { translation 3 -1 0 }");
   SoMaterial *wrapperMat
      = (SoMaterial *) myWrapperKit->getPart("material",TRUE);
   wrapperMat->diffuseColor.setValue(.8, .8, .8);

   // Create a cube with its own transform.
   SoSeparator *cubeRoot = new SoSeparator;
   SoTransform *cubeXform = new SoTransform;
   cubeXform->translation.setValue(-4, 0, 0);
   root->addChild(cubeRoot);
   cubeRoot->addChild(cubeXform);

   SoMaterial *cubeMat = new SoMaterial;
   cubeMat->diffuseColor.setValue(.8, .8, .8);
   cubeRoot->addChild(cubeMat);
   cubeRoot->addChild(new SoCube);
```

```
// Add a sphere node without a transform
// (one will be added when we attach the manipulator)
SoSeparator *sphereRoot = new SoSeparator;
SoMaterial *sphereMat = new SoMaterial;
root->addChild(sphereRoot);
sphereRoot->addChild(sphereMat);
sphereRoot->addChild(new SoSphere);
sphereMat->diffuseColor.setValue(.8, .8, .8);

// Create the manipulators
myHandleBox = new SoHandleBoxManip;
myHandleBox->ref();
myTrackball = new SoTrackballManip;
myTrackball->ref();
myTransformBox = new SoTransformBoxManip;
myTransformBox->ref();

// Get the draggers and add callbacks to them. Note
// that you don't put callbacks on manipulators. You put
// them on the draggers which handle events for them.
SoDragger *myDragger;
myDragger = myTrackball->getDragger();
myDragger->addStartCallback(dragStartCallback,cubeMat);
myDragger->addFinishCallback(dragFinishCallback,cubeMat);

myDragger = myHandleBox->getDragger();
myDragger->addStartCallback(dragStartCallback,sphereMat);
myDragger->addFinishCallback(dragFinishCallback,sphereMat);

myDragger = myTransformBox->getDragger();
myDragger->addStartCallback(dragStartCallback,wrapperMat);
myDragger->addFinishCallback(dragFinishCallback,wrapperMat);

SoXtExaminerViewer *myViewer
    = new SoXtExaminerViewer(myWindow);
myViewer->setSceneGraph(selectionRoot);
myViewer->setTitle("Attaching Manipulators");
myViewer->show();
myViewer->viewAll();

SoXt::show(myWindow);
SoXt::mainLoop();
}
```

```
// Is this node of a type that is influenced by transforms?
SbBool
isTransformable(SoNode *myNode)
{
   if (myNode->isOfType(SoGroup::getClassTypeId())
      || myNode->isOfType(SoShape::getClassTypeId())
      || myNode->isOfType(SoCamera::getClassTypeId())
      || myNode->isOfType(SoLight::getClassTypeId()))
      return TRUE;
   else
      return FALSE;
}


// Create a path to the transform node that affects the tail
// of the input path.   Three possible cases:
//   [1] The path-tail is a node kit. Just ask the node kit for
//       a path to the part called "transform"
//   [2] The path-tail is NOT a group.  Search siblings of path
//       tail from right to left until you find a transform. If
//       none is found, or if another transformable object is
//       found (shape,group,light,or camera), then insert a
//       transform just to the left of the tail. This way, the
//       manipulator only affects the selected object.
//   [3] The path-tail IS a group.  Search its children left to
//       right until a transform is found. If a transformable
//   *   node is found first, insert a transform just left of
//       that node.  This way the manip will affect all nodes
//       in the group.
SoPath *
createTransformPath(SoPath *inputPath)
{
   int pathLength = inputPath->getLength();
   if (pathLength < 2) // Won't be able to get parent of tail
      return NULL;

   SoNode *tail = inputPath->getTail();

   // CASE 1: The tail is a node kit.
   // Nodekits have built in policy for creating parts.
   // The kit copies inputPath, then extends it past the
   // kit all the way down to the transform. It creates the
   // transform if necessary.
   if (tail->isOfType(SoBaseKit::getClassTypeId())) {
      SoBaseKit *kit = (SoBaseKit *) tail;
      return kit->createPathToPart("transform",TRUE,inputPath);
   }
```

```
SoTransform *editXf = NULL;
SoGroup     *parent;
SbBool       existedBefore = FALSE;

// CASE 2: The tail is not a group.
SbBool isTailGroup;
isTailGroup = tail->isOfType(SoGroup::getClassTypeId());
if (!isTailGroup) {
   // 'parent' is node above tail. Search under parent right
   // to left for a transform. If we find a 'movable' node
   // insert a transform just left of tail.
   parent = (SoGroup *) inputPath->getNode(pathLength - 2);
   int tailIndx = parent->findChild(tail);

   for (int i = tailIndx; (i >= 0) && (editXf == NULL);i--){
      SoNode *myNode = parent->getChild(i);
      if (myNode->isOfType(SoTransform::getClassTypeId()))
         editXf = (SoTransform *) myNode;
      else if (i != tailIndx && (isTransformable(myNode)))
         break;
   }
   if (editXf == NULL) {
      existedBefore = FALSE;
      editXf = new SoTransform;
      parent->insertChild(editXf, tailIndx);
   }
   else
      existedBefore = TRUE;
}
// CASE 3: The tail is a group.
else {
   // Search the children from left to right for transform
   // nodes. Stop the search if we come to a movable node
   // and insert a transform before it.
   parent = (SoGroup *) tail;
   for (int i = 0;
       (i < parent->getNumChildren()) && (editXf == NULL);
       i++) {
      SoNode *myNode = parent->getChild(i);
      if (myNode->isOfType(SoTransform::getClassTypeId()))
         editXf = (SoTransform *) myNode;
      else if (isTransformable(myNode))
         break;
   }
```

```
        if (editXf == NULL) {
            existedBefore = FALSE;
            editXf = new SoTransform;
            parent->insertChild(editXf, i);
        }
        else
            existedBefore = TRUE;
    }

    // Create 'pathToXform.' Copy inputPath, then make last
    // node be editXf.
    SoPath *pathToXform = NULL;
    pathToXform = inputPath->copy();
    pathToXform->ref();
    if (!isTailGroup) // pop off the last entry.
        pathToXform->pop();
    // add editXf to the end
    int xfIndex   = parent->findChild(editXf);
    pathToXform->append(xfIndex);
    pathToXform->unrefNoDelete();

    return(pathToXform);
}


// This routine is called when an object
// gets selected. We determine which object
// was selected, then call replaceNode()
// to replace the object's transform with
// a manipulator.
void
selectionCallback(
    void *, // user data is not used
    SoPath *selectionPath)
{
    // Attach the manipulator.
    // Use the convenience routine to get a path to
    // the transform that affects the selected object.
    SoPath *xformPath = createTransformPath(selectionPath);
    if (xformPath == NULL) return;
    xformPath->ref();
```

```
      // Attach the handle box to the sphere,
      // the trackball to the cube
      // or the transformBox to the wrapperKit
      if (selectionPath->getTail()->isOfType(
            SoSphere::getClassTypeId())) {
         handleBoxPath = xformPath;
         myHandleBox->replaceNode(xformPath);
      }
      else if (selectionPath->getTail()->
            isOfType(SoCube::getClassTypeId())) {
         trackballPath = xformPath;
         myTrackball->replaceNode(xformPath);
      }
      else if (selectionPath->getTail()->
            isOfType(SoWrapperKit::getClassTypeId())) {
         transformBoxPath = xformPath;
         myTransformBox->replaceNode(xformPath);
      }
   }

   // This routine is called whenever an object gets
   // deselected. It detaches the manipulator from
   // the transform node, and removes it from the
   // scene graph that will not be visible.
   void
   deselectionCallback(
      void *, // user data is not used
      SoPath *deselectionPath)
   {
      if (deselectionPath->getTail()->
            isOfType(SoSphere::getClassTypeId())) {
         myHandleBox->replaceManip(handleBoxPath,NULL);
         handleBoxPath->unref();
      }
      else if (deselectionPath->getTail()->
            isOfType(SoCube::getClassTypeId())) {
         myTrackball->replaceManip(trackballPath,NULL);
         trackballPath->unref();
      }
      else if (deselectionPath->getTail()->
            isOfType(SoWrapperKit::getClassTypeId())) {
         myTransformBox->replaceManip(transformBoxPath,NULL);
         transformBoxPath->unref();
      }
   }
```

```
// This is called when a manipulator is
// about to begin manipulation.
void
dragStartCallback(
   void *myMaterial, // user data
   SoDragger *)         // callback data not used
{
   ((SoMaterial *) myMaterial)->diffuseColor=SbColor(1,.2,.2);
}

// This is called when a manipulator is
// done manipulating.
void
dragFinishCallback(
   void *myMaterial, // user data
   SoDragger *)     // callback data not used
{
   ((SoMaterial *) myMaterial)->diffuseColor=SbColor(.8,.8,.8);
}
```

Customizing a Dragger

This section describes how to modify the appearance of a dragger. This customization is performed either by changing the default geometry for a part or by changing the part after an instance of a dragger has been built. Although the look and feel of a dragger can be changed or removed in this manner, no new functionality can be added.

Using the **SoTrackballDragger** as an example, this section describes the *parts* of a dragger and how they combine to make the whole dragger. It explains how the *geometry* for each part can be changed or removed, and how that can affect the functionality of the dragger. Example 15-4 illustrates how parts of an **SoTranslate1Dragger** can be changed after it has been built.

Parts of a Dragger

Every dragger is a node kit that is constructed out of parts. A *part* is simply a piece of the dragger that has some task associated with it. Often, two parts act as a pair. One part is displayed when it is in use (or *active*), and the other is displayed when that part is not in use (or *inactive*). For example, for the trackball's inactive "XRotator" part, a white stripe is displayed, and for its active "XRotatorActive" part, a yellow stripe is displayed.

Each dragger has a resource file associated with it that contains an Inventor scene graph describing the default geometry for each part. By creating a new resource file, you can override the default and give the part a new shape or new properties such as color or drawing style. In the resource file, scene graphs are labeled with their unique resource names.

Many classes of draggers use the same part names. For example, the trackball, rotate-disc, rotate-cylindrical, and rotate-spherical draggers each have a part named "rotator." Since the default parts are stored in the global dictionary, each part in each class must have a unique resource name. In all cases, the class name (without the "So" or "Dragger") is prepended to the part name. Table 15-2 shows how the resource names and part names relate.

For example, the **SoTrackballDragger** has twelve parts. Table 15-2 lists the resource and part names of eight of these parts (for brevity, the "userRotator" and "userAxis" parts are omitted). When you interact with a trackball dragger, you are actually interacting with its parts. For example, if the mouse goes down over the trackball's "XRotator" part, a rotation about the *x*-axis is initiated.

Resource Names	Part Names	Task
trackballRotator trackball RotatorActive	rotator rotatorActive	Free rotation
trackballXRotator trackballXRotatorActive	XRotator XRotatorActive	Rotation about x-axis
trackballYRotator trackballYRotatorActive	YRotator YRotatorActive	Rotation about y-axis
trackballZRotator trackballZRotatorActive	ZRotator ZRotatorActive	Rotation about z-axis

Table 15-2   Selected Parts of the SoTrackballDragger

Changing a Part after Building the Dragger

To change the part of a dragger that has already been built, use the **setPart()** or **setPartAsPath()** method provided by **SoInteractionKit**. The **setPart()** method takes the root of a scene graph as a parameter, while **setPartAsPath()** accepts an **SoPath**.

For example, to change the "rotator" part of **myDragger**:

```
myDragger->setPart("rotator", myNewRotatorSceneGraph);
```

To change the "rotator" part of a dragger within a manipulator:

```
myManip->getDragger()->setPart("rotator",
                        myNewRotatorSceneGraph);
```

You can also provide **setPartAsPath()** with the path to a particular instance of an object in the scene graph. The dragger then uses that object for the part. For example, if you have an arrow used as a weather vane mounted on a post, you could provide the path to the arrow and rotate the arrow itself. (Note the difference here between specifying a node and specifying a path. If you specify the arrow *node* using **setPart()**, a new instance of that node is created and two copies of the same geometry appear on the screen. If you specify the *path* to the arrow using **setPartAsPath()**, the dragger actually uses the existing arrow node and waits for the user to press the mouse on the same weather vane that is sitting on the barn.)

```
myRotateManip->getDragger()->setPartAsPath("rotator",
                        pathToMyWeatherVaneArrow);
```

Example 15-4 shows how to change the geometry of the draggers in Example 15-2. The "translator" and "translatorActive" parts are now cubes instead of arrows. The **setPart()** method is used to replace the default parts with the new scene graphs specified here. Figure 15-10 shows the new dragger geometry.

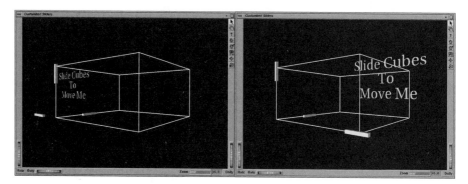

Figure 15-10   Changing the Dragger Parts to Cubes

Example 15-4   Changing Parts after Building a Dragger

```
// Create myTranslator and myTranslatorActive.
// These are custom geometry for the draggers.
SoSeparator *myTranslator = new SoSeparator;
SoSeparator *myTranslatorActive = new SoSeparator;
myTranslator->ref();
myTranslatorActive->ref();

// Materials for the dragger in regular and active states
SoMaterial *myMtl = new SoMaterial;
SoMaterial *myActiveMtl = new SoMaterial;
myMtl->diffuseColor.setValue(1,1,1);
myActiveMtl->diffuseColor.setValue(1,1,0);
myTranslator->addChild(myMtl);
myTranslatorActive->addChild(myActiveMtl);

// Same shape for both versions.
SoCube *myCube = new SoCube;
myCube->set("width 3 height .4 depth .4");
myTranslator->addChild(myCube);
myTranslatorActive->addChild(myCube);

// Now, customize the draggers with the pieces we created.
xDragger->setPart("translator",myTranslator);
xDragger->setPart("translatorActive",myTranslatorActive);
yDragger->setPart("translator",myTranslator);
yDragger->setPart("translatorActive",myTranslatorActive);
zDragger->setPart("translator",myTranslator);
zDragger->setPart("translatorActive",myTranslatorActive);
```

Changing the Default Geometry for a Part

Every class of dragger has a resource file associated with it that contains Inventor scene graphs defining default geometry for that class. The default geometry for a given class is also compiled in, so that if the dragger resource files are lost, the dragger will still operate.

Where a Dragger Looks for Defaults

When a dragger is constructed, it checks whether a resource file for overriding the defaults has been created. When reading from this file (if found), if the dragger encounters a second definition of a particular geometry, the new geometry replaces any previously defined geometry of the same name.

Inventor will look for files only if the environment variable SO_DRAGGER_DIR has been set. If it has, Inventor will look in that directory.

In all cases, a given dragger class will read only files of its same name: the **SoTranslate1Dragger** class reads only resource files named translate1Dragger.iv, the **SoTrackballDragger** class reads only files named trackballDragger.iv.

Changing the default geometry of a dragger part is a simple matter of creating a new file that contains a scene graph defining the new resource. When encountered, this new definition overrides the default definitions of that resource. The next two sections show how to do this using the **SoTrackballDragger** as a foundation.

How to Edit Your File

To change the default geometry of a part, you merely redefine the scene graph for the geometry used by the part. When creating new resource files, it is necessary to define only the geometry that you wish to change. Other geometry will use the default values.

Keep in mind that you should never edit the resource files in Inventor/resources. If you want your application to use alternate resources, put your files in a convenient place and set the SO_DRAGGER_DIR environment variable to point there.

As an example, let's replace the **trackballRotator** resource of the trackball with a cube. (For more information on the Inventor file format, see Chapter 11.) Looking at the default geometry file for the trackball, we see that the **trackballRotator** resource is defined by this scene graph:

```
# default geometry for SoTrackballDragger's "rotator" part (inactive)

DEF trackballRotator Separator {
   DrawStyle { style INVISIBLE }
   Sphere {}
}

# default geometry for SoTrackballDragger's "rotatorActive" part

DEF trackballRotatorActive Separator {
   DrawStyle { style INVISIBLE }
   Sphere {}
}
```

Note that, in the case of the trackball, the resources specify that the **rotator** and **rotatorActive** parts have the same geometry, an invisible sphere. Although this is common, some draggers may have completely different geometry for when they are inactive and active (and most manipulators have more complicated scene graphs than just a sphere).

To change the **trackballRotator** and **trackballRotatorActive** resources from an invisible sphere to a visible cube, you simply replace the sphere with a cube in both scene graphs:

```
# default geometry for the SoTrackballDragger's "rotator" part

DEF trackballRotator Separator {
   BaseColor {
      rgb 1. 1. 1.          #white
   }
   Cube {}
}

# default geometry for the SoTrackballDragger's "rotatorActive" part

DEF trackballRotatorActive Separator {
   BaseColor {
      rgb .5 .5 0.          #yellow
   }
   Cube {}
}
```

Using this mechanism, you can not only change the geometry of a given part, but also remove the functionality of that part entirely. For example, to disable the trackball's "rotator" part but still leave the cube visible, you can make the cube unpickable:

```
# default geometry for the SoTrackballDragger's "rotator" part

DEF trackballRotator Separator {
   BaseColor {
      rgb 1. 1. 1.           #white
   }
   PickStyle {
      style UNPICKABLE
   }
   Cube {}
}

# default geometry for the SoTrackballDragger's "rotatorActive"
part

DEF trackballRotatorActive Separator {
   BaseColor {
      rgb .5 .5  0.          #yellow
   }
   PickStyle {
      style UNPICKABLE
   }
   Cube {}
}
```

To remove the trackball's rotator part altogether, leaving a trackball that can only rotate about its *x*, *y*, and *z* axes, you could redefine its geometry to be an empty scene graph:

```
# default geometry for SoTrackballDragger's "rotator" part

DEF trackballRotator Separator {
}
# default geometry for SoTrackballDragger's "rotatorActive" part

DEF trackballRotatorActive Separator {
}
```

You can also read the geometry from a file instead of defining it inline:

```
DEF trackballRotator Separator {
   File { name "myCustomRotator.iv" }
}
DEF trackballRotatorActive Separator {
   File { name "myCustomRotatorActive.iv" }
}
```

Note: Never set a dragger part to NULL. Internal methods require a node to be present, even if it's simply an empty separator as shown in the previous example. (Often, the dragger parts are the children of a switch node. Changing a node to NULL could result in an incorrect ordering of the switch node's children.)

## Part VI

Using the Toolkit with Other Libraries

## Chapter 16

Inventor Component Library

Chapter Objectives

After reading this chapter, you'll be able to do the following:

- Construct, build, and use an **SoXtRenderArea**

- Use the Inventor utility functions provided for initialization and window management with the Xt Intrinsics

- Render a simple scene graph in the overlay planes

- Construct and build Inventor components and manage them as Xt widgets

- Attach a component directly to a scene graph and pass data to the application

- Use callback functions to pass data from a component to the application

- Add your own application buttons to a standard Inventor viewer

- Use the Inventor clipboard to copy and paste data

This chapter describes the Inventor Component Library, which includes utility functions, a render area, and a set of Xt components. Components are reusable modules with a built-in user interface for changing the scene graph interactively. Designed for easy integration into your program, each component is built from Motif-style Xt widgets and can be used alone or in combination with other widgets. Important concepts introduced in this chapter include the two types of components, *editors* and *viewers*, and the steps for *constructing* and *building* components and for managing them as Xt widgets. Since all components are interactive and are used to edit parts of the 3D scene, this chapter also describes how different types of components pass data back to the application.

Introduction to Components

The Inventor Component Library consists of three major parts:

- Xt utility functions for initialization and window management

- An Xt render area for static display of a scene graph

- A set of Xt components, which include their own render area and a user interface for changing the displayed scene

The following sections describe each part in more detail. This chapter assumes you have already read Chapter 10, which describes the relationship between the Xt library and the Open Inventor toolkit, which is window-system–independent.

Xt Utility Functions

This section outlines the basic sequence for initializing Inventor for use with the Xt Intrinsics, a library built on top of the X Window System library. An Xt widget contains an X window, along with extra functions for controlling the widget behavior. Because they contain a window, widgets can receive events from the X server.

The **SoXt::init()** routine returns an Xt widget that serves as the application's main shell window. In the following example, the widget is named **myWindow**. An **SoXtRenderArea** is later put into this window.

The basic steps are as follows:

1. Initialize Inventor for use with the Xt Intrinsics (**SoXt::init()**).

2. Create the **SoXtRenderArea**.

3. Build other Inventor objects and Xt widgets.

4. Show the render area and Xt widgets (**myRenderArea->show()**; **SoXt::show()**).

5. Enter the event loop (**SoXt::mainLoop()**).

Here is an example that follows this sequence:

```
#include <X11/Intrinsic.h>
#include <Inventor/So.h>
#include <Inventor/Xt/SoXt.h>
#include <Inventor/Xt/SoXtRenderArea.h>

main(int argc, char **argv)
{
   // Initialize Inventor and Xt
   Widget myWindow = SoXt::init(argv[0]);

   SoXtRenderArea *myRenderArea =
        new SoXtRenderArea(myWindow);

   SoSeparator *root = new SoSeparator;
   // Build other Inventor objects and Xt widgets
   // and set up the root
   // ...

   myRenderArea->setSceneGraph(root);
   myRenderArea->setTitle("Simple Xt");
   myRenderArea->show(); // this calls XtManageChild
   SoXt::show(myWindow); // this calls XtRealizeWidget

   // Realize other Xt widgets
   // ...

   // Go into main event loop
   SoXt::mainLoop();
}
```

Tip: Be sure your program calls **show()** for the child widgets before it calls ❖ **show()** for the shell widget. If you try to show the shell widget first, you receive this error: "Shell widget x has zero width and/or height."

Render Area

The **SoXtRenderArea** is an Xt widget that performs OpenGL rendering. When it receives X events, it translates them into **SoEvents**, which are then passed to the scene manager for handling.

Methods

The scene graph to be rendered is set into the render area with the **setSceneGraph()** method. (This method increments the root's reference count.) The **getSceneGraph()** method returns the root node of this scene graph.

Other useful methods on **SoXtRenderArea** include the following:

setTransparencyType()
          specifies how transparent objects are rendered (see the section on the render action in Chapter 9 for details).

setAntialiasing()   specifies the antialiasing methods.

setBorder()   shows or hides the window border.

setBackgroundColor()
          specifies the window background color.

The render area attaches a node sensor to the root of the scene graph and automatically redraws the scene whenever the scene graph changes. Use the following method to change the priority of the redraw sensor:

setRedrawPriority()
          specifies the priority of the redraw sensor (default priority is 10000)

Use the following two methods if you wish to disable automatic redrawing:

setAutoRedraw()   enables or disables the redraw sensor on the render area.

render()   redraws the scene immediately. If AutoRedraw is TRUE, you don't need to make this call.

See the *Open Inventor C++ Reference Manual* on **SoXtRenderArea** for more information on these methods.

Xt Devices

If you use the default values when you create an **SoXtRenderArea**, mouse and keyboard events are handled automatically. The constructor for **SoXtRenderArea** is

SoXtRenderArea(Widget *parent* = NULL,
     const char * *name* = NULL,
     SbBool *buildInsideParent* = TRUE,
     SbBool *getMouseInput* = TRUE,
     SbBool *getKeyboardInput* = TRUE);

To disable input from either the mouse or the keyboard, specify FALSE for the *getMouseInput* or *getKeyboardInput* variable. For example, to disable mouse input:

```
SoXtRenderArea *renderArea = new SoXtRenderArea(parent,
        "myRenderArea", TRUE, FALSE, TRUE);
```

Inventor defines three Xt devices:

- SoXtKeyboard

- SoXtMouse

- SoXtSpaceball

Use the **registerDevice()** method to register additional devices, such as the spaceball, with the render area. When this method is called, the render area registers interest in events generated by that device. When it receives those events, it translates them into **SoEvents** and passes them to the scene manager for handling. For information on creating your own device, see *The Inventor Toolmaker*.

Using the Overlay Planes

The overlay planes are a separate set of bitplanes that can be used for special purposes in Inventor. (Check your release notes for the number of overlay planes, which is implementation-dependent.) The overlay planes are typically used for objects in the scene that appear on top of the main image and are redrawn independently. Although you are limited with respect to color and complexity of the scene graph placed in the overlay planes, using them enables you to quickly redraw a simple scene graph without having to redraw the "complete" scene graph. The overlay planes provide a useful mechanism for providing user feedback—for example, for rapidly drawing geometry that follows the cursor.

Use the following methods to place a scene graph in the overlay planes:

setOverlaySceneGraph()
> sets the scene graph to render in the overlay planes

setOverlayColorMap()
> sets the colors to use for the overlay bit planes; the overlay planes usually use color-index mode

setOverlayBackgroundIndex()
> sets the index of the background color for the overlay image (the default is 0, the clear color)

The overlay scene graph has its own redraw sensor and is similar to the "regular" scene graph, with these restrictions:

- If you have a small number of overlay planes (for example, two), specify BASE_COLOR for the **model** field of **SoLightModel**. (If your implementation has more than two overlay planes, you may be able to obtain crude lighting effects by using the **SoMaterialIndex** node; otherwise, use the **SoColorIndex** node to specify color indices.)

- Keep the scene graph simple. Use line draw-style, rectangles, and 2D text that draws quickly. Do not use textures. Because the overlay planes are single-buffered, the redraw will flash if the scene is too complex.

- Be sure to load the color map. There is no default color map for the overlay planes.

The color map for the overlay planes contains a limited number of colors. Color 0 is *clear* and cannot be changed. With two bitplanes, you can use indices 1 through 3 for colors. The syntax for **setOverlayColorMap()** is as follows:

setOverlayColorMap(int *startIndex*, int *num*, const SbColor **colors*);

To render a shape with a particular color, use an **SoColorIndex** node to set the current color index. Do not use an **SoMaterial** node or **SoBaseColor** node to set colors when you are in color-index mode (they are ignored).

Example 16-1 illustrates use of the overlay planes with a viewer component. By default, color 0 is used for the overlay plane's background color (the *clear* color), so this example uses color 1 for the object.

Example 16-1 Using the Overlay Planes

```
#include <Inventor/SoDB.h>
#include <Inventor/SoInput.h>
#include <Inventor/nodes/SoNode.h>
#include <Inventor/nodes/SoCone.h>
#include <Inventor/Xt/SoXt.h>
#include <Inventor/Xt/viewers/SoXtExaminerViewer.h>

static char *overlayScene = "\
#Inventor V2.0 ascii\n\
\
Separator { \
   OrthographicCamera { \
      position 0 0 5 \
      nearDistance 1.0 \
      farDistance 10.0 \
      height 10 \
   } \
   LightModel { model BASE_COLOR } \
   ColorIndex { index 1 } \
   Coordinate3 { point [ -1 -1 0, -1 1 0, 1 1 0, 1 -1 0] } \
   FaceSet {} \
} ";

main(int , char **argv)
{
   // Initialize Inventor and Xt
   Widget myWindow = SoXt::init(argv[0]);

   // Read the scene graph in
   SoInput in;
   SoNode *scene;
   in.setBuffer((void *)overlayScene, (size_t)
        strlen(overlayScene));
   if (! SoDB::read(&in, scene) || scene == NULL) {
     printf("Couldn't read scene\n");
     exit(1);
   }

   // Allocate the viewer, set the overlay scene and
   // load the overlay color map with the wanted color.
   SbColor color(.5, 1, .5);
   SoXtExaminerViewer *myViewer = new
        SoXtExaminerViewer(myWindow);
   myViewer->setSceneGraph(new SoCone);
   myViewer->setOverlaySceneGraph(scene);
```

```
    myViewer->setOverlayColorMap(1, 1, &color);
    myViewer->setTitle("Overlay Plane");

    // Show the viewer and loop forever
    myViewer->show();
    XtRealizeWidget(myWindow);
    SoXt::mainLoop();
}
```

Xt Components

Components are widgets that provide some 3D-related editing function. All components in the Inventor Component Library return an Xt widget handle for standard Motif-style layout and control. The render area is an example of a simple component. Viewer components are derived from **SoXtRenderArea**.

Each component contains a user interface with such things as buttons, menus, and sliders that allow the user to change the scene graph interactively. One example of a component is the material editor, used in Examples 16-2, 16-3, and 16-4. With this editor, the user can customize objects shown in the Inventor window by interactively changing values for ambient, diffuse, specular, transparent, emissive, and shininess elements and immediately see the effects of those changes. Another example is the examiner viewer, which enables the user to move the camera through the scene, providing real-time changes in how the scene is viewed. Figure 16-1 shows the component class tree.

An **SoXtComponent** is an Inventor C++ wrapper around a Motif-compliant widget. This means that you can layer components in a window with other Motif widgets using standard layout schemes such as bulletin boards, form widgets, and row/column widgets. The material editor itself is an **SoXtComponent** made up of other components and Motif-style widgets. (Its color sliders are derived from **SoXtComponent**, and the radio buttons, toggle buttons, and menu are Motif-style widgets.) You can pass in a widget name to each component, which can then be used in resource files as the Motif name of the widget.

Components fall into two general classes, viewers and editors, depending on which part of the scene graph they affect. *Viewers* affect the camera node in the scene, and *editors* affect other nodes and fields in the scene, such as **SoMaterial** nodes and **SoDirectionalLight** nodes.

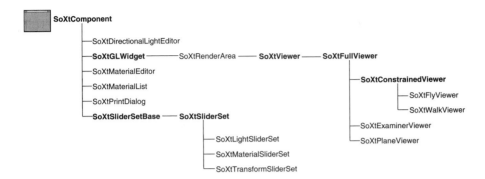

Figure 16-1   Component Classes

General Model

Follow these general steps to use any component in your program. (Additional considerations for specific components are outlined in the following sections.)

1. Create the component using its constructor. Pass in the parent widget, the widget name, and whether it should build itself inside the parent widget.

2. Show or hide the component.

3. Pass data from the component to the application.

Construct the Component

Create the component using its constructor. The constructor has the form:

SoXtComponent(Widget *parent* = NULL,
                const char * *name* = NULL,
                SbBool *buildInsideParent* = TRUE,
                SbBool *getMouseInput* = TRUE,
                SbBool *getKeyboardInput* = TRUE);

For example:

```
SoXtMaterialEditor *editor = new
        SoXtMaterialEditor(parentWidget);
```

This step initializes local variables and structures and builds the component. You supply the parent widget you want the component to appear in. If you do not supply a parent widget, or if you pass FALSE for the *buildInsideParent* parameter, the component is created inside its own shell. An important side effect is that if the component is put in its own window, it can resize itself when necessary. If the component is built into the widget tree, it cannot resize itself. If you do not supply a name, the name is the class name—"SoXtMaterialEditor," in this case.

If you specify FALSE for the *buildInsideParent* parameter, the component is built inside its own shell, but it uses the passed parent as part of the widget hierarchy for X resource lookup.

Show and Hide the Component

The **show()** and **hide()** methods are routines that allow you to manage the component widget. In summary, the **show()** method is used to make the component visible. The **hide()** method is used to make the component invisible. However, in Motif-compliant applications, the topmost parent of the widget tree must be *realized* before its children are displayed. Additionally, only the children that are *managed* are displayed.

If the Inventor component is a top-level shell widget (that is, no parent widget was passed to the constructor), the **show()** method causes the component to call **XtRealizeWidget()** on itself, and **XtManageChild()** on its children.

If the component is not a top-level shell widget, the **show()** method causes the component to call **XtManageChild()** on itself and all its children. These widgets won't be visible, though, until **XtRealizeWidget()** is called on the top-level widget.

The **show()** and **hide()** methods on **SoXtComponent** do some additional work that the component relies on. When you use a component, be sure to call its **show()** method, not **XtManage()** or **XtRealize()**, and **hide()**, not **XtUnmanage()** and **XtUnrealize()**. For instance:

```
SoXtRenderArea *ra = new SoXtRenderArea();
ra->show();
```

Each component also has a series of specialized methods for changing its behavior while the program is running. (See **SoXtComponent** in the *Open Inventor C++ Reference Manual*.) These methods include the following:

setTitle()	places a title in the title bar of a component that is a top-level shell widget
setSize()	sizes the component (uses **XtSetValue()**)
getSize()	returns the size of the component (uses **XtGetValue()**)
isVisible()	returns TRUE if the component is currently mapped and realized on the display

Passing Data to the Application

There are two ways for a component to pass data back to the application:

- Use a callback list to inform the application when certain changes occur in the component (see Example 16-2). Callbacks are useful when you want to affect more than one node (you can attach a component to only one node at a time).

- Attach the component to a node (or field) in the scene graph (see Example 16-3). For viewers, this is the *only* way to pass data back to the application; viewers are attached to an entire scene graph.

Using Callbacks

Editor components such as the material editor can also use callback functions to pass data back to the application. Example 16-2 illustrates the use of a callback procedure with the material editor.

A list of callback functions and associated data, **SoCallbackList**, is automatically created when a component is constructed. You can add functions to and remove functions from this list and pass a pointer to the callback data.

Some widgets, such as viewers, use lists of callback functions:

- *Start callbacks*—called when interaction starts (for example, on a mouse down event)

- *Finish callbacks*—called when interaction finishes (for example, on a mouse-up event)

The following methods add functions to and remove functions from these callback lists:

addStartCallback(*functionName, userData*)
removeStartCallback(*functionName, userData*)

addFinishCallback(*functionName, userData*)
removeFinishCallback(*functionName, userData*)

The material editor invokes its callbacks or updates the nodes it is attached to according to a programmable update frequency. Use the **setUpdateFrequency()** method to specify this frequency. Choices are as follows:

CONTINUOUS   continuously update the field as the value changes (the default)

AFTER_ACCEPT   update the field only when the user hits the accept button

Example 16-2 builds a render area in a window supplied by the application and a material editor in its own window. It uses callbacks for the component to report new values.

Example 16-2   Using a Callback Function

```
#include <Inventor/SoDB.h>
#include <Inventor/Xt/SoXt.h>
#include <Inventor/Xt/SoXtMaterialEditor.h>
#include <Inventor/Xt/SoXtRenderArea.h>
#include <Inventor/nodes/SoDirectionalLight.h>
#include <Inventor/nodes/SoMaterial.h>
#include <Inventor/nodes/SoPerspectiveCamera.h>
#include <Inventor/nodes/SoSeparator.h>

// This is called by the Material Editor when a value changes
void
myMaterialEditorCB(void *userData, const SoMaterial *newMtl)
{
    SoMaterial *myMtl = (SoMaterial *) userData;

    myMtl->copyFieldValues(newMtl);
}
```

```
main(int , char **argv)
{
   // Initialize Inventor and Xt
   Widget myWindow = SoXt::init(argv[0]);

   // Build the render area in the applications main window
   SoXtRenderArea *myRenderArea = new SoXtRenderArea(myWindow);
   myRenderArea->setSize(SbVec2s(200, 200));
   // Build the Material Editor in its own window
   SoXtMaterialEditor *myEditor = new SoXtMaterialEditor;

   // Create a scene graph
   SoSeparator *root = new SoSeparator;
   SoPerspectiveCamera *myCamera = new SoPerspectiveCamera;
   SoMaterial *myMaterial = new SoMaterial;
   root->ref();
   myCamera->position.setValue(0.212482, -0.881014, 2.5);
   myCamera->heightAngle = M_PI/4;
   root->addChild(myCamera);
   root->addChild(new SoDirectionalLight);
   root->addChild(myMaterial);

   // Read the geometry from a file and add to the scene
   SoInput myInput;
   if (!myInput.openFile("dogDish.iv"))
      exit (1);
   SoSeparator *geomObject = SoDB::readAll(&myInput);
   if (geomObject == NULL)
      exit (1);
   root->addChild(geomObject);

   // Add a callback for when the material changes
   myEditor->addMaterialChangedCallback(
         myMaterialEditorCB, myMaterial);

   // Set the scene graph
   myRenderArea->setSceneGraph(root);

   // Show the main window and the Material Editor
   myRenderArea->setTitle("Editor Callback");
   myRenderArea->show();
   SoXt::show(myWindow);
   myEditor->show();

   // Loop forever
   SoXt::mainLoop();
}
```

Attaching a Component to a Scene Graph

One way to affect a scene graph directly is to *attach* an editor component to a node in the scene graph. Example 16-3 shows using the **attach()** method to attach the material editor to a material node:

```
myEditor->attach(myMaterial);
```

The syntax for attach() here is

attach(SoMaterial *material*, int *index* = 0);

material   the node to edit

index   for multiple-value materials, the index within the node
                    of the material to edit

In the same way, viewers are "attached" to the scene graph whose camera they edit. For example:

```
SoXtFlyViewer *spaceShip = new SoXtFlyViewer;

spaceShip->setSceneGraph(root);
```

See "Viewers" on page 438 for a detailed description of what happens when a viewer is attached to a scene graph.

Example 16-3 builds a render area in a window supplied by the application and a material editor in its own window. It attaches the editor to the material of an object. Figure 16-2 shows the image created by this example.

Example 16-3 Attaching a Material Editor

```
#include <Inventor/SoDB.h>
#include <Inventor/Xt/SoXt.h>
#include <Inventor/Xt/SoXtMaterialEditor.h>
#include <Inventor/Xt/SoXtRenderArea.h>
#include <Inventor/nodes/SoDirectionalLight.h>
#include <Inventor/nodes/SoMaterial.h>
#include <Inventor/nodes/SoPerspectiveCamera.h>
#include <Inventor/nodes/SoSeparator.h>

main(int , char **argv)
{
   // Initialize Inventor and Xt
   Widget myWindow = SoXt::init(argv[0]);
```

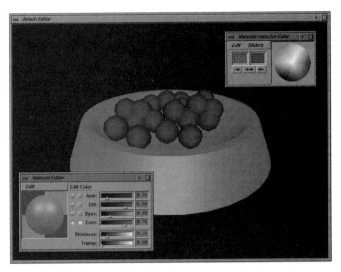

Figure 16-2   Material Editor and Render Area Created in Separate Windows

```
// Build the render area in the applications main window
SoXtRenderArea *myRenderArea = new SoXtRenderArea(myWindow);
myRenderArea->setSize(SbVec2s(200, 200));

// Build the material editor in its own window
SoXtMaterialEditor *myEditor = new SoXtMaterialEditor;

// Create a scene graph
SoSeparator *root = new SoSeparator;
SoPerspectiveCamera *myCamera = new SoPerspectiveCamera;
SoMaterial *myMaterial = new SoMaterial;

root->ref();
myCamera->position.setValue(0.212482, -0.881014, 2.5);
myCamera->heightAngle = M_PI/4;
root->addChild(myCamera);
root->addChild(new SoDirectionalLight);
root->addChild(myMaterial);

// Read the geometry from a file and add to the scene
SoInput myInput;
if (!myInput.openFile("dogDish.iv"))
   exit (1);
```

```
   SoSeparator *geomObject = SoDB::readAll(&myInput);
   if (geomObject == NULL)
      exit (1);
   root->addChild(geomObject);

   // Set the scene graph
   myRenderArea->setSceneGraph(root);

   // Attach material editor to the material
   myEditor->attach(myMaterial);

   // Show the application window and the material editor
   myRenderArea->setTitle("Attach Editor");
   myRenderArea->show();
   SoXt::show(myWindow);
   myEditor->show();

   // Loop forever
   SoXt::mainLoop();
}
```

Example 16-4 builds a render area and a material editor in a window supplied by the application. It uses a Motif-compliant form widget to lay both components inside the same window. The editor is attached to the material of an object. Figure 16-3 shows how this example initially looks on the screen.

Example 16-4   Placing Two Components in the Same Window

```
#include <Xm/Form.h>
#include <Inventor/SoDB.h>
#include <Inventor/Xt/SoXt.h>
#include <Inventor/Xt/SoXtMaterialEditor.h>
#include <Inventor/Xt/SoXtRenderArea.h>
#include <Inventor/nodes/SoDirectionalLight.h>
#include <Inventor/nodes/SoMaterial.h>
#include <Inventor/nodes/SoPerspectiveCamera.h>
#include <Inventor/nodes/SoSeparator.h>

main(int , char **argv)
{
   // Initialize Inventor and Xt
   Widget myWindow = SoXt::init(argv[0]);
   // Build the form to hold both components
   Widget myForm = XtCreateWidget("Form",
           xmFormWidgetClass, myWindow, NULL, 0);
```

```
// Build the render area and Material Editor
SoXtRenderArea *myRenderArea = new SoXtRenderArea(myForm);
myRenderArea->setSize(SbVec2s(200, 200));
SoXtMaterialEditor *myEditor =
        new SoXtMaterialEditor(myForm);

// Lay out the components within the form
Arg args[8];
XtSetArg(args[0], XmNtopAttachment, XmATTACH_FORM);
XtSetArg(args[1], XmNbottomAttachment, XmATTACH_FORM);
XtSetArg(args[2], XmNleftAttachment, XmATTACH_FORM);
XtSetArg(args[3], XmNrightAttachment, XmATTACH_POSITION);
XtSetArg(args[4], XmNrightPosition, 40);
XtSetValues(myRenderArea->getWidget(), args, 5);
XtSetArg(args[2], XmNrightAttachment, XmATTACH_FORM);
XtSetArg(args[3], XmNleftAttachment, XmATTACH_POSITION);
XtSetArg(args[4], XmNleftPosition, 41);
XtSetValues(myEditor->getWidget(), args, 5);

// Create a scene graph
SoSeparator *root = new SoSeparator;
SoPerspectiveCamera *myCamera = new SoPerspectiveCamera;
SoMaterial *myMaterial = new SoMaterial;


root->ref();
myCamera->position.setValue(0.212482, -0.881014, 2.5);
myCamera->heightAngle = M_PI/4;
```

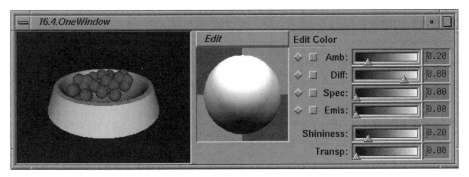

Figure 16-3   Using the Material Editor Component to Edit a Scene

```
root->addChild(myCamera);
root->addChild(new SoDirectionalLight);
root->addChild(myMaterial);

// Read the geometry from a file and add to the scene
SoInput myInput;
if (!myInput.openFile("dogDish.iv"))
   exit (1);
SoSeparator *geomObject = SoDB::readAll(&myInput);
if (geomObject == NULL)
   exit (1);
root->addChild(geomObject);

// Make the scene graph visible
myRenderArea->setSceneGraph(root);

// Attach the material editor to the material in the scene
myEditor->attach(myMaterial);

// Show the main window
myRenderArea->show();
myEditor->show();
SoXt::show(myForm); // this calls XtManageChild
SoXt::show(myWindow); // this calls XtRealizeWidget

// Loop forever
SoXt::mainLoop();
}
```

Viewers

Viewers, such as the examiner viewer and the fly viewer, change the camera position and thus affect how a scene is viewed. The examiner viewer uses a virtual trackball to rotate the scene graph around a point of interest. With the fly viewer, mouse movements have the effect of tilting the viewer's head up, down, to the left, and to the right, as well as moving in the direction the viewer is facing.

All viewers have the following elements built into them:

- A render area in which the scene is being displayed
- Thumbwheel and slider trim at the sides, which function differently for each viewer
- A pop-up menu controlled by the right mouse button
- Viewer icons in the upper right corner that are shortcuts for some of the pop-up menu operations
- Optional application icons in the upper left corner

Figure 16-4 shows an example of the examiner viewer.

Constructing a Viewer

When you construct a viewer, you can specify whether the viewer is a browser viewer (BROWSER; the default) or an editor viewer (EDITOR). If the browser creates a camera node (see the following section), this camera node is removed from the scene graph when the viewer is detached. If an editor viewer creates a camera node, the camera node is retained when the viewer is detached.

The constructor for each viewer takes an additional parameter that specifies what to build. By default, the decoration and pop-up menu are created. For example, the constructor for the examiner viewer is as follows:

```
SoXtExaminerViewer(Widget parent = NULL,
                   const char * name = NULL,
                   SbBool buildInsideParent = TRUE,
                   SoXtFullViewer::BuildFlag buildFlag = BUILD_ALL,
                   SoXtViewer::Type type  = BROWSER);
```

The *buildFlag* can be one of the following values:

BUILD_NONE   the decoration and pop-up menu are not created

BUILD_DECORATION
                only the decoration is created

BUILD_POPUP   only the pop-up menu is created

BUILD_ALL   the decoration and pop-up menu are created

❖ Tip: If the user doesn't need the viewer decoration, you can disable the creation of the decoration at construction time using the *buildFlag*; this will improve performance.

Specifying the Scene Graph for the Viewer

When you call **setSceneGraph()** for a viewer, several things happen automatically. First, the viewer searches the scene graph for a camera. If it finds one, it uses that camera. If it doesn't find a camera, it adds one. Second, it adds headlight, draw-style, and lighting-model nodes to the scene graph. (The following paragraphs describe these steps in detail.)

Call **setSceneGraph(NULL)** to disconnect the scene graph from the viewer component. If the viewer created a camera and the viewer is a browser, it removes the camera. If the viewer is an editor, it leaves the camera, since the view is saved along with the scene graph. For both types of viewers, the headlight group is removed when the scene graph is removed.

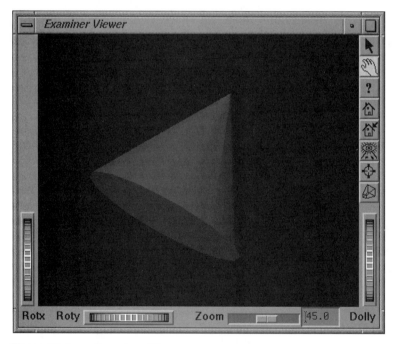

Figure 16-4   Examiner Viewer

Cameras

All viewers search from the scene graph root downward for the first camera. If the viewer finds a camera, it uses it. If it doesn't find one, it creates a camera (of class **SoPerspectiveCamera** by default). If the viewer is an editor, it inserts the camera under the scene graph root, as shown in Figure 16-5. When you save the scene graph, this new camera is saved with it. If the viewer is a browser, it inserts the camera above the scene graph, as shown in Figure 16-6. This camera is not saved with the scene graph and is removed when the viewer is detached.

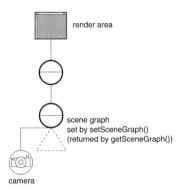

Figure 16-5   Inserting a Camera for an Editor Viewer

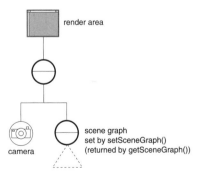

Figure 16-6   Inserting a Camera for a Browser Viewer

Lights

Viewer components by default also add a directional light source to the scene. The viewer continuously changes the position of this light so that it tracks the camera and functions as a headlight shining on the camera's field of view. This headlight group is added just after the camera in the scene graph. To write the scene graph to a file without the headlight, you can either detach the viewer or turn off the headlight (see the **setHeadlight()** method for **SoXtViewer** in the *Open Inventor C++ Reference Manual*).

Viewer Draw-Style

All viewers include a pop-up menu that allows you to change the draw-style of the entire scene. Sometimes, when the viewer changes the draw-style, it also changes the lighting model (for example, wireframe draw-style uses base-color lighting). When a viewer is attached, it inserts draw-style and lighting-model nodes above the scene graph, as shown in Figure 16-7. The following list describes the choices for draw-style and the accompanying changes in lighting model:

VIEW_AS_IS   ignores viewer's draw-style and lighting-model nodes (the default).

VIEW_HIDDEN_LINE

      forces all shapes to be wireframe and changes lighting to BASE_COLOR. This style displays only the edges of front-facing polygons (back lines are hidden).

VIEW_NO_TEXTURE

      forces all shapes to be rendered without textures.

VIEW_LOW_COMPLEXITY

      forces all shapes to be rendered with a low complexity and no textures.

VIEW_LINE   forces all shapes to be wireframe and changes the lighting model to BASE_COLOR.

VIEW_POINT   forces all shapes to be points and changes the lighting model to BASE_COLOR and the point size to 3.0.

VIEW_BBOX   forces all shapes to be rendered as bounding boxes.

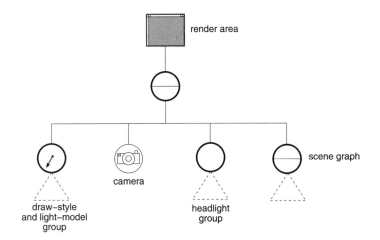

render area

camera

scene graph

draw–style
and light–model
group

headlight
group

Figure 16-7   Inserting Drawing Style and Lighting Model Nodes

Viewer Draw-Type

The draw-styles above can affect the scene while the camera is still, or while
the user is interactively moving the camera. When the draw-style is set, you
can choose between two settings, STILL and INTERACTIVE, to show which
state should be affected. Use the **setDrawStyle()** method for **SoXtViewer** to
specify the draw style and draw type:

setDrawStyle(SoXtViewer::DrawType *type*,
            SoXtViewer::DrawStyle *style*)

For example:

```
setDrawStyle(SoXtViewer::INTERACTIVE,
            SoXtViewer::VIEW_LINE);
```

The viewer pop-up menu, shown in Figure 16-8, lists the draw-style choices
for STILL, the choices for INTERACTIVE, and the choices for buffering type.

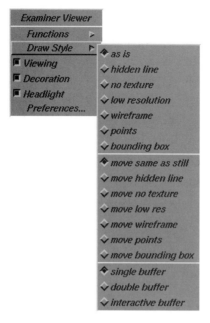

Figure 16-8   Viewer Pop-up Menu

Methods for SoXtViewer

Use the **setBufferingType()** method for **SoXtViewer** to specify whether the viewer should use single buffering, double buffering, or a combination. The default buffering type is double buffering. Double buffering provides smoother redraws, but offers fewer colors. Buffering types are as follows:

SoXtViewer::BUFFER_SINGLE

> uses only one buffer; the image flickers between redraws

SoXtViewer::BUFFER_DOUBLE

> redraws in the back buffer and then swaps buffers

SoXtViewer::BUFFER_INTERACTIVE

> uses double buffering only when the user is doing interactive work; otherwise, uses single buffering

Other useful methods for **SoXtViewer** include the following:

setHeadlight()   turns the headlight on and off. The headlight is ON by default.

setViewing()   allows you to turn the viewer on and off. When the viewer is turned off, events over the render area are sent to the scene graph.

viewAll()   automatically views the entire scene graph.

setAutoClipping() turns autoclipping on and off. When ON, the near and far camera clipping planes are continuously adjusted around the scene's bounding box to minimize clipping. Autoclipping is ON by default.

saveHomePosition()
     saves the current camera values so that the camera can quickly be reset to this position later.

resetToHomePosition()
     sets the camera position to the previously saved home position.

setStereoViewing()
     renders the scene twice, offsetting the camera in between. Stereo glasses must be used when this scene is viewed. (This feature is hardware-dependent. See your release notice for information on whether this feature is supported.)

setSteroOffset()   sets the spacing between the eyes for stereo viewing.

See **SoXtViewer** in the *Open Inventor C++ Reference Manual* for further details.

Methods for SoXtFullViewer

The **SoXtFullViewer** class, derived from **SoXtViewer**, is the abstract base class for all viewers that include decoration around the render area. This decoration is made up of thumbwheels, sliders, and push buttons. The **setDecoration()** method allows you to show or hide the component trims. The **setPopupMenuEnabled()** method allows you to enable or disable the viewer pop-up menu.

You can add optional application icons to the upper left corner of the component. Use the following methods to add these icons:

addAppPushButton()
> adds a push button for the application to the end of the button list

insertAppPushButton()
> places a push button at the specified index in the button list

removeAppPushButton()
> removes a push button from the button list

See **SoXtFullViewer** in the *Open Inventor C++ Reference Manual* for further details.

Example 16-5 creates a simple scene graph with a material and a dish. It then creates a browser examiner viewer and attaches it to the scene graph. The camera and light in the scene are automatically created by the viewer.

Example 16-5   Using a Browser Examiner Viewer

```
#include <Inventor/SoDB.h>
#include <Inventor/Xt/SoXt.h>
#include <Inventor/Xt/viewers/SoXtExaminerViewer.h>
#include <Inventor/nodes/SoSeparator.h>

main(int , char **argv)
{
   // Initialize Inventor and Xt
   Widget myWindow = SoXt::init(argv[0]);

   // Build the viewer in the application's main window
   SoXtExaminerViewer *myViewer =
      new SoXtExaminerViewer(myWindow);

   // Read the geometry from a file and add to the scene
   SoInput myInput;
   if (!myInput.openFile("dogDish.iv"))
      exit (1);
   SoSeparator *geomObject = SoDB::readAll(&myInput);
   if (geomObject == NULL)
      exit (1);

   // Attach the viewer to the scene graph
   myViewer->setSceneGraph(geomObject);
```

```
    // Show the main window
    myViewer->show();
    SoXt::show(myWindow);

    // Loop forever
    SoXt::mainLoop();
}
```

Using the 3D Clipboard

This section describes the convenience routines provided by Inventor for exchanging Inventor data between applications. Inventor's copy and paste methods conform to the X Consortium's *Inter-Client Communication Conventions Manual* (ICCCM), July 1989, which presents guidelines on how processes communicate with each other when exchanging data.

Inventor currently supports two data types, Inventor and string. If you need to copy and paste additional data types, or if you need more control over copy and paste functions than is provided by Inventor's convenience routines, you can use the Motif or Xt data-exchange routines directly. For more information, see the *X Toolkit Intrinsics Programming Manual* by Adrian Nye and Tim O'Reilly (Sebastopol, Ca.: O'Reilly & Associates, 1990).

The **SoXtClipboard** class handles the details of exchanging data according to the ICCCM guidelines. This class includes a constructor, as well as **copy()** and **paste()** methods.

Creating an Instance of SoXtClipboard

The constructor for **SoXtClipboard** has the following syntax:

SoXtClipboard(Widget *w*, Atom *selectionAtom* = _XA_CLIPBOARD_);

The clipboard is associated with a particular widget, such as a render area widget or a top-level widget. For example, you could pass in

```
renderArea->getWidget()
```

as the first parameter of this constructor.

The X Toolkit supports several types of selections (primary, secondary, and clipboard; these are also referred to as *selection atoms*). By default, Inventor supports the clipboard selection (_XA_CLIPBOARD_). If you need to perform data transfers from the primary or secondary selections, you can specify the selection type in the constructor for **SoXtClipboard**. In most cases, however, you use the default selection type.

Copying Data onto the Clipboard

Use one of Inventor's three **copy()** methods to copy data onto the **SoXtClipboard**. You can specify a node, a path, or a path list to copy:

copy(SoNode *node*, Time *eventTime*);

copy(SoPath *path*, Time *eventTime*);

copy(SoPathList &*pathList*, Time *eventTime*);

The **copy()** and **paste()** methods require an event time, which is the time stamp from the user event that triggered the copy or paste request. This event could be a keyboard press event or a menu pick event, for example, and is used by the X server to synchronize copy and paste requests. Behind the scenes, the data is copied into a bytestream and made available to any X client that requests it.

Pasting Data from the Clipboard

The **paste()** method also requires a callback function that is invoked with the paste data. The paste data is always a path list, regardless of what was copied originally:

paste(Time *eventTime*, SoXtClipboardPasteCB *pasteDoneFunc*,
        void *userData* = NULL);

The **paste()** method requests data from the X server and calls the *pasteDoneFunc* when the data is ready. A paste is asynchronous. It simply makes a request to the X server for data to paste and then returns. When the data is delivered, the *pasteDoneFunc* is called and passed the user data along with a list of paths that were pasted. If no data is delivered, the *pasteDoneFunc* is never called. It is up to the application to delete the path list for the paste data when the application is finished with it.

Tip: SoXtClipboard can easily be used along with **SoSelection**. You can obtain a path list from the selection node and then tell the clipboard to copy that path list.

Using Inventor with OpenGL

Chapter Objectives

After reading this chapter, you'll be able to do the following:

- Create Inventor callback nodes that include calls to the OpenGL Library

- Explain how Inventor uses and affects OpenGL state variables

- Write a program that combines use of Inventor and OpenGL and uses the **SoGLRenderAction**

- Use color index mode

This chapter describes how to combine calls to the Inventor and OpenGL libraries in the same window. It includes several examples of programs that combine use of Inventor and OpenGL in different ways. Tables 17-1 through 17-9 show how Inventor affects and is affected by OpenGL state. This entire chapter can be considered advanced material.

Introduction

This chapter is for the experienced OpenGL programmer and is not intended as an introduction to OpenGL. Before you read this chapter, be sure to read *at least* Chapters 1 through 5 and Chapter 9 of this programming guide. You'll need a basic understanding of the Inventor database (Chapters 1 through 4), Inventor actions (Chapter 9), and Inventor event handling (Chapter 10) before you begin combining features of OpenGL with Inventor.

The preferred way to combine use of OpenGL and Inventor is by subclassing. When you subclass, you create a new node that makes calls to OpenGL. This process, which is beyond the scope of this chapter and is described in detail in *The Inventor Toolmaker*, allows you to build on an existing node. Another advantage of subclassing is that your new class has access to Inventor reading and writing (callback nodes, described in this chapter, do not read and write detailed information to a file).

It is important to note that Inventor inherits state from OpenGL for *rendering only*. Additional Inventor features, such as picking, computing bounding boxes, and writing to a file, do not use OpenGL and are unaware of changes made directly to the OpenGL state variables. For example, it is possible to send a viewing matrix directly to OpenGL and then use Inventor to draw a scene without a camera. However, if you then try to pick an object, Inventor will not know what viewing transformation to use for picking, since it doesn't use OpenGL for picking.

You can combine Inventor with OpenGL in several ways. An easy way to add custom OpenGL rendering to a scene database is to add a callback node (**SoCallback**; see Example 17-2). This node allows you to set a callback function that is invoked for each of the various actions that nodes perform (rendering, picking, bounding-box calculation). The **SoCallback** node differs from the event callback node in that it provides callbacks for all scene operations rather than just for event handling.

A second way to combine Inventor with OpenGL is to create a GLX window, make OpenGL and Inventor calls, and then apply an **SoGLRenderAction**, as shown in Example 17-3. For instance, you could create a GLX window, clear the background, do some initial rendering into the window, set up the viewing matrix, and then use Inventor to draw a scene by applying a GL render action to the scene graph. Or, you could use Inventor to set up the camera, lights, and materials, and then use OpenGL code to draw the scene. As long as you follow the general rules described in the following section on OpenGL state usage, you can mix OpenGL and Inventor rendering as you wish. (Note that this is an advanced feature, not for the faint of heart.)

OpenGL State Variables and Inventor

If you need to combine Inventor and OpenGL calls, Tables 17-1 through 17-9 list the OpenGL state variables and describe which Inventor nodes (or actions) change those variables. If Inventor uses the current value of an OpenGL state variable and never changes it, the variable is omitted from this set of tables. See the *OpenGL Programming Guide* for a complete list of all OpenGL state variables and their default values. The recommended value for these variables is the default value, with two exceptions: turn on z-buffering and use RGB color mode.

Remember, the constructor for **SoGLRenderAction** takes a parameter that specifies whether to inherit the current OpenGL values. If you specify TRUE, Inventor inherits values from OpenGL. If you specify FALSE (the default), Inventor sets up its own reasonable default values (see Chapter 9).

To save and restore OpenGL state, use the OpenGL **pushAttributes()** and **popAttributes()** commands. For example, if you change variables in the OpenGL state in a callback node, you need to restore the state when the callback node is finished. Note that if your callback node begins with a **pushAttributes()** and ends with a **popAttributes()**, but a render abort occurs in between, **popAttributes()** is never called and the state is not restored.

OpenGL State Variable	Inventor Nodes That Change This Variable
GL_CURRENT_COLOR	Shapes, Material, Base Color
GL_CURRENT_INDEX	Color Index node, Shapes
GL_CURRENT_TEXTURE_COORDS	Shapes, TextureCoordinate2
GL_CURRENT_NORMAL	Shapes, Normal
GL_CURRENT_RASTER_POSITION	Text2
GL_CURRENT_RASTER_COLOR	Text2
GL_CURRENT_RASTER_INDEX	Text2
GL_CURRENT_RASTER_POSITION_-VALID	Text2

Table 17-1   OpenGL State Variables: Current Values and Associated Data

OpenGL State Variable	Inventor Nodes That Change This Variable
GL_MODELVIEW_MATRIX	Transformation nodes, Cameras
GL_PROJECTION_MATRIX	Cameras
GL_TEXTURE_MATRIX	Texture2Transform
GL_VIEWPORT	Cameras
GL_DEPTH_RANGE	Cameras
GL_MODELVIEW_STACK_DEPTH	Transformation nodes
GL_TEXTURE_STACK_DEPTH	Texture2Transform
GL_MATRIX_MODE	Cameras, Texture2Transform

Table 17-2   OpenGL State Variables: Transformation State

OpenGL State Variable	Inventor Nodes That Change This Variable
GL_FOG_COLOR	Environment node
GL_FOG_INDEX	Environment node
GL_FOG_DENSITY	Environment node
GL_FOG_START	Environment node
GL_FOG_END	Environment node
GL_FOG_MODE	Environment node
GL_FOG	Environment node
GL_SHADE_MODEL	Light Model, if in color index mode

Table 17-3   OpenGL State Variables: Coloring

OpenGL State Variable	Inventor Nodes That Change This Variable
GL_LIGHTING	Light Model
GL_COLOR_MATERIAL	Shapes
GL_MATERIAL_PARAMETER	Shapes
GL_MATERIAL_FACE	Shapes
GL_AMBIENT	Shapes, Material
GL_DIFFUSE	Shapes, Material
GL_SPECULAR	Shapes, Material
GL_EMISSION	Shapes, Material
GL_SHININESS	Shapes, Material
GL_LIGHT_MODEL_AMBIENT	Shapes, Material
GL_LIGHT_MODEL_LOCAL_VIEWER	Shapes, Material
GL_LIGHT_MODEL_TWO_SIDE	Shape Hints
GL_AMBIENT	Lights

Table 17-4   OpenGL State Variables: Lighting

OpenGL State Variable	Inventor Nodes That Change This Variable
GL_DIFFUSE	Lights
GL_SPECULAR	Lights
GL_POSITION	Lights
GL_CONSTANT_ATTENUATION	Environment
GL_LINEAR_ATTENUATION	Environment
GL_QUADRATIC_ATTENUATION	Environment
GL_SPOT_DIRECTION	Lights
GL_SPOT_EXPONENT	Lights
GL_SPOT_CUTOFF	Lights
GL_LIGHT*i*	Lights
GL_COLOR_INDEXES	Lights

Table 17-4 (continued)   OpenGL State Variables: Lighting

OpenGL State Variable	Inventor Nodes That Change This Variable
GL_POINT_SIZE	Draw Style
GL_POINT_SMOOTH	Render action
GL_LINE_WIDTH	Draw Style
GL_LINE_SMOOTH	Render Action
GL_LINE_STIPPLE_PATTERN	Draw Style
GL_LINE_STIPPLE	Draw Style
GL_CULL_FACE	Shape Hints
GL_CULL_FACE_MODE	Shape Hints

Table 17-5   OpenGL State Variables: Rasterization

OpenGL State Variable	Inventor Nodes That Change This Variable
GL_FRONT_FACE	Shape Hints
GL_POLYGON_MODE	Draw Style
GL_POLYGON_STIPPLE	Shapes if SCREEN_DOOR transparency

Table 17-5 (continued)   OpenGL State Variables: Rasterization

OpenGL State Variable	Inventor Nodes That Change This Variable
GL_TEXTURE_x	Texture2 node
GL_TEXTURE	Texture2 node
GL_TEXTURE_WIDTH	Texture2 node
GL_TEXTURE_HEIGHT	Texture2 node
GL_TEXTURE_COMPONENTS	Texture2 node
GL_TEXTURE_MIN_FILTER	Complexity node
GL_TEXTURE_MAG_FILTER	Complexity node
GL_TEXTURE_WRAP_x	Texture2 node
GL_TEXTURE_ENV_MODE	Texture2 node
GL_TEXTURE_ENV_COLOR	Texture2 node
GL_TEXTURE_GEN_x	Texture Coordinate Function nodes
GL_EYE_LINEAR	Texture Coordinate Function nodes
GL_OBJECT_LINEAR	Texture Coordinate Function nodes
GL_TEXTURE_GEN_MODE	Texture Coordinate Function nodes

Table 17-6   OpenGL State Variables: Texturing

OpenGL State Variable	Inventor Nodes That Change This Variable
GL_BLEND	Render action, Texture2 node
GL_BLEND_SRC	Render action, Texture2 node
GL_BLEND_DST	Render action, Texture2 node

Table 17-7   OpenGL State Variables: Pixel Operations

OpenGL State Variable	Inventor Nodes That Change This Variable
GL_UNPACK_ALIGNMENT	Texture2 node
GL_*_SCALE (* = RED; GREEN; BLUE; ALPHA)	Texture2 node
GL_*_BIAS (* = RED; GREEN; BLUE; ALPHA)	Texture2 node

Table 17-8   OpenGL State Variables: Pixels

OpenGL State Variable	Inventor Nodes That Change This Variable
GL_LIST_BASE	Text2, Text3 nodes
GL_LIST_INDEX	Separator, Text2, Text3 nodes
GL_LIST_MODE	Separator, Text2, Text3 nodes

Table 17-9   OpenGL State Variables: Miscellaneous

Color-Index Mode

You can open an X window that supports OpenGL rendering in either RGB mode or color-index (also referred to as *color-map*) mode. If you use color-index mode, be sure to load the color map. Example 17-1 shows how to set the color map for the **SoXtRenderArea**. See also the *Open Inventor C++ Reference Manual* on **SoXtRenderArea::setColorMap()**.

If you are using BASE_COLOR lighting, use the **SoColorIndex** node to specify the index into the color map.

If you are using PHONG lighting, use the **SoMaterialIndex** node to specify indices into the color map for the ambient, diffuse, and specular colors. This node also includes fields for specifying the shininess and transparency values (but not the emissive value). It expects the color map to contain a ramp from ambient to diffuse to specular colors.

Tip: You can design a scene graph that can be used in RGB or color index windows by putting both **SoMaterialIndex** and **SoMaterial** nodes in it.

Example 17-1   Using Color Index Mode

```
#include <Inventor/SoDB.h>
#include <Inventor/SoInput.h>
#include <Inventor/nodes/SoNode.h>
#include <Inventor/Xt/SoXt.h>
#include <Inventor/Xt/viewers/SoXtExaminerViewer.h>
#include <GL/glx.h>

// Window attribute list to create a color index visual.
// This will create a double buffered color index window
// with the maximum number of bits and a zbuffer.
int attribList[] = {
   GLX_DOUBLEBUFFER,
   GLX_BUFFER_SIZE, 1,
   GLX_DEPTH_SIZE, 1,
   None };

// List of colors to load in the color map
static float colors[3][3] = {{.2, .2, .2}, {.5, 1, .5},
         {.5, .5, 1}};

static char *sceneBuffer = "\
#Inventor V2.0 ascii\n\
\
Separator { \
   LightModel { model BASE_COLOR } \
   ColorIndex { index 1 } \
   Coordinate3 { point [ -1 -1 -1, -1 1 -1, 1 1 1, 1 -1 1] } \
   FaceSet {} \
   ColorIndex { index 2 } \
   Coordinate3 { point [ -1 -1 1, -1 1 1, 1 1 -1, 1 -1 -1] } \
   FaceSet {} \
} ";
```

```
void
main(int , char **argv)
{
   // Initialize Inventor and Xt
   Widget myWindow = SoXt::init(argv[0]);

   // Read the scene graph in
   SoInput in;
   SoNode *scene;
   in.setBuffer((void *)sceneBuffer, (size_t)
           strlen(sceneBuffer));
   if (! SoDB::read(&in, scene) || scene == NULL) {
      printf("Couldn't read scene\n");
      exit(1);
   }

   // Create the color index visual
   XVisualInfo *vis = glXChooseVisual(XtDisplay(myWindow),
      XScreenNumberOfScreen(XtScreen(myWindow)), attribList);
   if (! vis) {
      printf("Couldn't create visual\n");
      exit(1);
   }

   // Allocate the viewer, set the scene, the visual and
   // load the color map with the wanted colors.
   //
   // Color 0 will be used for the background (default) while
   // color 1 and 2 are used by the objects.
   //
   SoXtExaminerViewer *myViewer = new
           SoXtExaminerViewer(myWindow);
   myViewer->setNormalVisual(vis);
   myViewer->setColorMap(0, 3, (SbColor *) colors);
   myViewer->setSceneGraph(scene);
   myViewer->setTitle("Color Index Mode");

   // Show the viewer and loop forever...
   myViewer->show();
   XtRealizeWidget(myWindow);
   SoXt::mainLoop();
}
```

Using an SoCallback Node

A typical use of an **SoCallback** node is to make calls to OpenGL. At the beginning of the callback function, you need to check the action type and then proceed based on the type of action that has been applied to the node. Typically, you are interested in the render action:

```
if(action->isOfType(SoGLRenderAction::getClassTypeId())){

    ...execute rendering code ..

}
```

Caching

The effects of a callback node may not be cacheable, depending on what it does. For example, if the callback node contains shapes whose geometry is changing, it should not be cached. In Example 17-2, the callback node creates a checked background, which can be cached because it is not changing.

If a callback node relies on any information outside of Inventor that may change (such as a global variable), it should not be cached. To prevent Inventor from automatically creating a cache, use the **SoCacheElement::-invalidate()** method from within a callback. For example:

```
void
myCallback(void *myData, SoAction *action)
{
    if (action->isOfType(SoGLRenderAction::getClassTypeId())){
        SoCacheElement::invalidate(action->getState());
            //makes sure this isn't cached
        //...make OpenGL calls that depend on a global variable...//
    }
}
```

Be careful when opening an OpenGL display list inside an **SoCallback** node. Recall from Chapter 9 that the Inventor render cache contains an OpenGL display list. Only one OpenGL display list can be open at a time, and a separator node above the callback node may have already opened a display list for caching. If your callback node opens a second display list, an error occurs. Use the **SoCacheElement::anyOpen()** method to check whether a cache is open.

Using a Callback Node

Example 17-2 creates an Inventor render area. It uses Inventor to create a red cube and a blue sphere and then uses an **SoCallback** node containing GL calls to draw a checked "floor." The floor is cached automatically by Inventor. Note that the **SoXtRenderArea** automatically redraws the scene when the window is resized. Example 17-3, which uses a GLX window, does not redraw automatically.

Both Examples 17-2 and 17-3 produce the same image, shown in Figure 17-1.

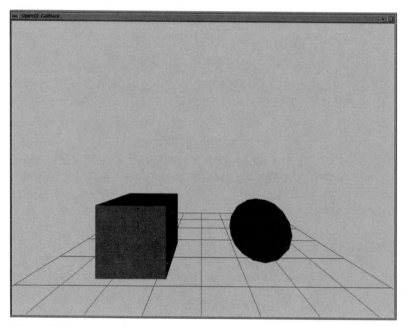

Figure 17-1   Combining Use of Inventor and OpenGL

Example 17-2 Using a Callback Node

```
#include <GL/gl.h>
#include <Inventor/SbLinear.h>
#include <Inventor/Xt/SoXt.h>
#include <Inventor/Xt/SoXtRenderArea.h>
#include <Inventor/nodes/SoCallback.h>
#include <Inventor/nodes/SoCube.h>
```

Chapter 17: Using Inventor with OpenGL

```
#include <Inventor/nodes/SoDirectionalLight.h>
#include <Inventor/nodes/SoLightModel.h>
#include <Inventor/nodes/SoMaterial.h>
#include <Inventor/nodes/SoPerspectiveCamera.h>
#include <Inventor/nodes/SoSphere.h>
#include <Inventor/nodes/SoSeparator.h>
#include <Inventor/nodes/SoTransform.h>

float    floorObj[81][3];

// Build a scene with two objects and some light
void
buildScene(SoGroup *root)
{
   // Some light
   root->addChild(new SoLightModel);
   root->addChild(new SoDirectionalLight);

   // A red cube translated to the left and down
   SoTransform *myTrans = new SoTransform;
   myTrans->translation.setValue(-2.0, -2.0, 0.0);
   root->addChild(myTrans);

   SoMaterial *myMtl = new SoMaterial;
   myMtl->diffuseColor.setValue(1.0, 0.0, 0.0);
   root->addChild(myMtl);

   root->addChild(new SoCube);

   // A blue sphere translated right
   myTrans = new SoTransform;
   myTrans->translation.setValue(4.0, 0.0, 0.0);
   root->addChild(myTrans);

   myMtl = new SoMaterial;
   myMtl->diffuseColor.setValue(0.0, 0.0, 1.0);
   root->addChild(myMtl);

   root->addChild(new SoSphere);
}

// Build the floor that will be rendered using OpenGL.
void
buildFloor()
{
   int a = 0;
```

```
      for (float i = -5.0; i <= 5.0; i += 1.25) {
         for (float j = -5.0; j <= 5.0; j += 1.25, a++) {
            floorObj[a][0] = j;
            floorObj[a][1] = 0.0;
            floorObj[a][2] = i;
         }
      }
   }

// Draw the lines that make up the floor, using OpenGL
void
drawFloor()
{
   int i;

   glBegin(GL_LINES);
   for (i=0; i<4; i++) {
      glVertex3fv(floorObj[i*18]);
      glVertex3fv(floorObj[(i*18)+8]);
      glVertex3fv(floorObj[(i*18)+17]);
      glVertex3fv(floorObj[(i*18)+9]);
   }

   glVertex3fv(floorObj[i*18]);
   glVertex3fv(floorObj[(i*18)+8]);
   glEnd();

   glBegin(GL_LINES);
   for (i=0; i<4; i++) {
      glVertex3fv(floorObj[i*2]);
      glVertex3fv(floorObj[(i*2)+72]);
      glVertex3fv(floorObj[(i*2)+73]);
      glVertex3fv(floorObj[(i*2)+1]);
   }
   glVertex3fv(floorObj[i*2]);
   glVertex3fv(floorObj[(i*2)+72]);
   glEnd();
}

// Callback routine to render the floor using OpenGL
void
myCallbackRoutine(void *, SoAction *)
{
   glPushMatrix();
   glTranslatef(0.0, -3.0, 0.0);
   glColor3f(0.0, 0.7, 0.0);
   glLineWidth(2);
```

```
    glDisable(GL_LIGHTING);   // so we don't have to set normals
    drawFloor();
    glEnable(GL_LIGHTING);
    glLineWidth(1);
    glPopMatrix();
}


main(int, char **)
{
    // Initialize Inventor utilities
    Widget myWindow = SoXt::init("Example 17.1");

    buildFloor();

    // Build a simple scene graph, including a camera and
    // a SoCallback node for performing some GL rendering.
    SoSeparator *root = new SoSeparator;
    root->ref();

    SoPerspectiveCamera *myCamera = new SoPerspectiveCamera;
    myCamera->position.setValue(0.0, 0.0, 5.0);
    myCamera->heightAngle  = M_PI/2.0;   // 90 degrees
    myCamera->nearDistance = 2.0;
    myCamera->farDistance  = 12.0;
    root->addChild(myCamera);

    SoCallback *myCallback = new SoCallback;
    myCallback->setCallback(myCallbackRoutine);
    root->addChild(myCallback);

    buildScene(root);

    // Initialize an Inventor Xt RenderArea and draw the scene.
    SoXtRenderArea *myRenderArea = new SoXtRenderArea(myWindow);
    myRenderArea->setSceneGraph(root);
    myRenderArea->setTitle("OpenGL Callback");
    myRenderArea->setBackgroundColor(SbColor(.8, .8, .8));
    myRenderArea->show();

    SoXt::show(myWindow);
    SoXt::mainLoop();
}
```

Applying a Render Action Inside a GLX Window

Example 17-3 creates a GLX window, makes Inventor and OpenGL calls, and then applies a GL render action. It uses OpenGL to render a checked "floor" and Inventor to render a red cube and a blue sphere, in the same window.

Example 17-3   Using a GLX Window

```
#include <GL/glx.h>
#include <GL/gl.h>
#include <GL/glu.h>
#include <stdio.h>
#include <unistd.h>

#include <Inventor/SoDB.h>
#include <Inventor/actions/SoGLRenderAction.h>
#include <Inventor/nodes/SoCube.h>
#include <Inventor/nodes/SoDirectionalLight.h>
#include <Inventor/nodes/SoLightModel.h>
#include <Inventor/nodes/SoMaterial.h>
#include <Inventor/nodes/SoTransform.h>
#include <Inventor/nodes/SoSeparator.h>
#include <Inventor/nodes/SoSphere.h>

#define    WINWIDTH    400
#define    WINHEIGHT   400

float    floorObj[81][3];

// Build an Inventor scene with two objects and some light
void
buildScene(SoGroup *root)
{
    // Some light
    root->addChild(new SoLightModel);
    root->addChild(new SoDirectionalLight);

    // A red cube translated to the left and down
    SoTransform *myTrans = new SoTransform;
    myTrans->translation.setValue(-2.0, -2.0, 0.0);
    root->addChild(myTrans);

    SoMaterial *myMtl = new SoMaterial;
    myMtl->diffuseColor.setValue(1.0, 0.0, 0.0);
    root->addChild(myMtl);
```

```
   root->addChild(new SoCube);

   // A blue sphere translated right
   myTrans = new SoTransform;
   myTrans->translation.setValue(4.0, 0.0, 0.0);
   root->addChild(myTrans);

   myMtl = new SoMaterial;
   myMtl->diffuseColor.setValue(0.0, 0.0, 1.0);
   root->addChild(myMtl);

   root->addChild(new SoSphere);
}


// Build a floor that will be rendered using OpenGL.
void
buildFloor()
{
   int a = 0;

   for (float i = -5.0; i <= 5.0; i += 1.25) {
      for (float j = -5.0; j <= 5.0; j += 1.25, a++) {
         floorObj[a][0] = j;
         floorObj[a][1] = 0.0;
         floorObj[a][2] = i;
      }
   }
}

// Callback used by GLX window
static Bool
waitForNotify(Display *, XEvent *e, char *arg)
{
   return (e->type == MapNotify) &&
            (e->xmap.window == (Window) arg);
}

// Create and initialize GLX window.
void
openWindow(Display *&display, Window &window)
{
   XVisualInfo*vi;
   Colormap cmap;
   XSetWindowAttributes swa;
   GLXContext cx;
   XEvent event;
```

```
static int attributeList[] = {
        GLX_RGBA,
        GLX_RED_SIZE, 1,
        GLX_GREEN_SIZE, 1,
        GLX_BLUE_SIZE, 1,
        GLX_DEPTH_SIZE, 1,
        GLX_DOUBLEBUFFER,
        None,
};

display = XOpenDisplay(0);
vi = glXChooseVisual(display,
        DefaultScreen(display), attributeList);
cx = glXCreateContext(display, vi, 0, GL_TRUE);
cmap = XCreateColormap(display,
        RootWindow(display, vi->screen),
        vi->visual, AllocNone);
swa.colormap = cmap;
swa.border_pixel = 0;
swa.event_mask = StructureNotifyMask;
window = XCreateWindow(display,
        RootWindow(display, vi->screen), 100, 100,
        WINWIDTH, WINHEIGHT, 0, vi->depth, InputOutput,
        vi->visual,
        (CWBorderPixel | CWColormap | CWEventMask), &swa);

XMapWindow(display, window);
XIfEvent(display, &event, waitForNotify, (char *) window);
glXMakeCurrent(display, window, cx);
}


// Draw the lines that make up the floor, using OpenGL
void
drawFloor()
{
   int i;

   glBegin(GL_LINES);
   for (i=0; i<4; i++) {
      glVertex3fv(floorObj[i*18]);
      glVertex3fv(floorObj[(i*18)+8]);
      glVertex3fv(floorObj[(i*18)+17]);
      glVertex3fv(floorObj[(i*18)+9]);
   }
```

```
      glVertex3fv(floorObj[i*18]);
      glVertex3fv(floorObj[(i*18)+8]);
   glEnd();

   glBegin(GL_LINES);
   for (i=0; i<4; i++) {
      glVertex3fv(floorObj[i*2]);
      glVertex3fv(floorObj[(i*2)+72]);
      glVertex3fv(floorObj[(i*2)+73]);
      glVertex3fv(floorObj[(i*2)+1]);
   }
   glVertex3fv(floorObj[i*2]);
   glVertex3fv(floorObj[(i*2)+72]);
   glEnd();
}


main(int, char **)
{
   // Initialize Inventor
   SoDB::init();

   // Build a simple scene graph
   SoSeparator *root = new SoSeparator;
   root->ref();
   buildScene(root);

   // Build the floor geometry
   buildFloor();

   // Create and initialize window
   Display *display;
   Window window;
   openWindow(display, window);
   glEnable(GL_DEPTH_TEST);
   glClearColor(0.8, 0.8, 0.8, 1.0);
   glClear(GL_COLOR_BUFFER_BIT | GL_DEPTH_BUFFER_BIT);

   // Set up the camera using OpenGL.
   glMatrixMode(GL_PROJECTION);
   glLoadIdentity();
   gluPerspective(90.0, 1.0, 2.0, 12.0);

   glMatrixMode(GL_MODELVIEW);
   glLoadIdentity();
   glTranslatef(0.0, 0.0, -5.0);
```

```
        // Render the floor using OpenGL
        glPushMatrix();
        glTranslatef(0.0, -3.0, 0.0);
        glColor3f(0.0, 0.7, 0.0);
        glLineWidth(2.0);
        glDisable(GL_LIGHTING);
        drawFloor();
        glEnable(GL_LIGHTING);
        glPopMatrix();

        // Render the scene
        SbViewportRegion myViewport(WINWIDTH, WINHEIGHT);
        SoGLRenderAction myRenderAction(myViewport);
        myRenderAction.apply(root);
        glXSwapBuffers(display, window);

        sleep (10);
        root->unref();
        return 0;
}
```

An Introduction to Object-Oriented Programming for C Programmers

Open Inventor is an object-oriented toolkit for developing 3D programs. It is written in C++, but it includes a C programming interface. This book is full of references to classes, subclasses, and other concepts from object-oriented programming. All examples are in C++. You will get the most from this book if you have a reasonable understanding of classes and objected-oriented programming before you begin reading it.

This appendix provides an informal introduction to object-oriented programming for C programmers and an overview of the concepts behind the C interface. If you are comfortable with object-oriented programming, you can skip the first section and just skim the example in this appendix. For the specifics of Inventor's C programming interface, see Appendix B.

This chapter contains the following sections:

- "What Is Object-Oriented Programming?" introduces you to the two fundamental concepts of object-oriented programming: data abstraction and inheritance.

- "An Example of a Class: Sphere" develops a substantial example of a C++ class that illustrates the concepts of object-oriented programming.

- "Suggested Reading" points you to further information on C++.

What Is Object-Oriented Programming?

Many successful programmers use object-oriented techniques without knowing it. You have probably heard programmers complimenting an implementation by describing it as *modular*. Modular code has a well-defined interface that works without requiring its users to know how it was written. Modular code can be reused by many applications, cuts down on programmer learning time, and allows the implementation internals to change without affecting the programs that use it. It protects the programmer from the implementation details. The programming interface defines the functionality.

Data Abstraction

For an example, look at the file I/O functions provided in the standard C library: **creat()**, **open()**, **read()**, **write()**, and **close()**. These routines clearly define the I/O functionality without revealing the file system details or implementation. Each function uses a file descriptor to identify the data representing the file, device, or socket. The data structures that represent these objects are different for each file type, yet they are completely hidden from you as a programmer. The open/close/read/write semantics apply consistently to each object.

This technique of hiding internal data structures is known as *data abstraction*—the first fundamental concept of object-oriented programming. It's good programming practice to confine access to data structures to the code that is intended to modify the structures. Revealing private data allows the programmer using the structure to modify things that perhaps he shouldn't modify. The programmer is then relying on details of the internal implementation, so the implementor can't make changes to that internal representation.

Objects represent the building blocks from which programs are constructed. They consist of data structures and some associated functions that operate on those data structures. Objects perform functions on themselves rather than allowing applications to have access to their internal implementation. In our example, the C file I/O routines define a generic file (the object) that is accessed through the open/close/read/write functions.

Inheritance

So far, we've described good, modular code, but not specifically object-oriented programming. *Inheritance* is the concept that sets object-oriented code apart from well-written modular code. Inheritance allows you to create new objects from existing objects. It makes it easy to customize and specialize your programs. Inheritance is the second fundamental concept of object-oriented programming.

You've probably often wanted to reuse some existing code, but you couldn't because you needed to make minor changes. So you copied the code with the changes into an independent implementation. This reinvention is tedious, error-prone, and a waste of your time. Inheritance provides you with a mechanism for reusing your existing code and adding small changes, without starting over.

The C file I/O routine example actually defines three object types: files, devices, and sockets. These objects are created from the generic file object, which defines the open/close/read/write semantics. Writing the I/O routines is just a matter of implementing those functions for each type of file object. The implementation differences stay hidden from the programmer.

Implementing Data Abstraction and Inheritance: Classes

Object-oriented programming languages use the techniques we've described in a formal manner. C++ provides a few extra constructs on top of C that enforce these techniques. The most basic of these constructs is the *class*. You can think of a class either as a data structure with relevant functions attached, or as a group of related functions with some data attached. It doesn't matter which model you prefer. The important concept to understand is that objects encapsulate related data and functions into a single package, called a *class*.

Functions within a class are usually called *member functions*, or more generically, *methods*. The data structures within a class are referred to as *member variables*. So a class is composed of member functions and variables.

Note that we're using the term *class* to represent the abstract notion of an object, much like a structure in C. The term *object* usually refers to an instance of a class. You create an object from a given class when you instantiate the class. The C parallel would be allocating memory to make a copy of a structure. You can refer to that copy of the structure as an *instance* of the structure, or as an *object* with the same type as the structure.

When new classes are defined, they can be derived from an existing class. The existing class is called a *base* or *parent* class, and the new class is called the *derived class* or *subclass*. New classes created this way typically inherit all of the methods and variables that were defined in the base class.

Class Hierarchies

Open Inventor is composed of a large set of related classes that implement many aspects of 3D programming. These classes are implemented in C++. The Open Inventor C programming interface allows you to use these classes from C programs. So you can write C programs that reap the benefits of C++ inheritance without needing to learn C++ first. But the C interface does not hide the fact that there are classes. Your programming tasks will be easier if you understand the Inventor classes and how they relate to each other. For example, you need to know which class each class is derived from to know which functions apply.

Class relationships in object-oriented systems are often illustrated through *class hierarchy diagrams*, or *class trees*. Figure A-1 is an example. It illustrates a fictitious class hierarchy. Note that this example is not based on Inventor. It is used to convey key concepts in a simple manner, but its sphere, cone and quad mesh are for example only and are not the same as the Inventor classes with similar names.

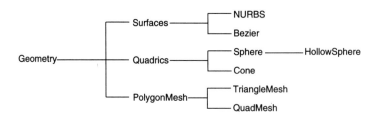

Figure A-1   Sample Class Hierarchy Diagram

Functions and variables defined in the class **Geometry** also exist for every subclass. So if **Geometry** has a variable **Bbox** and a function **getBbox()**, all the subclasses of **Geometry** also have **Bbox** and **getBbox()**.

See Chapter 1 for a summary of the Open Inventor class tree.

An Example of a Class: Sphere

This section discusses an example of a C++ class and its member functions. The class we'll consider is one from the fictional class tree shown in Figure A-1: **Sphere**, which represents and operates on a sphere. The **Sphere** class is defined below with several member functions and some member variables:

```
class Sphere {
public:
    Sphere();           // creates a sphere with default values
    ~Sphere();          // destructor, which deletes a sphere
    void render()       // renders the sphere
    Boolean pick(int x, int y); // picks the sphere

    float radius;       // radius of the sphere
    float center[3];    // center of the sphere
};
```

Sphere is a class that creates, manages, and operates on a geometric sphere object. The internal implementation details of the sphere are not exposed to you.

Notice that the functions of **Sphere** do not have a sphere argument. When you invoke these functions from C++, you invoke them from the class itself. Each function has an implied sphere argument. For example, this is how you would create a sphere, set its radius, and then render it in C++:

```
Sphere *mySphere;       // pointer to a sphere object
mySphere = new Sphere(); // creates and initializes sphere
mySphere->radius = 3.0;  // sets the radius
mySphere->render();      // renders it
```

The **sphere->** syntax accesses a member variable or invokes a member function in the same way that C accesses structure members. For example, **mySphere->render()** invokes the **render()** function on **mySphere**. The **new Sphere()** syntax creates a sphere, allocating memory for the object and initializing it.

This is how the sphere class would look in the corresponding C interface:

```
Sphere *SphereCreate();
void SphereDelete(Sphere *sphere);
void SphereRender(Sphere *sphere);
Boolean SpherePick(Sphere *sphere, int x, int y);
```

(This example follows the naming conventions for Inventor C functions. For details on those conventions, see Appendix B.)

The C interface would also define a structure for the sphere:

```
struct Sphere {
    char    pad[48];            /* padding generated by Inventor */
    float   radius;
    float   center[3];
};
```

The **pad[48]** is generated automatically from the C++ code. These **pad** statements are a by-product of the generation of the C interface from the C++ classes. They protect private data that you as a programmer shouldn't need to access.

To create a sphere, set its radius, and render it from C, you would write code like this:

```
Sphere *mySphere;       /* my sphere object */

mySphere = SphereCreate();
mySphere->radius = 3.0;
SphereRender(mySphere);
```

Notice how similar this code is to the C++ example. The main difference is syntax. (Again, note that this is a hypothetical example; this is not exactly how the radius for a sphere is specified in Inventor programs.)

An Example of Inheritance: HollowSphere

Recall that inheritance is the ability to build specialized classes from existing classes. In C++, you can create *subclasses* of a class, which are identical to the parent class with exceptions you can select. These exceptions can be different implementations of functions on the parent class, or extra added functions. Subclasses are said to be *derived from* or *subclassed from* the parent class.

For example, we can build a subclass of **Sphere** called **HollowSphere**. **HollowSphere** is identical to **Sphere**, except that it has a thickness value and a new function that tells it whether to render translucently. **HollowSphere** is derived from **Sphere**. Since it's a subclass of **Sphere**, all member functions of **Sphere** also apply to **HollowSphere**. Our definition of **HollowSphere** does not have to define **delete()**, **render()**, or **pick()** functions. **HollowSphere** inherits these functions from the **Sphere** class. The same is true of **Sphere**'s member variables, **radius** and **center**: **HollowSphere** inherits those as well.

Here is the C++ class definition for **HollowSphere**:

```
class HollowSphere : public Sphere {        // subclass of Sphere
    void   showEquator();                    // show equator during render
    float  thickness;                        // stores thickness value
}
```

The following C++ code fragment creates a hollow sphere, sets its radius and thickness, turns on the equator options, and renders it:

```
HollowSphere *mySphere;
mySphere = new HollowSphere();
mySphere->radius = 3.0;
mySphere->thickness = 0.25;
mySphere->showEquator();
mySphere->render();
```

To do the same using the C interface:

```
HollowSphere *mySphere;
mySphere = HollowSphereCreate();
mySphere->radius = 3.0;
mySphere->thickness = 0.25;
HollowSphereShowEquator(mySphere);
HollowSphereRender(mySphere);   /* inherited from parent class */
```

Note that when you invoke a method from the parent class, the method name is prefixed by the name of the subclass. See Appendix B for a fuller explanation of how the Inventor C interface names inheritance methods.

Suggested Reading

If you want to learn more about C++ and object-oriented programming, the following books are good starting points:

- Dewhurst, Stephen C., and Kathy T. Stark, *Programming in C++*. Englewood Cliffs, N.J.: Prentice-Hall, Inc., 1989.

- Ellis, Margaret A., and Bjarne Stroustrup, *The Annotated C++ Reference Manual*. Reading, Mass.: Addison-Wesley, 1990.

- Lippman, Stanley B., *A C++ Primer*, 2e. Reading, Mass.: Addison-Wesley, 1991.

- Pohl, Ira, *C++ for C Programmers*. Redwood City, Ca.: The Benjamin/Cummings Publishing Co., 1989.

- Shapiro, Jonathan, *A C++ Toolkit*. Englewood Cliffs, N.J.: Prentice-Hall, Inc., 1991.

- Weiskamp, Keith, and Bryan Flamig, *The Complete C++ Primer*, 2e. San Diego, Ca.: Academic Press, 1992.

An Introduction to the C API

Read this chapter if you will be programming in C! If you are unfamiliar with object-oriented programming, you should first read Appendix A, which introduces some of the features of C++ and some of the conceptual underpinnings of the Open Inventor C interface.

Though the C++ syntax is different, the concepts described in earlier chapters of this book still apply to the C implementation of Open Inventor. As you read the rest of this book, you can refer to this appendix as necessary to translate the C++ examples into C. If you have purchased Open Inventor, you can also compare the C version of each online example program to the C++ version in this book. See the release notes for information on finding and using the online example programs and for details on how to compile and link an Inventor program written in C.

The following sections explain the differences between the Open Inventor C and C++ interfaces. They discuss these topics:

- Naming C functions

- C function name abbreviations

- Creating and deleting objects from C

- Calling C functions

The Open Inventor C interface is generated by an automated translation program. This interface defines a C structure for each C++ class, which is actually a direct mapping to the C++ class. This structure is defined in the C include file for the class. Fields within the C structure are either hidden or public. Public fields (member variables) are documented in the reference manual page for each class. Hidden fields (private member variables) are named **pad[]**. You should not modify hidden fields.

The sample code fragments in these sections are drawn from Chapter 2.

Naming C Functions

The name of each C function is the C++ member function prefixed by the class name. Suppose there were a class named **SoGenericType**, with a member function **doOp()**. The C name for that function would be **SoGenericTypeDoOp()**. The object to be operated upon by the member function appears as the first argument to the C version of the function. A C prototype for our generic hypothetical function would look something like this:

```
SoGenericTypeDoOp(SoGenericType *);
```

To give a more specific example, the function to add a node to a group looks like this in C++ and C:

C++:
```
root->addChild(material);
```
C:
```
SoGroupAddChild(root, (SoNode *) material);
```

The C function name has the prefix **SoGroup**. Since **addChild()** is a member function of **SoGroup**, the first argument to the C function must be a pointer to an object of type **SoGroup**. Since **addChild()** expects a pointer to an object of type **SoNode** as its second argument, use a cast to **SoNode *** if you need to.

Now, suppose that you want to apply the function **doOp()** to a member of a subclass of **SoGenericType**, like **SoGenericSubType**. The C subclasses inherit all the member functions of their parent classes in the form of macro functions. The macros simply call the parent class function and cast the object to the parent's object type. The names of the inherited macro functions, though, are prefixed with the name of the subclass, not the parent class. So the C function name for **doOp()** would be **SoGenericSubTypeDoOp()**. You could use the parent class funtion, **SoGenericTypeDoOp()**, if you cast the object to **SoGenericType**.

In the real Inventor example **addChild()**, you're more likely to be adding children to subclasses of **SoGroup**. For example, the C macro function to add a child node to a separator is

C:
```
SoSepAddChild(separator, (SoNode *) material);
```

Abbreviating C Function Names

Here is another example of an Open Inventor C function:

C++:
```
viewer = new SoXtExaminerViewer(myWindow);
viewer->setSceneGraph(root);
```

C:
```
viewer = SoXtExamVwrCreateStd(myWindow, NULL);
SoXtExamVwrSetScene(viewer, (SoNode *) root);
```

The C++ function **setSceneGraph()** is a member of the class **SoXtRenderArea**, but the viewer is a pointer to type **SoXtExamVwr**. So the C macro function name is prefixed with **SoXtExamVwr** and has a pointer to an object of that type as its first argument.

But as you can see, the C function name is abbreviated. The function in the preceding example, if it were unabbreviated, would be **SoXtExaminer-ViewerSetScene()**, which is long and unwieldy. Table B-1 lists the abbreviations used in the C function names. Whenever the C++ function name contains one of the strings listed in the table, the corresponding C function uses the abbreviation in the second column.

C++ Function Name	Abbreviation
Action	Act
Attenuation	Atten
Binding	Bind
BoundingBox	BBox
Button	Btn
Callback	CB

Table B-1   C Function Name Abbreviations

C++ Function Name	Abbreviation
Camera	Cam
Catalog	Cat
Character	Char
Color	Col
Component	Comp
Cylinder	Cyl
Decoration	Decor
Detail	Dtl
Direction	Dir
Directory	Dir
Editor	Ed
Environment	Env
Event	Ev
Examiner	Exam
FaceSet	FSet
Function	Func
Highlight	HL
Index	Ind (Indexed->Index)
Input	In
Integer	Int
Keyboard	Key
Light	Lgt
LineSet	LSet
Location	Loc
Locator	Loc

Table B-1 (continued)   C Function Name Abbreviations

C++ Function Name	Abbreviation
Manager	Mgr
Manipulator	Mnp
Material	Mtl
Matrix	Mx
Normal	Norm
Orthographic'	Ortho
Output	Out
Perspective	Persp
Plane	Pln
Point	Pt
PointSet	PSet
Pointer	Ptr
Position	Pos
Primitive	Prim
Profile	Prof
Projector	Proj
QuadMesh	QMesh
RenderArea	RA
Rotate	Rot
Searching	Search
Section	Sect
Slider	Sldr
String	Str
Sphere	Sph
Texture	Tex

Table B-1 (continued)   C Function Name Abbreviations

C++ Function Name	Abbreviation
Tolerance	Tol
Transform	Xf
Translate	Xlate
TriangleStripSet	TSet
Vec	V(Vec3f-> V3f)
Vertex	Vtx
Viewer	Vwr
Visibility	Vis
Wheel	Whl
Window	Win

Table B-1 (continued)   C Function Name Abbreviations

Creating and Deleting Objects from C

The C versions of constructors and destructors are named following a convention slightly different from the one for most member functions. The C constructor for an object of our imaginary type **SoGenericType** would be **SoGenericTypeCreate()**. This example shows the C++ and C constructors for the **SoSeparator** type:

C++:
```
SoSeparator *root = new SoSeparator();
```
C:
```
SoSep *root;
root = SoSepCreate();
```

Destructors are named similarly. A destructor for an object of type **SoGenericType** would be **SoGenericTypeDelete()**. To delete a viewer, for example, you might call **SoXtExamVwrDelete(viewer)**. To delete nodes and groups, you use functions that *unreference* the node or group, instead of using destructors. See the discussion in Chapter 3 for details on deleting nodes.

Overloaded C++ Methods

The C++ language allows more than one method of a class to have the same method name, as long as the lists of arguments to the methods are different. This cabability is not provided by the C language, so different function names must be made for each identical method name from C++. Here is an example from the **SoAction** class:

C++

```
void apply(soNode * node);
void apply(SoPath *path);
```

C:

```
void SoActApply(SoAction * act, SoNode * node);
void SoActApplyPath(SoAction * act, SoPath * path);
```

Calling Functions

You should be aware of a few differences between the way C++ calls functions and the way C does. The C++ versions of the Open Inventor methods fill in default values for some arguments. If you omit those arguments, C++ simply calls the function with the defaults. C does not fill in those defaults for you, though. You must supply values for each argument. Here's an example of a C++ call to create an **appWindow** object, and the equivalent C call:

C++:

```
Widget appWindow = SoXt::init(argv[0]);
```

C:

```
widget appWindow;
appwindow = SoXtInit(argv[0], "Inventor");
```

C Classes and Manual Pages

There is an online C reference manual page for every Inventor class. For detailed information on a class, see its reference manual page, which lists the functions available to that class and any data structures available. The "Inherits From" section tells you which class the current class is derived from. For many classes, this hierarchy can be several layers deep. If you want to know all the functions available to a given class, you need to know the functions available to the parent class. These are listed as part of the synopsis of the manual page. Each class has a separate include file, named after the class.

The reference manual pages also list the suggested default value for function arguments as follows:

```
void setSomeValue(x, y, z = 1.0)
```

where z = **1.0** means that 1.0 is the recommended default value for the argument *z*.

The reference manual pages use both the abbreviated and the unabbreviated versions of the C class names. Your programs can use both versions as well.

A Sample Open Inventor Program in C

You now know nearly enough to rewrite Example 2-4 in C. Here's one way you might do so:

```
main(int argc, char **argv)
{
    Widget        myWindow;
    SoSep         *root;
    SoMtl         *myMaterial;
    SoCone        *myCone;
    SoXtExamVwr   *myViewer;

    myWindow = SoXtInit(argv[0], "Inventor");
    if (myWindow == NULL) exit(1);

    root = SoSepCreate();
    SoSepRef(root);
    myMaterial = SoMtlCreate();
    myCone     = SoConeCreate();
    SoMColSetR_G_B(&(myMaterial->diffuseColor), 1.0, 0.0, 0.0);
    SoSepAddChild(root, (SoNode *)myMaterial);
    SoSepAddChild(root, (SoNode *)myCone);

    /* Set up viewer: */
    myViewer = SoXtExamVwrCreateStd(myWindow, NULL);
    SoXtExamVwrSetScene(myViewer, (SoNode *)root);
    SoXtExamVwrSetTitle(myViewer, "Examiner Viewer");
    SoXtExamVwrShow(myViewer);
    SoXtShow(myWindow);
    SoXtMainLoop();
}
```

Error Handling

Inventor provides a basic error handling mechanism for use with both the optimized and debugging versions of Inventor. As shown in Figure C-1, three classes are derived from the base class, **SoError**. *Read* errors occur during reading of an Inventor file. *Memory* errors occur when an application runs out of memory. *Debugging* errors occur as the result of a programming error. Most debugging errors are generated only in the debugging version of Inventor and are not checked in the optimized version. A correct application does not generate any debugging errors. In the beginning, it's a good idea to link with the debugging version of Inventor to ensure that your program is correct. Later, when no errors are generated, you can switch to the optimized version.

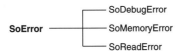

Figure C-1　　SoError Class Tree

For example, suppose Inventor encounters an unrecognized field name when it is reading a file. The following steps occur:

1. Inventor calls the static **SoReadError::post()** method and passes in the correct arguments.

2. The **SoReadError** class creates an instance of itself. Within this instance, it stores the *debug string*, a character string that represents a detailed error message. (Use **getDebugString()** to obtain the debug string.)

3. The **SoReadError** class passes the error instance to its error handler. The default error handler for all error classes simply prints the debug string to **stderr**. You can register your own error handler for specialized behavior. For example, in this case, you might want to bring up a window displaying a message saying that an error occurred during reading. Use the **setHandlerCallback()** method to register your own handler for an error class.

Runtime Type-Checking

Standard Inventor runtime type-checking for error classes is provided by the base class **SoError**. Each error class contains a runtime class type ID that can be used to determine the type of an instance.

Posting an Error

Each subclass of **SoError** has its own **post()** method. Posting is performed primarily by Inventor, but application writers can post their own errors as well.

Handling an Error

You can override the default error handler by specifying a callback function to be invoked when an error is posted. Each subclass of **SoError** supports a static **setHandlerCallback()** method. You can register the callback on **SoError**, so that it is called for all errors, or you can register it on one of the classes derived from **SoError**. The callback for the most derived class of a specific error instance is used to handle the error. Note that the error instance passed to a callback is deleted immediately after the callback is invoked. The application must copy this data ahead of time if it needs to use it later.

Debugging

If you are using an interactive debugger, you may be able to set a breakpoint in **SoError::handleError()**, which is called whenever an error is handled. You can also create your own error handler, register it, and use the callback function to investigate the error condition.

Index

animation, 6
   engines, 332, 337, 340
   nodes used for, 354
   using realTime field, 337
antialiasing, 218
   built into render areas, 254
appearance icon, 41
application, sending events directly to, 266
applying an action, 39, 72, 213, 214, 257
approximating curve, 184
architecture, Inventor, 5
arithmetic engines, 332, 347
array manipulation, engines used for, 332
arrays, 72
ASCII file format, 284
assignment (=) operator, 64
attaching components, to the scene graph, 434
attenuation, of light, 121
attributes, text, 140
autoclipping, 445
automatic
   field conversion, 335
   normals, 101
   render caching, 225

B

B-spline
   basis function, 187, 188, 194
   curve, example of, 194
backface culling, 123
balance scale, creating with node kits, 377
base classes, 16
base color, 118
   lighting model, 120, 426
basic types, 30
   in Inventor, 29
basis function, B-spline, 187, 188, 194
beveled text, 144
Bezier surface, example of, 199

binary format, for Inventor files, 302
binding materials, 127
   per vertex, 130
binding normals, 132
bit masks, writing to a file, 289
black and white image, printing, 219
blend color, for a texture, 166
blend texture model, 161
blending
   additive, 216
   alpha, 216
blinker node, 355, 357
   example, 86, 358
Boolean engine, 347
   example, 348
Boolean values, writing to a file, 290
bounding box
   caching, 224
   complexity, 124
bounding boxes, used for culling, 228
breakpoint, in a curve, 186
browser examiner viewer, 446
browser viewer, inserting a camera for, 441
buffer, for off-screen rendering, 219
buffering
   double, 444
   single, 444
   single and double, 444
buildFlag, for viewers, 439
buildInsideParent parameter, for components, 430

C

C functions,
   abbreviations, 481
   names, 480
   subclass names, 480
C programs,
   include files for, 32
   adding functionality to the scene graph in, 246

culling, 227
  and caching, 228
  for picking, 227
  for rendering, 227
current geometric transformation, 81
  and lights, 90
cursor position, 255
curvature continuity, 186
curved profiles, 147
curves
  approximating, 184
  breakpoints in, 186
  cubic, 186
  cubic Bezier, 191, 192
  defining, 184
  interpolating, 184
  nonrational, 193
  parametric, 183
  passing through endpoints, 191
  piecewise, 185
  quadratic, 185
  rational, 193
  uniform cubic B-spline, 191
custom
  highlighting, 273
  selection policy, 261
customizing a dragger, 411
cutting and pasting, 4, 447

D

data sensor, 310
  how to set up, 312
  notifying, 311
  in render area, 312
data types, supported by Inventor, 447
database, 12
  initializing, 36
  objects, 6
  primitives, 4, 12
  reading a file into, 37, 284

database *(cont.)*
  scene, 5
  traversing, 39
debugging error, 336
decal texture model, 161
decrementing the reference count, 70, 72
DEF keyword, in file format, 297
default
  coordinates, for textures, 168
  geometry, for draggers, 415
  lighting model, 80, 90
  texture mapping, 168
  values, 42
degree, of a curve, 192
delay queue
  for sensors, 311
  time-out interval for, 325
deleting
  an action, 213
  engines, 336
  nodes, 38, 68, 70
derivedFrom()
  SoType method, 75
deselect()
  SoSelection method, 268
deselectAll()
  SoSelection method, 269
deselecting objects, 269
deselection callback function, 273
details
  class tree for, 241
  classes that store, 242
devices, Xt, 425
diagrams, scene graph, 44
diffuse color, 117
digital clock, 338
directed acyclic graph, 37
direction
  of a spotlight, 94
  of lights, 92
  of profile curve, 202

directional
  light, 92
  light editor, 16
directory search path, 285
disconnect()
  SoField method, 334
display list, 9
  OpenGL, 224, 461
dodecahedron, 106
dots-per-inch (DPI), of a printer, 220
double buffering, 444
drag-point dragger, 390
draggers
  and callback functions, 397
  changing a part's geometry, 415
  changing parts after building, 413
  class tree for, 391
  complex, 390
  customizing existing, 411
  definition of, 390
  disabling a part, 417
  geometry of, 412
  parts of, 411
  removing a part, 417
  simple, 390, 395
  types of, 390
  typical uses of, 390, 392
  using multiple, 398
draw-style, 118
  for viewers, 442
draw-type, for viewers, 443
dynamic loading, of compiled objects, 302

E

editing scene graph nodes, 15
editor viewer, inserting a camera for, 441
editors, 15, 254
  compared to viewers, 428

efficency
  and material binding, 130
  sharing textures, 159
  using SoBaseColor, 118
efficient scene graphs, 104
elapsed time engine, 340, 379
elements, 214, 248
  of traversal state, 40
emissive color, 117
enable()
  SoEngineOutput method, 336
enableConnection()
  SoField method, 336
Encapsulated PostScript format, 220
engines, 12
  and lights, 91
  animation, 332, 340
  arithmetic, 332, 347
  Boolean, 347
  calculator, 350
  class tree for, 333
  compared to sensors, 329
  deleting, 336
  elapsed time, 340
  example of, 24
  file format for, 292
  gate, 344
  general uses for, 329
  multiple connections, 335
  names for, 75
  network, 335
  one-shot, 342
  outputs, 331
  reference counting for, 336
  sample applications using, 330
  time-counter, 342
  triggered, 332
  types of, 332
  updating values of, 337
  used for array manipulation, 332

H

handle box manipulator, 11, 14, 258, 394
  example of using, 403
handling events, 257
haze, environment node, 121
HDTV, camera aspect ratio for, 81
headlight, 445
height angle, of perspective camera, 83
hidden children, 303, 361
hidden fields, C, 480
hiding components, 430
highlighting, 272
  callback functions for, 273
  custom, 273
highlights, class tree for, 272
Hold_Final flag, 342

I

icons, 12
  for property nodes, 41
  key to, x
idle sensors, setting up, 318
Ignore flag, 67
  writing to a file, 290
image, for texture map, 219
image components, 219
immediate sensors, 316
inactive parts, of a dragger, 411
include files, 32
including other files, file format for, 301
incrementing, reference count, 70
index, of a child, 45
indexed
  binding, for materials, 128
  face set, example of, 105, 106
  shape nodes, 132
inheritance, 16
  within the scene graph, 46
inheriting values, from OpenGL, 453

initialization functions, 15, 253
initializing, the database, 37
input devices, 256
insertAppPushButton()
  SoXtFullViewer method, 446
insertChild()
  SoGroup method, 45
intensity
  ambient, 121
  of light, 91
  map, 162
Inter-Client Communication Conventions
  Manual (ICCCM), 447
interaction, user, 14
interpolating curve, 184
Inventor, and OpenGL, 9
Inventor Component Library, 12, 22, 32, 253, 254,
  323, 422
Inventor files, file header for, 286
Inventor Toolkit
  extending, 20
  parts of, 11
isConnected()
  SoField method, 334
isHandled()
  SoEventCallback method, 265
  SoHandleEventAction method, 258
isIgnored() method, 67
isOfType()
  SoNode method, 75
isOverride() method, 67
isSelected()
  SoSelection method, 269
isSmoothing()
  SoGLRenderAction method, 218
isValidHeader()
  SoDB method, 286
isVisible()
  SoXtComponent method, 431

J

justification, of text, 140, 145

K

keyboard, 425
  events, 255, 425
knot
  multiplicity, 189
    maximum, 192
  sequence, 182, 184, 188
    common, 191
  vector, 188
knots, 188

L

large scenes, culling of, 227
left-hand rule, 105
level of detail, 115
library, components, 422
light
  ambient color of, 121
  ambient intensity, 121
  attenuation, 121
  color of, 91
  directional, 92
  intensity, 91
  model, base color, 426
  node
    class tree for, 92
    position of in scene graph, 90
  point, 92
  spotlight, 94
lighting
  ambient, 121
  model, 120
    and viewer draw-style, 442
    Phong, 100, 120, 121
  two-sided, 123
lights
  accumulation of, 91
  added by viewers, 442
  comparison of, 92
  direction of, 92
  example of using, 94
  turning on and off, 91

lights *(cont.)*
  types of, 93
  using SoTransformSeparator with, 91
line pattern, 119
line width, 119
linear profiles, 147
linking profiles, 147
list parts
  file format for, 299
  for node kits, 377
location
  of a spotlight, 94
  of lights, 92

M

macros, for getting node kit parts, 371
main loop, 15, 253
managing
  the selection list, 268
  widgets, 430
manipulators, 4, 11, 14, 17
  and event handling, 258
  class tree for, 393
  compared to draggers, 393
  different ways to use, 401
mapping
  environment, 177
  reflection, 177
  textures, 168
material
  binding, 126
    default, 127
    example of, 130
  editor, 312, 428
  node, 117
materials
  binding per vertex, 130
  indexed, 105
  indexed binding for, 128
  specifying per face, 127
matrices, premultiplication of, 232
member function, static, 313

memory, storing texture maps in, 162

memory errors, 72

meters, 125

methods, for Sb- classes, 31

metrics icon, 42

mode
color index, 458
RGB, 458

models, texture, 160, 166

modulate, texture model, 160

Motif-compliant widget, 422, 428

Motif-style list, for selecting objects, 269

motion callbacks, for draggers and manipulators, 397

motion hierarchies, 377

mouse, 26, 28

mouse events, 255, 425

multiple engine connections, 335

multiple-value field, 61
in file format, 287

multiplicity, of knots, 189

multVecMatrix()
SbMatrix method, 31

N

names
example of using, 76
in file format, 297
for nodes, paths, engines, 75
searching for, 234, 235
of text font, 141

naming C functions, 480
abbreviations, 481
subclasses, 480

naming conventions, in Inventor, 29

network, of engines, 335

new operator, 38

node, 12, 38
replacing with a manipulator, 401
root, 37, 49
searching for a, 234

node kits, 11, 13, 368
base model for, 363, 365
catalog for, 363, 369
class tree for, 363
creating, 367
creating a motion hierarchy with, 384
creating paths to parts, 374
example
of editing parts, 374
getting parts, 374
setting each part, 372
using with editors, 381
file format for, 298
group methods for, 377
list parts, 377
part names, specifying, 372
selecting, 282
setting several parts in one command, 377
simple example of, 379
uses for, 360

node sensors, 311

node type, searching for, 234, 235

nodes
blinker, 355
categories of, 38
creating, 38
deleting, 38, 68, 70
fields in, 38, 60
groups, 12
icons for, x
names for, 75
pendulum, 354
property, 12, 115
rotor, 354
shapes, 12
sharing instances of, 54
shuttle, 355
used for animation, 354
with zero references, 72
writing to a file, 286

nonrational curves, 193

normal binding, 132

normals
automatic, 101
generating automatically, 132
indexed, 105

notifying, a data sensor, 311
NURBS shapes, 182
  acronym, 194
  and SoComplexity, 124
  and caching, 199
  control points, 184
  knot sequence, 184
  mapping parameter space to object space, 183
  order of a curve, 185
  parameters
    relationships among, 192
  suggested readings on, 207
  trimming, 147
NURBS surfaces, 199
  and SoComplexity, 202
  default texture mapping for, 173
  trimming, 202

O

object coordinate space, 32
object space complexity, 124
object-oriented programming, 9
objects, scene, 6
obtaining results, from picking, 239
off-screen renderer, 219
one-component texture, 162
  format for storing, 163
one-shot
  engine, 342
  sensor, 318
    setting up, 318
openFile()
  SoWriteAction method, 233
OpenGL Library, 4, 213, 214, 217, 218, 221, 226, 452
  and Inventor, 9, 452
  display list, 224
  render action, 39, 215
  state, 453
  values, inheriting, 453
OpenGL Programming Guide, 216

order
  and control points, 185
  of a curve, 185
  of a scene graph, 46
  of transformations, 134
  of vertices, 122
ordering, of children, 45
origin, of text, 141
orthographic camera, 84
  height, 84
  view volume of, 85
outputs, engines, 331
overlay
  planes, 425
  scene graph, 426
Override flag, 67
  and file format, 68

P

parameters, for actions, 213
parametric curves, 183
parts
  of 3D text, 146
  of a dragger, 411
  of text, 145
  specifying materials for, 127
paste() method, 447, 448
pasting data, from the clipboard, 448
path
  trigger, 316
  writing to a file, 292
path sensors, 311
paths, 58, 69
  cutting and pasting, 285
  example of, 59
  names for, 75
  SoPath and SoFull Path, 375
  types of, 362
  uses of, 60
  versus full paths, 361
  writing to a file, 289
pendulum node, 354

X

Z